A SUCCESSOR VISION

THE UNITED NATIONS ASSOCIATION IS MAKING THE U.N. WORK. THROUGH POLICY RESEARCH, PUBLIC OUTREACH, AND INTERNATIONAL DIALOGUE, UNA–USA IS BUILDING A NATIONAL AND INTERNATIONAL CONSTITUENCY FOR GLOBAL CO-OPERATION. A NONPROFIT, NONPARTISAN MEMBERSHIP ORGANIZATION, UNA–USA PARTICIPATES ACTIVELY IN THE PUBLIC DEBATE ABOUT AMERICA'S ROLE IN THE WORLD, SERVING AS A MAJOR SOURCE OF INFORMATION FOR CONGRESS, THE EXECU-TIVE BRANCH, STUDENTS, AND THE MEDIA. STEP BY STEP, UNA–USA IS BRINGING THE U.S., THE U.N., AND THE GLOBAL COMMUNITY CLOSER TOGETHER.

A SUCCESSOR VISION

The United Nations of Tomorrow

Edited by
PETER J. FROMUTH

UNITED NATIONS ASSOCIATION OF THE
UNITED STATES OF AMERICA

Library of Congress Cataloging-in-Publication Data

A Successor vision : the United Nations of tomorrow / edited by Peter J. Fromuth.
p. cm.
Analysis and proposal from an international panel which met during
1986 and 1987 under the auspices of the UNA-USA and some of the
supporting essays from the panel staff.
Includes bibliographies.
1. United Nations. I. Fromuth, Peter J. II. United Nations
Association of the United States of America.
JX1977.S817   1988
341.23—dc 19   88-23440 CIP
ISBN 0–8191–6905–6 (alk. paper)
ISBN 0–8191–6906–4 (pbk. : alk. paper)

All University Press of America books are produced on acid-free paper.
The paper used in this publication meets the minimum requirements of
American National Standard for Information Sciences—Permanence of Paper
for Printed Library Materials, ANSI Z39.48–1984.

UNITED NATIONS MANAGEMENT AND DECISION-MAKING PROJECT

1985–1987

The U.N. Management and Decision-Making Project was a two-year research program of the United Nations Association of the USA (UNA-USA), dedicated to strengthening the effectiveness of the United Nations and its immediate affiliated organs by offering constructive criticism regarding the management, governance, and role of the world organization. Financed by a grant from the Ford Foundation, the project reflected an effort to identify ways of making the United Nations work better in an era of increasing interdependence and of growing demands on the world body.

The project consisted of two parts. Its centerpiece was a high-level, 23-member international panel that united individuals with senior political experience and those with outstanding managerial skills. This panel published a final report (Part One of this volume) in the summer of 1987 that set out a rationale, priorities, and feasible agenda for the United Nations for the remainder of the century and proposed the type of changes in structure, procedures, and management that are necessary to carry out such an agenda. A preliminary report entitled *U.N. Leadership: The Roles of the Secretary-General and the Member States* was released in early December 1986.

Second, in addition to the meetings and reports of the Panel the project staff produced several research papers over the course of 1986 and 1987. These papers provided a background for the deliberations of the Panel and served as a source of information and analysis for the wider policy-making public in the United States and other countries. The research papers, included here as Part II, were reviewed by the panelists before publication, but do not necessarily represent the views of the Panel as a whole or the position of any individual member.

INTERNATIONAL PANEL

U.N. Management and Decision-Making Project

Elliot L. Richardson (chairman)
Chairman, UNA-USA
Former Secretary of Commerce
Former Attorney General of the United States
Former Secretary of Defense
Former Secretary of Health, Education and Welfare

Andres Aguilar Mawdsley
Permanent Representative of Venezuela to the United Nations
Former Ambassador of Venezuela to the United States

Otto Borch
Danish Ambassador to NATO
Former Ambassador of Denmark to the United States
Former Permanent Representative of Denmark to the United Nations

Andrew F. Brimmer
President, Brimmer & Company
Former Governor, Federal Reserve System

Enrique V. Iglesias
Minister of Foreign Affairs, Uruguay

Senator Nancy L. Kassebaum

Prince Sadruddin Aga Khan
Former U.N. High Commissioner for Refugees

T. T. B. Koh
Singapore Ambassador to the United States
Former Permanent Representative of Singapore to the United Nations

K. B. Lall
Chairman, Indian Council for Research on International Economic Relations
Former Indian Ambassador to the Economic Community, Brussels and
   Luxembourg
Former Permanent Representative of India to UNCTAD and GATT

Jacques Leprette
Former Permanent Representative of France to the United Nations
Former French Ambassador to the EEC

Robert S. McNamara
Former President of the World Bank
Former Secretary of Defense

Frederic V. Malek
President, Marriott Hotels and Resorts
Former Deputy Director, Office of Management and Budget

Olusegun Obasanjo (Major-General)
Former President of Nigeria

Philip A. Odeen
Regional Managing Partner, Management Consulting Services
Coopers & Lybrand
Former Principal Deputy Assistant Secretary of Defense

Sadako Ogata
Professor, Sophia University (Tokyo)
Former Minister, Mission of Japan to the United Nations

Paul H. O'Neill
Chairman and CEO, ALCOA
Former Deputy Director, Office of Management and Budget

Olara A. Otunnu
Former Foreign Minister, Uganda
Former Permanent Representative of Uganda to the United Nations

Mohamed Sahnoun
Algerian Ambassador to the United States
Former Permanent Representative of Algeria to the United Nations
Former Algerian Ambassador to France and Germany

*Members of this panel serve in their individual capacities. The conclusions
and recommendations set forth in this report and other publications of this
project do not necessarily reflect the official views or negotiating positions of
any country or group of countries.*

TABLE OF CONTENTS

EXECUTIVE SUMMARY

Crises in the lives of organizations often spark a rethinking of basic purposes, strategies and agendas. The purpose of this report is to help ensure that the current situation of the United Nations, which is one of deep crisis, leads to a sharper definition of goals, a more effective deployment of means, and a revitalized mandate.

A paradoxical situation confronts the U.N. and other international organizations today. On one hand the gap between the legal and political sovereignty of nation states and their ability to give sovereignty concrete shape—whether in air quality, energy security, jobs, surety against nuclear warfare, etc.—has never been larger. Yet while this "sovereignty gap" seems to cry out for international solutions, it has actually produced very little innovation to equip our existing international machinery to do the job. In parts of the international system some cautious modernizing is taking place. At the center of the system, however, there is deep skepticism about the present capacity of the United Nations to respond usefully to most global problems.

Many factors lie behind this skepticism: frustration with the U.N.'s ineffectiveness in the security field; its frequent failure to contribute usefully to the management of many global problems outside the traditional security area; deficiencies in its management and in its public information programs; the junior level of many of the delegates who sit on its many main intergovernmental committees, especially those in the economic and social area, etc.

In the face of such problems the prevailing skepticism is unsurpris-

NB: The United Nations numbers more than 24 organizations of varying degrees of independence from the center of the system, i.e. the "U.N. proper." The subject of this report is the U.N. proper which is composed of those programs that are included in the U.N.'s regular budget and those which, while funded voluntarily, are subordinate to the General Assembly and ECOSOC.

ing, yet it does not reflect a balanced evaluation either of U.N. performance or of the nature of the factors which affect that performance. The U.N. has rendered many services of incalculable value to its members and to the world community: the fostering of decolonization; peacekeeping and peacemaking efforts; defense of human rights; assistance to refugees; the development and extension of international law; promotion of collective action on such common problems as environment, population, resource strain, et al.

While this is an impressive record, many of the achievements mentioned belong to a time when the U.N. played a more central part in the cooperative management of world problems than it does today. Many diagnoses have been offered to explain this increasing marginalization: management handicaps embedded in the staff structure and institutional culture; lack of intellectual leadership; lack of political will; excessive politicization. The panel considered each of these but found none of them completely satisfactory. Instead, it believes that the U.N.'s current situation derives from two more basic problems: the ambiguity of its specific world role and its failure to change that role as the world has changed.

The panel believes that the role of the U.N. at the close of the 20th century is determined by two factors, each pulling in opposite directions: the causes and the effects of most major challenges facing governments are international, while the authority for dealing with those problems remains vested in nation states. This mix of opportunity and constraint dictates a responsibility to promote international cooperation by connecting an unsentimental assessment of national interests with an uncontestable vision of common goals.

Yet the present system of international organizations, of which the U.N. is theoretically the center, is not organized to carry out this mission due to weaknesses in its structure and flaws in the assumptions that determine how it defines its work. To correct that situation, this report proposes a new vision for the United Nations:

Relating Functions to Structure

1. the U.N. should identify common interests among its members;
2. it should convert those common interests into common views; and
3. it should strive to convert those common views into cooperative action.

This formula already typifies the United Nations' most successful efforts, but for the generality of U.N. activities it remains the exception rather than the norm. A sharper definition of the functions of the U.N. in relation to the U.N. system, and a new structure, particularly in the economic and social area, are indispensable.

Global Watch

In order to identify the issues on which convergence of interests exists, the U.N. needs: (i) a setting where emerging issues of urgent global significance can be spotlighted and their implications for national and international policy choices and human welfare given prominent international attention by a small senior body; (ii) a capacity at the staff level to monitor, and put into usable form, data on "global watch issues," to systematically examine implications for national and international security and welfare, and to identify overlapping interests and the margins for potential agreement.

Consensus-Building

A more systematic approach to consensus-building at the United Nations is indispensable. It should incorporate the following elements:

- affected parties: Communities of interest are more easily formed and collective action taken when negotiations and decisions include only those countries most directly affected by the issue.
- equity-security: Links between economic equity and security (in the broadest sense of *human* security) are increasingly direct, and future consensus-building efforts, particularly as they relate to the cross-over between economic, technological, and environmental concerns, must reflect that linkage.
- representational diplomacy: To assure speed of consultation, minimal procedural and parliamentary delay, and participation at senior levels, global watch discussions should not be conducted in universal membership bodies but in a forum which, while of limited size, would be composed of countries drawn from the entire membership of the U.N. according to a system of rotating representation.

Consensus Conversion: Stimulating Collective Action

As the need for effective management of international issues grows more acute, a more direct U.N. role in defining and proposing specific mechanisms for cooperation—occasionally even in helping to set up the necessary logistical apparatus—will be necessary.

Strengthening Structure

The panel has given considerable attention to the deficiencies of the present U.N. structure in the economic and social area, these include: a generally low level of representation; overlap between the General Assembly, the Economic and Social Council, and UNCTAD; a lack of intellectual authority; the absence of a system for identifying emerging global issues; and the weakness of coordination and joint planning in the U.N. system. While institutional changes are clearly needed, a balance has to be struck between what may be desirable ultimately, and the kinds of constructive practical steps which member states could undertake immediately. Consequently, the panel has made the following recommendations:

Ministerial Board

To provide a high-level center for the conduct of global watch consultations described above, a small Ministerial Board of not more than 25 governments should be established in affiliation with ECOSOC. The Board would be composed of delegates with the seniority and expertise to consult effectively, issue communiques and initiate or propose ad hoc actions with regard to matters on which there is agreement that enhanced international management is essential.

- *Functions*: GLOBAL WATCH—high-level consultations and exchange of views on any urgent international problems not within the jurisdiction of the Security Council; CONSENSUS-BUILDING—through ad hoc working groups of the most affected countries the Board will forge communities of interest on matters before it; CONVERTING AGREEMENTS INTO ACTION—when appropriate the Board shall propose actions by or under the aegis of the U.N. proper (General Assembly would have to authorize), by other international agencies, by individual U.N. member countries.
- *Agenda*: The Board could address any issues of imminent or clearly foreseeable consequence for human security and welfare not within the jurisdiction of the Security Council, e.g., matters associated with natural disasters, the global biosphere, the spe-

cial problems of the least developed countries, international debt, disease control, illegal capital flight, international narcotics trafficking, cross border population movements, urban overpopulation, etc.

- *Composition and procedures*: The 25 members would consist of a core of permanent members made up of the largest developing and developed countries, and a larger number of rotating members (criteria for determining "permanent" and "rotating" might be population and economic size); it is expected that governments would be represented at a high level by ministers or other officials from the ministries which are most directly relevant to the agenda subject; meetings would be held on an as-needed basis, normally 1–3 days in duration; all decisions would be taken by consensus.

- *Support*: The Board would be supported by a Bureau of Global Watch located in the Department for International Economic and Social Affairs (DIESA). Drawing heavily upon electronic and computer-based information networks such as UNEP's Earthwatch, and utilizing the existing resources of DIESA, the Bureau would gather, update, monitor and analyze a global data base on each item which the Board has placed on its "human security" agenda.

- *Organizational status*: While ultimately the Board should be given an explicit basis in the Charter, for the present it should be attached to ECOSOC but report to the Assembly directly once a year at the same time as the ECOSOC makes its report.

- *Why a new body?*: Existing U.N. machinery is inadequate to address, authoritatively and effectively, urgent issues of human security and welfare. The Second and Third Committees and ECOSOC are too large, too comprehensive in their agendas, and their delegations often too junior to have the authority for so important a task.

A Two-Step Approach Toward a More Integrated U.N. System

Why is a more integrated system necessary?: It is essential to create an apparatus for identifying, analyzing and proposing responses to the kinds of issues described above that is integrated intellectually and employs the sectoral expertise of the U.N.'s economic and social agencies in a coordinated manner. Most problems requiring international management overlap the spheres of several agencies and U.N.

programs. YET THERE IS NO CENTER AT THE CENTER OF THE U.N. SYSTEM and therefore no means for putting to work the system's rich potential for interdisciplinary analysis to identify the global issues on which national interests converge and where high levels of cooperation are necessary and feasible.

The Two-Step Approach: The panel recommends creation of a single commission, composed of the Directors General of all the main agencies in the economic and social fields, mandated to develop integrated responses to global issues through joint programming, and development of a consolidated U.N. system budget. Such a Commission however is not feasible for immediate implementation due to the scale of the constitutional, structural and budgetary changes involved. The panel therefore adopted the Commission as a medium-term goal toward which the U.N. system should evolve. As an immediate step in the direction of the U.N. Commission it calls for a commission with advisory powers only.

Step 1—The U.N. Advisory Commission:

COMPOSITION: the Advisory Commission would consist of 5 persons, selected by the Secretary-General, with outstanding international reputations in the economic and social field.

FUNCTION: It would identify emerging issues of a global or regional scale that cross over several agencies fields of concern. Following consultations with agency heads, it would propose joint approaches to these problems. It would also present proposals to the new Ministerial Board suggesting actions by member states or international institutions regarding these "crossover" issues. It would conduct regular reviews of the major program emphases in the economic and social area in light of global trends. Finally, it would prepare the agendas and follow-up on the decisions of the annual U.N. system summits (a proposal of the Group of 18 adopted last December), and participate in the summits on a co-equal basis with the specialized agency heads.

SUPPORT: The Advisory Commission would be served by a small inter-agency staff seconded from the U.N.'s main economic and social agencies.

Step 2—The U.N. Commission:

COMPOSITION: The Commission would be composed of 15 to 18 Commissioners, including Directors General of the principal specialized agencies and the Bretton Woods organizations. The Commission would be nominated by the Ministerial Board and confirmed by the General Assembly, except for the heads of the IMF, World Bank and GATT whose appointment procedures would not change.

FUNCTION: The Commission would have the same functions as the Advisory Commission except that it would also prepare a consolidated U.N. system program budget from the submissions of every participating agency (except for the IMF, World Bank and GATT) for submission to the General Assembly for its approval.

SUPPORT: The Commission would have its own budget and, like the Ministerial Board, would draw upon DIESA for substantive support.

Development Assistance Board

In order to improve the quality and coherence of U.N. development assistance and to reduce overlap and duplication, the separate executive boards of UNDP, UNFPA, WFP, and UNICEF should be replaced by a single Development Assistance Board. The Board would exercise oversight of all program proposals, conducting reviews before the start of fundraising efforts in order to ensure influence upon the overall scope and content of work programs. The Board would also be responsible for development of a conceptual framework for U.N. development assistance which leads gradually to appropriate specialization.

Elimination of Second and Third Committees; Expansion of ECOSOC to Plenary Size

To eliminate the nearly complete duplication of agendas and debates between the Economic and Social Council (ECOSOC) and the General Assembly's committees dealing with economic and social matters (Second and Third), and to end the waste of scarce human resources which results from this duplication, the Second and Third Committees of the General Assembly should be discontinued and their duties assumed by ECOSOC, which would be enlarged to plenary size and strengthened by structural and procedural reforms, including addition of a Reports and Agenda Committee.

Merger of the Special Political Committee into the Fourth Committee

In view of the steady decline in the agenda and responsibilities of the Fourth Committee as the global movement toward decolonization nears completion; in view of the overlap in significant parts of the agendas of the Fourth Committee and the Special Political Committee; and in view of the Secretary-General's recent decision to combine the secretariats for special political questions, regional cooperation, decolonization and trusteeship, and the Council on Namibia into a single Department, the Special Political Committee and the Fourth Committee should be merged. The new committee should be called "Committee for Non-Self-Governing Territories and Special Political Questions."

Merger of the Department of International Economic and Social Affairs (DIESA) with the Office of the Director-General for International Economic Cooperation (DIEC)

To improve the identification, study and management of interrelated economic and social issues by the U.N., the main economic and social secretariats (DIESA and DIEC) should be combined into a single department headed by the Director-General. The expanded DIESA should be reorganized along interdisciplinary lines, it should support the work of the Ministerial Board and the Advisory Commission and it should have expertise and data-monitoring capability in every major economic and social area embraced by the U.N. system.

Peace and Security

The panel believes that the U.N.'s limitations in the peace and security field are more the product of contemporary international relations than of shortcomings in U.N. management or structure. Unlike social, economic and humanitarian affairs, major structural changes in U.N. peace and security mechanisms appear unpromising. Instead, consensus-building, practical implementation, and selectivity in focusing on tasks where the U.N. has a comparative advantage are critical to improving U.N. performance. This will entail some rethinking of priorities, strategies, goals and directions along lines elaborated in the report. Among the specific proposals recommended are the following:

Strengthening Cooperation With Regional Bodies

The Secretaries-General of the United Nations and of regional organizations and their deputies should meet on a regular basis to exchange information regarding emerging disputes that might threaten international peace and security, to discuss joint measures where appropriate, and to consider common problems of financial, logistical and political support.

Multilateral Inspection Teams

Arms reductions, because they impose higher security risks than traditional arms control steps, demand thorough, reliable and impartial verification, often beyond the capabilities of national technical means based largely on satellites. In cases involving the production or storage of weapons, satellite reconnaissance is clearly not sufficient and on-site inspection by one's adversary is generally unacceptable. There may be instances where the U.N. could provide multilateral inspection teams from a politically balanced mix of countries for third-party inspection and reporting.

Ad hoc Compliance Review Groups

Ad hoc review groups could be established under the aegis of the Security Council to examine compliance questions related to multilateral agreements and questions arising from the reports of the proposed Multilateral Inspection Teams. After considering reports of questionable practices or apparent violations, review groups could initiate consultations between the parties, and could refer serious breaches to the full Security Council.

The Secretary-General

1. In choosing an individual to serve as Secretary-General, the most important international civil servant, member states have a responsibility to select someone with the qualities of leadership, integrity, vision and intellect necessary to carry out this enormously demanding job.
2. The Secretary-General should vigorously defend his duties and prerogatives as chief executive and recognize that his responsibilities under the Charter require him to be an initiative-taker rather than a caretaker in the service of efficient management.
3. The Secretary-General should make explicit and binding delegations of authority to capable individuals with executive responsibility for: (i) planning and development of the program budget; (ii) financial and administrative policy with particular emphasis

on the personnel area; (iii) and coordination of related activities of the U.N. proper and the U.N. group.

4. To establish a coherent administrative structure of manageable proportions, responsibility for the departmental activities funded by the U.N.'s regular budget should be coordinated in a small cabinet chaired by the Secretary-General and including among its members the Under-Secretary-General for Administration and Management and the Director General.

5. Effective as of the next election, Secretaries General should be elected for a single term not to exceed seven years.

ABOUT THE AUTHORS

Prince Sadruddin Aga Khan is President of the Groupe de Bellerive and co-Chairman of the Independent Commission on International Humanitarian Issues. He is currently serving as the Coordinator of the U.N.'s Humanitarian and Economic Assistance relating to Afghanistan. Prince Sadruddin was the United Nations High Commissioner for Refugees from 1965 to 1977 and has also served as Special Consultant to the U.N. Secretary-General, as Special Consultant to the Director-General of UNESCO and as Executive Secretary to the International Commission for the Preservation of Nubian Monuments.

Maurice Bertrand was on the faculty of France's National School of Administration from 1946 to 1954 when he became, successively, senior counsellor to the Defense Ministry and then to the Prime Minister. Mr. Bertrand served as the French representative to the U.N.'s Joint Inspection Unit from 1968 to 1985. His publications include numerous reports on U.N. management, personnel and programming issues and most recently a comprehensive proposal for reform entitled *Some Reflections on Reform of the United Nations*.

Peter Fromuth was the Staff Director of the U.N. Management and Decision-Making Project. Before coming to the United Nations Association he was on the legislative staff of the Alaska State Legislature, and of US Senator Ted Stevens and served as an international economist with the Commerce Department. He has published numerous articles and editorials on U.N. issues and currently serves as Executive Director of the UNA-USA Economic Policy Council.

Frederick K. Lister served the United Nations for 34 years in a variety of positions in the economic, social and administrative area. After his retirement in 1981 he authored *Decision-making Strategies for Inter-*

national Organizations (University of Denver, 1984). During 1986 and 1987 Mr. Lister served as consultant to the U.N. Management and Decision-Making Project.

Edward C. Luck is President of the United Nations Association of the USA. He has been a consultant to the Rand Corporation and has published and testified widely in the fields of arms control, national security policy, Soviet foreign policy, and multilateral diplomacy. Mr. Luck is editor of the book, *Arms Control: The Multilateral Alternative* (New York University Press, May 1983).

Ruth Raymond is a public affairs officer at the Food and Agriculture Organization in Rome. In 1986 and 1987 she served as principal research associate with the U.N. Management and Decision-Making Project.

INTRODUCTION

Future historians may come to view the 1980s as an age of paradox, in which international politics was dominated by two contradictory facts: increasing nationalism, and decreasing national power. On the one hand, governments are increasingly forced to acknowledge that the means for managing a lengthening agenda of national problems—unemployment, economic welfare and growth, environmental risks, large movements of population, trafficking in narcotic drugs, etc.—are beyond their grasp when acting alone. On the other hand, the last several years have seen the rise and persistence of "go-it-alone" policies, often of a demonstrably symbolic nature.

But many of the same problems also seem beyond the means of existing international machinery. In the security area the U.N., its collective security apparatus made obsolete by deteriorating great power relations, has been compelled to improvise. As a result, it has frequently found itself confined to the margins of dangerous conflict, unable to fulfill even the more modest tasks of mediation or peacekeeping. In the sphere of international economics, the collaborative efforts of the International Monetary Fund (IMF), World Bank, the U.S. Federal Reserve and Treasury, and debtor governments are staving off risks of immediate default by Third World debtors, but nowhere is the long-term sustainability of the current approach to international debt discussed by the affected parties. During the highly successful first phase of its existence, the General Agreement on Tariffs and Trade (GATT) brought massive reductions in tariff levels. Today it is not only irrelevant to the settlement of most serious trade disputes but to an increasing proportion of world trade as well.

If limits upon governmental action are drawing tighter and international institutions are not keeping up, the 1980s would seem to be a time for adapting our international equipment to meet new needs. Through a process of cautious incrementalism, some slight modernizing is occurring.

Concern over the magnitude of developing country debt has led the IMF to more flexible conditionality. The same concern led the World Bank to focus more on balance of payments support and macro-policy conditionality than on its traditional project lending. Driven by the twin dangers of protectionism and increasing cartelization, the membership of the GATT has agreed to a new trade round where the possibility of expanding GATT norms to cover services and agricultural trade will at least be discussed. Annual Western economic summits, while essentially consultative, at least help to organize and adjust the expectations of participants about each other's policies. The Plaza meeting of September 1985, and the increasingly frequent get-togethers of the U.S., Japanese and German finance ministers which have followed, suggest growing support for the idea that currency stability is a common obligation—and may foreshadow acceptance of other joint responsibilities too. And in the environmental area, the recent U.N.-based agreement freezing production of ozone-depleting chemicals could provide a model for international cooperation on other environmental hazards.

At the regional political level there has also been progress. The European Economic Community has expanded its membership, broadened the range of tariff-free products and services and, with the adoption of majority voting in the Council, gained greater political cohesion. The ASEAN countries have achieved a significant degree of foreign and economic policy coordination. The signatories of the Antarctica Treaty have maintained a working cohesion despite the prospect of conflicts over mineral and fishing rights within the territory of Antarctica itself.

At the global level, however, and at the U.N. in particular, emergence of new problems for statecraft—whether in kind or degree—has usually not given rise to significant structural or procedural adaptations. Where effective regional or ad hoc arrangements exist, the cost of inaction at the U.N. may be acceptable. Risks accumulate, however, when a problem—because of the number and distribution of affected parties, the collective nature of the relevant response, the sources of relevant data, the breadth of strategy and perspective required—is inescapably global but is not addressed globally. Underlying the absence of innovation at the global level is a deep skepticism, among developed and developing countries alike, about the utility of the existing U.N. machinery for managing most truly global problems.

Many explanations have been offered for the U.N.'s increasing marginalization. In one view the U.N. is debilitated by inefficiencies and management handicaps embedded in its staff, structure and institutional culture. Another explanation holds that the U.N. bureaucracy is no less efficient than any other and that the real problem lies in a lack of political will to implement U.N. resolutions. A third stresses the controversial political nature of so many issues referred to the world body, effectively immobilizing it from making useful contributions to their settlement. Still another sees the U.N. as mainly a casualty of the general deterioration in the climate for international cooperation.

While there is certainly much truth in such observations, none of them is a complete explanation of the U.N.'s malaise. In the view of the members of the international panel, the U.N.'s situation derives from two more basic problems: the ambiguity of its specific world role, and the failure to change that role as the world has changed.

Ambiguity and Ambivalence

Over the last several years the U.N. has been increasingly incapacitated by an identity crisis which prevents it from articulating a coherent vision of its role in today's world that is at once compelling and attractive to a balanced majority of its members. It is a crisis rooted in the evolution of the U.N.'s political ethos over 42 years. During this period, institutional momentum came first from the developed West, passed next to the Third World and then, by the late 1970s, entered a third stage, in which there was near stalemate between the forces of the first two, with no group of countries supplying initiative or direction.

While major achievements marked both of the first two stages, the strategies for making use of the U.N. that were followed by the West and the Third World successively entered a cul-de-sac. By the late 1960s, the Western vision, which though supportive of decolonization, also found in the U.N. a means for reinforcing and extending the postwar economic status quo, proved too gradualist to accommodate Third World aspirations, particularly in the economic area. The Third World vision, which saw in the U.N. a tool for accelerating the pace of systemic change, ultimately proved too ambitious to engage the West.

The period since the U.N.'s 40th anniversary represents at least the possibility of a fourth stage. On one hand, the severity of the Organization's financial crisis has produced wide and, in fact, unprecedented interest among member states in pursuing ways to "rationalize" the

U.N. and make it more "efficient."[1] This has already resulted in the adoption of measures proposed by the U.N.'s Group of 18 experts to improve the Organization's administrative functioning, as well as the adoption of a revamped procedure for budgetary decision-making recommended by the full UNA panel, and by some members of the Group of 18, to give U.N. budgeting the stability and self-discipline it badly needs. While this marks progress, recent disagreements over the size of the U.N.'s relatively modest budget mirror the more fundamental breakdown in consensus described above—in short, about the role of the United Nations itself. Unfortunately, there is little movement on this more basic task of developing a "successor vision" of the Organization for the 1990s and beyond—and little evidence that any group of countries is actively in search of one.

The World Has Changed Since 1945

Uncertainty about *what* a practical U.N. role should be has made its member nations ill-prepared to adapt and refine the U.N.'s central structure when changes in the world call for such adaptations. Yet, many of the conditions which prevailed when the Charter was drafted 42 years ago have changed profoundly. Consequently, even with stronger agreement about its specific role, without change in structure and approach, the U.N. would be poorly equipped to exercise it.

The first change, and the most far-reaching, was in the structure of world power. The collective security provisions of the Charter, founded on an arguably unrealistic premise anyway, were designed for a "world that never happened." The rapid replacement of the wartime alliances with bipolarity and the advent of nuclear weapons made the collective enforcement of the peace a near-impossibility, since no combination of states could prevail over an aggressor unless it had the support—or at least acquiescence—of both nuclear superpowers. When this condition has been present, the U.N. has played an important, even determinative, role. All too often, however, disagreement between the U.S. and the Soviet Union has confined the U.N. to potentially important but narrow roles: the Secretary-General's "good offices," e.g., mediation, dispute settlement and, when invited by the parties to a dispute, peacekeeping actions.

A second change is the almost threefold increase in the number of independent countries since 1945, confronting the international system with new and taxing social, economic and security challenges. A great many of the new states have had difficulty establishing effective domestic political authority, a task complicated by the fact that they have inherited colonial borders incorporating sharply different demographic groups, often with little sense of belonging to a single national unit. Further complicating their nation-building task is the frequent absence of economies with the carrying capacity to sustain growth— or even stability—in standards of living or to finance the civil infrastructure that makes for national cohesion. As a consequence, they are susceptible to security threats not only from external sources but from inside as well.

Such phenomena, eroding the surface of sovereignty *from within,* mark a third structural change: the nature of conflict during the postwar period is shifting away from the "aggressor-victim" model to one in which distinctions between domestic and international wars are difficult to establish. The most commonplace conflicts now fall beyond the primary scope of action envisioned in the security provisions of the U.N. Charter. They include: civil wars; wars between a superpower and a Third World regime (fought directly or through proxies); terrorist campaigns; attacks upon the civil authorities by powerful outlaw groups, such as narcotics gangs; and so on. While, technically, the Charter permits actions on behalf of international security to override a country's right to noninterference in its domestic concerns, since the U.N. action in the Congo there have been no significant applications of this principle—and there is, in fact, a very strong bias against its exercise. The result is that the U.N. tends to be marginal to the prevention, containment and resolution of most modern-day conflict.

The effects of the fourth structural change—the globalization of economic activity—may be seen daily in virtually every part of the world. In a way that could not have been foreseen at the time of the creation of the Bretton Woods institutions and the U.N., the dense interpenetration of world trading and financing networks has reduced the effective autonomy of national policy over the entire range of national economic conditions. In the areas of employment, sectoral job creation, structural adjustment, fiscal policy, trade policy, monetary policy, and even tax policy, both goals and means are far more constrained by extranational variables than they have ever been in the past. The political fate of Congressmen from Pittsburgh or Lincoln, Nebraska, or Silicon Valley can be determined by decisions taken in Brussels, Sao Paulo or Tokyo. The fortunes of a Christian Democratic German Chancellor or a Socialist French President can rise or fall on the wheel of U.S. fiscal and monetary policies.

Through the medium of trade, a second stratum of exchange has developed—the transmission of the costs and effects of social policies. Thus, through lower prices and lost jobs, some countries with unionized labor and environmental and workplace regulations which raise production costs are paying for the lower costs of their unregulated competitors. Such integration has occurred without parallel development of the means for managing its consequences, either at the bilateral level or at the multilateral level. Although many countries now seek better processes for joint macro-economic management, the size of U.N. deliberative bodies—and the near inevitability of extraneous issue linkage which comes with their size and broad mandates—has left the U.N. on the sidelines of this search.

The increase in economic interdependence, while massive, is a change in degree rather than in kind. The Bretton Woods institutions were an effort to manage interdependence and avoid the collisions of national interest that helped ignite the Second World War.

The fifth structural change—the emergence of environmental risks of a global character—clearly *is* a qualitative one. The world ecosystem is undergoing severe strain as a result of processes largely beyond the control of individual countries or groupings of allied countries. Such phenomena as ozone depletion, acid rain, global warming, ocean pollution, disposal of nuclear waste, regional drought, civilian nuclear accidents, chemical contamination of common waterways, the declining quality of ground water, deforestation, and many others generally share characteristics which make them difficult to address at the national level. The source point and the target areas are often separated by hundreds or thousands of miles; the "affected zone" is generally indivisible; noncooperation by a few would often entail high cost to the many; and, in most cases, outcomes cannot be determined by one or two countries acting together (acid rain may be an exception, since the U.S., China, the Soviet Union and Europe are the principal producers). These features suggest that the U.N. ought to be a major player in the care, preservation and management of the global ecosystem. Despite the useful and innovative work of the U.N. Environment Program, such objectives have not received high-level support or attention at the U.N.

A sixth major development also unforeseen by the framers of the U.N. Charter is the now semipermanent presence of massive numbers of stateless, displaced persons. Although the original task of the High Commissioner for Refugees (UNHCR) was seen as limited and temporary—to care for those, in Europe and elsewhere, made homeless by the Second World War—it has never ceased to operate. Rather than representing a temporary humanitarian need, due to the dislocation of a world war, today's refugees are the result of repeated systemic breakdowns. In Africa, Asia and Latin America, millions have fled or been forced to flee their home countries—either because of civil warfare or some other collapse of domestic order, or because the economic carrying capacity of the country they have fled can no longer sustain them. While the faces change, the phenomenon seems permanent. Although organizations like UNHCR, the International Red Cross and many others are kept busy trying to contain and care for these new tidal movements of refugees, they are rapidly being overwhelmed and are not equipped to address the growing economic and security causes and dimensions of the problem.

The Need to Clarify the U.N.'s Role

The U.N. is not always well-equipped to address the issues arising from every structural change described here. But that is not the real problem. The list of issues for which the U.N.'s features *do* create actual or potential opportunities for significant impact is a long one. Its difficulties have more to do with the phenomenon mentioned above—the ambiguity and ambivalence in its members' view of its role. Without overcoming this more basic problem, there is little chance of improvement in the Organization's effectiveness or its credibility. Now necessary is a "successor vision" of the U.N.'s role which (1) attracts the support of a balanced majority of its members, (2) utilizes the features which make the U.N. unique, (3) reflects the current and foreseeable conditions of the world in which it exists, and (4) offers a clear set of directions and goals to guide the desire for institutional change widely expressed in the international community today.

Part I seeks to illuminate such a "successor vision" by examining specific U.N. successes and failures and the reasons why (Chapter One); by identifying flaws in its management, in the assumptions guiding its work, and in popular perceptions of international organizations in general (Chapter Two); by offering a new set of orientations to replace them, and a clarification of the U.N.'s role (Chapter Three); and by proposing several changes to give that role fuller expression (Chapters Four and Five).

Notes

1. As outlined in Chapters Two and Five, the panel believes that the management of the U.N. must be strengthened in fundamental ways. But panel members also wish to caution that conventional means for measuring efficiency in the business world—outputs per units of input, for example—are not adequate for judging the efficiency or effectiveness of U.N. bodies. Enormous expenditures of time and energy, for example, may go into a cease-fire resolution of the Security Council, which ultimately saves lives.

Part One

CHAPTER 1

REVIEWING THE RECORD

International Security and Conflict Management

The U.N's track record in the peace and security realm has been mixed, combining quiet successes with all-too-visible failures of collective will and imagination. Far too often, paralyzing differences among the major powers have prevented the U.N. from playing more than a marginal role in addressing the most intransigent and explosive threats to world peace. Despite its readily apparent limitations, however, the U.N. has managed to make an important, sometimes critical, difference in resolving a wide range of disputes and conflicts, in forestalling their escalation, and in establishing global arms control and disarmament norms.

In general, the U.N. has been far better at doing the things that draw relatively little public attention, such as mediation, fact-finding, good offices, and consensus-building, than at playing power politics or public diplomacy. It has been more successful at preventing things from getting worse than at compelling nation-states to do its bidding. The following examples of U.N. successes and failures will illustrate the institution's comparative advantages and disadvantages as it seeks to respond to an increasingly complex set of challenges to international security.

It has been over 25 years, dating from the Congo operation, since significant enforcement action has been taken under U.N. auspices. The two major cases of U.N. military action, in Korea and the Congo, did achieve their immediate objectives of restoring peace and stability to the areas. But at the same time, the controversial operations so polarized the major powers and so damaged the institution's political

3

foundation that they will not soon be repeated. Sanctions, such as the arms embargoes imposed on Southern Rhodesia and South Africa, while not universally respected in practice, have provided a way for U.N. members to put some teeth in their resolutions without resorting to military action. It has come to be recognized that enforcement actions under Chapter VII of the Charter (whether military or non-military) are only viable if there is major power unanimity, so that in this divided world the U.N.'s first task has become consensus-building or serving as "a center for harmonizing the actions of nations in the attainment of these common ends" (Article 1, Paragraph 4). The difficulties this often entails are illustrated by current efforts to limit arms transfers to the combatants in the Persian Gulf war.

In the absence of enforcement action, the U.N. has been much more creative and persistent in developing ways to fulfill Chapter VI's mandate for the "peaceful settlement of disputes." One of the most successful innovations has been the introduction of U.N. peacekeeping forces to add an element of stability to troubled regions in order to ease the peacemaking process and to lessen the possibility of disruptive incidents. Sometimes referred to as Chapter VI½, peacekeeping operations have brought stability to Kashmir, Sinai, Cyprus and the Golan Heights. It is conceivable that they might be employed in the future in Namibia, Afghanistan and the Persian Gulf, should the parties to those conflicts decide to seek a peaceful alternative. While peacekeeping forces have been consistently successful at bolstering regional stability, they have not in themselves been able to (nor were they designed to) ensure the success of peacemaking efforts in areas, such as Southern Lebanon and Cyprus, where there is no unanimity on the desirability or conditions of a peaceful settlement of the underlying disputes. Regarding those operations, it has become increasingly unclear whether the international community is prepared to provide the necessary political, human and financial support indefinitely without greater progress on the diplomatic front.

As an essentially political organization, the U.N. has provided its good offices in mediating countless disputes in order to prevent violence or its escalation. The U.N.'s most striking successes have been associated with the decolonization process, in which it has served as the midwife to the birth of many new states, ranging from Israel to Bahrain. The U.N. has played an important role in the resolution of each major Middle Eastern conflict, most critically in the 1973 war, which threatened to escalate into an East-West confrontation. Resolutions of the Security Council still provide the most widely accepted formulas for settling the intractable problems of the Middle East and Namibia. In recent years, the U.N.'s record has been more modest, centering on the efforts of the Secretary-General's office in arbitrating the Rainbow Warrior dispute between France and New Zealand, in discouraging the use of chemical weapons and attacks on cities in the Iran-Iraq war, in conducting ongoing negotiations on Afghanistan and Cyprus, and currently in convening intensive discussions among the five Permanent Members of the Security Council on ways to resolve the war between Iran and Iraq.

The politics and the decision-making processes of the U.N., however, have not always aided its peacemaking efforts. As a near-universal intergovernmental body, the U.N. has tended to be reactive to crises, rather than anticipatory, becoming involved only after the two sides have become intransigent or after all else has failed. Too rarely has the international community sought U.N. involvement at the early stages of an emerging dispute, when preventive diplomacy could be most effective. The Iran-Iraq war is a sad case in point. The U.N. failed to address the issue until after Iraq had invaded Iran. The Security Council then passed a resolution calling for a cease-fire without calling on Iraq to withdraw its forces from Iranian territory. The resolution not only failed to do any good, it reinforced Iranian suspicions that the Security Council is biased against it. Likewise, the tendency of the General Assembly, and increasingly of the Security Council as well, to pass judgment repeatedly on controversial issues, particularly relating to the Middle East, Southern Africa and Central America, has made it more difficult for the U.N. to play its traditional role of an honest broker in these regions. The office of the Secretary-General, however, has worked to maintain its credibility with the key parties in those regions.

Similar lessons can be drawn from the U.N.'s efforts in arms control and disarmament. When the world body has addressed issues that are multilateral in scope and of general concern to the international community, it has been relatively successful. When the majority of its members have sought through the passing of resolutions to persuade the most powerful countries to do things they were otherwise reluctant to do, then the distance between words and deeds—the U.N.'s credibility gap—simply grew. While the annual laundry-list approach of the General Assembly, focusing largely on East-West nuclear issues, has done little to advance the prospects for disarmament, in Geneva the 40-nation Conference on Disarmament and its predecessors have played a critical and sometimes creative role as a multilateral negotiating forum midway in size and function between Soviet-American negotiations and the universal deliberative bodies in New York. Nine multilateral arms control agreements gained broad international acceptance through this process during the 1960s and early 1970s, among them treaties on nuclear non-proliferation, outer space, partial test ban, environmental modifications, the sea bed and Antarctica. It has only been in recent years, however, that U.N. members have begun to deal with the questions of limiting non-nuclear arms and forces, to which a global body could make a truly unique contribution. There has been encouraging progress recently in the Conference on Disarmament talks on banning chemical weapons and on establishing a U.N. agency to monitor such an accord, similar to the way the U.N.'s International Atomic Energy Agency has applied safeguards to nuclear reactors throughout the world to discourage further nuclear proliferation.

Economic and Social Issues: Debate and Negotiations

At once the most disputed and ambiguous aspect of the U.N.'s role is the nature and extent of its involvement in the determination of politically sensitive aspects of its members' relations. The largely unsuccessful efforts to negotiate a New International Economic Order which transpired at the U.N. under the general rubric of "Global Negotiations," and the more fruitful negotiations on the Law of the Sea which took place under U.N. auspices, provide some beneficial insights.

Global Negotiations and the "North-South Dialogue"

Since 1973, U.N. discussions between North and South concerning economic policy have occurred on the basis of—or in response to—the proposition that the world economic system is in fundamental respects inequitable and that both justice and world prosperity demand sweeping systemic change. A New International Economic Order (NIEO), a manifesto of new principles and a package of proposals to give them shape, was proposed by the Group of 77 as a basis for redressing the situation. Although many of the early statements of the NIEO were adopted by consensus, and although its stepchildren—Global Negotiations and the North-South dialogue—occupied center stage and consumed a tremendous amount of human resources for over a decade, virtually none of their contents were ever "negotiated." Disappointment with this fact led many developing country delegates to use U.N. forums to vent frustration over the North's "bad faith," which in turn triggered a progressive disaffection with these forms on the part of many developed countries. The several reasons why negotiations did not take place are instructive:

• *Global agendas.* Every significant branch of the economic relationship between industrialized and developing countries was proposed for negotiation. This involved the piecing together of disparate objectives into global issue packages that gave equal emphasis to each part of the package and to the connections between them. Consequently, the trade-offs and mutual gains that might have been identified for the ripest issues became hostage to the general negotiability of the issue that was least ripe.

• *Global bargaining.* U.N.-based consultations and "negotiations" on North-South issues tended to follow the principle of universal—and equal—participation *on all issues,* making issue-specific coalitions and bargaining groups impossible.

• *Non-convertible linkages.* It proved impossible to translate specific forms of interdependence, e.g., between exporters and importers of oil or commodities or capital, into a comprehensive agreement linking all major economic issues and all countries of the North and South.

• *Weak rationales.* Governments will not negotiate unless the costs of refusing to do so are higher than the costs of negotiating. But because the "global packages" approach prevented the offering of specific concessions in exchange for specific gains, the costs of refusing to negotiate were negligible.

• *Lack of a common information base.* Lack of relevant expertise among negotiators, and an overstretching of human resources due to the universal nature of agendas and participation, caused many diplomats to have an inadequate database for conducting informed negotiations. Major differences in the quality of the data available to different governmental representatives caused debates to bog down over the accuracy of an adversary's information and analysis, preventing discussion of possible solutions to a common problem.

• *Disagreement about venue.* Apart from divisions over substance, a large number of the countries whose participation was essential to the conduct of any real negotiation believed that the NIEO agenda encroached upon the jurisdiction of other institutions.

Negotiations on the Law of the Sea

Ironically, while the members of the U.N. were toiling in ultimately fruitless pseudo-negotiations on the NIEO, the same governments engaged in one of the most comprehensive, complex, and largely successful multilateral negotiations of recent years. The Third Conference on the Law of the Sea (UNCLOS in 1973–1982) produced a convention that is often likened in its broad scope to a "constitution for the oceans." While some obstacles, such as disagreement over the International Seabed Authority, are slowing down ratification by the signatories, the convention largely succeeded in reconciling an immense array of interests, and many of its provisions—regarding the breadth of the territorial seas, passage through straits, fisheries, the exclusive economic zone, the definition of the continental shelf, etc.— are widely observed by the world community. Several of the distinguishing features of UNCLOS III have potential relevance for U.N. negotiations generally.

• *agreement to a multilateral approach.* By 1970 there was wide agreement that the old maritime order had collapsed and that a new cooperative regime governing sea use would present fewer risks and costs and better results to the broad range of interested parties than would continuation of an increasingly anarchic status quo.

• *agreement about goals.* Parties differed on specifics but all believed it was in their national interests to reach agreements, e.g., on limits of territorial seas and fishing zones, precise continental shelf definitions, air and marine passage through straits, rules to protect the marine environment, guidelines for mineral exploitation of the seabed.

• *agreement about venue.* Unlike the NIEO, which implied some transfer of negotiation and decision-making authority on trade and financial questions from the Bretton Woods institutions to the U.N. General Assembly, UNCLOS could engage in authoriative negotiations without inpinging on the mandate of any other institution and, therefore, without generating opposition to the very concept of such a negotiation.

• *binding consensus.* Because UNCLOS sought an agreement which would receive the widest possible support and because this required protection of the interests and views of minorities, it adopted decisions by consensus only. Furthermore, since decisions were to be binding upon the signatories, each was painstakingly negotiated in order to strike an acceptable balance of interests.

• *coalitions of the like-minded.* Traditional regional, political and economic groups played a very minor role. In their place were groups composed of countries with similar specific interests: straits states, archipelagic states, coastal states, landlocked states, etc.

• *flexible form and process*. The consensus requirement, the number of countries represented (156 by the conclusion of the Conference) and the comprehensiveness of the subject matter required numerous innovations, including: small representative negotiating groups, compulsory "cooling off periods" when debate became too heated, etc.

• *prohibition on reservations*. In order to increase the inducement to agree, reservations were not allowed.

Economic and Social Issues: Policy Research and Cooperation

U.N. activities in this area seek to promote common norms and standards, to foster convergence of national policies with regard to those standards, to assist countries in the formation of joint undertakings, and finally to assist developing countries in the identification of effective development policies. Obviously, to advance goals of this kind, the links between research and cooperation should be direct and dynamic. U.N.-based research, as distinct from research in an academic environment, should: identify issues on which international cooperation is necessary; pinpoint dimensions of a problem where enhanced cooperation is possible; improve the U.N.'s ability to serve as a catalyst—either for the understanding of a problem or for responding to it directly; provide a common factual and conceptual basis to guide consideration of issues at the political level; explore policy options for actions by individual countries or groups of countries.

The U.N. record in providing this kind of catalytic analysis, and spurring cooperation based upon it, is very mixed. Two areas in which it has had some impact are population and environment.

The United Nations' work in population combines global monitoring, authoritative research, and consciousness-raising to produce both cooperation and policy convergence at the international level.

Three phases are evident. First, the years between the time of the United Nations' origin and the 1974 U.N. World Conference on Population in Bucharest, Romania, were a time of ambivalence, marked on the one hand by growing realization of the need to control population growth, and on the other by resistance on the part of many countries to family planning programs. By acknowledging the relationship between population, development, and the international economic system, the adoption of the World Population Plan of Action at the Bucharest Conference represented a significant, albeit modest, step toward multilateral cooperation in stabilizing population growth.

During the subsequent decade the UNFPA worked in collaboration with specialized agencies and non-governmental organizations to integrate population planning into the development process. By dispatching teams of regional experts to assess population needs and provide technical assistance at the national level, the UNFPA was able to build a consensus among governments in favor of population stability as a national goal. This led to the subsequent adoption of national policies to stabilize population in a large number of developing countries, including Mexico, South Korea, Thailand, Morocco, Indonesia, Pakistan, Bangladesh, Vietnam and India. In 1984 the emerging consensus was reflected in the declaration and recommendations calling for universal availability of family planning services that were adopted by the Mexico City Conference on Population held that year.

The ingredients behind the U.N.'s influence in world population policy—global monitoring, an authoritative and reliable data base, and effective consciousness-raising—also helped it produce greater policy convergence and cooperation in the environmental area. The 1972 U.N. Conference on the Human Environment held in Stockholm, Sweden, stimulated a dramatic evolution in awareness of environmental risks and triggered the establishment of mechanisms for managing these risks. These included the creation of environmental ministries in nearly every country, the formation of UNEP, the creation of a framework of treaties and conventions to protect and preserve the environment, including the recent accord on protection of stratospheric ozone. Finally, U.N. initiatives in the environmental area, such as the plan to halt pollution in the Mediterranean Sea (Appendix I), provide some of the best examples of national policy convergence and cooperation stimulated by an international organization.

Unfortunately, the U.N.'s performance in the research and cooperation area in general is not nearly so strong as its record in population and environment. One of the greatest disappointments, in fact, has been in the economic field, where the contributions of the present-day United Nations compare very unfavorably with its contributions in the 1950s and 1960s. Then, U.N. economists exerted considerable influence over the evolution of new approaches to the international economy, development and the role of international institutions. The formation of the International Development Agency of the World Bank, the Compensatory Financing Facility of the IMF and the Generalized System of Preferences, all can be traced to discussion and writings emanating from the United Nations.

Today such originality is rare. While some U.N. enclaves still occasionally contribute new approaches to the problems of the international economy and development, the Organization's total output in this area, so vital to its role, has dwindled to a rivulet. Although DIESA's *World Economic Survey* and UNCTAD's *Trade and Development Report* sometimes provide interesting information, they tend to be descriptive rather than analytical, and repetitive. Their potential as vehicles for identifying new issues, for exploring possible complementarities in national positions, or for developing consensus approaches to existing sources of division is largely unexploited.

With the exception of modest progress in the field of drugs, transport and transnational corporations, the record of the U.N.'s intergovernmental bodies is no better, and often worse, than that of the Secretariat. For example, the *International Development Strategy,* a negotiated document intended to foster the evolution of consensus on the goals and methods of development, is usually a litany of virtuous ends with no attention to means.

Several factors lie behind the weakness of the U.N.'s record in conducting policy-relevant research or in providing a setting for policy-relevant deliberations:

• *universality without synthesis.* There is virtually no facet of human activity that is left untouched by the universal scope of the United Nations system. But this rich fund of data is largely unexploited, since there is no structural means for gathering and synthesizing it from a global perspective, converting it into usable form, and presenting it to member states.

• *Lack of interdisciplinary approach.* Extereme sectorialization within the Organization as a whole, and within individual departments, prevents the U.N. Secretariat from identifying linkages between economic-social-military-environmental-etc. issues. The absence of emphasis on such "crossover" issues at the Secretariat level prevents their systematic consideration at the political level.

• *Research that is poor in quality.* The general quality of U.N.-based research has deteriorated noticeably over the last 20 years (work on population is one of a few exceptions) due to several factors: increasing political pressure has discouraged originality; close links to the major international centers of research—universities, foundations, institutes—have not been maintained; data collection and monitoring have suffered from a lack of synthesis; research that should pose new questions and explore new issues has tended instead to produce only syntheses of existing knowledge and to describe rather than analyze; and there has been little effort to define audiences in advance.

• *Membership bodies: no center at the center*. None of the intergovernmental bodies that might provide a political focal point for monitoring global developments and consulting on joint responses regards this as its mandate. Nor, if such a mandate were adopted, is it likely that any could fulfill it. In the three potential bodies—the Economic and Social Council, the UNCTAD Trade and Development Board, and the Second Committee—the membership is too large, too junior in rank, too lacking in expertise to deal credibly with a global agenda.

• *ECOSOC and the Second Committee: overburdened and overlapping*. There is near total absence of distinct, specific mandates and areas of responsibility between ECOSOC and the U.N. Second Committee and very significant overlap between these two bodies and UNCTAD's Trade and Development Board. The picture is one in which large political bodies are saddled with an impossible oversight load on the one hand (159 bodies and expert groups report to ECOSOC and the Second Committee), while, on the other hand, their general debates tend to recirculate the same issues year after year.

• *No intellectual center at the Secretariat level*. At the same time, there is no structural means at the senior Secretariat level for focusing on the interlocking aspects of major problems which the system addresses in a sectoral fashion but might be addressed in a more coordinated way. (The Administrative Committee on Coordination might have carried out such a function, but its focus has always been chiefly confined to administrative coordination.)

Economic and Social Activities: Technical Assistance

About $2 billion in development assistance, representing 5% of total ODA, is provided by the agencies of the U.N. Group annually, mainly through UNICEF, UNDP, WFP, and UNFPA, with lesser amounts provided by UNEP and the U.N.'s Regular Program of Technical Assistance. These programs, which (except for the last mentioned) are financed voluntarily, tend to be very popular with donors and recipients: UNICEF's successful efforts to combat child mortality, WFP's emergency food assistance, UNFPA's family planning programs, and UNDP's contributions to rural agricultural development and to developing country fund-raising efforts with other international agencies are among the best known.

Despite its relatively favorable reputation, and the relatively small amount of resources involved, it seems clear that the aid provided in this way could enjoy a greater impact if a number of constraints were addressed. First, the most serious drawback of U.N.-supplied aid, which is particularly true of the assistance provided through UNDP, is that it has not carved out its own niche or speciality. Consequently, much of U.N.-delivered aid is indistinguishable—except by its smaller size—from assistance provided by bilateral and other multilateral donors. Secondly, despite its modest size, U.N. aid tends to be fragmented, not just among the four main programs of the U.N. Group, but among all the specialized agencies and a large number of smaller semi-independent programs as well. Such proliferation causes U.N. development agencies to compete for the same resources (total U.N. technical assistance has declined 4% in real terms since 1981) and makes coordination difficult, risking duplication or overstretching of resources. Finally, the sheer number of U.N.-affiliated but effectively independent aid suppliers causes recipients to spend scarce human resources in organizing and coordinating them all—a task that is scantily rewarded by the small amount of resources available from any single U.N. source.

Economic and Social Activities: Humanitarian Assistance

A natural monopoly of the U.N., which has unfortunately grown in significance over the course of its existence, is the provision of basic humanitarian assistance to victims of disasters and emergencies—both natural and man-made, both episodic and of long duration. Such assistance commonly involves the supply of food, shelter and medical care to victims, legal protection for stateless refugees, and more permanent assistance to individuals remaining in a highly vulnerable status for an indefinite time. Because the international community regards such services as obligations between peoples, not governments, the U.N.'s universal character confers potential advantages—a degree of moral authority, a humanitarian right of access—shared by no other political entity.

Generally, the U.N. has made excellent use of this near "monopoly." A record of difficult but successful humanitarian interventions—in the Congo in the early 1960s, in Biafra in 1969, in Bangladesh in 1972, in Cambodia from 1979 to the present, to the Vietnamese and Chinese boat people in 1980 and 1981, during the most severe period of the African Emergency from 1984 to 1986, and on behalf of the Palestinian refugees from the 1950s to the present—has produced a harvest of credibility demonstrated annually by mobilization of large voluntary resources ($750 million to UNRWA and UNHCR in 1986).

Humanitarian actions, among the best managed of U.N. operations, have often had similar features, many of which played a part in the success of the United Nations Office for Emergency Operations in Africa (OEOA), which is worth examining briefly for that reason.

Designed to coordinate the African relief efforts of a large number of international organizations, the OEOA (January 1985–October 1986) faced formidable obstacles that it managed to overcome during the 22 months of its existence: the high number of agencies involved in various aspects of the effort and the poor integration of their activities; a degree of competitiveness among the large, semi-autonomous U.N. agencies involved and a tendency on the part of some to view OEOA's broad mandate as a threat; and a general lack of information regarding the status of relief needs and the logistical character and volume concentration of relief efforts. Despite these and other potential impediments, OEOA was highly successful, serving as the focal point and organizational center of the relief operation and helping to raise at least $1 billion for the many organizations actually delivering relief.

Several factors seem to have contributed to OEOA's success. First, its mandate was concrete and specific. Second, it benefited from strong and dynamic leadership. Third, its temporary character meant that it did not inherit a preexisting staff and style of operation but was able to select the best possible staff, through secondment from U.N. agencies and by special short-term recruitment, and was able to define its own ad hoc mode of operation that was well suited to the tasks with which it was charged. Fourth, though it never enjoyed a consensus of support from U.N. members, it did receive forceful and enthusiastic backing from a core of countries, and, as a consequence, those that were not enthusiastic eventually acquiesced. Fifth, by building a constituency among active and influential non-governmental organizations, it was able to broaden the degree of both financial and political support for its efforts well beyond what would otherwise have been forthcoming from governments and, in so doing, to multiply its effectiveness. Finally, and most important of all, by creating an authoritative, totally up to date, computerized information system about country needs— what, where, how to supply it, etc.—OEOA was able to provide a set of information tools that were so useful that governments could not fail to use them.

In the humanitarian realm, the major area in which the U.N. has fallen very far short of its potential is that of *immediate response* to disasters. When a disaster strikes a country that is unable to cope with its effects on its own, there is generally an outpouring of offers of assistance from U.N. agencies, NGOs and individual governments from all over the world. While helpful to the recipient, the response brings organizational tasks that are often far more than the already overtaxed civil authorities can possibly deal with. The U.N.'s Office of Disaster Relief (UNDRO) was created to help stricken countries obtain rapid relief and to help them manage that relief, by quickly assessing damage and coordinating what is usually a multiagency, multinational response. For a variety of reasons, many of which have been beyond its control, UNDRO has lacked the organizational capacity to play such a role.

First, UNDRO has never been explicitly and authoritatively designated as lead agency in first-stage disaster response and thus made the natural focal point of needs and damage assessment in the early hours of disaster. Second, perhaps in part as a consequence, UNDRO has never developed the capacity to play such a role. It is unable to field a team of experts qualified to assess the scope of a disaster and the needs of the stricken government and thus ensure that *appropriate* international assistance will be identified and mobilized. Third, because it is unable to assist other responding parties or local authorities in this way to any significant degree, it has little influence when it comes to coordinating their efforts.

Human Rights and Normative Action

Today more than 50% of the world's nations recognize human rights standards established since the U.N.'s founding. In 1948, under the leadership of individuals like Eleanor Roosevelt and Renee Cassin, the Commission on Human Rights (formed under Article 68 of the U.N. Charter) adopted the Universal Declaration on Human Rights. Eighteen years later, the International Covenants on Civil and Political Rights were created, along with other instruments which established basic civil, political, economic, and social rights, as well as provisions against genocide, torture, and racial and sexual discrimination.

In the mid-1970s, the United Nations turned to implementation and enforcement of the now codified human rights standards. Committees were established, with the requirement that states parties to existing treaties report on their compliance. In addition, the U.N. Commission on Human Rights expanded its scope to include working groups and rapporteurs on forced or involuntary disappearances, torture, extrajudicial killings, and religious intolerance. The Commission established and enlarged procedures whereby offending governments had to account in a confidential session for complaints of human rights abuses documented by non-governmental organizations (NGOs) and other bodies.

This successful record may be attributed largely to four key elements. First, the United Nations solidly established its norms *before* embarking on implementation, thus enabling the executing bodies to proceed with a clear purpose. Second, the United Nations benefited from the dynamic leadership of a few individuals in launching human rights efforts with a strength that fostered ongoing momentum. Third, the assignments of the working groups and rapporteurs are limited to specific themes or countries, so their tasks are sharply defined and manageable in scope. Finally, the working groups and rapporteurs are authorized to conduct investigations on an autonomous basis and call for governmental reforms if they deem it necessary. This enables them to investigate and expose human rights violations quickly and assertively, often eliciting at least partial cooperation from the governments in question.

Lessons for More Effective U.N. Action

The successes described above shared features which the failures generally lacked. Viewed as a whole, the common components of the success stories reveal criteria essential to the U.N.'s ability to address in a useful way issues that are important to the world community.

• *Convergence of interests*
The U.N. Secretariat, often with the involvement of certain member states, accurately identified issues in which common interests were demonstrable and in which the advantages of cooperative action (in lieu of, or in addition to, unilateral action) could be persuasively presented. Examples include: the widespread costs, risks and potential inequities associated with increasing disintegration of the maritime order in the 1950s, 1960s and 1970s; gains in world prosperity associated with development; injury to human beings resulting from depletion of the ozone layer; and threats to the sustainability of human life associated with uncontrolled population growth.

• *Converting common interests into common views*

Through successful consensus-building, member states *acknowledged* common interests and then *narrowed the range of permissible means* to protect them. The U.N. used a variety of methods to bring this about. Examples include; consciousness-raising, as in the international conferences on environment and population; and creation of a commonly accepted data base so that the parties agree on the nature and extent of a problem—as in UNEP's monitoring of the rate and effects of ozone depletion or DIESA's demographic statistics.

• *Converting common views into cooperative action.*

Consensus was then converted into outcomes directly useful to the affected parties. In some cases this meant the conduct of negotiations in which policy differences were narrowed further, followed by the establishment of a cooperative regime where none existed before: e.g., the Law of the Sea Convention, the scale-down agreement on hydrofluorocarbon emissions under the Ozone Accord, the International Covenants on Civil and Political Rights, and the "thematic" rapporteurs and working groups established by the Human Rights Commission. In other cases the conversion of consensus involved U.N. initiatives which stimulated effective regional action, as in the case of UNEP's plan to combat pollution of the Mediterranean and such operational actions as the Office for Emergency Operations in Africa or UNHCR's refugee operations.

CHAPTER 2

SOME LESSONS FROM EXPERIENCE

Unfortunately, occasions on which the three-stage process described above has been followed tend to be the exception at the U.N. rather than the norm. Areas of convergence of national interest seldom receive systematic attention and are identified at levels that are too abstract to stimulate useful dialogue. The wish list quality of the International Development Strategies mentioned in Chapter One typifies this failing. In addition, the task of bringing forth common views from a given set of common interests has not been made a priority. Inadequate resources are given to the creation of common data bases, to the exploration of policy options on which national governments could agree, etc. Consequently, when successes occur, it is generally as a result of the presence of special circumstances—exceptional leadership, imaginative initiatives with the backing of influential member states, and so on.

If the United Nations is to provide the kinds of "public goods" that the world community increasingly needs, then the three-part approach summarized at the end of Chapter One must become the new axiom of U.N. work. A transformation of this order means fundamental change: in the administration and management of the Organization; in the assumptions underlying its structure and functions; and in thinking about the role of international organizations in general. Chapters Two and Three address the nature of the shortcomings and the changes that must take place in each of these areas.

U.N. Management

Arguably the United Nations' most valuable resource is the agreement on core program goals that it is able to generate among member countries. Putting that agreement to work thus becomes the Organization's most important management task. As Chapter One has shown, in some instances this "consensus resource" has been employed with great effect. However, on too many occasions this has not happened. Part of the explanation may be found in deficiencies in the U.N.'s management. The U.N.'s system—if it may be called a system—for choosing *priority* tasks, *staffing* them satisfactorily and *monitoring* their outcomes is not adequate to ensure either that it is doing the right things with its resources (i.e., pursuing goals with the right means) or that it is doing those things well. It is also clear that the U.N. has lost opportunities to generate public understanding and support for program goals as a consequence of weakness in its public information effort. This section focuses on the major areas where improvement is needed in U.N. management and the crucial leadership role of the Secretary-General. While several of the observations which follow are strongly critical, it should be emphasized that many of the practices which weaken U.N. management, particularly in the personnel area, also exist in the bureaucracies of member states.

U.N. Personnel Policy Issues

The unusual difficulties encountered in personnel management at the U.N. are partly due to the very characteristics—universality of membership, multicultural nature of staff, comprehensiveness of mission—that make the world body unique among organizations. Although a standardized approach to personnel management is more difficult in a multicultural environment than in a more homogeneous cultural setting, it is not impossible to achieve. At the United Nations, however, the challenges posed by cultural diversity are heightened by two more troublesome phenomena: a lack of clarity, at the level of working staff units, about the Organization's mission and a remarkably low level of interest, on the part of most member states, in ensuring administrative efficiency. It is this member state attitude, which is tolerant of personnel inefficiencies and guilty of fostering them, that is the single most important explanation for the U.N.'s very troubled personnel situation.

The Role of the Secretary-General. No really significant improvement in personnel matters is likely to take place without a fundamental change in the attitude of the U.N.'s top leadership. Over the past 15 years the Assembly has moved deeply into the details of policy-making in personnel matters (indeed, into the entire range of management issues) in large part because Secretaries-General have not sufficiently asserted their administrative prerogatives under Chapter 15 of the U.N. Charter. Articles 97 and 101 of Chapter 15 give to the Secretary-General exclusively the powers of chief executive officer. These powers must be defended against challenges, not just by member states acting as "micro-managers" or as lobbyists, but by the various staff associations and other competing sources of influence in the Organization's decentralized management structure as well. In the words of one former senior U.N. official, "job lobbying is a bit like an appetite that grows the more you are willing to feed it. Deny it meals, and the clamor to be fed will go away." One of the reasons why the U.N. has found it difficult to resist overtures by foreign ministers or ambassadors on behalf of their nationals is the fear that refusal may cause dissatisfaction that will ricochet—resulting in the denial of financial assistance to some extrabudgetary program, for example. But it would appear that the Secretariat's fears about spillover have been exaggerated. Another important prerogative of the Secretary-General, in which, again, too much is ceded to others, is the power of appointment at the senior level. Because political considerations are permitted to play so great a role, unqualified individuals are frequently appointed to key administrative posts.

The Role of the General Assembly. While the Assembly clearly has an important role in the setting of broad policy goals, on a number of issues it has adopted a "command and compliance" approach to reaching them. For example, the Office of Personnel Services (OPS) is directed to implement the goal of equitable geographical distribution— obviously an essential characteristic of any global organization—but to do so in such a way as to impose serious obstacles to the speed and efficiency of U.N. recruitment. Other, less well-intentioned, Assembly policies have had a sharply counterproductive effect. For example, a resolution of the 1980 session gave legislative sanction to the practice of reserving certain fixed-term posts for nationals of the same country. In another action, the General Assembly effectively increased the obstacles to a merit-based approach to recruitment by urging the Secretary-General to convert temporary staff to permanent status after they had served for five years.

Politicization. In a recent report the U.N. staff union concluded: "Politicization of the Secretariat has spread from the original notion whereby political appointments were limited to the D-2 level and above, into every level and aspect of work, thereby undermining the overall technical and managerial competence of the staff."

Politicization takes a wide variety of forms. There is, for example, the requirement of some countries that their citizens serve only on the basis of short-term "secondments," that they relinquish part of their salaries to their governments, and that their recruitment by the U.N. be limited to a prescribed list of candidates.

Other forms of political interference are also very damaging. One of these is the tradition of considering certain posts, offices, or divisions the domain of particular member states or groups of member states— a situation that makes concepts of efficiency in workforce management and fairness in career development impossible to apply. Even more injurious is the nearly universal propensity of member states to try to influence the outcome of personnel decisions. Though especially egregious in the recruitment area, in recent years this lobbying has also focused on promotions and has even gone so far as to include the marks given a staff member on evaluation reports.

Recruitment. There are effectively two formal recruitment procedures for U.N. professional staff. One, for junior staff (P-1 and P-2 grades), utilizes competitive examinations and has generally raised the caliber of entering U.N. professionals since its introduction in 1981. The other, for employees entering at the middle levels and above (the vast majority), is flawed in such fundamental respects that there is a general tendency to circumvent it. The most serious of these flaws is the fact that the U.N. has no common objective, job-specific standards to guide recruitment at the mid-professional (P-3/P-4) or managerial (P-5/D-2) levels. As a result, the U.N. inevitably relies too heavily upon haphazard, subjective, highly personalized processes. This ad hoc system limits the pool of qualified candidates and the possibility that the best person will be chosen for the job. In addition, the informal approach lowers staff morale, since it fosters the impression that advancement depends upon personal contacts and patronage.

Evaluations. Personnel evaluations should: measure employee performance; identify candidates for promotion; and identify nonperformers who may be candidates for termination. The U.N.'s performance evaluation process, though intended as the backbone of its quality control, is too weak to perform any of these useful functions. It provides almost no basis for objective task-related appraisal, and reports are subject to lengthy employee rebuttal procedures that generally overturn supervisor's recommendations. Most managers avoid the risk of time-consuming rebuttal by giving high marks irrespective of performance (90% of staff consistently receive "A" ratings); those faced with poor performers tend to overrate them and then seek their transfer.

Promotions/Terminations. There are no clear across-the-board criteria for advancement in the professional grades, and whether promotions are granted on a rigorous or permissive basis depends on the individual supervisor and on the strength of the patronage an employee may have developed elsewhere in the Organization or the mission community. Terminations are virtually nonexistent once an employee has been granted a permanent contract.

International Civil Service Commission (ICSC). Established in 1974 to advise the General Assembly on salaries, allowances and other conditions of service (policies on recruitment, promotion career development) to develop a unified international civil service, the Commission's effectiveness has been limited by several factors: inadequate qualifications of Commissioners; preoccupation with matters with financial implications to the exclusion of personnel policy issues; and a tendency to base its decisions on positions developed by its staff, who are governed by the same system of salaries and allowances as the U.N. system employees that the Commissioners are intended to regulate.

Planning, Programming, Budgeting, and Evaluation

Under the U.N.'s present structure, both the Secretariat and the member states are expected to participate in the task of selecting priorities and planning the various program pieces that flow from them. The Secretariat input is supposed to be provided by the Secretary-General, the Director General and their staffs at six-year intervals when the Medium-Term Plan is prepared, and again every two years when the proposals for the program budget are being prepared. Member state direction, on the other hand, should come from the Committee for Program and Coordination, ECOSOC, and the main committees of the General Assembly when the program budgets are being adopted.

The actual practice is totally different. The collective nature of decision-making on the U.N.'s programs makes it difficult to shape priorities in a coherent manner. While ultimate responsibility rests with member states, as a practical matter the sheer size and diversity of the activities funded by the U.N. regular budget means that member states are less likely to "lead" in a legislative sense than to respond to a set of broad strategic choices proposed by the Secretary-General. Vehicles for such a role already exist: the Secretary-General is required to propose priorities for the Organization over a six-year period in the Medium-Term Plan and to indicate which of the U.N.'s ongoing programs should be phased out and which reinforced.

But Secretaries-General have avoided such initiatives in order to steer clear of positions that would bring them into conflict with different member states. Because priority-setting has not been acknowledged as a leadership role, the U.N.'s leadership is largely unequipped to conduct it. What is missing is a strong technocratic and interdisciplinary team able to carry out the program evaluations and appraisals of new issue areas and provide sufficient intellectual support for the program budget.

As a result of this lack of input, the documents intended to link common goals at the conceptual level with specific objectives at the level of planning and programming budgetary expenditures become in reality little more than an extension of existing activities. In fact, program objectives are described in such a vague and routinized manner ("information will continue to be provided on . . . to help the developing countries to . . . ," "issue-oriented in-depth studies will be undertaken . . .") as to be nearly meaningless, making the program budget little more than an aggregation of a multitude of decisions and recommendations with little to connect them.

Passivity and lack of direction from the U.N. Secretariat are matched by the absence of coherent oversight by the senior intergovernmental bodies. In fact, until changes were adopted by the General Assembly in December 1986, the program implications and budgetary effects of resolutions that call for new activities were never considered in the same place at the same time. Instead of forcing trade-offs between competing programs, the committee structure tended to have the opposite effect. Failure to provide overall programmatic direction, by either member states or Secretariat leadership, has effectively left individual program managers with free rein, at a considerable cost in terms of coherence, relevance, and strategic direction.

The situation has not been helped by the poor state of the U.N.'s evaluation system. In general the evaluation process is not timed to coincide with the planning and budgeting cycle so that the conclusions of the former can inform the decisions of the latter; the quality of evaluations and "program performance reports" is uneven at best; data is scanty on the results of previous evaluations; and evaluation is generally overlooked by intergovernmental bodies, which devote little time to reviewing the outcomes of the programs they have authorized.

In December 1986 the General Assembly adopted reforms (Appendix II) that have the potential for strengthening the planning and programming process by requiring the member states and the Secretary-General to engage in a dialogue on priorities early enough to have an impact on the budget and by unifying considerations of budget and program matters, at the broad policy level, in a single committee. If the reforms produce greater member state involvement at the beginning of and throughout the planning and budget process—which is their goal—then a more assertive role for the Secretary-General in shaping and proposing major program emphases will be essential to their success.

Public Information

The reach and impact of U.N. efforts often depend on the extent to which they arouse the active support not just of governments but of peoples. Mobilizing public support is very difficult without a vigorous information program capable of using the international media to nurture an informed understanding of the aims and activities of the Organization and the realities with which it must cope. In fact, the credibility of the U.N. often depends as much upon the public perception and media coverage of its actions as on the effectiveness with which they are carried out.

There are several ways in which the ability of the Department of Public Information to carry out this key function could be strengthened. A few of the more important points are mentioned here. First, DPI is not aggressive enough in its dealings with the press. On too many occasions DPI has missed excellent opportunities to communicate a U.N. success story or has relayed it in so passive a way that the press has not picked it up. Second, press releases are far too numerous and DPI coverage is not selective enough. DPI press officers are assigned to cover too many meetings with too little news value to the international press while some important U.N. events receive scant DPI attention. Third, as a result of what appear to be weak links between the Office of the Secretary-General and DPI, newsworthy statements or actions by the Secretary-General—the U.N.'s most important spokesman, and in a sense, its most valuable news asset—are often poorly exploited. Fourth, there is a continuing need for high-quality feature stories covering the Organization's activities in fields that greatly benefit from public support. Unfortunately, too much of what is produced in this area makes for very dull reading. Finally, because of their importance to international public perceptions of the

U.N. and its work, it is essential that the accuracy, fairness, and balance of DPI information products be closely monitored.

The Leadership Role of the Secretary-General

The political and managerial responsibilities of the Secretary-General have evolved rather paradoxically. Despite their modest foundation in Articles 98, 99, and 100, his political responsibilities have grown extensively. His powers as the U.N.'s chief executive, on the other hand—and notwithstanding a more explicit constitutional writ in Articles 7, 97, 98, 100, and 101—have actually eroded through lack of exercise.

A slow contraction of the prerogatives of managerial leadership has taken place over many years as Secretaries-General have lost ground to a variety of challengers. In the administrative area, governments routinely attempt to influence personnel decisions, while the staff has in many instances amassed powers and rights that effectively make them co-managers who are capable of curtailing the Secretary-General's freedom of action. Too often the leadership's prerogatives have been ceded after very little struggle, suggesting that the problem is not the inroads that staff and member states have been able to make but the lack of resistance to such pressures.

In the programmatic area, the lead role rests with the member states. But, as indicated above, intractable East-West and North-South divisions repeatedly frustrate the consensus-building process in the U.N.'s deliberative organs, raising the importance attached to "legislative" directions suggested by the Secretary-General. In fact, the Secretary-General's office must adopt a more expansive view of its role, taking initiatives that would elicit more explicit policy guidance from member states when none is forthcoming. In the absence of such leadership, the Organization faces continued paralysis in many contentious but vitally important areas.

For nearly a quarter-century now, Secretaries-General have been cautious in their exercise of administrative power, and, like executives anywhere, none has been eager to risk breaking with the tradition set by his predecessors. Yet one of the characteristics of a good leader is the ability to go beyond the limits of tradition and custom and seek to redefine the parameters of what is possible. The political and psychological pressures, after all, need not always go in one direction. While Secretaries-General do lack economic and military power, they command an unusually visible pulpit from which to seek to shape both public and official opinion around the world. A Secretary-General who begins with a true mandate for leadership, even while redefining the management role of the office, is in a good position to begin reshaping the conditions under which the office operates, especially in the realm of administration and management. For all of these reasons, it is imperative that member states give greater emphasis than in the past to the qualities of leadership, experience and intellect essential to meet the enormous challenges of the post of Secretary-General.

Flawed Assumptions

Collective Security. The U.N. Charter was drafted on the eve of a profound transformation of the international security environment, whose course could not be anticipated or understood by the U.N.'s founding fathers. Today, many of the assumptions behind the collective security provisions of the Charter seem almost quaint, though the security machinery established by the Charter has shown remarkable resiliency through the years in the face of one unanticipated challenge after another. With the collapse of civility, much less unity, among the victorious allies, the Military Staff Committee had very little to do in terms of fulfilling its initial mandate of protecting against threats to their collective security. The Charter, moreover, was a prenuclear document. Nuclear deterrence quickly replaced collective security as the dominant factor defining the international security (or insecurity) environment, adding a modicum of stability to what had suddenly become a bipolar world but also rather strictly limiting how far the U.N. could go in policing the world.

No sooner had people become adjusted to these new realities than the U.N. helped to spawn a second fundamental shift in the nature of international politics. Through the decolonization process, scores of newly independent countries emerged with a host of very difficult security problems, often with domestic roots; an independent view of what ought to constitute U.N. priorities; and doubts about the equity of major power dominance of U.N. decision-making processes. Security problems came to assume not only East-West but North-South and South-South dimensions never envisioned by the founders of a "United" Nations. Soon the U.N. had all the earmarks of a universal organization. Full of internal contradictions and squabbles, it shed any pretense of representing an alliance of the like-minded. With the spread of advanced weaponry and the rise of regional military powers, the trends first seen on the political level were confirmed in military terms. While bipolarity still reigns in strategic nuclear arms, on lower rungs of the strategic ladder multipolarity appears to be the mode of the future, posing a more complex but potentially more important challenge for the U.N.

The U.N. Role in Global Economic Policy. In Articles 1 and 55 and elsewhere in the Charter, the U.N. is given important but ambiguous responsibilities in international economic policy. It is charged with "achieving international cooperation in solving problems of an economic character . . . [and] with promoting "higher standards of living, full employment, conditions of economic progress; solutions of international economic and related problems," etc. But the precise role of the U.N. relative to these goals is nowhere clarified by the Charter and when the U.N. has been viewed as an instrument for their direct pursuit, serious obstacles have arisen.

First, significant action affecting employment, higher standards of living, etc. requires multiple supportive decisions by governments on trade, fiscal and monetary policies, and so on. Yet such collaboration is in practice very difficult to achieve, and the U.N. has never been the chosen venue for attempting it. For constitutional and political reasons the GATT, the IMF, the World Bank, and their joint committees are the settings for incipient efforts at coordination when they involve large groups. Less formal gatherings, such as the OECD summits, are the venues of choice for smaller get-togethers.

Second, "full employment," "economic progress," and so on, are the kinds of propositions to which all can agree on *outcomes,* but few can agree on *means.* Means-ends controversies regularly prevent countries as economically comparable and politically compatible as the United States, Japan, and the Federal Republic of Germany from settling on coordinated actions to correct structural imbalances that all *agree* should be corrected. Experience suggests little probability that larger and more disparate groups would have greater success.

Notwithstanding these impediments—constitutional, political, substantive—a majority of U.N. members dissatisfied with the gradualist approach to economic change that is followed by the industrialized West sought to use U.N. forums to conduct binding political negotiations to restructure economic relationships between developed and developing countries. Though doomed to failure, the effort occupied enormous human resources and public attention. Indeed, the exaggerated view of the capacity of U.N. economic forums was even codified in the ambitious language of a resolution designed to restructure the

U.N.'s economic and social role (A 32/197), which proposes that the General Assembly be the "principal forum for policymaking and the harmonization of international action" on international economic, social, and related matters.

Although adopted without vote, the ambitious vision of the restructuring resolution had few true believers among the most important capitals of North and South. Ministers of trade or of finance in both groups had not the slightest intention of giving—to ECOSOC, for example—the principal responsibility for deciding or even discussing the major economic questions in their sectors. The pseudoconsensus behind the resolution gave way to hollow rhetoric and open skepticism and never led to a reappraisal of assumptions or a search for a more compelling political rationale or a U.N. policy role to fit a new rationale.

Dialogue Versus Parliamentary Decision. The political and substantive reasons for the breakdown in the North-South dialogue at the U.N. have been touched upon above and elsewhere in this report. Institutional deficiencies have also played a role. Because the U.N. is the only setting in which developed (both market and socialist) and developing countries can discuss the full range of issues confronting them, institutional obstacles to dialogue have serious implications not only for economic matters but for every aspect of their relations.

At the root of these obstacles is a mistaken assumption that the forms and principles of parliamentary decision-taking are an appropriate model for the conduct of most U.N. business, but the analogy is inappropriate. Because the members of a national parliament are subject to a common authority, it is possible to produce binding outcomes by majority vote. However, no "parliament of sovereigns" could possibly function this way, and U.N. decisions are treated as recommendations only. Here enters a second problem with the analogy. In a democracy, parliament is the ultimate authority and, consequently, its obligation to act outweighs its need to maximize consensus. At the U.N. the obligation is precisely the opposite. Because national governments determine their own actions and those actions together may be made more or less harmonious due to international dialogue and conciliation, the U.N.'s *primary* concern must be to promote such conciliation.

This is not to suggest that the General Assembly's practice of passing general resolutions should be discontinued; they serve an important consciousness-raising function and help to establish an agenda of global issues. It does mean that the current balance between dialogue and decision, now skewed heavily toward the latter, should be drastically redressed.

Altering the balance will require a change in old parliamentary habits: the length of debates, the repetitiousness of speeches, the volume of meetings, the desire to "negotiate" when negotiation can only produce paper outcomes, and, most important, a kind of "vote happy" instinct to offer resolutions for every agenda item at every meeting of plenary bodies and subsidiary groups alike.

Big Problems, Little Boxes: Intellectual and Organizational Compartmentalization. To shield international functional cooperation from disruption by extraneous political controversies, the founders of the U.N. system designed a weak political center, loosely linked to functional satellites. This buffering in fact made possible impressive examples of functional cooperation, but it has also brought handicaps that are increasingly costly.

First, it has frozen the U.N. in a highly sectoral world view that has less and less connection to what we now understand is the multisectoral and interdisciplinary nature of the challenges facing humanity. Increasingly, the experience of governments and the counsel of groups like the World Commission on Environment and Development has revealed the determinative character of "crossover" issues—that is, of the impact on one sector of policies in another.

One conspicuous example of this law of unintended consequences at the global level is the cumulative drag on world prosperity resulting from the import-compression policies urged upon developing country debtors to satisfy interest payments on their debt. Similarly, many poor African nations are increasing their reliance on primary product income to meet debt payments, despite the fact that the overcultivation of commodity crops is turning good soil to desert and that the terms of trade for such goods themselves are in long-term decline. Another example of crossover is the rapid disappearance of large Latin American tropical forests—an ecological resource essential to avoidance of the global greenhouse effect—as many of the Latin countries attempt to improve their balance of payments.

Recognition of the importance of crossover issues domestically and globally has led many governments to begin to establish some means for more integrated analysis and operational coordination so that the actions of individual departments reinforce each other—or, at least, are not directly counterproductive. Unfortunately, the adaptations—albeit crude and modest—now taking place at the national level have not yet begun at the United Nations.

The budgetary, statutory, and political independence of the specialized agencies and the de facto autonomy of most of the funds and programs has created a centrifugal pull away from the center that three decades of "coordination" reforms have not altered. The persistence of this situation despite periodic scoldings from governments and intergovernmental groups is largely a result of the fact that the bounded and sectoral attentions of the individual agencies reflect the biases and institutional outlooks of the governmental departments that oversee them.

Throwing Institutions at the Problem. Of course there is nothing to prevent the U.N. proper from serving as a center for interdisciplinary research, analysis, and development of policy options, irrespective of the state of cooperation and collegiality in its relations with the specialized agencies. Here, however, a different set of problems has intervened.

Since the early 1970s the growth of the Secretariat has proceeded along a kind of U.N. reproductive ladder, with the result that the financial and intellectual resources it can bring forcefully to bear on any issue have been greatly diminished. Typically, the first rung of the ladder is the identification of a particular problem in a consensus resolution of the General Assembly. Frequently the resolution emphasizes (i) that the issue is intersectoral and requires a response that integrates a number of different fields, and (ii) that its solution will require global cooperation. Rung two is usually an international conference, which produces an action plan of some kind (rung three), which in turn usually involves an intergovernmental committee and a minisecretariat (rungs four and five). The latter is then installed, usually in perpetuity, in the U.N.'s program budget (rung six).

For more than a decade of U.N. institution-building, this process was repeated, with each new or newly acknowledged issue giving birth to its own institutional counterpart. This generation of new "centers" and "funds" undoubtedly extended the scope of international cooperation, and in some cases has built new constituencies and augmented resources available for technical assistance. But it is increasingly clear that the costs of this fractionalizing of global issues outweigh the benefits.

First, while "action" plans on women, youth, the disabled, science and technology, environment, human settlements, and so on always emphasize the need for an integrated, crosssectoral approach, the actual programs are invariably compartmentalized and have a marginal impact on the U.N. or on the agency programming through which they are supposed to promote their concerns. Second, the rationales that may justify holding an international conference—such as consciousness-raising—often do not justify a permanent secretariat and lead to poor use of resources. Third, many of these funds and centers engage in operational assistance of a cloistered character that is not integrated with U.N. technical assistance overall, reducing the total resources available for such assistance. Fourth, many of these small units cannot function effectively in isolation and, given their limited capabilities, are not taken seriously by governments, specialized agencies, or by such funding entities as UNDP or UNICEF. Finally, this proliferation of semi-independent units has not been offset by any parallel effort to coordinate their activities, synthesize their data, or understand and act upon their interrelationships.

Bridging the Sovereignty Gap: The Role of International Organizations in an Age of Nation-States

Too often prescriptions for an expanded role for international institutions are volunteered to national policymakers in a language that has little meaning. It is a language of generalities about "interdependence" or "mutual gains" that are passionately averred and specifics about means and modalities that are weakly conceived and unconvincingly presented. Clearly, the mere facts of interdependence and the growth of national limits, while axiomatic among most governments, will not themselves induce governments to choose a multilateral tool over the alternatives. Unfortunately, advocates of internationalism, after invoking "interdependence" as a kind of abstract imperative to cooperate, frequently fail to show how such cooperation would translate into a method of issue management that is more attractive than unilateral alternatives. Nor can the rationale for the existence as well as the refurbishing of international organizations be established by abstract assertions of collective self-interest or mutual gains. Gains are often mutual but rarely equal. In fact, the nature of most international problems is such that the risks, costs and sacrifices involved in managing them are rarely distributed evenly. Finally, impatient internationalists do their cause little service when they respond to growing constraints upon national power with proposals for some form of world government.

The case for international institutions can be compelling, but only if articulated in the language of national self-interest and combined with uncontestable common goals. An easy way to understand their role in an era of sovereign states is to consider that while the term "sovereignty" means absolute power within a limited geographical sphere, it is only in the legal and political sense that state power *is* absolute. In every other way that matters—military security, the economy, the environment, public health, and social conditions—authority may be unlimited but effective power is not. In the late 1980s that gap between abstract sovereignty and the means to exercise it has grown particularly large, even for the so-called "superpowers." If participation in international institutions is seen as helping to close this "sovereignty gap," then a greater investment in them will seem justified; if it is seen as widening the sovereignty gap, then it will not.

The task for international institutions and for those who would expand their use in the 1990s and beyond is, therefore, to strengthen their appeal to national governments as a means to bridge the sovereignty gap without encroaching upon sovereignty's still very vital core. To do that, the U.N. needs to command a better knowledge of the nonmilitary issues that are most threatening to sovereignty, to offer a flexible system of consultation and negotiation regarding their management, and to be an inspired catalyst, bringing affected governments together and "selling" ideas and ad hoc mechanisms to policymakers in need of a means to cooperate.

CHAPTER 3

DEFINING AND DEPLOYING COMPARATIVE ADVANTAGES

Chapter Two outlined several conceptual and institutional factors that, in the view of the panel, prevent the U.N. from fulfilling the three-part process proposed in Chapter One—a process that already typifies the U.N.'s most successful activities. Chapter Three prescribes a new set of premises and functions to replace, reform, or modify the status quo at the United Nations and enable the world body to exercise its natural comparative advantage more effectively.

New Premises

International Security

In devising a U.N. strategy for handling future security problems, the panel recognizes the need to make judgments about the evolving security environment *and* about the U.N.'s comparative advantages and disadvantages. The U.N. has no choice but to deal, step by step, with the world as it is: difficult, divided, dangerous, and in disarray. The U.N., after all, is needed for precisely the reasons that have inhibited its success. Because peace is a fragile commodity and security never absolute, it is essential to take steps that will strengthen the U.N. institutionally, putting it in a better position to respond to unpredictable challenges and opportunities as they arise over the long haul. This will entail tailoring its priorities and action agenda to the range of issues on which a U.N. contribution is most needed and to which the institution is best suited to respond. If the U.N. tries to be all things to all people in the security realm, spreading its modest political and financial resources too thinly, it will most likely fall short of expectations across the board.

The emergence of an era of subnational and transnational conflict in the developing world has raised a particularly important and difficult set of challenges for the U.N. system. Although scholarly and official attention still tends to be focused on Europe, a series of internal, transnational, and international conflicts are under way in most other regions of the world. Few of these—which range from holy wars to humanitarian interventions, from civil wars to challenges to the sovereignty of ministates—conform to traditional patterns of interstate conflict, where aggressors and victims are rather more readily identified and dealt with. Many of the conflicts now under way involve one or more major powers directly or through proxies or via arms transfers, making it difficult for the Security Council to handle them publicly, especially with the reluctance of powerful countries to bring "their" problems to the Council. Yet most of these conflicts do not impinge on the central strategic interests of the major powers in ways that foreclose the possibility of cooperative efforts to find a peaceful settlement through quiet consultations, fact-finding, and mediation. At times it may be awkward for the U.N., as an interstate body, to deal with nontraditional forms of conflict, but the U.N. does offer the surest route for engaging the interest and concern of the larger international community. Through greater cooperation with regional organizations and peacemaking efforts, as envisioned in the Charter, the U.N. could multiply its potential for resolving some of these sticky local issues.

The continuing erosion of the bipolar system is also creating new challenges for the United Nations. The gradual loosening of military blocs—in the East, the West, and between the major powers and allies or clients in the developing world—could lead to an increasing emphasis on multilateral bodies for problem-solving in the security realm. On the other hand, it may make it more difficult to develop a consensus on what to do in particular situations and to limit negotiations to a relatively small number of interested parties. This trend, along with the global diffusion of military capabilities, has contributed to a lessening of the cohesiveness and power of blocs within the U.N. Although this may be welcome news to those countries, particularly the United States, that consider themselves a victim of bloc voting, these trends could also contribute to the growing sense of a leadership void in the world organization.

The worldwide spread of military capabilities and sophisticated weapons—including the capability to produce nuclear weapons—has made it more difficult to draw a clear distinction between countries that are militarily powerful and those that are militarily weak. Fewer and fewer countries can now claim, as did many of the developing countries during the few debates on conventional weapons in the 1960s and 1970s, that efforts to control arms transfers would be tantamount to "disarming the unarmed." The substantial worldwide growth of the conventional arms trade over the past two decades—including the increasing means of arms production in, and of military exports from, developing countries—has begun to change the nature of North-South, as well as South-South, security relationships. With the emergence of important regional military powers and the demonstrations of near-impotence by the so-called superpowers when it comes to exerting decisive military force in many parts of the world, it has been less and less feasible to think of security and disarmament in simple "we-they" terms. As a result, the need for multilateral approaches to the arms control and disarmament agenda should become increasingly apparent. (At the same time, however, the breakdown of bipolarity may make the negotiations that much more complex and difficult in the future.)

Now that the leaders of the U.S. and USSR, the world's chief nuclear powers, are at least talking about substantial nuclear arms reductions, it seems somewhat less utopian to envision the U.N. as the institutional catalyst for a series of steps that would make the world safe for nuclear disarmament. As the debate over the proposed elimination of interme-diate nuclear forces in Europe makes clear, resistance to deep cuts in nuclear weaponry will continue until there are sufficient alternative institutions, procedures, and norms to provide a general sense of reassurance during the proposed transition to decreased dependence on nuclear weapons to provide national security.

Although the primary burden may fall on regional institutions and arrangements, the U.N. could play a constructive role in the develop-ment and propagation of the norms and principles that would be part of a process of confidence-building, enhanced communications, and ongoing contact. These are prerequisite to the development of "politi-cal will." U.N. concepts of interpositional peacekeeping forces, fact-finding, monitoring, good offices, mediation, and arbitration would, of course, have their analogs on a regional basis, if steps toward military disengagement could be negotiated.

International Economic Policy: Elements of a New Role

The international economic agenda is so vast and the issues involved so complex that progress will not depend upon the action of any one organization or any one coalition of governments. Nor is progress likely to come about as the result of negotiations on some comprehensive and definitive "deal" between North and South. Instead, it is more probable that the common goals of world economic growth, equity, and stability will, as in the past, be the subject of negotiation on specific issues. Although on certain circumscribed subjects some of these negotiations may take place in U.N. venues, for the statutory, political, and substantive reasons mentioned above, it is to be expected that most of them will not. But the relevant question for the United Nations is not *where* a particular negotiation will take place, but *how* its special institutional features can be used to enlarge consensus and set the terms of dialogue, thereby contributing to the success of the negotiations wherever they may take place.

1. Exploiting institutional features:

A complementary relationship between the U.N. and the Bretton Woods and regional economic groupings can be constructed on the basis of actual or potential distinguishing features:

—*inclusivity:* Market, developing, and CMEA economies are all represented.

—*integrated approach:* The U.N. offers a place to discuss economic trends and issues in a holistic way—not just the inadequately examined trade-debt-macroeconomic growth relationship, but such things as foreseeable social, political, and environmental impacts of patterns of economic activity, etc.

—*early warning:* With much higher quality trend analysis than exists in the Secretariat today, the U.N. could be *the* setting for flagging emerging phenomena with global implications and to promote consultations.

—*setting the global agenda:* High-level consultations between North, South, and CMEA on a common, accurate data base resulting in agreement about the likely growth path of a particular problem or trend, and resulting in *brief communiques,* could help establish agendas for cooperation.

—*identify areas of potential agreement:* Instead of proclamations about worthy aims (e.g., the IDS declarations), Secretariat intellectual resources should be applied to (a) defining areas of possible agreement about goals, and (b) exploring plausible policy options for agreement on means.

—*negotiation of priorities, policies, and notional distribution of official development assistance.*

2. Elements of a new consensus:

To give meaning to the role proposed above, the secular breakdown in North-South relations must be addressed in such ways as to suggest a desirable direction for the international economy on which all can agree:

—Recognition that a return to stable, low-inflationary growth requires:

    a. adjustment by deficit as well as surplus countries: extreme imbalances in current and capital accounts are equally injurious internationally;

    b. minimizing interference in trade and restrictive attempts to penalize or counter such interference;

    c. attention to minimum income security of primary product producers.

—The need to assure the soundness, resilience, and fairness of the world financial system in order to respond to the needs of developed and developing countries in an equitable global economy, requiring:

    a. improved strength and resources of international financial institutions;

    b. enlargement of the role and responsibilities of the IMF regarding global liquidity—should it have a role in reserve creation and regulation?

    c. an effective long-term solution to management of international debt.

—Recognition of the unique problems and needs of least-developed countries and least-developed regions of developing countries.

—Increasingly direct linkage between *equity* with regard to economic *aspirations* of developing countries and *security*.

—Avoidance of another global oil crisis, or minimizing its potential damage to the global economy.

—As developing-country population and urbanization increase, education and awareness are also expanding through modern means of technology, greater literacy, mass communications, etc. As a result, tremendous growth in popular aspirations is pushing governments toward providing more opportunities for private *economic initiatives*. Consequently, an appropriate balance between the public and private sector will have to be developed in order to maximize the efficiency of both.

3. Contents of a new dialogue:

—Desirable elements of a solution to Third World debt. Debt packages will not be negotiated at the U.N., but a small high-level U.N. forum could be an influential setting for consideration of criteria that should shape a new approach. Communiques issued by such a body could open a dialogue addressed to all institutions with responsibilities in this matter.

—Package of proposals to reduce dependence of developing countries on primary product income—and to ensure some degree of income stability during the period of reducing dependence.

—Elements of a unique approach to the problems of least-developed countries and least-developed regions of developing countries, giving special attention to increasing rural agricultural productivity, strengthening managerial infrastructure, and institutional changes to define and implement a U.N. philosophy of technical assistance to the least-developed.

—Discussion of ingredients of new normative framework to guide investment-led trade.

—The necessity to move to a more open trading system with equal opportunities for all trading nations.

—The development of effective means to narrow the widening technology gap between developed and many developing countries.

The Emergence of Human Security Issues and the U.N. Role

In the 42 years since San Francisco, a generation of formidable but largely unforeseen challenges to the basis, quality, and sustainability of mankind's future have emerged more quickly than the institutional means or the international consensus required to manage them effectively. Because they pose the genuine possibility of injury to human society, because they are in many ways less controllable than the more obvious risks of nuclear conflagration, and because they may be more decisive in their impact as a result, they are referred to here as issues of human security. While human security concerns arise from the sheer mass and intensity of human activity in general, they are propelled by two forces of constantly increasing momentum and complexity: the growth and distribution of *population;* and the volume and character of *economic activity.* Although the primary effects are most noticeable in developing countries, secondary and tertiary consequences affect the entire world:

Immediate factors:

• *population growth*
The 90% increase in world population that is expected (in fact a

doubling or tripling is possible) before world population stabilizes in the second half of the 21st century will take place in the developing world, and 90% of that growth will occur in cities.

• *food*

Current reports of the FAO and WFC find world hunger increasing at a gathering rate, from 460 million hungry people in 1970 to 475 million in 1980 to 512 million in 1985—at a time when world per capita food supply has never been greater. Without fundamental change in world food production and distribution policies, massive starvation will occur on an unprecedented scale.

• *Third World urban conditions*

Current overpopulation of Third World urban centers produces high levels of homelessness, inadequate access to water, sewage and waste disposal problems and high and increasing incidence of disease and mortality, yet population increases of the kind estimated will require a 65% increase in funds simply to maintain existing—and poor—urban infrastructures, services, and shelter.

• *employment*

Under existing population growth estimates, the developing-country labor force will grow by nearly 900 million between 1985 and 2000, generating a need for 60 million new jobs per year.

• *economic activity*

Between 1950 and 1980, developing countries increased their production of goods and services sixfold while production of industrial goods grew by a factor of eight. Extrapolating from these trends and from estimated population change, tremendous growth in economic activity can be expected even without any improvement in relative standards of living.

Foreseeable consequences:

• *aspirations*

As education and awareness expand through mass communication and higher literacy, the 80% of the world's population living in developing countries will seek accelerated change in the present economic conditions that confine most to poverty and some half-billion to hunger.

• *participation or chaos*

Unless the benefits of the global economic system are more widely distributed, many marginalized segments of developing-country populations will have no incentive to cooperate in its security and stability.

Absence of accommodation will cause major increases in migration to developed countries, a resort to radically nationalistic policies, further increase in humanitarian emergencies, civil and regional strife, and greater suffering.

• *resource strain*

To bring developing countries' energy consumption to a level equal to that of the industrialized countries, world energy consumption would have to increase by a factor of eight; to equal per capita consumption of manufactured goods in industrialized countries, world industrial output would have to grow by a factor of 2.6. Such resource use would increase demands on essential environmental assets and life-support systems already heavily taxed by developed-country economic activity.

• *increased need for policy coordination*

Greater developing-country participation in the international economy will also raise mutual vulnerability of developed and developing countries from already acute levels.

The U.N. role:

• *dialogue*

The magnitude of such systemic growth and change will require intensified dialogue between countries. Only at the U.N. are all represented.

• *early warning*

Dialogue and the possibilities for common policy or joint action would be strengthened by up-to-date, accurate data to flag emerging trends or danger signals in enough time to take corrective or anticipatory action.

• *regime building*

The U.N. could provide a setting for pursuit of consensus regarding the management of specific human security issues, the roles of particular countries, the range of permissible means, etc.

• *ad hoc mechanisms*

When existing arrangements are inadequate, U.N. consultations could provide the stimulus for ad hoc cooperative actions, whether in joint ventures involving two or more countries or in more formal arrangements.

Multilateral Technical Assistance: An Uncertain Identity

Chapter One touched upon several shortcomings of U.N.-channeled or U.N.-originated technical assistance that, despite the popularity and obvious success of many of the activities funded, diminish the overall impact of the Organization's direct contribution to development. Among these drawbacks are the fractionalizing of U.N. assistance among a growing number of programs, funds, and agencies; and a miniaturization of the aid available, since resources have contracted slightly as institutions have grown—two trends that have intensified the degree of "aid salesmanship" and its diversionary pressure on recipient-government development programs. Other shortcomings are the desultory and pro forma quality of the overall policy direction provided by the various governing bodies and oversight groups and the increased difficulty of coordination at the agency level, despite some useful recent innovations (Consultative Groups organized by the IBRD; Roundtables initiated by the UNDP).

Related to all of these shortcomings and partly responsible for their severity is a more fundamental problem: the absence of a clear understanding of the role, or a coherent ordering of the priorities, of U.N. technical assistance. Apart from activities that are sui generis, such as the humanitarian assistance provided by UNHCR and UNRWA, the emergency food assistance given by the World Food Program, and the attention given to the problems of child and maternal health care by UNICEF, U.N. development assistance is indistinguishable from that provided by many other donors. While the panel is not prepared to propose what the exact nature of a distinguishing U.N. role ought to be, it urges that such a study be undertaken as soon as possible and that it direct its attention to:

1. Substantive areas that should be made a U.N. priority and existing priorities that should be given even greater emphasis:
   - Assistance to enable the least-developed countries and least-developed regions of developing countries to meet *basic humanitarian needs* (food, public health, shelter, education, etc.);
   - Assistance to raise general levels of *education and literacy* in the developing world;
   - Assistance to strengthen the development of *managerial infrastructure in least-developed countries,* with particular emphasis on improving indigenous capacity to: direct external assistance for development; handle emergency situations; improve the efficiency and allocation of resource use; carry out the basic tasks of public administration.

2. Institutional changes to support such a role:
   - *Intermediation*

More than 90% of the funds provided through UNDP, the largest of the U.N. technical assistance suppliers, goes to projects executed by other agencies; UNDP also devotes considerable effort to advising recipients with regard to projects financed by other donors and has had considerable success in persuading these donors to observe recipients' priorities. Both of these activities would be far more effective if UNDP had a level of expertise sufficient to: advise recipients and donors on the basis of a *general equilibrium analysis* of a country's development needs, and not solely to advise them about a specific project or the situation in a particular sector; provide project "backstopping" in order to evaluate the merits of a project proposal, oversee its execution, and appraise its results.

* *Oversight*
Overall policy coherence and consistency, and implementation of the kind of U.N.-specific priorities proposed here, would benefit from a unification of the governing boards of the main U.N. technical assistance programs.

New Functions

The three-part approach to U.N. work repeatedly advocated in this report obviously demands a clarification of the U.N.'s key functions. This section examines in detail the three new functions proposed above: *global watch*—to identify the issues on which convergence of interests exists; *consensus building*—to bring about common views with regard to those interests; and *consensus conversion*—to translate, usually by some form of collective action, common views and communities of interest into outcomes useful to the affected countries. While all of these functions have played a role in the United Nations' most successful activities they have not been given the prominence, priority, or systematic attention that their importance to the U.N. and to the world community at large requires.

Global Watch

The first requirement is for a setting in which emerging human security issues of global significance can be spotlighted and their implications for national and international policy choices and future welfare can be given high-level international attention.

Most regional issues are best dealt with at that level; others, however, may be difficult to contain regionally, while a third set is effectively multi-regional (acid rain, for example). When a regional problem cannot be managed effectively locally, or when an issue is inescapably global, the international community needs a means by which it is at least possible to take note of its existence. A global watch activity would perform the following functions:

1. proposal of global human security agendas by tagging issues that fit the sovereignty-gap criteria;

2. gathering, updating, and monitoring of a reliable global data base on each major item on the human security agenda;[1]

3. providing links between the relevant scientific or expert community and national policymakers;

4. providing a setting for high-level consultations, at the request of affected countries, on items included on the global agenda;

5. publicizing matters on the global agenda internationally, when a consensus of affected countries considers it appropriate.

The following are examples of the kind of issues that appear an appropriate subject for global watch:

natural disasters: If one central authoritative global watch facility had existed in late 1983 and early 1984 when the conditions for the African famine were already in evidence, the response time of the world community might have been greatly reduced. Global communication, global data-gathering capability, and major scientific advances in the understanding of different types of disaster, and breakthroughs in the means for containing and combatting disasters of all types, could be harnessed more effectively by rapid monitoring, exchange of information, and consultation at the global level.

global biosphere: Scientists believe that the next 20 years will see such rapid changes in the earth's biosphere that there will be little possibility of anticipatory responses. On issues such as deterioration of the ozone layer, global warming, ocean pollution—which require international cost-sharing and common strategies—the problems themselves seem to be developing faster than the world scientific community's understanding of them, and so are also outstripping cooperative political responses.

least-developed countries: Economic development in some low-income countries is now so depressed and the resource and environmental asset base so weak, particularly in many African countries, that there is a possibility of semipermanent humanitarian emergency on an enormous scale. Exposed to every blight of nature, with inadequate physical and administrative infrastructure, and prone to breakdown in civil order and other security threats resulting from increased refugee flows, these countries represent a "Fourth World" that merits a different approach to assistance on the part of the world community. A global watch setting could provide a comprehensive up-to-date data base and an opportunity for governmental consultations on the shape of such a unique approach and the countries that would qualify as recipients. Elements of such an approach might include: joint reductions in or outright elimination of "tied aid," greater balance of payments support, debt relief, greater security and incentives for long-term investment programs, and maximum coordination of project and non-project aid.

international debt: Existing machinery and policies for managing the international debt problem have been sufficient to stave off a collapse of the international financial system—and so far—the threat of a major deflationary contraction in credit. However, there are growing signs that the approach followed from 1982 to the present cannot provide a basis for a return to debtor-country growth, that it has caused an increasing drag on world economic output generally, and for these and related reasons may not be sustainable. However, the effect upon the world economy and the aggregate sustainability of the present approach is not being systematically examined in any international body at the political level.

disease control: Better links between the international expert community of medical professionals, epidemiologists, etc.—and policymakers—are essential to development of, e.g., a concerted international approach to the treatment and containment of AIDS.

illegal capital flight: Economic recovery in developing countries, the eventual restoration of per capita GNP growth, and the successful long-term management of developing country indebtedness have all been hampered by the illegal outflow of extremely large amounts (up to one-third of private and official loan disbursements in some cases) of the capital loaned to some countries for national development and balance of payments purposes. Since capital flight increases liquidity constraints on Third World debtors, it is also a concern to developed-country governments and financial institutions. Information-sharing between North and South, consultation, and common strategy are necessary.

international narcotics trafficking: Global availability of illegal drugs continued to increase in 1986 due to burgeoning demand in the United States, Europe, Latin America, and Asia and the successful efforts of traffickers to circumvent enforcement programs.
Ironically, most of the increased production occurred in countries participating in international anti-narcotics efforts. Reversing the trend will require greater attention and cooperation at the global level.

cross-border population movements: Massive, tidal movements of people across borders and often across entire regions have increased over time. Whether these migratory flows are caused by social, economic, political, or other factors, they have often had a destabilizing effect on the receiver country or region. The identification of factors that may lead to new outbreaks of refugee or other movements of population groups, and consultation on appropriate international responses—prevention, containment, repatriation, creation and protection of legal rights of displaced persons, etc.—would help to avoid situations that result in either human injury or threats to regional and international security. The "early warning" and rapid-response capability of the U.N. should benefit by the creation in March 1987 of an Office for Research and Collection of Information, linked to the Secretary-General and charged with monitoring factors "related to refugees flows."

urban overpopulation: By the year 2000 more than 50% of the world's population will live in cities. Most of this growth will occur in the Third World, where urban populations are already growing twice as fast as rural populations. In Latin America, for example, the population is already almost 70% urban. Of the six cities expected to exceed 15 million inhabitants, four will be in the developing world—Sao Paulo, Mexico City, Calcutta, and Bombay. Growth in this magnitude raises major challenges for meeting the most basic needs—shelter, food, health, schooling—that appear far beyond the capacity of many developing countries, given current economic growth expectations. Failure to anticipate these needs will result in major international problems of both a humanitarian and security nature. Again, provision of high-level attention through global watch is the first step toward devising a method for managing the problem.

Consensus-building

In an era of sharply declining national autonomy, greater use of international "regimes"—internationally agreed norms of behavior that make it possible to deal with problems as they arise—becomes indispensable. But when the decline in effective national autonomy triggers increases in nationalistic behavior, in part out of frustration, the decision to join a "regime" will require a higher degree of proof that such an approach to issue management offers better options than those available to states acting on their own. For some subjects— certain international environmental questions, for example—the expediency of a regime is self-evident. But for many other types of problems the advantages are less clear. Unlike such things as a tear in the ozone layer, many international issues do not affect every country— or, if they do, do not affect all countries equally. Yet the regime model most often favored at the U.N. calls for universal participation. In such situations, potential parties to a regime are often discouraged by the prospect of unequal sharing of costs, benefits, and decision-making power and the linkage of extraneous issues.

A more systematic approach to consensus-building at the United Nations is now indispensable. The following elements provide the basis for a new approach to this function:

affected parties only: Communities of interest are more easily formed and collective decisions more readily taken when it is possible to distinguish between significantly affected and non-significantly affected countries—as in the case of acid rain, for example. Regimes, wherever they are negotiated, should include only those countries whose absence would stand in the way of reaching the intended goal.

representational diplomacy: Often only the broadest possible representation will confer legitimacy upon an agreement—as in the case of one whose effectiveness depends upon the consent and subsequent action of a very large number of states—or will ensure that a problem is examined in all its important aspects. This is especially true of issues on the global watch agenda illustrated above, most of which must be addressed in the context of their global dimensions. Yet there is no realistic prospect of convening regular U.N. meetings for consultations on these issues in which the largest developed and developing countries would participate at a senior level unless they can be addressed in a forum of limited size operating on some type of representational basis.

Small size is even more essential when it is feasible to move beyond consulting to actual negotiations on certain matters. To achieve agreement in such cases, the number of negotiating parties must be small enough to permit fluid give and take and make genuine bargaining possible, but the composition of negotiating groups should provide, through some means of representation, for input from all parties.

level and quality of representation: Two features of the discussions in the UNCTAD Trade and Development Board, the Second and Third Committees, the Economic and Social Council, and the General Assembly that prevent them from effectively carrying out a "global watch" function or from conducting significant negotiations are the delegates' low rank and insufficient qualifications in the areas under discussion. Indeed these discussions are often conducted at the level of second and third secretaries with no direct links to the ministries concerned with the subjects of the resolutions voted upon.

equity-security: Links between equity and security are increasingly explicit, and successful consensus-building will have to recognize that linkage, particularly as it relates to crossovers between economic and technological interests and environmental ones. Agreements on such issues as ozone depletion, global warming, cross-border air pollution, the atmospheric and climatic effects of desertification and deforestation, etc. will have to include some means of equalizing costs and benefits.

Consensus Conversion: Stimulating Collective Action

Outcomes likely to flow from the kind of community-building agreements described above will increasingly involve joint action by individual governments. Except for some activities that are sui generis-humanitarian relief, peacekeeping, human rights investigations—for which the U.N. is uniquely suited, the world body is no more qualified to undertake large-scale operational programs than is the United States Congress to administer the U.S. foreign aid program.

In general, once a community of interests has been identified and agreement nurtured to the point where joint action is possible, the U.N.'s role is to be the catalyst rather than the primary agent of collective action. Here again, a systematic approach is needed. In some instances it will be enough to identify domains where cooperation is mutually attractive—as is now the case with the joint U.S.-Soviet Antarctic research on ozone change and the EEC's European Center for Nuclear Research, the Airbus enterprise, and Arianespace. But as the need for international issue management grows increasingly acute, a more direct U.N. role—in defining and proposing specific mechanisms for cooperation or helping to set up the necessary logistical apparatus—will be necessary. In such cases much can be learned from the successful experiences the U.N. has already had in this field. The Med Plan described in Appendix I outlines a number of key components: administrative responsibility located as close as possible to the affected area, participation by affected countries only, effective use of an authoritative data base on the problem, and ultimate transition to self-sufficiency.

International Security

Although the three functions described above—global watch, consensus-building, and consensus-conversion—are as relevant to the political and military security area as they are to the broad range of human security concerns described in this report, the potential role they can play in security-related areas merits special attention.

Given the global strategic trends described earlier, the security role of the U.N. may be on the verge of a renaissance. If the international community chooses to use the U.N. intelligently and selectively, then the world body could well become a more important and effective instrument for global problem-solving on security as well as humanitarian issues. The pragmatism that has increasingly characterized U.N. political and security work may be an indication of its ability to seize the opportunities before it.

The U.N. may not often have the power to compel states to carry out its decisions, but it can offer positive incentives for states to cooperate with it on a wide range of security-related tasks. The U.N. can provide so many useful services for resolving international conflicts and for negotiating and monitoring disarmament agreements that more and more national leaders should come to recognize that strengthening the U.N. is in their best interests. There are signs that the major powers are coming to understand that if viable, peaceful settlements are to be reached on such issues as Afghanistan, Southern Africa, the Middle East, Cyprus, or Iran-Iraq, the U.N. will have to be brought into the process to supplement their own national efforts.

At the same time, the majority of the members of the U.N. need to recognize that if they want the institution to play a problem-solving role, then they cannot always seek to identify the U.N. with one side of a problem, and hence make it part of the problem rather than part of its solution. In particular, it is a misuse of the Security Council to treat it as a tribunal for determining the rights and wrongs of most violent disputes, given the complex nature of contemporary conflict and the fact that it can rarely enforce its decisions. It would be far more productive if states sought to use the Council for what it is relatively good at—behind-the-scenes negotiations, consensus-building, providing a face-saving way out when the parties are ready to terminate hostilities, and posing alternatives to the parties for their consideration—rather than for what it does less well—conferring legitimacy, passing resolutions with teeth, and enforcing its judgments.

Over the years the U.N. has demonstrated the value of multilateral services that can facilitate (1) the search for formulas for resolving individual conflicts and for posing peaceful alternatives to the combatants, (2) the development of an international consensus in support of these approaches, (3) the process of negotiation and conciliation between parties to a conflict, (4) the provision of peacekeeping forces to assist the peacemaking process, and (5) the verification and monitoring of multilateral arms control and disarmament agreements. By building on its relative success in carrying out these roles and by striving to be more selective in terms of the range of issues it attempts to tackle at one time, the U.N. can both revive its founding mandate and restore its credibility as a peacemaker and a peacekeeper.

Notes

1. As Chapter Five outlines in detail, effective global watch consultations among governments will require sophisticated staff support utilizing the full range of electronic data gathering and analysis techniques, including trends analysis, model-building, etc.

CHAPTER 4

MAIN RECOMMENDATIONS

The successor vision of the United Nations advocated in this report—a new approach to its role, and clarified functions to give it fullest expression—all require institutional change. The most important changes and the reasons the panel adopted them are described below. A series of complementary proposals are detailed in Chapter Five.

Strengthening U.N. Intergovernmental Bodies in the Economic and Social Area

It is now indispensable for the well-being of the world community and the credibility of the United Nations as an institution that the U.N. be equipped to address, authoritatively and effectively, the urgent issues of human security and welfare that are not within the jurisdiction of the Security Council. Yet the existing machinery of the United Nations is inadequate for this purpose. The Second and Third Committees of the General Assembly, and the Economic and Social Council, are too large and too comprehensive in their agendas and too lacking in political or intellectual authority for such an important task. What is needed is a small, representative body whose members have the seniority and expertise to undertake consultations, issue joint communiques, and initiate or propose ad hoc actions on behalf of the governments represented with regard to matters on which there is agreement that enhanced international management is essential.

A variety of ways to create such a body were examined. One option—creation of an altogether new body—was rejected by the panel because it threatened to add to existing problems of overlap and duplication. Constitutional change of major proportions would also be required, since such a body would have many of the responsibilities assigned to ECOSOC in Chapters 9 and 10 of the Charter. While its establishment would logically require ECOSOC's elimination, it would also create new overlap problems between itself and the Second and Third Committees.

The panel also considered two other approaches. The first was to amend Article 61 of the Charter to return ECOSOC to its original size (or to at most 27), and to require it to give priority to economic and social issues of urgent consequence for "human security and welfare" not within the jurisdiction of the Security Council. The advantages of this option were that it did not create another body and preserved both the importance of ECOSOC and the approximate size intended for it by the framers of the Charter. Its drawback was that it required reversal of the historic trend favoring expansion of the Council and, for that reason, raised the prospect of insurmountable resistance. It also offered no opportunity to reduce the high level of duplication.

The second approach also centered upon ECOSOC but, rather than reducing the Council, it offered a three-part package to restructure the economic and social bodies of the central U.N.: creation of a small senior Ministerial Board within ECOSOC to carry out the functions described above; procedural reforms to strengthen ECOSOC, accompanied by its expansion to include all member states; and elimination of the Second and Third Committees of the General Assembly. After lengthy consideration of the many complicated issues raised by such an approach, the panel found the advantages to be compelling.

First, it provides what the U.N. now lacks: a small political center for high-level consultations on urgent matters of human security and welfare. Second, it does so while reducing the overlap and duplication that weakens the U.N.'s ability to deal with these matters today. Third, while it requires Charter amendment to expand ECOSOC once more, such a change merely carries an established trend to its logical culmination and, in the process, corrects an increasingly anomalous situation. That is, as presently constituted, ECOSOC is "neither fish nor fowl": too large for effective high-level consultations and fast, flexible decision-making, it is not large enough to perform credibly as a plenary body. The three-part package was endorsed by a consensus decision of the panel. It is outlined in detail below.

1. Ministerial Board

A Ministerial Board of not more than 25 governments should be established in affiliation with ECOSOC.

Functions of the Ministerial Board

a. *Global Watch:* High-level consultations and exchange of views on any international problem having grave and foreseeable consequences for human security and well-being that Board members or the Secretary-General choose to bring before it.

b. *Consensus-building:* Through consultative sessions, through formation of ad hoc working groups of countries most affected by a particular issue, through issuance of advisory opinions to other international organizations, the Board will seek to forge communities of interest on the matters before it.

c. *Converting agreements into action:* To stimulate outcomes useful to member states, the Board shall: propose action by or under the aegis of the U.N. proper; call upon U.N. or other international agencies to take specific actions by means of advisory communiques to the relevant governing body; and serve as a framework for the undertaking of joint ad hoc actions by individual U.N. member countries.

Powers of the Ministerial Board

a. *Communiques:* Meetings of a global watch type may often produce agreement about the nature of an issue and the likely path of its development, which, in the interests of global recognition of its scope and urgency, it is desirable to publicize as a bulletin or communique. Such a communique might be comparable to those released after ministerial or summit meetings of the major political and regional groups.

b. *Advisory communiques:* When meetings produce agreement not only on the nature and implications of an issue but on desirable courses of action, the Ministerial Board may issue an advisory communique urging the relevant parties (e.g., GATT, IMF, Security Council, General Assembly) to take such actions.

c. *Power of initiative.* Occasionally, a Ministerial Board consensus will permit various types of direct action: initiation of ad hoc joint ventures by member countries or members in affiliation with other countries most affected by a particular issue; directives to the Secretary-General or Director-General to undertake specific measures.

Structure and Procedures of the Ministerial Board

a. *Size:* The Board shall not exceed 25 members. The largest developed and developing countries would have permanent seats, while the remaining seats would be allocated on a temporary and rotating basis in order to provide for complete and balanced representation of the entire membership of the U.N.[1]

b. *Meetings and meeting subjects:* Board meetings would be held on an as-needed basis, normally no longer than two to three days at a time;

c. *Participation:* It is expected that governments would send ministers to these meetings, although the precise choice of senior official would vary with the subject matter scheduled for discussion. Because Board meetings will often deal with matters beyond the technical competence of foreign ministries, their usefulness will often depend on the willingness of member countries to provide representatives from the relevant ministries who are qualified in the agenda subject and senior enough to engage in substantive negotiations on particular measures, actions, or communiques with regard to it.

d. *Decisions:* All Board decisions and actions would be taken by consensus.

e. *Reporting:* In addition to specific communiques which may be addressed to the General Assembly in the normal course of the Board's work, the Ministerial Board would report to the Assembly once a year at the same time the Economic and Social Council makes its report.

Agenda of the Ministerial Board

The Board would meet on an as-needed basis in order to address matters of imminent or clearly foreseeable consequence for human security, with the exception of issues involving hostilities, which would continue to be reserved for the Security Council. The panel believes that the Board's broad mandate represents a potenially far-reaching extension of existing provisions for international cooperation. Whether the Board is to realize this potential, or play only a marginal role, will depend upon the credibility it earns by dealing with a few issues well. With that caveat, panel members believe that for the first period of its existence the Board's agenda should have a limited focus:

a. trends with medium- to long-term but clearly foreseeable large-scale consequences for the basis and conditions of human security;

b. events and developments, such as natural disasters, with immediate or imminent large-scale consequences for human security and requiring collaborative global or regional responses.

2. Expansion of ECOSOC to Plenary Size, Procedural Reform of ECOSOC, and Discontinuation of the Assembly's Second and Third Committees

To eliminate the nearly complete duplication of agendas and debates between the Economic and Social Council (ECOSOC) and the General Assembly's committees dealing with economic and social matters (Second and Third), and to end the waste of scarce human resources that results from this duplication, the Second and Third Committees of the General Assembly should be discontinued and their duties assumed by ECOSOC, which would be enlarged to plenary size.

a. The Economic and Social Council should be enlarged so that every Member of the United Nations would have a seat;

b. ECOSOC should have a *single* annual session held concurrently with the General Assembly;

c. The General Assembly should refer all economic and social matters on its agenda to ECOSOC for preliminary consideration;

d. ECOSOC would report to the Assembly in the same way that the Second and Third Committees have been doing, including draft resolutions, where necessary, for adoption by the Assembly;

e. The reports of ECOSOC would be taken up during the last two weeks of each Assembly session in its plenary meeting;

f. To help accommodate the increased workload, the Council should establish a Reports and Agenda Committee;

g. The Reports and Agenda Committee would screen and discuss the reports emanating from all of ECOSOC's many subsidiary bodies, including its functional and regional commissions and committees, the Human Rights Commission, the UNEP Governing Council, the Trade and Development Board, the Executive Committee of UNICEF and UNHCR, the Development Assistance Board, if established, etc.;

h. For these purposes the Committee would meet several weeks in advance of the Council and the Assembly;

i. The Reports Committee should be the same size as the Ministerial Board; its membership should be geographically balanced to ensure equitable representation;

j. Following its review of reports from subsidiary bodies, the Reports Committee should recommend texts for adoption by ECOSOC and/or the Assembly; it should also single out matters requiring ECOSOC's consideration either because of their inherent importance or timeliness or because lower-level agreement could not be reached on them.

k. ECOSOC's sessional Economic and Social Committees would be eliminated; in their place ad hoc negotiating groups would meet when necessary to deal with specific issues and the draft resolutions associated with them;

l. The Committee for Program and Coordination would continue to report to both ECOSOC and the Assembly; a number of adjustments would have to be made with regard to medium-term planning and program budgeting to accommodate the new intergovernmental arrangements.

The panel recognized that special attention must be given to establishing under the Council's aegis additional arrangements for dealing with some of the special questions now being considered by the Third Committee, particularly human rights, drug abuse, and the advancement of women.

Human Security Issues: Toward an Integrated U.N. System Response

It is essential to create within the U.N. system an apparatus for identifying, analyzing, and proposing responses to human-security issues that is integrated intellectually and employs the sectoral expertise of the U.N. system's economic and social agencies in a coordinated manner. As discussed above, most problems requiring international management overlap the spheres of several agencies and U.N. regional commissions. Yet, as is the case for the main intergovernmental organs, there is "no center at the center" at the agency level either.[2] The U.N. lacks a means for putting to work the system's rich potential for interdisciplinary analysis to identify the global issues on which national interests converge and where—but for lack of a catalyst—higher levels of cooperation are feasible.

The "Complementary Proposals" in Chapter Five of this report propose establishment of a Bureau of Global Watch within the U.N. proper to provide the interdisciplinary analytical and data base necessary for the Ministerial Board to function. Although the Bureau is an essential first step, the panel believes that a more structural remedy will eventually be required. Such an approach should directly incorporate all the system's main economic and social agencies in the task of identifying human security issues and, on behalf of the U.N. system, proposing to the senior intergovernmental bodies a range of integrated responses.

The panel considered two alternatives. The first approach, the most direct and far-reaching response to the problem, called for a major step toward centralization of the U.N. system with the creation of a single commission on the EEC model. This commission would be composed of the Directors-General of all the main agencies in the economic and social fields and mandated to perform the tasks referred to above and to prepare a consolidated U.N. system budget. The second approach, proposed as a step in the direction of the first, would also create a commission but with advisory powers only. This advisory commission, composed of five individuals with outstanding international reputations in the economic and social field, would be expected to offer the sort of intellectual approach that would enable the Ministerial Board and the General Assembly to give more interdisciplinary consideration to human-security problems.

The panel found the first approach the more promising long-term solution to the problems of weak coordination and the absence of an integrated approach. They also believed, however, that the constitutional, structural, and budgetary changes required were of such a scale as to make it unfeasible for immediate implementation and therefore recommended that the commission be regarded as an objective toward which the U.N. system should evolve over the next five to seven years. The advisory commission, on the other hand, provided a means to help implement a recommendation of the Group of 18 that called for annual U.N. system summits, did not involve profound restructuring, and therefore could be implemented very rapidly. It was also believed that experience with the advisory commission would help smooth a transition to the commission as well as refine the commission's ultimate form. The panel proposed the advisory commission for immediate adoption by the General Assembly. Both proposals are detailed below:

1. Advisory Commission

The Secretary-General should appoint a commission of five persons, chosen on the basis of their substantive expertise and leadership in the economic and social area.

a. *Function*

i. identify emerging issues of a global or regional scale that cut across several agencies' fields of concern;

ii. consult with executive heads of the U.N. agencies on joint approaches to these problems during the U.N.'s annual system summits (recommendation 10 of G-18) and in shorter meetings with the relevant agency heads during the year;

iii. develop proposals for the new *Ministerial Board* suggesting appropriate action by member states or international institutions regarding these issues;

iv. regularly review the major program emphases in the economic and social sector in light of global trends;

v. prepare the agendas and follow-up on the decisions of the annual system summits;

vi. participate in the annual U.N. system summits as co-equal parties with the Directors-General of the specialized agencies.

b. *Support*

The Advisory Commission would be served by a small, interagency staff composed of individuals with outstanding credentials in each of the main sectoral areas of the U.N.'s economic and social activities. The staff would be seconded from, or would have served in, the secretariats of the U.N.'s main economic and social agencies.

2. Commission

a. *Function*

The Commission would:

i. identify and conduct consultations on emerging issues of a global or regional scale that cut across several agencies' fields of concern;

ii. develop proposals for the Ministerial Board regarding appropriate action, e.g., specific improvements in coordination of policies of U.N. organizations with Bretton Woods organizations, joint undertakings by individual member states;

iii. conduct annual reviews of the major program emphases in the economic and social area in light of global trends; and

iv. prepare a consolidated U.N. system program budget from the submissions of every participating agency (except the IMF, World Bank, and GATT) for submission to the General Assembly for its approval.

b. *Membership*

Commissioners would be nominated by the Ministerial Board on the basis of expertise and leadership in the area concerned and confirmed by the General Assembly. The Commission would consist of 15 to 18 commissioners representing specialized U.N. agencies:

i. The Director-General of the United Nations would serve as the Commission's chairman and would be nominated by the Secretary-General and confirmed by the General Assembly;

ii. The Directors-General of all the principal specialized agencies—ILO, WHO, FAO, IAEA, UNIDO, UNESCO—and the Director-General of UNCTAD; all Commissioners would be assisted in the day-to-day operations of their agencies by one or two deputies;

iii. The heads of the IMF, GATT, and World Bank would also serve on the Commission, although no changes would be made in the manner in which they are appointed to their posts;

iv. Other functional agencies (UPU, ITU, etc.) would be represented by a single commissioner, as would the technical cooperation programs (UNDP, UNICEF, UNFPA, WFP).

v. Finally, three to five additional members might also be elected. These commissioners would not have direct responsibilities for any secretariat or agency and would contribute on a full-time basis to the functioning of the Commission and the preparation of its work.

c. *Support*

The Commission would have its own budget and would, like the Ministerial Board, draw upon DIESA, which would be restructured along interdisciplinary lines (see Chapter Five), for substantive support.

Technical Assistance for Development: A Simplified Framework

The panel believes that the most effective antidote to the problems of congestion, duplication, recipient overload, etc. described above, lies in the creation of a "central coordinating organization," as proposed in the Jackson Report of 1969, or a "single Development

Administration,'' as recommended in the 1975 Report of the Group of Experts on the Structure of the United Nations System. For political and institutional reasons, such proposals do not seem feasible today but, like the U.N. Commission, should be adopted as a desirable medium-term goal. For the present, the panel believes that a Development Assistance Board that merged the executive boards of all U.N. operational funds and programs that are subordinate to the U.N. General Assembly or ECOSOC would be more feasible and would also immediately contribute to the quality and coherence of U.N. development assistance.

1. Development Assistance Board

a. *Structure, Composition, Procedures*
i. The individual executive boards of UNDP/UNFPA, UNICEF, and WFP would be dissolved and in their place there would be created a single Development Assistance Board.
ii. The Development Assistance Board would be of the same size as the Ministerial Board and its members selected on the same permanent/rotational basis.
iii. Located in New York City, the Board would divide its annual calendar of sessions into separate meeting periods dedicated to each program or fund.
iv. While at the beginning the composition of delegations would vary to reflect the different types of expertise required for each part of the oversight calendar, eventually this would not be necessary, since it is hoped that the expertise of the permanent delegation would extend to all program areas.
b. *Responsibilities*
i. Oversight of all program proposals. Board review of program proposals would occur before the start of fund-raising efforts, so as to ensure influence upon the overall scope and content of work programs. The Board would be assisted in its oversight efforts by periodic addresses from the Director-General in which the Director-General would call attention to new cross-cutting issues that affect delivery of technical assistance. The most important of these addresses would occur once every two years; its purpose would be to present a notional framework for the allocation of development assistance funding in the next biennium.

ii. Oversight of all financial and administrative matters of the operational programs (incorporating standardized budget formats).

iii. Progressive elaboration of a conceptual framework for U.N. development assistance that sets the U.N. clearly apart from other providers of development assistance and gradually leads to appropriate forms of specialization.

Peace and Security: Focusing on What the U.N. Does Best

The panel believes that the U.N.'s limitations in the peace and security field are much more the product of contemporary international relations than of shortcomings in U.N. management or structure. Where U.N. peace and security mechanisms are concerned, major structural changes will not yield the sort of results anticipated in the realm of social, economic, and humanitarian affairs. They would yield uncertain benefits at best, while creating enormous political problems for the already hard-pressed organization. Fine-tuning or micro-management adjustments are also unlikely to produce significant advantages.

Although the voting procedures and composition of the General Assembly and the Security Council are hardly ideal, they too are not promising candidates for reform efforts. These arrangements, as established in the Charter, reflect finely balanced political considerations and are deeply rooted. It is the panel's view, moreover, that the path to more effective management of security issues lies not through "better" voting but, rather, through less emphasis on voting itself as a means of solving intractable problems. In general, the sooner it is recognized that the U.N.'s greatest contributions to world peace are made by persistence, hard work, and quiet diplomacy rather than by eloquent speeches or winning votes, the sooner will be restored the U.N.'s credibility and its reputation as the world's premier engine of peaceful change.

As in other substantive areas addressed in this report, consensus-building, practical implementation, and selectivity in focusing on tasks where the U.N. has a comparative advantage are critical to improving U.N. performance. This will entail some rethinking of priorities, strategies, goals, and directions along the lines described earlier in the report—tasks sometimes called strategic management—but relatively few structural changes. The four recommendations that follow are designed to take advantage of opportunities to expand U.N. effectiveness in areas where there is multilateral consensus and where the world body could make a marked, positive contribution.

1. Strengthening Cooperation With Regional Bodies

The U.N. is not the only international institution capable of dealing with threats to international peace and security. In fact, the Charter (Article 33) envisioned that parties to a dispute should first utilize "other peaceful means," including "regional agencies or arrangements," before bringing their differences to the U.N. The Security Council was not intended to be the first resort in solving all of the world's problems. The Council would be more effective if it rationalized its agenda and focused its efforts on those relatively few conflicts that might draw in outside powers and escalate into a global confrontation. Most conflicts, particularly those with local roots and a subnational or transnational character, can be addressed best by regional organizations, where they exist (the Organization of African Unity [OAU] in Chad, ad hoc coalitions of concerned regional countries, the Contadora Group in Central America, for example). Regional organizations may be more sensitive to the complexities of the local political environment, may avoid the appearance of interference by outside powers, and in some parts of the world—particularly Europe, Africa, and to some extent Latin America—have had a good track record at mediating local disputes. They tend to be weak, however, in finance, logistics, and peacekeeping expertise—areas where the U.N. community might be able to lend a helping hand in some cases.

• The Secretaries-General of the United Nations and of regional organizations and their deputies should meet on a regular basis to exchange information regarding emerging disputes that might threaten international peace and security, to discuss joint measures where appropriate, and to consider common problems of financial, logistical and political support.

• The United Nations should send liaison officers to those regional bodies and ad hoc groups that are actively dealing with potential threats to international peace and security.

• Before deciding whether to take up a particular issue which has been brought to its attention, the Security Council should first ascertain whether regional remedies have been attempted.

2. Rationalizing the U.N. Arms Control and Disarmament Agenda

As discussed earlier, there has been an unfortunate tendency inside and outside the U.N. to stress the importance of those aspects of disarmament—especially its East-West and nuclear dimensions—to which the U.N. can make the least contribution and to downplay those aspects of security—including its non-nuclear, multilateral, and regional dimensions—to which the U.N. has made the most positive contribution. In recent years, issues of limiting arms transfers, of developing confidence-building measures, and of moving toward conventional disarmament have begun to receive serious attention in U.N. studies and to be acknowledged by U.N. deliberative bodies, but more needs to be done to correct this imbalance.

• In their statements, policies, and resolutions, the U.N. and its member states should show greater appreciation for the critical importance of measures to control conventional arms, their transfer and their use, as a way to avoid the outbreak and escalation of conflicts that might lead to nuclear war. Another high priority and perhaps as important as negotiations on arms-control measures is the bolstering of U.N. peacemaking and peacekeeping capabilities. Progress should therefore be pursued simultaneously on both fronts.

• As part of its "global watch" effort outlined earlier, the U.N. should take the lead in developing and projecting a more comprehensive concept of security, one that takes into account such factors as economic and social development, environmental change, human rights, and large-scale migration.

• The U.N. should further develop its role as a catalyst for fresh thinking about the meaning of security in a changing world. By articulating a more comprehensive and fundamentally multilateral approach to security, the U.N. could encourage affiliated non-governmental organizations, research institutes, and the "peace movement" to consider broader-based approaches to the subject and to develop a keener appreciation for the potential contributions of the U.N. and other international institutions to the peace process.

3. Multilateral Inspection Teams

It appears that significant progress has been made at the U.N.-related Conference on Disarmament in Geneva on negotiation of a global ban on the production, stockpiling, and use of chemical weapons. To monitor such an accord, consideration is being given to the establishment of a U.N. agency to carry out on-site inspections, much as the IAEA does at nuclear facilities. Whether or not such a step is realized, it suggests a critical service that the U.N. could provide in an era when significant disarmament measures are under consideration. Because arms reductions impose higher security risks than traditional arms control steps, they demand the sort of thorough, reliable, and impartial verification that is often beyond the capabilities of national technical means, largely based on satellites. In cases involving the production or storage of weapons, satellite reconnaissance is clearly insufficient, and on-site inspections by the nationals of one's adversary are bound to be intrusive and open to charges of espionage or excessive zeal.

There may be instances in which the U.N. could provide multilateral inspection teams for third-party inspection and reporting. This would be a far cheaper, less controversial, and more unique contribution for the U.N. than the one it could make were it to follow through on such proposals as an international space agency or satellite-verification capability under U.N. auspices. Multinational inspection teams, moreover, would be a logical outgrowth of the successful U.N. experiences with fact-finding and peacekeeping. Their contingents could come from a politically balanced mix of countries and their use, whether on demand or by schedule, would be determined by the provisions of the particular agreement they are called upon to help monitor. As arms control and disarmament become a truly global affair, monitoring and verification too will have to assume a multilateral character, as in the case of the nuclear nonproliferation treaty.

4. Ad hoc Review Groups

Under Article XIII of the 1972 ABM Treaty, the United States and the Soviet Union established the Standing Consultative Commission (SCC) to consider questions that either side might raise about compliance with the treaty. Although it has not been possible to resolve all controversies surrounding observance of the treaty through this means, the SCC has served as a channel for airing numerous misunderstandings. Under the aegis of the Security Council the U.N. could establish a similar mechanism, in the form of ad hoc review groups which could meet on an as needed basis to address compliance questions related to multilateral agreements and receive reports of the proposed Multilateral Inspection Teams. After considering reports of questionable practices or apparent violations, a review group could either initiate a series of confidential consultations or refer serious breaches to the Security Council for further action. The Security Council could also develop a small expert secretariat for researching and assessing new techniques for technological or human inspections of compliance with agreements. When dealing with fundamentally multilateral issues, such as nuclear nonproliferation, conventional arms transfers, and chemical weapons, the need for global or regional institutional arrangements is obvious. As disarmament takes on a multilateral scope, so must the means of verification, reporting, and adjudication of disputes.

Strenghtening U.N. Leadership: The Role of the Secretary-General

The Secretary-General

a. Nothing carries more far-reaching significance for the effectiveness of U.N. performance than the choice of Secretary-General—the single most important international civil servant—and the support he or she receives from member states. The enormous demands of the job, and the central role which the Secretary-General must play in the revitalization of the U.N. urged by this report, call for governments, especially permanent members, to give the greatest priority to qualities of leadership, integrity, vision and intellect when choosing an individual for the post.

b. The Secretary-General should vigorously defend all the duties and prerogatives of the chief executive and recognize that if the responsibilities assigned to this office by the Charter are to be carried out efficiently, the Secretary-General must be an initiative-taker rather than a caretaker.

c. In view of the enormous demands upon the Secretary-General's time and the necessity of devoting great energy and personal resources to diplomacy in the political and security area, it is necessary that the Secretary-General make explicit and binding delegations of authority to capable individuals, giving them executive responsibility for: (i) planning and development of the program budget; (ii) financial and administrative policy, with particular emphasis on the personnel area; and (iii) coordination of related activities of the U.N. proper and the U.N. group.

d. Complementing the Secretary-General's duties as a program leader is his/her responsibility to act as the initiator and focal point of a "global watch" function. It should be the Secretary-General's task to address the General Assembly whenever necessary to focus world attention on emerging issues that require a multilateral response at the regional or global level.

e. To establish a coherent administrative structure of manageable proportions, responsibility for the departmental activities funded by the U.N.'s regular budget should be coordinated by a small management committee chaired by the Secretary-General and including among its members the Under-Secretary-General for Administration and Management and the Director-General.

f. The management committee should meet on a weekly basis to assist the Secretary-General in the formulation of decisions on any matter in the programming and administrative area that the Secretary-General chooses to place before it. Ultimate decision-making power should remain with the Secretary-General.

g. Effective as of the next election, Secretaries-General should be elected for a single term not to exceed seven years.

h. The term of the Director-General and of all Under-Secretaries-General and Assistant Secretaries-General whom the Secretary-General appoints in his own capacity should coincide with that of the Secretary-General, although any of these officers could be reappointed.

CHAPTER 5

COMPLEMENTARY RECOMMENDATIONS

1. *Reorganization of the Department for International Economic and Social Affairs (DIESA)*

To improve the quality of its contributions to the identification, study, and management of interrelated economic and social issues, the economic and social secretariats of the United Nations should be combined in a single department, an expanded DIESA.

    a. Structure:

      i. The expanded DIESA should be directed by the U.N. Director-General for Development and International Economic Cooperation;

      ii. The Office of the Director-General for Development and International Economic Cooperation (DIEC) and the Department for International Economic and Social Affairs (DIESA) should be merged;

      iii. DIESA should be reorganized along interdisciplinary lines and should have substantial expertise and data-monitoring capability in every major economic and social area embraced by the U.N. system of agencies.

    b. Function:

    The reorganized Department would:

      i. support the Bureau of Global Watch (recommendation 2 below) by providing in-depth sectoral and intersectoral analysis of economic and social issues;

      ii. monitor the coherence and consistency of U.N. system policies regarding those issues placed by the Ministerial Board on the global watch agenda;

iii. provide, in a carefully organized collaboration with the secretariat of UNCTAD, applied research on specific positive-sum opportunities for North-South and South-South economic complementarity;

iv. provide substantive support for the programming of operational activities conducted by UNDP and the operational programs,

v. provide substantive support for negotiations on economic and social matters in the General Assembly, the Ministerial Board, or ECOSOC;

vi. continue to provide to U.N. bodies and to member states substantive research services (e.g., DIESA's statistical work on trade, transport, population, national accounts, maritime transport, energy, industry and construction).

The panel believes that among the substantive U.N. activities in the economic and social area that should be consolidated are those parts of the UNCTAD secretariat that are unrelated to shipping and commodities, or other sectoral trade issues, and their negotiation. Attention should also be given to the merits of incorporating the U.N. Centre for Transnational Corporations.

2. *Establishment of a Bureau of Global Watch Within DIESA to Support the Work of the Ministerial Board*

The work of the Ministerial Board would be supported by a small Bureau of Global Watch located in the U.N.'s Department for International Economic and Social Affairs (DIESA), which would be restructured along interdisciplinary lines (see above). As the principal substantive backstop for the Board, the Bureau would gather, update, monitor, and report on human security issues placed on the global watch agenda by Board decision, and would establish links between policymakers and the scientific and expert communities on these issues.

Underlying the proposal for a global watch secretariat is the panel's belief that by providing timely, reliable information in usable form on matters of consequence to human security, the U.N. can have a very significant influence in shaping international attitudes and, ultimately, behavior. In fact, the very process of producing credible information will itself help to foster political will to act on the information.

Office of Global Scanning

To perform this function effectively the Bureau would have to consist of two closely related offices. One, the Office of Global

Scanning, would serve as a small nerve center orchestrating the monitoring of global watch issues by retrieving, assembling, synthesizing, and putting into usable form the data gathered from hundreds of widely scattered sources worldwide—U.N. agencies, governments, media, universities, scientific groups, NGOs, etc. Eventually, the full range of information and electronic data-gathering techniques would be required to ensure the success of the Scanning Office, as well as to establish the potential utility of the Ministerial Board.

Office of Global Watch Research
The second office would carry out applied research, as requested by the Board or the Secretary-General, on specific global watch issues, employing the data base provided by the Office of Global Scanning. The Office of Global Watch Research would examine implications for national and international welfare and security, exploring the range of choices for international action and helping to identify overlapping interests and margins for potential agreement.

Staff
In view of the need to apply the most up-to-date information skills and knowledge, the importance of having a constant inflow of fresh thinking and approaches, and the extremely taxing nature of the work involved, the panel suggests that both offices be composed of temporary employees only. Staff should include a mix of individuals seconded from other U.N. organizations and others drawn from outside research centers, government institutes, and so on.

3. *Merger of the Special Political Committee Into the Fourth Committee for Non-Self-Governing Territories and Special Political Questions*
In view of the steady decline in the agenda and responsibilities of the Fourth Committee as the global movement toward decolonization nears completion; in view of the overlap in significant parts of the agendas of the Fourth Committee and the Special Political Committee; and in view of the Secretary-General's recent decision to combine the secretariats for special political questions, regional cooperation, decolonization, trusteeship, and the Council on Namibia into a single department, the Special Political Committee and the Fourth Committee should be merged. The new committee should be called "Committee for Non-Self-Governing Territories and Special Political Questions."

4. *Programming, Planning, Budgeting, and Evaluation*

The proposals described in Recommendations 4 and 5 below draw heavily upon staff research papers prepared for the panel on the subject of planning, programming, budgeting and evaluation and on personnel, which were reviewed by panel members during 1986.

Recommendations that flow from the present analysis are the following:

Recommendation 1: A clear distinction should be made between programs aimed at the search for consensus and those aimed at converting existing consensus into useful results. This distinction should be taken into account in the design of the Medium-Term Plan and the definition of programs.

Recommendation 2: For programs dealing with joint management in the areas of limited consensus, time-limited objectives should be established and followed.

Recommendation 3: In order to strengthen the U.N. global watch function and to promote consensus-building, the process of identifying problems that the U.N. could usefully address should be better organized by (a) use of the Introduction to the Medium-Term Plan to pinpoint those emerging issues requiring collective response in which a U.N. role is feasible; (b) adoption of regulations describing the type of global watch studies to be conducted, the means for deciding upon them, and the calendar for their preparation and review by member states; and (c) establishment of a list of international centers of research and expertise that, in addition to relevant secretariats of the U.N. system, could contribute to a global watch function.

Recommendation 4: A capacity for timely and in-depth program evaluation should be developed within the Secretariat. To ensure the independence of evaluations, the head of the evaluation office should: report directly to the Secretary-General; have the title of Inspector General, equivalent in rank to an Under-Secretary-General; be nominated by the Secretary-General and confirmed by the General Assembly; and should release reports, both confidential and public, to the appropriate oversight body in his/her own name and not through any other office, including the Office of the Secretary-General.

Recommendation 5: All programs, subprograms, and program units in the U.N. regular budget should be subject to six-year "sunset" provisions, losing their authorization after the sixth year unless reauthorized by the General Assembly.

Recommendation 6: The calendar for the preparation of the Medium-Term Plan should be so organized as to permit all intergovernmental and expert bodies to participate in the preparation of the relevant parts of the Medium-Term Plan. Approval of the Medium-Term Plan should replace the usual process of definition of mandates through resolutions.

Recommendation 7: To ensure that the new consensus requirement for decisions by the Committee for Program and Coordination strengthens rather than weakens the ability of member states to provide fiscal and programmatic direction, "consensus" should not be interpreted as requiring unanimity on all details of the program budget but only on the *level of the budget* and the *allocation of resources among major programs.*

5. Personnel
Role of the Secretary-General
a. The Secretary-General should defend his prerogatives as chief administrative officer in the formulation and execution of personnel policy.

b. A high-level, independent search and review committee should be appointed by the Secretary-General to assist with all appointments at the level of D-2 and above, providing him with a short list of candidates.

Role of the General Assembly
The General Assembly should discontinue its "command and compliance" approach to personnel matters and restrict itself to broad issues of policy.

International Civil Service Commission
a. ICSC commissioners should be required to have substantial experience in the area of personnel management in the public or private sector.

b. The staff of the ICSC should be recruited from outside the U.N. on the basis of secondments or renewable fixed-term contracts not to exceed a cumulative total of five years.

Recruitment
a. The external competitive examination should be extended to grades P-3 and P-4.

b. Writing tests and occupation-based oral examinations should be conducted for recruitment at the P-5 and D-1 levels.

c. All recruitment should be conducted by occupational groups, and the appointment and promotion machinery should be reorganized for this purpose.

Promotions and Terminations
a. No "permanent" contract should be granted before an employee has served for a minimum of six years.

b. Two successive negative evaluations should result in dismissal.
Performance Evaluation
a. The current evaluation form should be replaced by one that rates the performance of specific tasks.
b. The evaluation rebuttal procedure should be replaced by a simple "right of review."
c. All professional employees should be evaluated annually.

6. *Improving the Disaster Management Capability of the United Nations Office of Disaster Relief (UNDRO)*
The recommendations for strengthening UNDRO which are presented below are based in large part upon a paper authored by panel member Prince Sadruddin Aga Khan and presented to the international panel in order to assist the panel in its review of U.N. disaster response.
a. UNDRO's mandate is too wide for its current human and financial resources and should be narrowed to give priority to two key functions: to make rapidly available expertise and information bearing upon all aspects of disaster management in order to assist local authorities and the humanitarian community immediately after a disaster has occurred; and to act as a service organization to assist member states and other official and non-governmental organizations in improving their disaster-management capability;
b. For this purpose the General Assembly and the Secretary-General should explicitly charge UNDRO with leading the first stage of international disaster response;
c. A restructuring of UNDRO is necessary if it is to fulfill the requirements of this role: to be the first on the scene with qualified personnel capable of providing rapid initial damage-and-needs assessment; to have access to a sophisticated satellite-based communications network capable of locating the resources and the skills necessary to make an *accurate assessment of any disaster,* whether natural or technological; and to have the financial means to place a team with the requisite assessment skills on the scene within 24 hours of a disaster;
d. UNDRO's role as lead agency in first-stage disaster response should be formally acknowledged by the major U.N. humanitarian agencies; once UNDRO has been restructured, agreements should be negotiated between UNDRO and the other principal disaster respondent agencies of the U.N. system to establish general modalities for cooperation so that in the event of a disaster precious time is not lost in gaining approvals for essential cooperation on the part of multiple agency heads;

e. The UNDRO coordinator should create a consultant panel of senior experts with demonstrated operational skills, field experience, and international reputation from which he could select an individual to lead UNDRO's operational efforts in disaster situations. Experts would be drafted according to the particular features of a disaster;

f. UNDRO should promote the elaboration of a special legal, administrative, financial and operational Code of Conduct to regulate the management of disasters. The cornerstone of the code would be the increasingly recognized principle that during a period of emergency, humanitarian criteria (e.g., right of access) should prevail over political or sovereignty considerations; and

g. With the assistance of the Secretary-General, UNDRO should seek to augment its present arrangements with donor countries in order that enough funds will be immediately available to permit disaster response.

7. *Making Better Use of Regional Organizations*

Much greater attention should be given to the potential contribution of regional organizations to the overall effectiveness of the U.N. In general, regional organizations, including the U.N.'s Regional Economic Commissions, share several advantages:

—They are closer to the participating governments and often have greater credibility than the U.N. in general;
—Their deliberations tend to be less political and controversial;
—At the regional level it is easier to take an integrated approach to economic issues;
—South-South cooperation is easier to organize, particularly in economic integration efforts; technical cooperation often benefits from greater knowledge of local conditions.

These advantages have been stressed very often and have led to numerous recommendations and resolutions for greater decentralization of various U.N. activities, especially technical cooperation. However, despite these recommendations and their partial implementation (for example, the U.N. Regional Economic Commissions now have a larger role in technical cooperation), various obstacles remain:

—The reluctance of numerous central bodies dealing with technical cooperation and with development problems in general to yield their responsibilities to regional organizations;

—The inadequacy of the resources provided for development aid at the regional level;
—The diversity of situations in the various regions;
—The difficulty of defining the geographic level at which regional activities are appropriate: "Regions" are often too vast, and the *subregional* level is often not feasible for cooperation and/or integration; the actual geographical definition of a region may vary from one U.N. agency to another; and many of the regional and subregional organizations have inadequate resources.

A fresh look at the present responsibilities of the U.N. and of the regional and subregional organizations is indispensable. The structure of this new relationship might be similar to the one this report proposes for the center of the U.N. system. This would, of course, require agreement on which *geographical areas* would lend themselves to such a structuring. Although the panel has not conducted a systematic study of the regional organizations and is therefore unable to offer specific recommendations, it believes that it is essential to reinforce and reorganize regional and subregional organizations, including the U.N. Regional Economic Commissions, and believes that a comprehensive study of this issue should be one of the main tasks of the new institutions recommended in this report.

8. *Reduction of Subsidiary Bodies*
The multiplicity of inter-governmental and expert bodies subordinate to the General Assembly and ECOSOC, now numbering more than 200, has resulted in a needlessly complex organizational structure, weak internal communication, and impediments to coordinated program planning. The Special Commission on Restructuring of the Inter-Governmental Machinery in the Economic and Social Fields should request the assistance of the Secretary-General and of independent outside experts in carrying out a systematic assessment of each of these organs, weighing their usefulness, and the opportunity for mergers and eliminations, whenever possible.

Appendix I

The United Nations Environment Programme and the Mediterranean Sea (Med Plan)
The United Nations Environment Programme's coordination of the effort to halt pollution in the Mediterranean Sea (Med Plan) is a rather dramatic example of regional cooperation "midwived" by U.N. action.

First, by targeting only those countries that border the Mediterranean and thus were most affected by the sea's pollution, UNEP established a limited scope for its task from the outset.

Second, UNEP's objective—cleaning up the Mediterranean—was both specific and feasible within the context of its resources.

Third, UNEP-supplied reliable evidence of the degree of pollution in the Mediterranean (e.g., widespread oil clusters, the disappearance of shore life, outbreaks of typhoid, etc.) was sufficiently compelling to persuade the affected countries that failure to remedy the situation would undermine national as well as global interests.

Fourth, UNEP coordinated the process in stages and was able to measure progress against a series of milestones over several years. Up to 1974, Mediterranean states and international organizations had focused on controlling oil pollution (the primary concern since the late 1960s).

Fifth, from 1974 to 1980, UNEP officials designed an agenda that represented the interests of all the affected countries and provided incentives for participation (equipment, control over a project of interest to a given country, etc.).

After 1980, as a result of skillful negotiation and mounting evidence of the seriousness of the problem, the countries involved supported a protocol calling for national controls over industrial and municipal waste emissions. Moreover, they committed themselves to measures that went beyond the concessions they had made during the bargaining process.

Because of the Med Plan, governments of countries bordering the Mediterranean have become more effective environmental managers. Oil spills and marine accidents have declined in size and frequency, and most states have adopted procedures for dealing with such occurrences. The quality of recreational waters has also improved.

Even more significant is the fact that Med Plan evolved from the status of a U.N.-based, -staffed and -funded operation to a fully autonomous one financed by the participating countries. In 1979, states approved a Mediterranean Trust Fund, supported by donations from participants in amounts that are proportional to their overall U.N. schedules. At the same time, they created a small Med Plan secretariat, which, while independent, reports to UNEP's Regional Seas Program. In 1981, Med Plan headquarters was transferred from Geneva to Athens, completing the transition to self-sufficiency.

In summary, the Med Plan succeeded because UNEP, under exemplary leadership, responded to a need expressed at the regional level, used the information available to bring about international cooperation, and ultimately allocated responsibility for the plan to the participants in the bargaining process.

Appendix II

The United Nations Relief Operation in Bangladesh:

The United Nations Relief Operation in Bangladesh (later the United Nations Relief Operation in Dacca—UNROD) is another example of successful multilateral disaster management. By providing complete, accurate information and effective consolidation of efforts, UNROD earned the trust and cooperation of governments throughout the world. Moreover, the fact that nearly 66% of the total aid generated was pledged bilaterally reflects UNROD's success as a catalyst for self-sustaining action at the national level.

From the beginning, the staff at headquarters was small; at UNROD's peak it consisted of only the Under-Secretary-General and three professional assistants. Instead of expanding its own bureaucracy, the United Nations drew upon existing headquarters services, most notably in field operations, purchase, transportation, and communication and the mission in Dacca employed local staff. Indeed, less than a year after hostilities had broken out, the monthly aid situation reports submitted as of May 1972 were prepared mostly by one international economist and his Bangali assistant.

UNROD also provided specific, crucial information and skills not available elsewhere. Concise briefing notes were circulated at regular meetings of donor countries at headquarters to keep delegations informed of both progress and unmet needs. An information room established at headquarters continually provided delegations with progress reports and tools for data analysis.

In April of 1972, the agencies and programs involved agreed to combine their efforts into one comprehensive program under UNROD, thus providing a central unit of leadership and information for governments and voluntary organizations alike.

(For a complete account of this effort, including its evolution from UNROB to UNROD, see Thomas W. Oliver, *The United Nations in Bangladesh,* [Princeton: Princeton University Press, 1979]).

Part II

CHAPTER 6

THE U.N. AT 40: THE PROBLEMS AND THE OPPORTUNITIES

Peter Fromuth

A U.N. Identity Crisis

A paradoxical situation confronts international organizations in the 1980s. It is a decade in which the "natural agenda" of the United Nations and the U.N. system is growing—in size, density, urgency, interconnectedness—a decade in which governments have come to recognize that such issues as human rights, development, environment, drug trafficking, population, natural resources, and terrorism are global in nature and call for global methods of management and amelioration. Yet there is a deep, internationally felt skepticism about whether the U.N. is equipped to deal effectively with such problems.

If there is a link among discussions of the United Nations today, it is their expression of a sense of drift, of an organization spinning its wheels. In his report to the 1983 General Assembly, Javier Pérez de Cuéllar painted a grim picture of the body he serves as Secretary-General. "The machinery is running," he said, "and the wheels are turning, but it is not moving forward as it should." A year later, Singapore's departing Ambassador, T. T. B. Koh, commented similarly, "Nothing is moving at the United Nations at the moment."; Throughout the General Debate at the opening of that session, the same theme of immobility, of lost momentum, and even of irrelevance was echoed in speech after speech. The Prime Minister of Suriname called for a United Nations that "will soon take more concrete steps that may be recognized throughout the world as recordable successes." In the words of Burma's delegate, "the time has come for a more conceptually clear and operatively more effective response to the numerous challenges and dilemmas of contemporary world problems."

There are many reasons for the U.N.'s loss of momentum. One—the result of regional rivalries and the continuance of an East-West divide—is the severe limitation on the Security Council's ability to take effective action. Another is the state of North-South negotiations at the U.N., which for a decade now have been unable to move beyond disagreement over the structure of the world economy and the direction and rapidity of even the most modest changes. Yet another cause is the diminished pool of resources available for U.N. operational activities—the result of fiscal and structural constraints on member states' economies as well as the more conservative view of international organizations taken by the U.N.'s principal donors.

But there is a more fundamental reason for the pervasive sense of drift in today's United Nations: the world body's own identity crisis. This is not to say that agreement regarding the "first principles" enshrined in the Organization's Charter has somehow disintegrated. The purposes listed in Chapter 1, Article 1 still command broad consensus.[1] The problem is that deep and often disabling disagreement is encountered when the attempt is made to translate these essentially abstract goals into proximate objectives and to indicate the means of achieving them.

One of the reasons why the U.N. so often fails to sustain the same level of agreement on current objectives that it still enjoys on ultimate goals is that its members interpret the role of the world organization very differently and, thus, perceive the priorities implied by Article 1 in sharply differing ways.

Whose United Nations? In the 41 years of its history, the U.N.'s political ethos has reflected the influence, successively, of a Western strategy for making use of the world organization and a Third World approach. While changes in Soviet bloc thinking over the same period of time are easily demonstrated—a restrictive, sometimes obstructionist approach during the 1940s and the 1950s and a selectively expansionist one in the 1970s—the Soviet posture has in general been responsive to changes in the U.N.'s political ethos and activities rather than responsible for them. Moreover, the countries of the Soviet bloc and those allied with them have always been a minority at the U.N. and have never enlisted general support for their own vision of world organization. Their support for the New World Information and Communications Order and the New International Economic Order notwithstanding, the Soviet bloc's effect on the U.N. is more often that of limiting its scope than of extending it to new fields.

During the first 20 years it was the initiatives and innovations of the Western group, especially the United States, that provided the U.N. with its momentum. Between the late 1960s and the global recession of 1982, the initiative passed to the developing world, and the tone and thrust of the world body—especially during the 1970s—reflected the agenda of the Movement of Non-Aligned Nations and the Group of 77. The third and current stage, which has its origin in the global recession of 1982 and the debt crisis it triggered, is marked by disarray, lack of direction, and near paralysis.

Although the United Nations recorded substantial achievements during the time of Western dominance and again in the period of Third World ascendancy, the intellectual underpinnings of both visions of world organization had a number of similar flaws. The West in the late 1940s and 1950s, and the South in the late 1960s and the following decade, tended to view the U.N. as a "transforming institution."[2]

In the early years, led by the enthusiasm of the United States, the governments of the industrialized democracies favored enlargement of both the powers and the sphere of activity of multilateral organizations. Fueling this enthusiasm was an overestimation of the U.N.'s ability, and the ability of the West via the U.N., to influence the behavior of sovereign states. The U.N.'s peacekeeping provisions, for example, so impressed President Truman that he indulged in uncharacteristic hyperbole, describing them as "machinery which will make future peace not only possible, but certain."[3] The West expected that if U.N. organizations prospered, they would broaden support for international law and for norms of interstate conduct, including respect for national sovereignty, and nurture the growth of political and economic liberalism in the developing world—ingredients of the kind of postwar international order the industrialized countries hoped to establish. While the U.N. *has* in fact strengthened international acceptance of such values—in part because many are widely shared in the Third World as well—it is clear that the West also held a number of unrealistic assumptions about how the U.N. would change—or be changed by—the newly decolonized states that by the 1970s formed the majority of its members.

This is especially true in the economic realm. For the industrialized nations, the U.N. was a means to extend and reinforce the postwar status quo. Although this strategy permitted a number of accomodations to Third World concerns—the formation of the United Nations Conference on Trade and Development (UNCTAD) and the International Development Agency (IDA), the addition of Part IV on trade and development to the General Agreement on Tariffs and Trade (GATT), the adoption of the Generalized System of Preferences, and other measures—by the end of the 1960s it had become too gradualist to satisfy the growing aspirations of the developing countries. When, under the influence of its new majority, the U.N.'s role, at least at the rhetorical level, shifted from system reinforcer to advocate of systemic change, Western disappointment did not lead to a reexamination of the powers of the institution or an adaptation of its methods for using them. On the contrary, little has changed in the Western strategy at the United Nations.

The Third World's approach to the U.N. during its own period of ascendancy was based on similarly unrealizable expectations. Where the West had overestimated how the U.N. as an institution could serve as a reinforcer and ratifier of Western economic and political interests, so the Third World overestimated the extent to which international institutions themselves could reshape international governance. In the decade that began with the first success of OPEC in 1971 and ended with the global recession of 1982, the Third World developed an exaggerated notion of economic power and strength. The leaders and membership of the Non-aligned Movement (NAM) and the Group of 77 sought to use U.N. forums to negotiate material changes favorable to the South across the entire economic spectrum—trade, finance, energy, aid, technology transfer, etc.—in order to redistribute global economic and, by implication, political power. Many developing countries expected to use the leverage of oil and other commodity cartels outside the world body, and a cohesive voting majority within it, to narrow the gap between their own economies and those of the wealthy industrialized countries—and to do so in short order. Although the political rationale for this ambitious agenda began to unravel at the end of the 1970s with the decline of commodity prices and of oil prices shortly after, seeming to disintegrate altogether with the onset of the global debt crisis and recession of 1982, the Third World offered no new organizing principle to replace it. Its response—or, more accurately, its relative lack of response—repeats the example of the West ten years earlier. That is, the failure of both attempts to use the U.N. as a tool of transformation has not stimulated a search for a viable alternative concept of world organization.

The current situation at the United Nations is a direct result of the common disappointment of expectations suffered first in the West and then in the Third World, and of the failure of both groups to adapt to the implications of these disappointments. Ironically, the loss of momentum at the U.N. and the world body's lack of direction has come about *despite* the view, now virtually axiomatic on both sides, that some form of collaboration above the level of nation states or political alliances is urgently needed. Without a successor vision of world organization, and perhaps out of a kind of intellectual battle fatigue, both sides increasingly resort to restatements of national interest and fail to agree either on the *ends* or the *means* of a more effective world organization. Nevertheless, the severity of the current financial crisis now forces a reassessment of precisely these kinds of questions. The unprecedentedly widespread willingness of member states to engage in such a reassessment creates a rare opportunity for far-reaching reform.

A More Practical Internationalism. To overcome the paralysis that besets the United Nations today will require putting aside what are, in a sense, false identities—conceptions of the world organization that misunderstand the U.N.'s purpose and overstate its powers. What the U.N. needs is a sense of purpose that has its own simple and irresistible logic—a purpose that (1) is inclusive and collaborationist; (2) exists at a level of specificity that is meaningful, and (3) can be translated into programs that undertake tasks which are at once important and likely to be fulfilled. Equally urgent is a hardheaded realism about what can be accomplished by a voluntary association of sovereign states that has a small treasury, no real enforcement powers, and a limited political mandate. This mix of opportunity and constraint suggests a simpler role for the United Nations: (1) to identify areas of consensus among its members; (2) to convert that consensus into practical, desirable, specific results; and (3) to seek to expand the margins of consensus by providing places for the exchange of views and vehicles for the incremental narrowing of differences.

Is the United Nations Equipped for the Task?

How well is the U.N. performing the role suggested above? On many occasions over the last 40 years, the U.N. *has* been able to pinpoint areas of consensus and to establish cooperative programs or regimes based upon them. In the field of collective security, for example, peacekeeping operations represent a type of collaborative action that the U.N. has evolved in order to adapt to—but also to make the fullest use of—a much lesser degree of consensus than is assumed in the Charter. Another instance of the U.N. effectively identifying and then exploiting consensus is its humanitarian activities, amounting to as much as $750 million per year, largely supplied by voluntary contributions. This matching up of censensus and action made possible U.N. relief to refugees in the Congo in the early 1960s, Biafra in 1969, Bangladesh in 1972, and Cambodia from 1979 through the present; to the Vietnamese and Chinese boat people in 1980 and 1981 and the Palestinian refugees from the 1950s to the present; and to still other millions in over a dozen African countries today. The same match makes possible efforts in the human rights area. Here, the U.N. has developed a quasi-judicial system of reporting, investigation, and norm-setting and, with the assistance of numerous nongovernmental organizations, has brought moral pressure to bear on some governments.

A contemporary success is the United Nations Environment Program's sponsorship of a series of self-regulated agreements banning pollution in regional seas, a program by which such unlikely partners as Greece and Turkey and Syria and Israel have adopted common goals and standards for reducing pollution of the Mediterranean. Another contemporary example is population: Influenced to a significant extent by activities in which the U.N. took a leading role, there is now much greater acceptance within the Third World of the necessity of controlling population growth.

The U.N. has also had a hand in the evolution of new approaches to the international economy, development, and the role of international institutions, and many ideas that found their way into practical governmental action can be traced to a U.N. source. For example, the writings of U.N.-based economists in the late 1940s helped gain wider understanding in political circles of the problems of development planning and of the importance of adequate food supplies and noninflationary growth. Raul Prebisch, working at the United Nations Conference on Trade and Development (UNCTAD) in the 1960s, suggested the outline of the Generalized System of Preferences (GSP), a system for multilateralizing preferential trade treatment. Phillipe de Seynes, Hans Singer, and other U.N. economists in the 1950s laid the theoretical groundwork for what has since become the International Development Agency (IDA), a World Bank fund for grants and low-interest loans to the poorest developing countries. Likewise, the Compensatory Financing Facility, an arrangement for offsetting export shortfalls adopted by the International Monetary Fund (IMF) in 1963, had its origins in U.N. discussions in the early 1960s.

Unfortunately, the past is richer in documented, if modest, successes in population, environment, and many other areas than is the present. Part of the cause, as already mentioned, lies in the external political environment, which, until recently, witnessed a steady decline in multilateral cooperation, especially in economic affairs. Over the last year, however, disintegrative trends in the international economic system have begun to bottom out—as evidenced, for example, in the interest of the industrialized countries in coordinated approaches to developing country debt, regulating interest rate movements and monetary flows, and supplying greater humanitarian assistance to African countries afflicted by the current crisis. Moreover, the "spillover" effects on the U.N. of the deterioration in the climate for multilateral cooperation have themselves been greatly exaggerated and are, in any event, an inadequate explanation for the perceived decline in U.N. effectiveness. There is, in general, too great a willingness to ascribe the U.N.'s credibility problem to developments that are external to it. This is a distortion that not only underestimates the extent to which the U.N. community—both delegations and Secretariat—bears responsibility for the problems facing the Organization but that also tends to "sell the U.N. short," by failing to indicate the range of opportunities for effective U.N. action that does in fact exist today.

Among the areas that will require fundamental improvement if the decline in the U.N.'s credibility is to be reversed is the manner in which the U.N. identifies spheres of actual or potential concern among its members and the Organization's arrangements for converting such convergence of interest about a specific problem into actions and outcomes that are helpful to the world community. We might dub the first, the "search for consensus"; the second, the "conversion mechanism."

The Search for Consensus

Nowhere is U.N. activity more important to the world community than in the effort to identify issues upon which there is a convergence of interest among U.N. members. Both the member states and the leadership of the U.N. have a role to perform if this function is to be fulfilled; neither, however, is performing it effectively.

The world body's primary role—and the justification for its existence—is to enlarge and refine a general convergence of views and, where feasible, translate it into practical action. Yet a review of the operation of the U.N.'s intergovernmental bodies turns up little evidence that the search for consensus has been conducted systematically or even made a priority.[4] Before discussing some of the obstacles to the more effective exercise of this role by U.N. intergovernmental bodies, it may be useful to summarize the different types of consensus-seeking, i.e. "forum function," they are expected to perform:

• *A platform for airing differences and exchanging views:* The United Nations General Assembly provides members states with a kind of pressure valve for "letting off steam" in disagreements with other states. On a number of occasions this has allowed time for diplomatic processes to avert a potential crisis.

• *A vehicle for identifying problems of global significance:* The plenary bodies of the U.N. have often been the place where issues of global, or at least multilateral, significance are first brought to world attention. Whether or not responsibility for follow-up action moves to national governments or to another agency—the International Bank for Reconstruction and Development (IBRD, or World Bank), the International Monetary Fund (IMF), regional development institutions, etc.—the U.N. has traditionally played an important role in setting the global agenda.

• *A meeting ground for constructive discussion of North-South issues:* At a time when the GATT remains narrowly sectoral, when the IMF and the World Bank are focusing chiefly on developing country domestic policies, and when the OECD hews to an exclusively Northern perspective, there is an opportunity for the U.N. to become the forum for a broader dialogue on the functioning of the international economy and its implications for national and international action.

• *A place for conducting negotiations of a multilateral character:* The difficulty of conducting meaningful negotiations at the world level between 159 parties of vastly different size and interests has been amply demonstrated, but the U.N. has had a role to play when one of the following conditions can be met: when the interests are regarded as common and equivalent, not relative and competing, as in conventions on the civil and political aspects of human rights; when the parties to a negotiation agree to let a smaller group act on their behalf, as in the frequent practice of forming "contact groups" to work out agreements (e.g., the U.N. peace plan for Namibia, the African Economic Resolution of the 39th General Assembly); and when the negotiation itself has been restricted to parties with a direct and substantial material stake in the outcome, as in the commodities negotiations at UNCTAD and, to a certain extent, in the Law of the Sea negotiations.

Yet there are numerous obstacles that impede the consensus-seeking process in U.N. forums. For example, ideally, U.N. forums should provide a global early warning system for identifying emerging issues with multilateral implications, examining the linkages between them, forecasting their probable future course, and discussing the range of feasible responses. Sometimes they *have* worked like this, but their successes owe a great deal to accident and ad hoc-ery. Indeed, a more regularized, "global watch" function currently faces large handicaps. For one thing, member states that favor such a role in the abstract have never translated this into an approach to ECOSOC, the General Assembly, or UNCTAD—the plenary bodies where a global watch function might be located—that might actually put these organs on a footing to perform in this way. At present, a considerable amount of clutter encumbers the agendas of those bodies, in part because they devote a great proportion of their time to reviewing reports of a plethora of subsidiary bodies.[5] Another obstacle is the fact that the secretariats do not provide the kinds of documentation—short, issue-specific, timely, technically sound studies—that would help to focus and inform a genuine global watch activity. Finally, if discussions of this kind are to receive a greater measure of global attention and impact, member states will have to reconsider their level of representation; at present it is sometimes too low and lacking in substantive qualifications.

An endemic U.N. problem, one that appears in relation to a variety of political as well as economic issues, is the overlapping of mandates and of areas of responsibility. The problem of blurred agendas and functions is probably most severe in the economic area and most extensive of all among such bodies as the U.N. General Assembly, the Second and Third Committees, ECOSOC, and the UNCTAD Trade and Development Board. Indeed, through a kind of "eternal recurrence," many of the same issues surface year after year in the general debates of each of these organs (and often in the plenaries of the major specialized agencies involved in development), only to reappear in debates over preambular or operative paragraphs of resolutions, which are themselves similar to resolutions on the same subject that were debated in prior years. For example, it is possible to find agenda items on the same trade and monetary issues in ECOSOC, UNCTAD's Trade and Development Board, and the U.N.'s Second Committee. Likewise, discussion of both Technical Cooperation among Developing Countries (TCDC) and Economic Cooperation among Developing Countries (ECDC) tends to occur in each of these forums.[6] The result is a waste not only of human resources but of the opportunity for raising issues to a level of prominence that would attract world attention.

Process too has often become the enemy of substance. Over the years U.N. forms have developed a number of procedures that weaken their ability to serve as a context for constructive debate and cause member governments to treat them less seriously. Included among these bad habits are: the length of debates, the repetitiousness of speeches, the absence of a germaneness rule, and the length and frequency of meetings. Just as harmful to the utility of proceedings is the approach often taken to decision-making. Problems in this area include: a predisposition to "negotiate," even when it is clear that a negotiation can only produce a paper outcome often heavily diluted with reservations; a tendency to offer and negotiate resolutions for every agenda item at virtually every meeting, not just of plenary bodies but of subsidiary groups as well, whether or not conditions are such as to make these resolutions meaningful; and a propensity for lengthy preambular paragraphs that, although devoid of operational status, must still be negotiated.

Ironically, the area in which U.N. forums seem to have their strongest claim to a natural monopoly—the nexus of North-South issues—is also the one in which the Organization's recent record is the most disappointing. The institutional and intellectual rigidities that have characterized both the Southern approach and the Northern response to the North-South dialogue have in general made discussion of international economic issues at the United Nations overly ideological and unproductive. In addition, many issues facing the more advanced developing countries do not lend themselves to treatment in a global context. Another problem, one encountered by any effort to conduct a U.N.-based negotiation, is that the institutional characteristics of the U.N. setting—universal participation on the basis of one-nation/one-vote, and the group system—are difficult to reconcile with the diversity of interests, power, and systemic responsibilities that characterize the countries participating in the international economy.

The Role of the Secretary-General. It is common to place the responsibility for the problems of the U.N. at the door of member states. This is to oversimplify matters. True, change of any kind is impossible without the support, or at least acquiescence, of member countries. Moreover, an "entrepreneurial" interpretation of the prerogatives of the Secretary-General would be difficult to sustain and might well damage the U.N. by antagonizing member states and the permanent members of the Security Council in particular. Yet the realm of what *is* possible directly depends upon the nature of the relationship that is cultivated between the leadership of the U.N. and its membership.

Chapter 15, Article 98 of the U.N. Charter authorizes the Secretary-General to "perform such functions as are entrusted to him" by the U.N.'s main organs. It is evident that in order to break the stalemate over the role of the U.N., to give greater coherence and definition to the Organization's short- and medium-term goals, and to develop viable and constructive solutions to the current political and financial crisis, a more expansive reading of Article 98's empowering clause is needed. The philosophy, shared by some Secretaries-General, that the U.N. leadership should function like senior civil servants serving a parliament is inappropriate to an era in which parliament is fractious and stalemated. A simple balancing of differences will not restore a sense of momentum or direction: The U.N. leadership must do more than *react* to member state mandates; it has a duty to *provoke* convergence about problems that are multilateral in origin and in solution but not yet recognized as such. The choice is between an initiative-taker and a caretaker. Although the first may be a controversial approach, the second is a debilitating one.

A role for the Secretary-General that would involve more active leadership, more risk-taking in the search for consensus, and generally greater influence upon U.N. decision-making raises the issue of the kind of Secretary-General member states want. Traditionally, the permanent members of the Security Council have had reservations about an activist U.N. leader, believing this might give him *too much* independence in the political area. It is not surprising, then, that the qualities which make for effective, dynamic, and visionary leadership have often been viewed with apprehension. And indeed, while most Secretaries-General have been devoted, tireless, and often courageous diplomats in the political area, they have rarely been strong and charismatic leaders or sufficiently engaged in the substance of the U.N.'s non-political programmatic and operational activities.

The Conversion Mechanism

In an organization whose chief resource is the convergence of views, the *exploitation* of such consensus becomes the most important management task.

Is the United Nations making the best use of the "consensus resources" available to it? Although it is difficult to give a definitive answer, two things can be said with certainty. First, there is a widespread impression, even within the U.N., that it is not easy to identify clearly the outcomes of many U.N. programs. Second, the U.N.'s system—if it may be called a system—for adopting programmatic or operational tasks, staffing them efficiently, and monitoring their outcomes is not adequate to ensure that the Organization is doing the right things with its resources or that it is doing those things well. These shortcomings are noticeable throughout most of the fields of operation of the U.N. group. However, they appear to be most evident in the economic and social programs that are carried out—at a cost of $650 million per year—by the various headquarters of the U.N. and the regional commissions, and in the tasks associated with technical cooperation for development that take place in the field (see table on Distribution of U.N. Resources—Economic and Social Programs—page 355).

One of the most serious defects in the conversion mechanism is the lack of priority-setting. For the most part, U.N. Secretaries-General have tended to treat the Organization's programmatic activities—as opposed to its political ones—as the preserve of member states. This has applied as much to the creation of new activities as to the redirection of existing ones. In general, their relatively passive stance has derived from the view that it is politically unwise for the U.N. leadership to be seen as challenging any program granted an intergovernmental mandate. Since virtually everything the U.N. does of a substantive or operational nature may be traced to some act of establishment, often in the distant past, this attitude on the part of Secretaries-General and their deputies is obviously an inhibiting one.

Because priority-setting has not been seen as the role of the U.N.'s leadership, it is today relatively unequipped to conduct it. This is true despite the fact that the General Assembly has adopted several measures ostensibly designed to require prioritizing of U.N. programs and activities. The Regulations and Rules Governing Program Planning (U.N. Document ST/SGB/204, June 1984), published pursuant to General Assembly Resolutions 37/234 and 38/227, indicate precisely how priorities should be determined in the United Nations. Regulation 3.7 states that the Medium-Term Plan "shall be preceded by an introduction, which will constitute a key integral element in the planning process and shall [. . .] contain the Secretary-General's proposals on priorities." Regulation 3.15 states that "the establishment of priorities among both substantive programs and common services shall form an integral part of the general planning and management process" and that "such priorities shall be based on the importance of the objective to member states, the Organization's capacity to achieve it and the real effectiveness and usefulness of the results." Regulation 3.16 defines the process whereby intergovernmental bodies recommend program priorities.[7] None of these rules, however, has been adequately implemented. One reason is member state resistance: It is one thing to ask countries to vote, in principle, for reallocating resources and phasing out obsolete programs and quite a different matter to request their support for terminating obsolete activities with which they may nonetheless have some connection.

Another problem is that priority-setting is usually left in the hands of the program and sub-program managers actually responsible for the activities in question. A third problem, one that applies as much to setting priorities for ongoing programs as to proposing new ones, is that the U.N. leadership is unprepared, both politically and analytically—in terms of accurate program evaluations or appraisals of new issue areas to undertake it.

Perhaps the most daunting barrier to more logical planning and selective programming, given the relative noninvolvement of the U.N. leadership, is the committee structure of the General Assembly. Under existing arrangements, the program implications and the budgetary effects of resolutions that call for new activities are never considered in the same place at the same time. The budget side of any new undertaking is reviewed by the Advisory Committee for Administrative and Budgetary Questions (ACABQ), which then recommends adjustments in expenditure—usually downward—based upon an analysis from an efficiency point of view. Recommendations of the ACABQ are then accepted or rejected by the U.N.'s Fifth committee, a body whose authority extends to the financial aspects of programs alone. The program side of things is handled through a parallel process carried out by a Committee for Program and Coordination (CPC) and the six other substantive committees of the General Assembly.[8] Unfortunately, the program track and the budget track never intersect in such a way as to provide for the meaningful examination of program goals and program capabilities *at the same time and in the same place.*[9]

In a more general way, the "collective management" role is not satisfactorily conducted by the existing intergovernmental machinery. First, there are too many intergovernmental bodies involved in the program-proposing business, making accountability and coordination difficult and waste and duplication impossible to control. Second, distribution of responsibilities is unclear and sometimes seems to follow no rational design. (For example, duplication in the economic area is as pronounced for the collective-management activities of ECOSOC, the Second Committee of the General Assembly, and UNC-TAD as it is for the consensus-seeking activities of these bodies described earlier. Third, the time devoted to management oversight is usually very brief. The main substantive committees spend very little time on program review, although the record of the various governing councils (UNDP, for example) is somewhat better. Fourth, main committee and ECOSOC agendas tend to be needlessly long, complex, and repetitious. For example, obligatory "general debates," in which the same countries repeat the same positions on the same issues, occur in ECOSOC, UNCTAD, the Second committee, and U.N. General Assembly each year. Fifth is the tendency to politicization. All of the main forums of the U.N. proper and the U.N. group are in some sense "political" bodies, since each properly concerns itself with issues about which its members may have different and conflicting national policies. Nonetheless, these legitimately political forums can become needlessly and excessively politicized when their members inject political issues into parts of the agenda where they are not relevant or when they seek to bring under the purview of the intergovernmental body subject matter that is beyond its mandate.

A number of other factors further complicate the process of informed priority-setting. Even those mechanisms designed as management and planning tools—the Introduction to the six-year Medium-Term Plan (MTP), the Plan itself, the biennial program budget, the program performance reports, and the evaluation reports—are not used effectively. Many of the reasons for this failure have already been suggested: the traditional mindset of the U.N.'s leadership; the absence of a strong technocratic and interdisciplinary group to give priority-proposing on the part of the leadership sufficient intellectual support; the absence of an intergovernmental context that would force consideration of trade-offs (the present context, until this year, has had the opposite effect); and the tendency, described in detail in "The U.N. in Profile," for program objectives to be described in a vague, routinized, and generally nondescriptive way. Moreover, in the area of economic and social development, the degree of specificity in the International Development Strategies—and in the descriptions of programs and subprograms that are purported to flow from them—is inadequate to establish clear-cut links between them.

Under the U.N.'s present structure the function of planning and programming should be conducted in two places: in the Secretariat, by the Secretary-General, the Director General, and their staff, at six-year intervals when the Medium-Term Plan is prepared, and again every two years when the proposals for the program budget are being established; and in the CPC, ECOSOC, and in the main committees of the General Assembly when the MTP and the program budgets are being adopted.

Up to the present, however, the process has not worked this way. For one thing, programs have been designed both at headquarters and in the Regional Economic Commissions by program managers and by the various intergovernmental or expert committees that are competent for each major program. Both the program managers and the intergovernmental bodies enjoy a considerable measure of de facto autonomy in this field, and there has been no central place, whether in the Secretariat or in the intergovernmental machinery, that actually shapes the programs of the Organization according to priorities.

When it comes to program *budgets*, the control that is exercised on the level of the expenditures by the Budget Division and the Secretariat and by the ACABQ and the Fifth Committee at the intergovernmental and expert level affects only that part of the budget which is financed through assessed contributions. This control is strict and conservative, tending to maintain the existing financial distribution of resources among the various programs and to avoid change or innovation.

However, no similar control exists for that part of the program budget which is financed through voluntary contributions. In the U.N. group some oversight of program and budget is exercised by the executive boards of the semi-independent entities—like UNEP and UNHCR (for these semi-independent organs the General Assembly examines only the very small part of their budgets financed through assessed contributions)—and by the executive organs of the entities that have separate budgets—likew UNDP, UNICEF, and WFP. But when it comes to the voluntary funds that are contributed to the programs of the U.N. proper, the degree of autonomy of the various departments or units that manage them is practically absolute. Despite the fact that the ACABQ reviews the budgets of independent entities, there is no unitary programming and budgetary process providing the General Assembly with a comprehensive vision of the financing of activities of the entire U.N. group.

U.N. practices show major shortcomings when it comes to providing the sort of credible, timely, and independent evaluation of program outputs and outcomes that is essential to selecting priorities among existing programs and when authorizing new programs. In general, the evaluation process is not timed to coincide with the planning and budgeting cycle so that the conclusions of the former can inform the decisions of the latter; the quality of evaluations and "program performance reports" is uneven at best, and data is scanty on the results of previous evaluations. Further complicating the task of evaluation is the fact that the specific objectives of programs and subprograms are, as mentioned above, often described in vague terms: "issue-oriented in-depth studies at both national and regional levels will be undertaken . . . ," or "information will continue to be provided on . . . to help the developing countries to . . . ," or "the devising of special measures will increasingly call for collaboration, not only with governments of recipient countries, but also with potential donors of voluntary contributions. . . ."

Unfortunately, evaluation and program review is generally overlooked by intergovernmental bodies like the Second or Third Committees or the Committee for Program and Coordination, which in practice devote a minuscule part of their meeting time to checking up on the outcomes of programs they have proposed. (For example, one delegate recently reported that the Fifth committee devoted only one hour to review of the Secretary-General's program performance report in 1985 and the same amount of time for the previous biennium.)

Program outputs and outcomes are determined to a considerable degree by U.N. personnel—who, after all, account for 75 percent of the expenditures of the U.N. proper and only slightly less than that among the affiliated agencies. Although it would be easy to cite many examples of high-quality staff work across a range of U.N. activities, there is a marked unevenness in the quality of outputs, and this is true across the board, whether one is discussing statistical bulletins or direct assistance to governments through a technical cooperation project. Improving the quality of U.N. staff performance will require action on several fronts.

Coordination of activities within the U.N. group itself has been largely frustrated by two powerful centrifugal forces. Exerting a decentralizing pressure from above is the large and growing number of independent U.N. bodies that are able to authorize activities. For example, one recent study estimated that as many as 30 independent U.N. entities channel development aid, usually in the form of project assistance, to developing countries.[10] Exerting a decentralizing pressure from below is the very nature of the activities themselves—the "major programs" that attempt to address every aspect of an issue—inevitably resulting in overlaps with other programs. Such programs tend to pursue these goals by breaking down their efforts into a multitude of tiny subprograms. (The average staff strength of the subprograms of the Regional Economic Commissions is 2.4 professionals.)[11]

Although this Sisyphean process may have done little harm during the first two decades of the U.N., the subsequent tremendous expansion of U.N. activities in the development field has made better internal coordination a necessity. This is because success depends upon the integration of activities ("projects," statistical studies, substantive research, etc.) that are themselves so closely interrelated.

What is true for the U.N. group alone is even truer for the U.N. system as a whole—that is to say, the U.N. group plus the specialized agencies. Here, however, there are extenuating circumstances. In Articles 57–58 and 63–64 the Charter's framers deliberately created a decentralized system offering very limited scope for any central direction. One reason for this approach was to prevent essentially technical agencies from becoming too involved in political issues. While this hope was realized in the earlier years of the U.N., the agencies have in recent times tended to become embroiled in such issues anyway. Also, with the great increase in development activities, the need for interorganizational cooperation has become infinitely greater than could have been foreseen by the U.N.'s founding fathers.

Since 1960 a vast superstructure resembling the institutional equivalent of a Calder mobile has been created in order to tie together this new generation of essentially development-oriented intergovernmental machinery.[12] Progress, however, has been negligible. On the few occasions on which the U.N. group *has*, in fact, spearheaded the U.N. system's response to an emergency—the African famine, for example—it has done so by creating special machinery that entirely bypasses its existing apparatus for coordination. The record is little different within the U.N. group itself and even within the U.N. proper, where it is not uncommon for serious overlaps to occur between separate entities like ECOSOC and UNCTAD or the Namibia Council and the Special Committee on Decolonization.

If something has been learned from the experience of the last 25 years, it is that committee-type coordination does not suffice. Within the U.N. group itself, the task requires a more forceful approach from the top of the Organization, one that makes possible member state backing and changes in the process of program planning. Coordination between the U.N. group and the rest of the system should perhaps be approached more discriminatingly than in the past, when it seems sometimes to have been "coordination for its own sake." At the same time, when programmatic coordination *is* desirable, the existing arrangements for coordination by ECOSOC and the Administrative Committee on Coordination are unsatisfactory on both the policy and managerial levels. And although U.N. development activities should perhaps be better integrated, the UNDP has so far lacked the capacity and the government support to enable it to serve as the focal point of such efforts.

• *There is no center at the center*: As the organs attached to the U.N. system and to the U.N. group in the system's center have proliferated, the U.N. proper has played a diminishing role. At the same time, there has been no offsetting evolution in the authority and intellectual influence of the Secretaries-General. The result is that in the crucial areas of priority-setting and of ensuring program complementarity where needed throughout the far-flung system, there is a near vacuum. Under existing institutional arrangements, there is little basis—and, given the traditional outlook of the U.N. leadership, little inclination—to counterbalance the U.N.'s extreme decentralization with an effort to propose common goals at the conceptual level and specific objectives at the level of planning and programming.

• *The elephant lays eggs*: While the resources of the U.N. and the U.N. system in the economic, social, and humanitarian area are a relatively small part (about 6.5 percent) of total global Official Development Assistance (ODA), they are far from trivial. In fact, in 1985 the entities belonging to the U.N. group will have spent more than $3.3 billion, most of it in the economic and social or the humanitarian area.[13] With so large a resource base, why are there not more frequent documentable successes on major global or regional matters? Much of the explanation lies in the extreme dispersal of U.N. activities, as described in "The U.N. in Profile," Chapter 15, and in the absence of a body at the center to at least propose and promote priorities for those parts of the system whose activities are closely interrelated. The result is that the U.N. group, and the U.N. system as a whole, lacks any regular basis for taking the sort of actions that will secure specific results on a few essential matters within a reasonable period of time.

• *Underfunded, understaffed, and uncoordinated programs and program fragments proliferate*: The absence of an effective control and information system, and of any way to require programming by objective, permits programs to go on for which there is very little possibility of achieving the purported goals with the available means. The Medium-Term Plan is replete with examples. In one case, the Program for Transport Development, the objective is "to overcome the bottlenecks and constraints of transport and communications facing the developing countries . . . to monitor and review the progress . . . to provide information on new transport technologies and institutional issues of global interest"—and more—with one lone professional staff member assigned to the task.[14] There is a "cover-the-map" quality to much of what the U.N. does, especially in the economic and social area. Contributing to this situation is an absence of accountability for program performances and the fact that program managers do not define objectives narrowly enough. Probably more significant than either of these two causes, however, is the fact that the pressure that member state delegates put on the U.N. to "do something" in a particular issue area is unaccompanied by any effort to match resources to specific desired results. Too often the outcome produced is merely symbolic. It may involve research and studies, public information, support for negotiation, efforts to coordinate national activities, and so on, which for the most part lead to meetings or documents—in effect, largely intellectual outputs whose effectiveness it is difficult to measure.

• *Quality-control problems are inevitable*: There is no systematic way to rationalize, to eliminate obsolescence, to pinpoint weaknesses, to avoid duplications, etc. To a very real extent, the absence of effective evaluation means that the U.N. is managing in the blind. And because there are no "sunset" provisions, many U.N. activities often take on a rather deathless quality. Member states know that effective evaluation systems do not end every anachronistic expenditure, but they can provide the U.N. with a mechanism for identifying such situations—one in which they would be forced to make decisions about their funding levels in the context of competing needs of a more current origin.

• *Lack of program flexibility breeds waste and resentment*: Over the years, the cumulative result of failure to set priorities and inability to evaluate performance has meant that the U.N.'s standard response to new needs is the introduction of new programs and the raising of new revenues. Quite apart from whether the U.N.'s budget, or the rate of growth in the budget, is large or small, such a manner of proceeding is bound to be wasteful and to generate increasing resentment among member states, who regard themselves as the bill-payers. In the national administrations of most countries, whether industrialized or developing, program turnover is considerable as governments respond to changing needs by phasing out some things to make way for new ones. The U.N.'s near total absence of terminations, consolidations, and transfers of resources is thus a type of "nonmanagement" that is virtually unique to this organization.

What Is to Be Done?

Possible Roles for the U.N.

The preceding discussion of the origin and nature of the U.N.'s current problems leaves a fundamental question unanswered: What should be the purpose of a United Nations reform? What kinds of things could the U.N. be doing for the world that it is failing to do today, or to do well enough? It is hoped that this project, and especially the members of the international panel, will help to provide an answer to that question. The goal of this concluding section is to assist in that search by suggesting some of the areas in which the United Nations seems to have an actual or potential comparative advantage over other international actors—an advantage which, it is hoped, the U.N. could be helped to use more effectively.

The U.N. as Peacekeeper and Crisis Manager. Despite simplistic criticisms that the U.N. fails to forward international peace and security, the last 40 years, particularly the period from 1950 to 1975, contain a number of examples of its having succeeded in this effort. U.N. peacekeeping activities, arbitration missions, or simply ad hoc troubleshooting may not have solved many conflicts on their own, but they have proved to be valuable mechanisms for crisis management and conflict containment, which have sometimes contributed to negotiated solutions or at least served to keep volatile situations from escalating. The U.N. is the only global actor in a position to provide this kind of essential "public good" to the world community. Indeed, the Security Council is an irreplaceable tool, which needs to be reinforced and properly used. Of course, the possibilities in this area depend to some extent on conditions in the international political climate. But the overriding importance of this function requires a continuous effort to exploit whatever opportunities for progress may exist.

The U.N. as Humanitarian Agent. So central to the U.N. as to be almost synonymous with its identity is the Organization's role as agent of the entire global community in carrying out certain basic humanitarian obligations. These obligations are distinct from those of development generally in that they are universally regarded as existing between peoples, not governments. One category of obligation involves organizing and leading the international response to disasters. This is a function for which the U.N.'s universal character gives it advantages—in terms of moral authority and the humanitarian right of access—that no other political entity possesses. A second obligation has been described as a "global welfare function." It involves meeting needs for food, shelter, medical care, and education that result from extreme economic deprivation. It is mentioned here rather than under the heading of development, since its purpose, like that of disaster response, is to relieve the most basic forms of human suffering.

One area in which there would appear to be a large margin for improvement is the U.N.'s capability for responding rapidly to disaster. During the African famine, the U.N. found itself without a proven method of coordinating a relief effort that involved many U.N. agencies, NGOs, and individual governments. The Office of Emergency Operations in Africa worked well enough, but it was a last-minute fix. Despite differences in the character of such disasters as the Mexican earthquake and the Colombian volcanic eruption, similar problems followed in the wake of each. The U.N. needs a proven, permanent process for coordinating a multiagency, multinational humanitarian response to disaster. UNDRO was created to do this but has so far failed. The U.N. may need to develop a facility with the political stature and the organizational horsepower to find and deploy resources in a hurry when disaster strikes.

The U.N. as Global Watch Organization. One way to give the notion of "global community" some material reality is for the U.N. to serve as a kind of global watch organization—for example, by spotlighting emerging issues that will require a collective response and calling world attention to them. This is a role that the U.N. has traditionally exercised through convening special sessions, calling major conferences, or raising issues in the Security Council or General Assembly debates. Yet on such occasions the record is disappointing in terms of the attention received from the public, press, scholarly community, and governments; the technical and substantive quality of the debates; and the lack of prominence the U.N. itself has given this type of "early warning" activity, either in terms of Secretariat support or by suggesting that a period of each General Assembly be set aside for this purpose. One area in which a global watch function could be immediately useful is in dealing with the burgeoning rate of migratory population movements, a phenomenon that still tends to be seen as a bilateral issue between governments in the major destination areas— North America and Europe—even though the management of this trend will require a combination of multilateral and bilateral means. A second set of emerging problems that ought to be dealt with more prominently at the U.N. is North-to-South environmental degradation.

The U.N. as Development Catalyst. From a humanitarian and a mutual gains point of view, there would appear to be a development role for an organization with a wider base of policy-making participation than the World Bank or the bilateral aid agencies themselves possess. Although the total amount of official development assistance provided by the agencies of the U.N. group (around 5 percent, or $2 billion per year) is small, the U.N. has a far greater opportunity to use its aid to influence thinking about development, and to affect the nature of development assistance, than the dollar amount of U.N. resources would imply. The ingredients of this opportunity would seem to lie in a conceptual approach that clearly sets the U.N. off from other development actors in order to emphasize to both donors and recipients that the U.N. has carved out a place and established a speciality in certain types of development assistance and not in others. If the U.N. were to adopt such an approach, one possible focus for its specialization could be assistance to the least-developed areas of the world.

The U.N. as Global Economic Forum. If the U.N.'s economic forums are able to overcome the problems described in "The Search for Consensus," they will have an opportunity to fill a vacuum in the present arrangements for managing the international economy. Current discussions of the world economy are of two types: narrowly focused multilateral exchanges taking place in a compartmentalized format in the Interim Committee of the IMF, the Development Committee of the World Bank, and GATT; and broadly focused discussions in the exclusive setting of the Western Economic Summits and the OECD ministerials. If the U.N. is to become more attractive as a forum for discussion of international economic policy, the structure of the intergovernmental machinery in the economic area may have to be reexamined, with some consideration given to consolidation, as well as to the advantages to be gained by the creation of a high-level economic body with a small but rotating membership. Such a framework might also prove to be a more congenial setting for treatment of the interrelated issues of North-South economic relations.

What Kinds of Reform Are Necessary?

The foregoing list is intended to stimulate discussion about where, precisely, the U.N.'s comparative advantages lie. Obviously, many changes, additions, and deletions could be made; the goal, however, is to pinpoint some of the areas in which a search for greater U.N. effectiveness might be conducted.

The challenge for reform is to locate opportunities for a much-enhanced U.N. impact that make the greatest use of its political and financial resources. Exploiting those opportunities requires addressing two questions: Is the U.N. doing the right thing with its resources, given their particular character and limitations and the range of feasible endeavor that these attributes imply? And is the U.N., as presently administered, doing what it does *efficiently?*

From the discussion in the previous section, "Is the U.N. Equipped for the Task?" it seems clear that the case for "efficiency reforms" is a good one. These could include, in *personnel:* improved methods of recruitment and training, a return to a more rational pyramid-shape for professional grade distribution, a more effective system of rewards and penalties for performance, etc.; in *budget:* improved procedures for reaching more general agreement on budgetary questions, creation of a unitary program and budget process, cost-control devices (including sunset clauses and parliamentary controls over supplemental appropriations), etc.; in *administration:* an independent monitoring and evaluation system, a senior Deputy Secretary-General for administration, etc.; in *financing:* changes in the scale of assessments to produce a more stable long-term basis for U.N. finances and consideration of a "resources envelope" basis for U.N. funding.

But it seems doubtful that such "technical" reforms alone, and others that might be mentioned (for example, those relating to decision-making procedures), would be sufficient to bring major improvement in the effectiveness of the outputs of the U.N. proper and the U.N. group. It has been the argument of this chapter that there is considerable basis for questioning (1) whether the U.N.'s goals, either programatically or politically (in terms of the main plenary bodies), fit its capabilities; and (2) whether the functioning of the Secretariat and the intergovernmental machinery serves to identify and promote such realistic goals. Consequently, it must be asked whether, and to what extent, structural reforms may be necessary to bring significant improvement in the manner in which the U.N. conducts the search for consensus and converts consensus into useful outcomes.

Notes

1. According to Article 1, Chapter 1 of the U.N. Charter, the main purposes of the United Nations are: (1) to maintain international peace and security . . .; (2) to develop friendly relations among nations . . .; (3) to achieve international cooperation in solving international problems of an economic, social, cultural, or humanitarian character and in promotion and encouraging respect for human rights . . .; (4) to attempt to harmonize the actions of nations in the attainment of these common ends. . . .

2. Department of State Bulletin, 13 (July 1, 1945). Quoted in Thomas M. Franck, *Nation Against Nation* (New York: Oxford University Press, 1985), p. 19.

3. *Ibid.*

4. The term "intergovernmental body" is used in this paper to refer to any official U.N. entity of limited or universal participation composed of representatives of member countries.

5. The findings of a 1984 Joint Inspection Unit Report entitled "Reporting to the Economic and Social Council" showed, for example, that more than 4,000 pages of reports were submitted to ECOSOC for review and oversight in 1983 (JIU/REP/84/7).

6. Duplication in the intergovernmental bodies often mirrors duplication in the secretariats themselves. Thus the overlapping subject matter of debates in ECOSOC AND UNCTAD reflects the fact that the supporting staff at DIESA and UNCTAD are working on the same issues.

7. The matter of priorities is pushed even further by Regulation 3.17, which calls for the establishment of an order or priority among sub-programs, and by Regulation 4.6, which requests the Secretary-General to identify within each program elements of high and low priority.

8. The committees are:
First Committee: Special Political and Security Committee
Second Committee: Economic Committee
Third Committee: Social, Humanitarian and Cultural Committee
Fourth Committee: Colonial Committee
Fifth Committee: Administrative and Budgetary Committee
Sixth Committee: Legal Committee

9. On December 19, 1986, several months after the preparation of this chapter, the General Assembly adopted a change in its procedure for making budgetary decisions which is designed to address this problem (A/Res/41/213). For a discussion of the reform and its implications see Chapter 12, p. 276–78.

10. Maurice Bertrand, *Some Reflections on Reform of the United Nations* (U.N. Doc. JIU/REP/87/7), 1985. p. 7.

11. *Ibid.*, p. 6.

12. *Ibid.*, pp. 9–10.

13. See Description of the Type of Activities by Main Function—Humanitarian Activities—*"The U.N. in Profile: How Its Resources Are Distributed,"* Chapter 15, by Maurice Bertrand.

14. Additional examples:

The Economic Commission for Africa: Marine Affairs, where efforts are to be directed at "assisting in the national development and management of the resources of the sea . . . in terms of policies, manpower, technologies, and institutions for the exploration, exploitation, development and management of the sea resources in order that member states can acquire sovereignty and jurisdiction over their territorial seas, exclusive economic zone, and continental shelf." Number of professionals: 1.

The Economic Commission for Latin America and the Caribbean: Science and Technology, dedicated to "strengthening of the technological capacity of the region." Outputs include: technical assistance (advisory missions; support to technical cooperation projects; design of regional system of technical cooperation; training courses), technical publications. Number of professionals: 2.

The U.N. Conference on Trade and Development: Trade Facilitation. The objective of this program is "to make international trade simpler by removing obstacles in the shape of unnecessary formalities, and excessive paperwork . . . to increase trade earnings through simplification and harmonization of trade procedures and documents." Outputs include various technical publications. Number of professionals: 2.

CHAPTER 7

RENEWING THE MANDATE: THE U.N.'S ROLE IN PEACE AND SECURITY

Edward C. Luck

For many years, it has been fashionable to dismiss the United Nations as a serious vehicle for advancing international peace and security. The U.N., afterall, has failed to attain anything close to the vision of a collective security system enunciated so boldly in its Charter. First the Cold War and then the emergence of large numbers of newly independent nation states have made it virtually impossible for the world body to engage in collective enforcement actions under Chapter VII of the Charter. For much of the 1970s and early 1980s, the U.N. was turned into a stage for playing out East-West and North-South tensions, rather than for resolving underlying security problems. Yet there is growing evidence that a new wind is blowing from the East and the South, bringing fresh opportunities for the world body to begin to regain some of its lost lustre.

The most dramatic sign has been the sudden Soviet embrace of U.N. peacemaking and peacekeeping efforts after four decades of marked wariness. Not only has General Secretary Gorbachev set out his vision of a far stronger U.N. in his *Pravda* and *Izvestia* article of September 17, 1987, but Moscow has undertaken regular payments for its share of the costs of the UNIFIL forces in Southern Lebanon, has pledged to pay its arrearages to the U.N. for past peacekeeping operations, and has proposed the deployment of a U.N. naval force in the Persian Gulf. The U.N. is now seen in Moscow as a potential aid in resolving its problems in Afghanistan and in easing tensions in other regions at a time when economic restructuring at home requires a relatively stable and predictable international environment. So, while this new thrust in Soviet policies toward the U.N. has overtones of propaganda at a time of uncertainty and drift in US relations with the world body, there are solid domestic and conceptual roots to the new Soviet approach.

Equally encouraging has been the virtual sea change in the tenor of the political discourse among U.N. member states, North-South as well as East-West. The incremental thawing of Soviet-American relations has been preceded by a progressive shift in the tactics of the non-aligned countries from the confrontational mode of the 1970s to an emphasis on pragmatism and compromise in the 1980s. There is a growing recognition among many developing countries that they have at least as much stake in limiting the spread of nuclear, chemical and advanced conventional weapons and in preventing the escalation of regional conflicts as do the global powers. And as the limits of Soviet and American military power in the third world have become increasingly evident, the need—and the possibilities—for bolstering multilateral institutions and arrangements has become more and more obvious.

Opportunities

If U.N. member states are willing to seize the initiative—a big "if"— the next few years could witness the growing use of U.N. mechanisms for addressing a wide range of regional and global security problems. As in the 1960s and early 1970s, progress on the bilateral level could well spur movement on the multilateral level (and vice versa). At each Soviet-American summit—including the 1986 meeting in Reykjavik and the 1987 one in Washington, DC—the discussions have floated from essentially multilateral issues like regional conflict to bilateral negotiations on arms control and economic topics. The possibilities for building a stronger and broader base for more stable East-West relations will depend in part on bolstering regional and global mechanisms for mediating and controlling local conflicts. Progress toward reducing Soviet and American nuclear arsenals, moreover, has already begun to refocus attention on the importance of multilateral efforts to limit non-nuclear forces and conflicts. The two processes, in other words, are symbiotic.

The 1986 and 1987 summit meetings may well have marked a watershed in official thinking and expert analysis about the role of nuclear weapons in Soviet-American relations. Based on the statements and proposals put forward by President Reagan and General Secretary Gorbachev, there appears to be a conscious effort on the part of the leaders of the two nuclear superpowers to downgrade the utility and value of offensive nuclear weapons. Both men have challenged the validity, even the morality, of the doctrine of mutual deterrence through assured destruction, which has been the accepted basis of their nations' strategic relations for the past three decades. They have repeatedly expressed frustration over the slow pace and meager results of past arms control negotiations and have put forward a series of proposals for deep cuts in the number of strategic weapons and have agreed to eliminate their intermediate nuclear forces. While part of their motivation surely is to gain political points, there is no doubt that they have altered the terms of strategic debate, whether or not their efforts ultimately bear fruit in terms of major reductions. Not only have they given an aura of official blessing to the concept of radical nuclear reductions, they have also, perhaps unconsciously, shifted the focus of analysis and debate to questions of conventional forces and of how to prevent the outbreak of conflict in an era of decreasing dependence on very large nuclear arsenals. It is in thinking about these questions, of course, that the role of the U.N. could become more relevant.

To a certain extent, it is possible to envision an emerging U.N. role as the institutional catalyst for a series of steps that would in essence make the world safe for deep nuclear reductions. As the debate over the treaty to eliminate intermediate nuclear forces makes clear, there will be continuing resistance to deep cuts in nuclear weaponry until issues relating to conventional forces and regional conflict are addressed satisfactorily. One of these issues is the development of alternative institutions, procedures and norms of a multilateral character to provide greater reassurance during the proposed transition to a less nuclear-dependent world. In many cases, as in Europe, the primary burden may fall to regional institutions and arrangements, as acknowledged in the U.N. Charter itself. The U.N., however, can play a critical role in the development and propagation of the norms and principles which would be part of a process of confidence-building, enhanced communications and ongoing contact. These are prerequisites to the development of "political will." U.N. concepts of interpositional peacekeeping forces, fact-finding, monitoring, good offices, mediation and arbitration would of course have their analogs on a regional basis if steps toward military disengagement could be negotiated.

These are very ambitious aims, but, in the wave of "new thinking" in Moscow, Washington and Beijing, formerly radical thoughts are becoming much more commonplace. While the "expert" communities are more comfortable with more traditional ways of thinking about security, their conceptions are under increasing challenge both by national leaders and by the publics at large. In each of these capitals, domestic economic and fiscal constraints, as well as the sometimes cross-cutting pressures of internal political considerations, appear to be playing an increasingly decisive role in shaping military and arms control decison-making. Each government seems to be looking for a relatively stable and predictable international environment, at least in the short-run, to permit a renewed focus on domestic problems and priorities. In recent years, the major military powers have tended to eschew the direct employment of their military forces in sustained armed combat abroad. The principal exceptions have been cases where they were already deeply engaged, such as in Afghanistan, or in brief interventions, such as in Grenada, Libya or Falklands/Malvinas.

And at the U.N., Secretary General Perez de Cuellar has been a somewhat cautious proponent of a broad rethinking—if not "new thinking"—of the way the world body seeks to meet its responsibilities toward world peace. He is widely credited for being a vigorous and persistent, if somewhat cautious, practitioner of multilateral diplomacy in sensitive trouble spots. General Secretary Gorbachev has given the U.N. a prime place in the exposition of his "new look" foreign policy, though it will take time to see how persistently he seeks to involve the U.N. in its implementation. President Reagan has visited the U.N. more often than any other US President and has warmly embraced the new U.N. administrative reforms, but again it is uncertain whether this administration in Washington—or its successor for that matter—will undertake a broader reassessment of the possible U.N. contributions to new global security arrangements.

It is perhaps ironic that in order to take advantage of these bold departures in official strategic thinking and to give the U.N. a significant place in their practical realization, the U.N. should project its own role in a more pragmatic and task-oriented manner than some of its more ardent and ambitious advocates might prefer. To be part of the "new thinking," the U.N. first needs to address continuing doubts about its credibility, effectiveness and relevance to the implementation, not just the impassioned advocacy, of international security. As the U.N. moves to reassert its utility for providing practical services to the international community in this realm, its utilization as an instrument for problem-solving will become a more attractive option to national leaders who will be facing their own growing credibility gaps between what they have promised and what they have been able to deliver in terms of disarmament and security accords.

Fortunately, the U.N. community is already moving in this direction. The growing pragmatism and moderation which many developing countries are displaying in economic and social arenas can also be seen in their approaches to security. The multilateral deliberations, resolutions and negotiations on global issues such as nuclear non-proliferation, chemical weapons and conventional arms transfers show a keener appreciation of the interrelatedness of various aspects of nuclear and non-nuclear arms control, as well as a recognition that all countries, not just the militarily most powerful, share responsibilities in this area. With the diffusion of military power, questions about who most threatens one's security and about what the U.N. can actually do to help bolster it are coming to replace the past phrases about arms control and disarmament being someone else's business. As reflected at the 1985 Review Conference of the Nuclear Nonproliferation Treaty, there is now far more talk about how to reinforce the nonproliferation regime than about abandoning it for its perceived inequities. Likewise, the 1987 U.N. Conference on disarmament and development resulted in a far more sophisticated and differentiated approach than the simple resource-transfer formulas so popular in the 1970's. At its 1987 session, the First Committee of the General Assembly streamlined its procedures for handling disarmament resolutions. And planning for the General Assembly's third special session devoted to disarmament—to take place in May-June 1988—has proceeded with relatively little controversy.

As in the field of U.N. administrative reform, these trends suggest that the international political environment is unusually favorable for a vigorous reassertion of the U.N.'s peace and security role. What is missing, at the moment, is dynamic leadership, a coherent vision, and an effective catalyst for constructive change. These exist in bits and pieces within the system, but the motivating force to put them together, as in 1945, ought to come from the member states themselves. Whether the United States is prepared, or equipped, again to serve as an intellectual and political engine for strengthening the global institution remains to be seen. And the Soviet Union, for all the vigor of Gorbachev's new initiatives, still lacks sufficient credibility to play that role.

Renewal

In considering specific proposals for strengthening the U.N.'s contributions to international peace and security at this promising junction, three criteria should be given particular attention. First, they should build on those functions in which the U.N., as a global and nearly universal body, has a comparative advantage over other international and national institutions. Second, they should be capable of attracting the enthusiastic support of a broad cross-section of the organization's membership. And third, they should fit into a coherent strategy for the U.N.'s future based on doing what it does best in depth rather than taking on or enlarging spheres of responsibility in which its contribution would be marginal, duplicative, or unnecessarily controversial.

The motto "do less but do it better" should be applied to the U.N.'s approach to international security. The universal nature of the organization and its scattered, open and ad hoc system of agenda setting make it extremely difficult for the U.N. to establish a limited and coherent set of priorities, particularly in the security field. But the proliferation of items brought before the General Assembly, Security Council and other deliberative organs, not to mention to the attention of the Secretary General, has made it virtually impossible to focus adequate attention or follow-up on any of them. It is understandable that the General Assembly is faced with a growing laundry list of "urgent" disarmament items, though since most of them in reality are hardy perennials it would make good sense to address these only every second year. The first Special Session on Disarmament identified over one hundred paragraphs of priority issues, incorporting almost everyone's wish list, while the participants in the Second Special Session could not agree on any final document at all. As plans go forward for a third Special Session, which unfortunately will take place in the middle of the US election campaign, thought should be given to aiming for something in-between, such as a short list of interrelated priorities of a global, multilateral character towards which the U.N. itself could make a real contribution. Neither laundry lists nor barren consensus documents will help heal the U.N.'s credibility problem or give it a significant input into the reinvigorated disarmament process.

The reputation of the Security Council also has been undermined by an inability to say "no." The Charter never envisioned the Security Council passing judgment on all or even most of the myriad disputes and armed conflicts in the world, assuming that regional organizations would first address the bulk of them. It was also not designed to be a debater's chamber, echoing the repetitious rhetoric of the General Assembly. Time and again, though, especially on issues of the Middle East, Southern Africa, and Central America, the Security Council has assumed the character of a mini-General Assembly, bent on gaining attention and passing resolutions rather than on quiet discussion of ways to resolve conflicts and settle disputes. The Council nevertheless remains a unique mechanism for building consensus among major players in the world scene, as illustrated by the ongoing effort to create the conditions for a peaceful settlement of the war between Iran and Iraq. In the years ahead, the Council may well help rally international support for a key U.N. role in the resolution of the conflicts in Afghanistan, Western Sahara and Namibia. But the cases in which it has made a demonstrable difference in dispute settlement are too few and far between, and in the interim it is not surprising that official and public attention has focused on the divisive clamor of its lengthy public sessions rather than on the sober deliberations of its private sessions.

The Security Council does not need to solve, or even ease, all of the world's problems to be valuable. It simply has to make a positive difference in resolving a few dangerous conflicts with the potential to escalate. Even one clear victory would begin to restore public faith in its potential. Therefore, less is more in terms of setting its agenda and concentrating, to the extent possible, over an extended period of time on a few key situations that hold some promise. In other cases, the Council should turn to regional organizations (OAU in Chad) or ad hoc coalitions of concerned regional countries (Contadora Group in Central America) to carry the initial burden with the political and logistical support of the U.N. system behind them wherever feasible. It is true that regional organizations in most parts of the world are weak, especially in political and security terms, but so is the U.N. and a more equitable burden sharing in this area over time might give some regional organizations a better raison d'etre and a much-needed shot in the arm.

The Council's credibility has also suffered from its total inability to enforce its decisions. National officials question the utility of seeking a Security Council decision if no effective sanctions, economic, diplomatic, or military, follow. The current deliberations on a possible arms embargo or other sanctions against Iran for its flouting of Security Council Resolution 598 is a good test case. Council actions, of course, may offer a degree of moral suasion in any case, but even this has declining utility when the prestige of the Council itself is faltering. The lack of enforcement power, of course, may simply tempt countries further to use the body instead as a place to seek public attention and partisan political advantage, fuelling a vicious cycle.

There is simply no possibility in this divided world, except in rare circumstances, for the Security Council to enforce its decisions. This is now a fact of life. The Security Council also is not an especially credible tribunal for determining the rights and wrongs of most violent disputes, especially given the complex nature of contemporary conflict. This suggests that it would be far more productive if states would seek to use the Council more for what it is relatively good at—behind-the-scenes negotiations, consensus-building, providing a face-saving way out when the parties are ready to terminate hostilities, and posing alternatives to the parties for their consideration—and less for those things where it lacks a comparative advantage, such as conferring legitimacy, passing resolutions, or enforcing its judgments.

The U.N. is evolving, in other words, into a service institution, one capable of providing the international community with a host of services which can facilitate 1) the search for formulas for resolving individual conflicts, 2) the development of an international consensus in support of these approaches, and 3) the process of negotiation and conciliation between the parties to a conflict. It cannot compel states to resolve their differences, but it can offer alternatives to violence and in some cases positive incentives for accepting them.

The Office of the Secretary General has demonstrated again and again the utility of such a service-oriented approach. By proffering his good offices, mediation, arbitration and fact-finding, the Secretary General and his colleagues have maintained their credibility and relevance in conflicts ranging from Afghanistan to the Middle East and from Iran-Iraq to the Rainbow Warrior episode. These efforts, however, have tended to be reactive rather than pre-emptive, often getting underway only after escalating tensions and violence have hardened positions and raised the stakes. More preventive diplomacy is needed, which will require better and more timely information, the greater use of special representatives of the Secretary General and the political courage on the part of the Secretary General to act quickly to bring emerging crises to the attention of the Security Council or to dispatch U.N. observers to the scene. The newly created Office for Research and the Collection of Information should help with the former, but it will take a more supportive membership and a more activist Secretary General to ensure the latter.

Peacekeeping, perhaps the most visible and effective service provided by the U.N., has fallen on hard times. The nature of contempo- rary conflict and the lack of major power unanimity have greatly narrowed the number of situations where peacekeeping forces can be sensibly utilized. Peacekeeping efforts face a number of serious short- comings in terms of finances, logistics and training for which a series of sensible steps have been recommended by various studies. These tend to reflect, however, a more serious underlying problem: the gradual slippage of political support for the concept of peacekeeping, especially in the United States. Where successful, peacekeeping oper- ations receive relatively little public attention and have sometimes been criticized for lessening the incentives for resolving the root causes of a dispute through their very effectiveness in dampening conflict and reinforcing the status quo. Where less successful, as their application in questionable circumstances such as UNIFIL in Southern Lebanon, peacekeeping efforts have gained both public attention and criticism. The unwillingness of Congress to provide full US funding for UNIFIL, after decades of strong American support for peacekeeping, does not augur well for the initiation of future operations. If the U.N. is successful in negotiating peace settlements in Afghanistan and Iran- Iraq, however, the situation could change dramatically since U.N. peacekeeping forces could well be required in both cases.

This political dilemma needs to be addressed squarely if peacekeep- ing is to regain its well-deserved reputation as a unique and valuable service to the international community. First, greater selectivity needs to be exercised in deciding whether peacekeeping is an appropriate instrument to be applied in particular circumstances. (U.N. profession- als, of course, warned that the situation in Lebanon was too chaotic for peacekeeping to work properly there, though the political exigen- cies and pressures of the moment, chiefly from the United States, prevailed.) Again, the U.N. may need to learn to say "no" in some cases. Second, peacekeeping should not be seen as a panacea when all else fails, but rather as one part of a larger fabric of peacemaking and arms control efforts which are mutually reinforcing. As part of a larger strategy, peacekeeping can contribute importantly to bolstering con- ditions for a peaceful settlement of underlying issues. Standing alone, without parallel restraints on arms imports into the area or progress on the diplomatic front, peacekeeping forces over time are bound to become increasingly exposed to both military and political assault. And third, in most situations planning for peacekeeping should include a "sunset" provision so that neither the parties to a conflict nor the larger U.N. community will be so prone to regard their presence as a permanent fixture of the local scene. One way to do this, as suggested in a recent UNA-USA report, would be to shift gradually the burden of their financial support to the adversaries whose differences required their presence in the first place. In the case of UNIFIL, an "interim" force over time has found itself caught in a very painful deteriorating limbo, with no attractive options.

In the arms control and disarmament realm, the role of the U.N. again can best be described in terms of services it provides to the international community. The U.N. can play a vital role as a catalyst, forum, educator, and inspector, but it has no power to compel recalcitrant states to conform to its visions of a less armed and more peaceful world. The General Assembly provides the only universal forum for the expression of the national viewpoints of the militarily weak as well as of the militarily strong, but its credibility and utility depend very much on its willingness to address the whole range of disarmament issues, not just those which the majority finds most convenient. It has also served, particularly in the 1960's and early 1970's, as a forum for debate and ratification of global treaties negotiated through the Committee on Disarmament and its predecessors in Geneva. By recognizing the linkages among different aspects of arms control and disarmament and by ackowledging the responsibilities which many countries share for progress in this field, the General Assembly can contribute to both a norm-setting and a consensus-building process. The first Special Session on Disarmament, by taking a very broad and balanced perspective, made an important contribution in this regard.

The U.N., working with non-governmental as well as governmental sources of ideas and inspiration, could play a major role in shaping the global security agenda and in stimulating new thinking about future trends and the nature of security. Undertaken as part of a more comprehensive "global watch" effort, the U.N., as a world body with social, economic and humanitarian responsibilities as well as a security mandate, could over time develop a comparative advantage over more narrowly based institutions in projecting a broader concept of security. In seeking to establish the conditions for peace, the U.N. should naturally include issues such as economic and social development, environmental change, human rights, and large-scale migration as factors in its analysis and projections. Through its ongoing series of studies, publications, expert groups, and training programs, the U.N. could begin to build a broader international consensus on the meaning of security in a post-nuclear, as well as a nuclear, era. In recent years, the Department of Disarmament Affairs has upgraded the quality and the breadth of its work and publications, and it should be encouraged to continue to expand its horizons beyond the traditional dogma which has dominated thinking in this field. Over time, the articulation and projection of a broader and more sophisticated multilateral approach to security could have the beneficial effect of encouraging the many non-governmental organizations affiliated with the U.N. which are active in the "peace movement" to consider broader-based approaches to the subject. In this way, the U.N. could multiply its utility as a norm-setting instrument.

The Conference on Disarmament in Geneva continues, year in and year out, to play a very useful role as an intermediate-sized negotiating body between the interactions of the major powers and the deliberations of the General Assembly. The track record of global agreements and negotiations compares quite favorably to the more widely publicized bilaterals between the US and USSR, though progress has been understandably slow in recent years. The Conference has managed to maintain a limited agenda and to focus on the multilateral aspects of a relatively few key issues, such as nuclear testing and chemical weapons. While Soviet-American differences have retarded progress in the former, there are more promising signs of movement on formulating an international agreement to ban the production, stockpiling and use of chemical weapons. The importance of such a step is underlined by the continuing use of chemical weapons in the Iran-Iraq war and by accusations of their use in other areas.

The principal obstacle to a chemical weapons ban—and it is a large one—is how it could be reliably monitored. There is serious discussion of establishing a U.N.-based institution which could carry out on-site inspections as the IAEA does of nuclear facilities. This would be an enormous and expensive undertaking, but one for which the U.N. is well suited. Whether or not such a step is realized, it is suggestive of a critical service which the U.N. could provide in an era of significant disarmament measures. Arms reductions, because they impose higher security risks than traditional arms control steps, demand thorough, reliable and impartial verification, often beyond the capabilities of national technical means based largely on satellites. In cases involving the production or storage of weapons, satellite reconnaissance is clearly not sufficient. On-site inspection by nationals of one's adversary may be seen as intrusive and may lead to charges of espionage or at least excessive zeal in some cases, though the inspection procedures of the INF agreement represent a major step forward in terms of what is negotiable. How they work in practice, of course, remains to be seen.

There may be instances where the U.N. could provide multilateral inspection teams for third-party inspection and reporting. This obviously makes sense in the case of multilateral agreements, such as on nuclear or chemical proliferation, but their use might be considered in other cases as well. This would be a far cheaper, less controversial, and more unique contribution for the U.N. than the various proposals which have been aired for an international space agency or satellite verification capability under U.N. auspices. Multinational inspection teams, moreover, would be a logical outgrowth of the successful U.N. experiences with fact-finding and peacekeeping. Its contingents could come from the traditionally neutral countries or from a politically balanced mix of countries.

In addition, the U.N. could establish a neutral forum to which apparent violations or questionable practices could be reported for further consultations or action. It should probably be a body with a lower political profile than the Security Council, and it might also develop an arm for researching and assessing new techniques for technological or human inspections of compliance with agreements. When dealing with fundamentally multilateral issues, such as nuclear non-proliferation, conventional arms transfers and chemical weapons, the need for global or regional institutions is obvious. As disarmament takes on a multilateral scope, so must the means of verification, reporting and adjudication of disputes.

These few examples could be multiplied many times. They are cited here only to suggest that a focus on those issues where the U.N. has a comparative advantage and on ways in which the U.N. could better serve the evolving security needs of the international community does not mean condemning the organization to a second-rate status. Indeed, in an era when the legitimacy and utility of massive nuclear arsenals are under increasing question, the role of the U.N. could well become richer, more challenging and more relevant to the central concerns of international security. With a bit of imagination, a touch of modesty, and a forward-looking agenda, the U.N. could well be on its way to a renaissance in terms of renewing its founding mandate and highest aspirations.

Expectations

To some readers, these suggestions may sound too tame, and to others too bold. It is really a question of perspective and of what one expects from the United Nations. From the very beginning in 1945, the U.N. has been a prisoner of expectations, which varied from country to country and person to person. Depending on what the observer expects from a world body, remedies for what ails the U.N.'s peace and security work tend to fall into three camps: systemic change, national change, or institutional incrementalism. The first school advocates fundamental or radical changes in the institution, its rules and operation. Basic Charter reform, such as eliminating the veto power in the Security Council, changing the one-nation, one vote formula in the General Assembly or creating more formidable U.N. enforcement powers, are cited as ways of transforming and multiplying U.N. capabilities for intervening in potential or ongoing conflicts. The second school of thought puts less faith in radical institutional innovations and instead calls on the member states to exert "political will" and to reassess their national interests, priorities, and predilections. The system would work, it is argued, if only the member states would permit it to do so.

Both of these lines of argument suffer from a basic circularity in which fundamental changes in the way the international system works are assumed to be prerequisites for allowing the U.N. to affect the system in a positive way. Neither approach in the end provides a sense of what steps the U.N. should undertake to deal with the world as it is: difficult; divided; dangerous; and in disarray. The U.N. is needed, of course, for precisely the reasons that make it so hard for it to succeed. The U.N. would have little to do in a Nirvana-like world.

The third school of thought has focused instead on incremental changes in the U.N.'s machinery, operations and conduct. Focusing largely on the central organs of the Security Council and the office of the Secretary General, this school has produced numerous studies of how the U.N. might go about its work a bit more efficiently and expeditiously. The basic problem, however, is not one of machinery or institutional tinkering. While quite useful and necessary, these efforts by and large have not addressed the difficult issue of public and official expectations, nor the larger question of defining and articulating a peace and security role for the world organization in the future that will be both compelling and capable of attracting the broad support of its member states.

If Charter reform is not necessary, reform of the international system not possible, and muddling through not a satisfactory alternative, then perhaps what is needed is conceptual reform, that is in the way those inside and outside the U.N. tend to think about its future role and contributions. There has been an unfortunate tendency, seen most vividly in the 1960's and 1970's, for the public, scholars, and diplomats in and outside the U.N. to stress the importance of those quantitative disarmament measures for which the U.N. is least suited and to downplay those aspects of security in which the U.N. has made the largest contributions and has the greatest potential. In particular, the obsession with Soviet-American nuclear disarmament, in U.N. forums as well as in the larger peace movement, has tended to obscure the critical importance of steps which could make the initiation of major or nuclear conflict less likely to begin with. For many years, the vast majority of the U.N. member states not only preferred to talk about the evils of the Soviet-American nuclear competition, but they went so far as to foreclose any serious discussion of the global competition in conventional armaments and general purposes forces. Everybody wanted to talk about someone else's arms race. Questions of limitations on arms transfers, confidence-building measures and steps toward conventional disarmament have only begun to receive serious attention in U.N. deliberative bodies and research efforts since they were given at least a second order blessing by the first Special Session on Disarmament in 1978. The U.N. Commission for Conventional Armaments, set up originally as the twin of the U.N. Atomic Energy Commission, never got off the ground due to Soviet objections and the two were merged into the U.N. Disarmament Commission in 1952.

The U.N. over-emphasis on East-West nuclear disarmament, while quite understandable in both political and emotional terms, had several unfortunate results. First, it was untenable in terms of achieving real results, because it was a case in which the majority of less powerful nations tried to compel the most powerful members of the U.N. to do things which they clearly were not prepared to undertake. This only added to the gap between performance and expectation in the world organization. Second, it implicitly denigrated the importance of the very useful work the U.N. could do in the areas of peacemaking, peacekeeping, and multilateral arms control and disarmament. If diplomats and spokespeople at the U.N. did not emphasize the importance of the organization's work, then it is not surprising that few outside the orgnaization paid attention to its efforts. Third, it shifted the focus from the global security agenda, including from a host of arms control and disarmament issues that were fundamentally multilateral in character and from a fuller understanding of the interplay among global social, economic and development efforts and arms control and disarmament measures. Fourth, it grew increasingly incongruous for the U.N., which exemplifies the values and the limitations of a step-by-step approach to problem solving, to be at the same time a voice calling for radical steps to alter the international security environment. Again, the gap between sweeping rhetoric and incremental action was all too obvious even to the most casual observer. And fifth, this tendency has made disarmament seem to be an abstract, even theoretical, concept, divorced from immediate security needs and defense planning, as if it was an end in itself rather than part of a larger security strategy. More attention came to be paid to the formal negotiating process and less to the underlying political-security relationships which could provide a more solid and enduring foundation for the disarmament process and to which the U.N. as a global forum could make an important contribution.

Challenges

In key respects, the U.N. Charter was formulated in an era very different from that faced by the United Nations today. It was not only a pre-nuclear document, but also one which assumed the traditional model of interstate conflict in which one party is widely recognized as the aggressor and others as victims. Collective security, of course, became a far more difficult concept to apply in cases either where there was a real possibility of nuclear escalation or where the parties were sub-national units, sometimes aided by third parties, and in which the question of who is the victim and who is the aggressor is muddled at best. When the United Nations has neither the military prowess to compel a solution to a conflict nor in some cases sufficient legitimacy to bring global moral suasion to bear, its tools for conflict resolution are bound to be at best one factor among many in bringing about a peaceful resolution.

The advent of nuclear weapons has been a mixed blessing in terms of the U.N.'s ability to play a part in ensuring international peace. The existence of large numbers of weapons of mass destruction has served to underlie in virtually everyone's mind the urgency and necessity of preventing a renewal of large scale conflict, particularly if it could lead to an armed confrontation between the major nuclear powers. The consequent development and dissemination of the concept of nuclear deterrence has also lent a certain degree of mega-stability to the international system, while at the same time permitting, perhaps even condoning, an enormous array of conflicts and disputes at lower levels of violence. Over time, as the risk that these lower level conflicts might escalate into nuclear conflagration has seemed to fade in public and official consciousness, the international community seems to have become somewhat inured to the human, social and economic costs of sub-nuclear levels of violence, particularly in the third world. And, as noted above, the fascination with the sheer enormity of existing nuclear arsenals has tended to distract attention from the day-to-day work of the U.N. and regional organizations in attempting to resolve or constrain violence on the local and regional levels.

The emergence of an era of sub-national conflict has raised a very difficult set of challenges for the U.N. system. The fabric of international security has been rent by a series of conflicts within or among developing countries. While the focus of scholarly and official attention still tends to be on Europe, wars or lesser conflicts are underway in most other regions of the world. To cite some of the examples of non-traditional forms of conflict in recent years, there have been 1) undeclared wars between major powers and regimes or rebellious groups in developing countries (Falklands/Malvinas, Afghanistan, China-Vietnam), often fought either with proxy forces (Angola, Ethiopia) or with aid to indigenous rebels (Nicaragua, El Salvador, Namibia, Angola, Cambodia); 2) civil wars of various stripes, some an excuse for intervention by neighboring countries (Chad, Sri Lanka, Lebanon, Cambodia, Western Sahara, Philippines, South Africa); 3) terrorist campaigns of either an intrastate or cross national variety (Iran, Libya, North Korea, Ireland); 4) intervention by neighboring countries justified in terms of humanitarian or legal considerations (Uganda, Cambodia, Grenada, South Africa); 5) holy wars (Iran-Iraq, Afghanistan); and 6) challenges to the security of mini-states (Grenada, Comoros, and Seychelles).

These tend to be particularly difficult problems for the U.N. to tackle for both political and conceptual reasons. There is rarely anything close to unanimity among either the Permanent Members of the Security Council or the larger U.N. membership regarding the facts, legality or morality of these situations. Since many of our contemporary conflicts fall in limbo between interstate and intrastate levels of violence and since rarely do states bother to declare war any more when they are interested in exerting military muscle, the U.N. has relatively few clear cut cases of violence between two sovereign nation states with which to deal (Iran-Iraq is a big exception). In extreme cases, such as Lebanon, it is difficult to find any legitimate entity to deal with which can claim real control over developments within its national borders. The U.N. is most likely to be called upon for assistance in those cases where it is either politically or militarily least capable of responding effectively.

The U.N. is also at times caught between the politics of those countries which are not interested in settling certain conflicts and those countries which would have the U.N. take a partisan political stance in particular disputes, even though that might undermine its ability to act as an impartial party in seeking their resolution. In theory, the U.N. exists as a monument to the cause of international peace and stability, though as a virtually universal institution not all of its members share that objective. Therefore its efforts will be resisted by those countries or groups which perceive either some benefit in the prolongation of a conflict or potential disadvantage in the likely terms of its resolution. Those which are dissatisfied with the status quo, or with the slow pace of peaceful economic, social and political change, will be at best selectively supportive of the organization's efforts to discourage the use of force as a means of accelerating change in the world. Most U.N. members quite naturally embrace situational ethics regarding what the appropriate role for the U.N. is depending on their perceived national interest in each case. Nevertheless, the U.N. has had some success over time in promoting norms such as the inviolability of national borders as a fundamental principle of interstate relations.

The U.N.'s role as a mediator and in some cases arbitrator of disputes has taken on increasing importance in light of the infeasibility of a more forceful U.N. role in dispute settlement. There is a basic incompatability, however, between these functions and the urge to use the organization as an advocacy body for a particular side in a dispute. On issues involving South Africa and the Middle East, for example, the General Assembly long ago chose to take sides on the principles involved. Too often, the Security Council has been used as a forum for general debate and the promotion of controversial resolutions on issues that divide the developing country majority and a handful of the more powerful members. This has necessitated drawing a distinction between the expressions of the deliberative bodies and the day-to-day peacemaking and peacekeeping activities of the Secretary General and the Secretariat. While this distinction has permitted the organization to play a useful role in the Middle East and Afghanistan, and perhaps will do so in the future in Southern Africa and Kampuchea, it has further weakened the organization's credibility, particularly in Western eyes.

The continuing erosion of the bipolar system is also creating new challenges for the United Nations. The gradual loosening of military blocs, in the East, the West, and between the major powers and allies or clients in the developing world, could lead to an increasing emphasis on multilateral bodies for problem-solving in the security realm. On the other hand, it may make it more difficult to develop a consensus on what to do in particular situations and to conduct negotiations with a relatively small number of interested parties. This trend, along with the increasing stratification of levels of military capabilities both among developed and developing countries, has contributed to a lessening of the cohesiveness and power of blocs within the U.N.. Although this trend may have considerable advantage for those countries, particularly the United States, which perceive themselves to be the victims of bloc voting, these trends could also contribute to the growing sense of a leadership void in the world organization. Now that neither the United States nor the non-aligned countries seem capable of dominating the U.N. agenda, it is unclear which countries or groups of countries will be able to seize the initiative in terms of setting forth a vision for the future of the organization.

The concomitant global defusion of military capabilities and sophisticated weapons—including the capability to produce nuclear weapons—has made it more difficult to think of a clear dichotomy between those countries which are militarily powerful and those which are militarily weak. There are fewer and fewer countries which can now claim, as many of the developing countries did during the few debates on conventional weapons in the 1960's and 1970's, that efforts to control arms transfers would be tantamount to "disarming the unarmed." The substantial world wide growth of the conventional arms trade over the past two decades, including the increasing means of arms production in and of military exports from developing countries, has begun to change the nature of North-South, as well as South-South, security relationships. With the emergence of important regional military powers and the demonstrations of the inability of so-called superpowers to exert and sustain decisive military force in many parts of the world, it has become less and less feasible to think of security and disarmament in simplistic "we-they" terms. Therefore, as noted above, the need for multilateral approaches to the arms control and disarmament agenda should become increasingly apparent. At the same time, the breakdown of bipolarity may make the negotiations that much more complex and difficult in the future.

As in other areas of U.N. endeavor, the enormous challenges before the world body in a rapidly evolving international security environment also represent an exciting opportunity. If the U.N. community responds to these challenges with sufficient vigor, pragmatism, and initiative, then the U.N. could well be on the verge of a renaissance in terms of its peace and security role. If these challenges are not met, then the organization could well become an increasingly marginal player in the effort to secure a more peaceful world.

CHAPTER 8

THE ROLE OF THE U.N. IN THE ECONOMIC AND SOCIAL FIELDS

Maurice Bertrand

The United Nations is facing a frustrating situation. On the one hand, everyone acknowledges that we are living in an ever-more interdependent world—and that we need *a suitable political framework* to manage this interdependence. On the other hand, because the only universal political organization we have is unable to deal usefully with the world's main economic and social problems, a sense of failure prevails. This paradox is not easy to explain, and, indeed, a number of different and often partial explanations are proposed. In the main, however, such explanations focus on the U.N. itself, emphasizing either its internal deficiencies *or* the "lack of political will" of governments and the so-called "crisis of multilateralism," without trying to establish a relation between the present conception and structure of the world organization and the unwillingness of many member states to use it.

In these analyses, no distinction is made between the political role of the U.N. in the field of peace and collective security and its economic and social functions. Economic and social activities are often treated as secondary or subordinate to political activities, as if a renewal of prestige and influence of the U.N. in the field of politics were the preliminary condition for the development or success of its economic functions.

A deeper analysis of the question shows that the problems facing the

127

U.N. in the economic and social sectors have their own importance and that a better understanding of the role the world organization should play in these sectors—and of the structure it should have to fulfill that role—is badly needed. Indeed, because improvement of the U.N.'s efficiency in the economic and social fields is a more likely prospect than improvement in the field of peace and security, it is the only *practical* way to create a better climate for international and peaceful cooperation.

Such a conclusion is inescapable when one has studied the nature of the present-day phenomenon of "interdependence" and the defects of our institutional response to it.

A clear indication of the shape of the structural reforms necessary for improving the U.N.'s efficiency in the economic and social fields flows from this study.

Interdependence and the Institutional Response

The institutional answer to the problem of interdependence between nations has been, since the first acknowledgement of the phenomenon toward the middle of the 19th century, the establishment of international organizations. Since then these institutions have grown enormously in variety, size, and number. Between 1900 and 1987 the number of intergovernmental organizations increased from 12 to approximately 340—a figure that includes 30 world, 50 intercontinental, and 260 regional organizations. In this network should be counted some 4,500 nongovernmental organizations that deal with everything from labor relations to environment, from human rights to disarmament. Every year the number of intergovernmental organizations increases by a figure close to 10, the number of NGOs by a figure close to 200, and all these organizations are growing in size.[1]

This quantitative development could justify optimism about solving the problems of an interdependent world, since increasing institutionalization should multiply the opportunities for the peaceful conduct of relations among nations. Yet, international organizations are often criticized for their inability to solve the most important global problems.

For this reason, the problems of interdependence deserve a more precise analysis. In such fields as transportation, communications, meteorology, technical problems, facilitation of trade relations between nations, health, and a few other sectors, where a relatively strong consensus has been easy to establish, the evolution of intergovernmental organizations has proceeded with ease. In fields where economic and political cooperation are required, however, the process has been far less simple and natural. Here, there has been a combination of two different approaches to the development of international organizations. In one approach, ideology and theory have a very important role; in the other, international organizations are looked upon as a means of increasing the influence of the major powers. It has been the first of these approaches—an *ideology* of peace—that has led to the various attempts to establish a global political organization. The process, at this level, has been one of trial and error. The first attempt was the creation of an International Court of Justice by the Peace Conferences of the Hague at the end of the 19th and the beginning of the 20th century, the second attempt was the League of Nations in 1919, and the third was the United Nations (and its system of specialized agencies) in 1945.

The development of economic cooperation at the regional and intercontinental levels has also been fostered by theory and intensive reflection. The idea that peace would result from the institutionalization of economic cooperation has played an important role in the development of a number of international organizations. The theory of "functionalism"[2] inspired the creation of the system of specialized agencies at the world level. At the European level, the establishment of the EEC has also been the result of reflection on the failure of the League of Nations and on the irrelevance of the U.N. when it comes to solving the problems of the Western European countries.

But the institutionalization of economic cooperation has also been viewed as a means of organizing the zones of influence of major countries, whether it be to maintain the political, cultural, and often military links between the former colonies and their mother country (British Commonwealth, etc.) or between a major power and developing countries in a geographic area (OAS, etc.); or to develop the solidarity of nations that are already members of political or military alliances (OCDE, CMIA) or have political and cultural affinities (Arab League, OAU, etc.). The result of this trend is a complicated network of independent and uncoordinated organizations, each having its own characteristics and roles and lacking a common approach to world problems. Indeed, governments are using this network of international organizations as much as possible to advance their own best interests with respect to military security, political influence, political propaganda, legitimation of their regimes and power, and such economic needs as security of supply, facilitation of exports, facilities of credit, and development assistance.

The importance given to such organizations varies according to its capacity to render the services expected of it and the type of international problem to be solved. For example, the critical nature of the debt problem of developing countries has enhanced the role of the IMF; the Chernobyl accident has drawn attention to the role the IAEA can play in such matters; and so on. Yet none of these organizations—with the exception of the European Community, which has its own dynamism and makes progress toward more intensive cooperation and even some degree of supranationality—is limiting the independence or sovereignty of any state. Multilateral diplomacy is inspired by the same philosophy of national interest as is bilateral diplomacy.

In the economic and social sectors, the U.N. is far from being a center of, or even an important partner in, the network of international organizations. The IMF concerns itself with the money, credit, and national economic policies of a number of countries; the World Bank and its affiliates are addressing the financing of development; the OECD, EEC, CMEA,[3] etc. are dealing with economic cooperation at the intercontinental and regional levels; and the specialized agencies of the U.N. system are addressing sectoral problems (industrial transport, agriculture, health, etc.)

The U.N. is fulfilling a unique role in the social sector as a result of its humanitarian activities, particularly those relating to refugees and human rights, but in the economic field its role is limited to some specific functions: superficial discussions of the world economy, ideological debates on North-South relations, collection and distribution of world statistics, some research in such fields as population and environment, the channeling of a very small proportion of official development assistance, certain specific negotiations (through UNCTAD) on various commodities, and discussions and negotiations on the Law of the Sea, transnational corporations, and the role of women in development. In some of these fields results have been obtained that have rendered important services to the international community, but these fall far short of expectations about the role the U.N. might play in economic matters.

One reason why the U.N. fails to exercise any intellectual or managerial leadership at all—even on the agencies of its own system—is that the member governments themselves are generally uninterested in the U.N.'s activities, as indicated by the low-level representatives they send to the various intergovernmental economic bodies. This is important to bear in mind when considering the ability of an uncoordinated network of international organizations to deal with the new and important problems that now confront it.

What has yet to be faced squarely—and the crisis of the U.N. is only one symptom of this—is that the rate of growth of economic interdependence in the world is such that the problems arising from it cannot be solved by existing institutions. In other words, the entire network of international organizations, including the U.N., is now confronted with problems it is not equipped to solve. This fact is on its way to being acknowledged.

Since the first oil crisis it has become commonplace to talk of interdependence, without fully analyzing its characteristics and consequences. It is apparent, however, that we are witnessing a phenomenon that is important, massive, and multifaceted, and one whose rate of growth is accelerating. The oil crisis, the Third World's debt, international migrations, nuclear accidents, the spread of international terrorism, drugs, exchange rate variations, and transnational corporations' strategies have demonstrated, and continue to demonstrate, that countries are no longer protected on their borders.

An historical analysis would show that the type of interdependence that has been developing since 1972[4] is different from the interdependence of the past. For a long time interdependence was limited to external trade. In the 19th century, as trade developed even further, it became necessary to regulate the means of transport and communications, and the advantages of cooperation in the field of health and science were discovered. In a parallel development, increased cooperation among the allies in two successive world wars—The Lend Lease Act and the Marshall Plan are the most significant examples—gave rise to a new type of interdependence and cooperation in important geographical areas. The world has now entered a third phase, in which interdependence is characterized by the existence of a world market, of a transnational production and distribution system through the network of transnational corporations, of a unique ecological zone, and of world problems that can be solved only if addressed globally.

It is being acknowledged more and more that the type of problems that beset today's world requires a global response and that existing multilateral and bilateral institutions are insufficient to meet them. Concepts and principles concerning individual problems are rapidly evolving, but no serious attempt has yet been made to approach them comprehensively despite their obvious interrelationship. Also lagging behind are efforts to improve the institutional setting within which to address the most urgent of these problems:

• Go-it-alone policies that threaten the world economy. In the last decade the uncontrolled growth of the debt of developing countries and sudden and erratic movements in the price of oil and other commodities and in exchange rates have appeared to threaten the stability of the world economy—indeed, the economy of every country. It is now being acknowledged that independent decisions taken by major economic powers on the level of interest rates, on the type of assistance given to their agricultural or industrial development, and on their budgetary policies could seriously endanger the global equilibrium necessary for maintaining growth and preventing recession and unemployment.

There are, of course, various perceptions and various types of reactions to the discovery of the importance of these new constraints: they sometimes give rise to nationalistic reactions, including a tendency toward increased protectionism or even xenophobia, as in the case of the increasing South-North migrations. At the same time, the necessity of applying common solutions to world problems is not yet obvious to public opinion in such a way as to become a part of the program of political parties.

Nevertheless, progress is being made in this direction: Governments are increasingly making known that they cannot solve such problems as unemployment, inflation, or the slowing down of the national growth rate without taking into account the situation of the world economy, and this is progressively being integrated in the explanations of national problems.

• The set of problems arising from what is referred to as the North-South relationship—the relationship between the rich countries of the world, which have entered the postindustrial age, and poor countries, whose people live in agro-pastoral conditions. Both North and South are at risk from the uncontrolled development of population in a number of developing countries in combination with the decline of population in the developed world. Both are also at risk from growing urbanization in middle-income as well as in poor countries, increasing the danger of famine, dire poverty, permanent unemployment, and disease in the South. And the development of irrational and uncontrollable political reactions among the Third World's new proletariat has serious economic consequences for the North (for example, in security of commodity supplies) and leads to a political destabilization at the world level, notably through an increase in migration.

• The set of problems linked to ecology, environment, global commons, etc.; the increasing capacity for destruction of chemical and nuclear industries; the increased risks of pollution; and the necessity of developing rational and coordinated policies for the exploitation of our "global commons" in space, oceans, etc.

• Cultural, ideological, and political problems, including those affecting security and peace, that must begin to be addressed in common fashion if all the other problems are to be solved.

The principles on which the nations of the world base their external policies have changed and are continuing to change, owing to three important developments:

1. The acknowledgement that there is no way to establish independent national strategies in the economic and social fields without taking into consideration the strategies, methods, and principles accepted by the other nations.[5]

2. The adoption of a principle of *reciprocal support,* according to which the good fortune of one country can no longer be built on the misfortune of others, and economic solidarity sometimes brings with it greater advantages than does competition. The United States' prosperity is indispensable to the prosperity of Europe and Japan, and the reverse is true as well. No major creditor country, major bank, or large corporation can accept the bankruptcy of a major debtor.

3. Governments are often ready to invest more time and effort to establish and encourage respect for common rules—for arms control or for the equilibrium of external trade—than to maintain their own systems for ensuring the country's security or prosperity.[6]

To say that the search for an institutional response to the reality of interdependence is lagging behind does not mean that the process has not already begun and given some results. These new perceptions have created the need for reliable political institutions at the global level— among them international treaties that include precise systems of inspection for arms control or medium-term commitments to implement economic policies. An attempt to obtain collective decisions that would have greater credibility than the resolutions of the U.N. General Assembly or the Security Council is seen in the decisions of the Western summits.

Mr. R. G Darman, then Deputy Secretary of the U.S. Treasury, in an interview with *The New York Times* in March 1986, likewise noted that interdependence creates the need for a solid world political framework that does not exist at present, saying "that it is absolutely essential to deal with the relations between what will be the monetary system, whatever its form, and the political system, the wider system in which the monetary system must work." This new type of relation is just in the process of being established, but outside the United Nations. Particularly since 1970, there have been regular summits between the two superpowers to discuss arms control, and between the major Western powers—the United States, Europe, and Japan—to address the harmonization of their monetary and economic strategies. The experimental involvement of some representatives of developing countries in the Western summits at Cancun in 1981[7] indicated the direction these consultations could take in the future.

The trend in these new political institutions seems to be toward the highest level of representation and the limiting of their membership to the most important countries—which means the exclusion of small countries and, in general (Cancun excepted), the Third World.

This rapid review shows that there is a need for: a comprehensive, institutional answer to world problems in view of the fact that the present system, particularly the present network of international organizations—established on an ad hoc basis and uncoordinated—is obviously unable to provide a global response; and a central institution able to provide, particularly in the economic field, intellectual and practical coordination.

The experience gained from the process of trial and error in establishing two successive global organizations and from a study of the role actually played by the U.N. teaches that a new modern global organization should not receive, as its main mission, the unrealistic mandate to "solve" all international problems or to "maintain" peace now and everywhere in the world but should be charged with trying to develop a better world consensus on economic and social questions, which is indispensable to the development of a better consensus in the political field.

Such an organization should, consequently, be equipped to:

- identify common problems in these fields

- facilitate discussions and negotiations on matters relating to them

- propose joint activities of member states in all fields where some consensus exists.

The Present U.N. Capacity in the Economic and Social Fields

Everyone acknowledges that the present capacity of the U.N. to fulfill the functions indicated above—identification, search for common approach, establishment of joint actions—is quite limited. Nonetheless, there is a variety of diagnoses to explain this weakness. One of the most popular blames "bad management," holding the Secretariat responsible for U.N. ineffectiveness in many fields, particularly when it comes to identifying world problems.

It seems fashionable to be severely critical of the performance, methods of work, level of qualifications, structure, and composition of the Secretariat. The Group of 18's report[8] has insisted on these aspects and has explained that "the quality of the work performed needs to be improved upon. The qualifications of staff, in particular in the higher categories, are inadequate and the working methods are not efficient. Today's structure is too complex, fragmented, and top heavy. The secretariat is divided into too many departments, offices and divisions." There is obviously some truth in this description. It is obvious that these deficiencies, particularly the insufficient level of competence—for too great a proportion of the professionals, including the high-level-post incumbents—is detrimental to efficiency.

It would be unfair, however, to state that the U.N. Secretariat has no capacity for identifying world problems on which some action is possible. In some sectors, this capacity exists, and it has sometimes been efficient. This has been the case, for example, in the population field, where improvement in collection of data, analysis of trends, studies showing the relationship between population and economic and social problems, and facilitation of exchange of views and experience have certainly contributed to a better acknowledgement of the various problems at stake, the definition of common approaches to solutions, and the adoption of effective population policies in a number of countries.[9] In the environment field, achievements of the same kind could be cited.

But it is correct to state, unfortunately, that this has not been the case in many other sectors. For example, the description of the problems facing developing countries in practically all sectors—science and technology, public administration, natural resources, human settlements, etc.—has not led to an identification of the manner in which the international community could help in solving them. In some cases, such as transnational corporations and commodities, the manner in which the problems have been identified has not obtained a general consensus. In other cases, such as drugs and disaster relief, the U.N. Secretariat has not been able, with the very small resources at its disposal, to cope with the magnitude of the problem.

It has also been noted that the traditional reports and studies prepared by the U.N. Secretariat on the world economy and on the world social situation are indeed not really directed at identifying issues the world organization could tackle and to which it could make a contribution to a better common understanding. These studies are in general more descriptive than analytical.[10]

It is also true that sectorialization, which leads to a relatively equal distribution of the U.N.'s manpower among a number of sectors, including those in which there is no great chance of having any effectiveness, does not attribute enough importance to interdisciplinary and comprehensive research. This situation is aggravated by the fact that it has not yet been possible, in carrying out this very difficult research,[11] to associate with any outside research center in the world. Finally, it can be said that international civil servants are not encouraged to develop new, original, or bold ideas, and that, consequently, they practice a self-censorship in the drafting of their reports.

But the reasons for this situation are not to be found in the Secretariat itself. Rather, it should be acknowledged that member states have never clearly requested the Secretariat to prepare carefully this type of identification of world problems, have not devoted the necessary resources to it, and have not established a structure for this purpose. On some occasions the Secretary-General has been encouraged to go in this direction. He has, several times, been invited to propose "priorities." The preparation of the Medium-Term Plan, and particularly of its Introduction, should have initiated this kind of research. But when these requests have failed to receive any satisfactory response, they have not been followed by new suggestions to encourage the Secretary-General to take the necessary measures to render these tasks possible.

Delegations have not really examined the consequences of their requests. They have not questioned either the exaggerated sectorialization of the U.N. proper or the decentralization of the U.N. system. They have not enforced a personnel policy that would have increased the capacity of the Secretariat. They have not changed the mandates concerning the world economic and social surveys, have not decided to develop an interdisciplinary work force, have not decided to facilitate the contribution of outside research centers, and have not considered whether improvements in the structure of the Secretariat might not be rendered easier to obtain through a serious reform of the structure of the intergovernmental machinery.

All these questions are now in the minds of an increasing number of people. In particular, the idea that. the necessary changes in the structure of the Secretariat are subordinate to a profound reform of the intergovernmental machinery has begun to make some progress. The Group of 18's report—which reflects the views of a majority of delegations on this point—has clearly stated that "the expansion of the agenda has led to a parallel growth in the intergovernmental machinery, which has in some cases resulted in duplication of agendas and work, particularly in the economic and social fields. The efficiency of the organization has suffered through this process, and there is a need for a structural reform of the intergovernmental machinery. . . . [T]here is also an urgent need for improved coordination of activities undertaken both within the United Nations itself and throughout the United Nations System. The structure of the present system makes coordination of activities a difficult undertaking. . . ."[12]

These strong statements have not led the Group to propose profound changes in the present intergovernmental structure. It is obvious—both in the recommendations made and the type of study recommended on this subject—that the majority of the members of the Group believed that some "corrections" to the existing structure would be enough to solve the major problems in this regard.

At least the road is open to a serious consideration of the problem. And, indeed, a thorough study of the present situation will show that it is impossible, without a complete reshuffling, to correct existing deficiencies. A review of these deficiencies helps to explain why.

The Level of Representation of Member States

The first feature that strikes any outside observer is the low level of representation of member states in these sectors. In the Security Council and elsewhere in the political sector, member states are represented by ambassadors (and efforts are made to supply ministerial-level representatives for some meetings), but in the economic and social bodies the majority of diplomats representing their countries are of lower (and sometimes far lower) grades. Indeed, discussions of economic problems in the Second Committee of the General Assembly, in the Economic and Social Council, or in the Trade and Development Board are held by secretaries or counsellors; and these diplomats have no direct links, in general, with the ministries of finance or economy that are not *directly* concerned by the resolutions taken in these bodies.

The dichotomy that exists between world financial institutions—the IMF and the World Bank—and the U.N. on economic matters is obviously detrimental to the U.N. In the financial institutions, the representatives of the ministries of finance and economy make decisions that have consequences for their economic and monetary policies; in the U.N., diplomats discuss general questions and approve resolutions that have no practical consequences (with some exceptions, as indicated, in such fields as population and environment). The only economic intergovernmental body in the U.N. in which ministers themselves are their countries' representatives is the World Food Council; for one week a year, ministries of agriculture of 30 countries have the opportunity to discuss problems of some interest for their own policies. One may wonder why what is possible for ministries of agriculture is not possible for other ministries. This question has to be borne in mind when one looks at the structure of the U.N. intergovernmental machinery.[13]

Structure of the U.N. Intergovernmental Machinery

The accompanying chart shows that the machinery for general discussion, studies, and negotiations in the economic and social sectors is not only very complicated but split among three different and never convergent branches that often deal with the same sectors, make the same types of studies, and have no common credible center for synthesis and reflection. A comparison of the agendas of ECOSOC, the Second Committee of the General Assembly, and the Trade and Development Board shows that very often the same topics are addressed without any real difference of approach, and that the general debates in the three branches are repetitive and not directed at identifying common approaches.[14]

Moreover, the distribution of tasks among expert groups and intergovernmental bodies and the determination of the number of members of each of them do not obey precise principles. This structure has been built over time; the reasons for decisions on the composition and mandates of various bodies have often been forgotten, and no review has succeeded to reorganize it on a rational basis. The historical trend to increase the number of members of all of these committees has, in general, been counterproductive, rendering the organization of the

MAIN INTERGOVERNMENTAL AND EXPERT BODIES DEALING WITH ECONOMIC, SOCIAL, HUMAN RIGHTS, ADMINISTRATIVE AND LEGAL MATTERS
(EXCLUDING EXECUTIVE BOARDS OF HUMANITARIAN OR TECHNICAL COOPERATION ORGANIZATIONS)

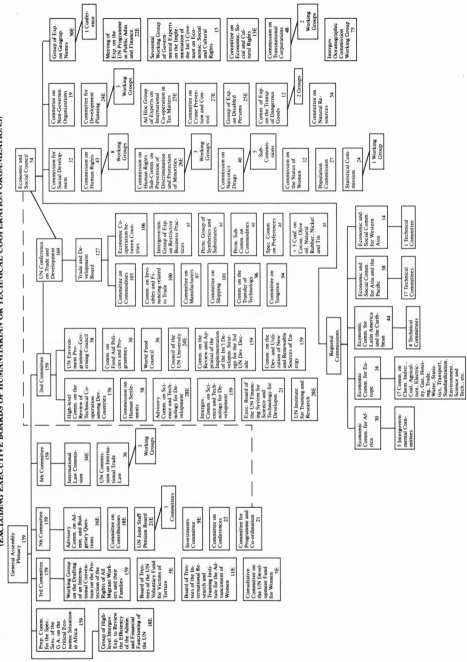

work more difficult, lengthening the debates, and leading to a very low level of representation.

Decentralization of the U.N. System

The type of deficiencies noted in the Secretariat of the U.N. proper exist throughout the U.N. system. At this level sectorialization reaches its apex; there is no aspect of human activity that is left outside the scope of the programs of the U.N. agencies. This universality should, in theory, facilitate the identification of the questions on which useful action is possible and allow the international community to concentrate its efforts on them. This is, unfortunately, not the case.

It is, of course, possible to cite some sectors in which proper identification has been made and useful action undertaken. While the contributions of each agency in the sectors in which it is specialized are difficult to evaluate precisely and are uneven, in a number of cases, such as education, health, labor relations, agriculture, and industry, they are not negligible. These partial achievements aside, the problems faced are the same as in the U.N. proper: Not only does an exaggerated sectorialization result in a failure to concentrate enough manpower resources and efforts on problems that may be capable of solution, but there is no system for facilitating global and comprehensive analysis and exchanges of views. The decentralization of the system, which renders it unable to define any integrated or comprehensive approach to the problems of development, is aggravated by the split between the Bretton Woods institutions—IMF, World Bank, and GATT—which are not universal (due mainly to the absence of the USSR) and have a system of weighted voting and the other agencies that use the system of "one country/one vote." The separation that exists in all countries between the Ministries of Economy and Finance and the Ministry of Foreign Affairs leads to a total absence of coordination and to contradictory policies between the Bretton Woods institutions and the rest of the U.N. system.

In this regard, the only instrument that ought to have ensured coordination, i.e., the Administrative Committee of Coordination (ACC), is neither equipped nor employed for this purpose. Despite a number of reforms and recommendations, the ACC and its system of subcommittees remains a total failure.

It is true that the ACC has not been created for intellectual coordination. The word "administrative" indicates its original purpose, and the agenda of its three short annual meetings does not deal with conceptual or programming matters.

All attempts to render ACC able to play a useful role in programmatic coordination have failed: creation of the Coordinating Committee on Social Questions (CCSQ) and the institution of "joint planning" in resolution 32/197; Regulation 3.7 of the U.N. Regulations and Rules on the Introduction to the Medium-Term Plan of the U.N., specifying that this introduction should "highlight" in a coordinated manner the policy orientations of the United Nations system; and attempts to use the Administrative Committee of Coordination-Committee on Program and Coordination meetings for discussions of major problems common to all agencies of the system. This last failure is not surprising, since the intergovernmental coordination is as weak as the intersecretariat one. Indeed, the coordination organized by the Charter (Article 58) was not intended to be very strong; and when the necessity of stronger coordination *has* been acknowledged, all the attempts to improve it have failed.[15]

Establishment of Joint Actions of Member States

Historically, the U.N. has succeeded in establishing two categories of joint actions of member states: humanitarian activities, particularly those on behalf of refugees; and some programs of multilateral technical assistance.

The assistance to refugees has been entrusted to organizations created for this purpose: High Commissioner for Refugees and the U.N. Relief and Works Agency (UNRWA—for Palestinian refugees). This humanitarian role is relatively well defined and well suited to the capacity of an international organization—which is often more politically sensitive and has greater independence and authority than a bilateral institution.

Unfortunately, this remark cannot be extended to the realm of technical-assistance activities. The multilateral aid that is delivered by the U.N. and the U.N. system has not found its specific focus; it has no characteristics to distinguish it from the bilateral technical-assistance activities. It is not inspired by a common approach to development problems and is not specific to any particular sector. Despite the relatively low level of resources it commands (6.5 percent of the total Official Development Assistance), technical assistance is fragmented among a variety of organizations—not only the four main programs affiliated with the U.N. (UNDP, UNICEF, WEP, UNFPA) and all the specialized agencies but also a number of independent bodies (including the 13 attached to UNDP, for example, the U.N. Volunteers Program, and the U.N. Sudano Sahelian Office). This structural complexity and dispersion are increased by the methods used—thousands of small projects and the system of "remote control advice" of the headquarters units. This type of joint action of member states cannot be cited as one of the successes of the United Nations.[16]

In fact, some "joint actions" are included in every program of the U.N. and its agencies. The collection and distribution of world statistics is one example. There are some "intergovernmental programs," such as the "World Weather Watch" in meteorology, "Man and Biosphere" in UNESCO, and numerous research programs, that can be considered the "joint actions" of member states and are carried out on a more modest level than are humanitarian or technical-assistance activities. Nonetheless, the identification of the types of activities in which member states could develop really important and efficient "joint ventures" is not systematically organized.

A Vision for Change

It is clear from the preceding developments that profound changes are necessary if the U.N. is to become an organization able to respond to the needs of the modern world. These cannot be limited to the type of measures recommended in the past by various expert groups involving some changes in the structure of the Secretariat or the reduction of the number of meetings or the removal of some overlaps.

The changes that are needed should allow for the establishment of an intellectual leadership for facilitating identification of issues; and an efficient intergovernmental machinery to search for common approaches and to establish and manage the joint activities of member states.

These functions cannot be fulfilled in the present setting. A profound reform of the secretariats—which are in charge of intellectual leadership—cannot be conceived in isolation—that is without a parallel reform of the intergovernmental U.N. machinery—and the role of the U.N. proper cannot be conceived in isolation from its system of specialized agencies, the restructuring of which has become imperative.

The changes that such a profound reform entails will, of course, not be obtained overnight. The understanding of the necessity of a reform, the definition of a common political approach to the various problems linked to the process of reform, and acceptance of the general scheme for such reform will be slow and gradual, and the resistance of the existing structures against the forces pushing for change will be enormous.

We are now at the very beginning of such a process. What is needed is *some vision of the changes* that must be undertaken and a well-defined *strategy for change*. This means, *first*, setting out a general idea of the new type of world organization that is becoming necessary; and, *second*, identifying the main obstacles and defining a step-by-step approach to overcoming them.

A reflection on the type of world organization that would be able to ensure adequate intergovernmental cooperation and identification of pertinent issues leads to a consideration of the existing models of international organizations. Among the existing ones, it might be interesting to draw some lessons from, for example, the Law of the Sea treaty, which created a new distribution of power among its main organs. But the institution of the European Community merits particular attention because it has succeeded in solving—at the regional level—problems that are comparable in many respects to the ones that are to be solved at the world level today.

Despite the media's constant criticism that the building of Europe is progressing at a slow pace, the institutions created by the Rome Treaty have an impressive record of achievement: Common, reasonable objectives have been defined; the number of countries cooperating in this endeavor has risen from 6 to 12; the process of cooperation and integration has regularly developed, and so too the intellectual leadership of the Commission and the process of quasi-permanent negotiation that takes place in the Council of Ministers; a number of joint ventures have been organized (from the European Center for Nuclear Research [CERN] to Airbus and Arianespace); and above all, so well-established is the habit of working together at solving common problems and reducing differences of view in a political situation that the idea of an armed conflict between the member countries is rendered scarcely imaginable.

Despite obvious differences between the political and the economic and social situations in Europe preceding the signing of the Treaty of Rome in 1957 and the world situation at the end of the 1980s, important similarities exist. This includes: an obvious growing interdependence; the need for an enlarged market; a need for a better and more precise identification of common problems; a new awareness of common interests; and effort to overcome the problems that had led to wars in the past; and a desire to institutionalize friendly relations.

Consequently, some inspiration for the vision of a new possible world organization could be drawn from various elements of the institution of the European Community. The lessons the Community teaches concern: the definition of common objectives, the search for a common approach at the intergovernmental level, the intellectual leadership and the identification of issues, the launching of joint ventures.

Definition of Common Objectives

One of the main difficulties the U.N. is facing is that its objectives in the economic and social fields have not yet been formulated in a realistic and practical manner. *Improving this formulation is an intrinsic part of a reform*, because it is only when these objectives are clear and agreed upon that the Organization can find the necessary dynamism to foster some progress. The differences in the methods of formulating objectives in the U.N. and in the European Community can be measured by considering Articles 2 and 3 of the Treaty of Rome.

Article 2 of this treaty states that the Community has the mission of establishing a *common market*, of progressively harmonizing economic policies of member states, and of promoting a harmonious development of national economic activities throughout the Community.

Article 3 lists 11 sub-objectives, among which are:

- the elimination of custom duties and of quantitative restrictions on the import or export of goods

- the establishment of common customs tariffs and of a common commercial policy toward third countries

- the abolition of obstacles to freedom of movement for persons

- the adoption of a common policy in the sphere of agriculture

- the adoption of a common policy in the sphere of transport

- the application of procedures by which the economic policies of member states can be coordinated and disequilibria in their balances of payments remedied

- the creation of a European Social Fund, a European investment bank, etc.

It is obviously because the main goal—the common market—is difficult to reach (30 years have passed since the process got under way, and 1993 is now the target date) that the Commission has been imaginative in making proposals and that the Council has been permanently engaged in the long process of negotiation; but this built-in process of reaching an agreed target is itself fostering progress.

It is obviously difficult to imagine that a world organization could adopt a comparable system of objectives. First, despite the progress made in acknowledging economic and social interdependence and the new policy principles recently adopted by the major countries (as described above), there is no consensus comparable to the one that existed among the nations party to the Treaty of Rome. The notion of a "common market"—considered as a reasonable "step" in the direction of the establishment of a political community in a non-distant future—was the result of a long process in the evolution of ideas about the "construction of Europe." Then came the considerable effort of Jean Monnet and his movement for "the United States of Europe" to prepare and educate public opinion as well as members of the political establishment, overcoming a very strong opposition to the establishment of such a treaty and the type of definition of objectives included in it.

At the world level, the political situation, the ideological differences, the economic and social disparities, and the recent failure of global negotiations between North and South do not permit the easy definition of a "step" of this type in the direction of a better world community.

The "taboo" on touching the Charter, which spread the idea that reform of the U.N. was impossible, has also contributed to obscuring the matter.

Indeed, the difficulty of defining common objectives for all member states at the world level has been a fundamental one ever since the drafting of the Charter, and the numerous methods used to try to overcome it have not yet given satisfactory results.

In general, objectives have been formulated in such general terms that there is room for different interpretations. The wording of the Charter in the economic and social area is the best example in this regard,[17] and the majority of resolutions establishing principles use the same type of formulation, too often adding to it a touch of unreality and utopian hope.[18]

The uneasiness created by this verbosity has led to various attempts at more precise formulations—as, for example, the indication in the International Development Strategies of desirable rates of growth for closing the gap between developed and developing countries—but this has remained wishful thinking. Other attempts at the sectoral level, such as health for all in the year 2000, the world population plan, other "world plans of action" in such fields as water, industry, science, and technology, even when accompanied by "strategies" for reaching these goals, have not yet been much more effective. Not only has sectorialization of objectives at the world level failed to give tangible results, but it fails to give rise to any global, common, reasonable, practical, and time-limited objectives in the whole economic and social field. On the contrary, by emphasizing the essential importance of one sector, some of these plans tend to offer "miraculous" solutions to the problem of development, but they never reach the threshold of credibility.

The establishment of medium-term plans in the U.N. and some specialized agencies has been another attempt to define objectives more clearly. But this considerable and thorough endeavor has not permitted either a definition of "priorities" or even the establishment at the program level of "time-limited objectives." The main reason for this failure quickly presents itself: the lack of a general intellectual framework showing how it could be possible to find a reasonable basis of agreement on the general trend to be followed, i.e., on the main general target toward which the U.N. and the U.N. system should move. This lack of common approach has fostered ideological debates. There was a certain logic to the belief that a common philosophy on economic and social problems was the preliminary condition to establishing a common plan of action, and it is not surprising that member states use the U.N. as a forum of propaganda for their preferred philosophical approach to this problem. The discussions about defining a new international economic order represented the main effort in this direction; research leading to better ways to implement human rights is another one. But at this ideological level, the three main economic and social schools of thought—the liberal, the socialist, and the non-aligned one—have not yet found some common ground.

Reaching some common approach to the type of world society acceptable to all nations and peoples is a distant but desirable ideal, and finding some "step" to take in this direction may indeed have been considered as the very basic mission of the U.N. The fact that all previous efforts have failed does not mean that this very difficult task should not be pursued—the more so when existing trends in the world allow some hope that a serious effort in this direction could give better results than in the past.

It has already been explained that the growing acknowledgement of interdependence has led to the adoption of new principles aimed mainly at the harmonization of economic policies. This new approach offers some possibility of formulating objectives in a more practical manner and even of reformulating some of those that have not been considered acceptable in the past, mainly for ideological reasons. The new idea of the desirability of some system of stabilization of exchange rates and the search for a solution of the developing countries' debt offer new opportunities for discussing seriously the relationship of these questions to the question of stabilization of the prices of commodities—the more so when developed countries have begun to experience the drawbacks of the variations in the price of some of them.

What has not been possible to negotiate effectively (despite, for example, the adoption of the Common Fund or of the Law of the Sea Convention) in a climate of exaggerated ideological confrontation should become easier to define as a part of a general trend toward practical harmonization of national economic policies.

This practical approach can be extended to the methods of delivering multilateral development aid. It is increasingly acknowledged that the use of experts is becoming obsolete and that the conception of this aid has to be reconsidered. The time has come to rethink "technical cooperation" (which still conveys a flavor of colonialism) and to replace it with some social system at the world level that focuses more than at present on the least-developed parts of the world and is more oriented toward education and training.

The progress toward democracy that has recently been made in Latin America and some other parts of the world should also facilitate a better understanding between the North and the South. Changes occurring in the USSR could work in the same direction.

All these changes are offering new opportunities. Obviously, it remains impossible to define a "step" that will be as clear and simple as the "common market" of the Rome Treaty. *The time is not ripe for adoption at the world level of a "comprehensive plan of action" that all member states could approve.* Nevertheless, it is irrelevant to take inspiration from the EEC system of objectives, which:

- make no reference to idealistic or utopian considerations, stating ambitions that seem possible to reach

- deal with economic matters

- combine substantive targets (establishment of a common market, free circulation of people) with institutional means for helping to reach them (common agricultural and transport policy, social fund, investment bank).

For defining useful and credible objectives at the world level, these three features should be kept in mind. In the economic field, what is today really important for governments and peoples of all countries is to facilitate the establishment of the conditions of economic prosperity and to avoid the risks of unemployment, inflation, recession, and the social and political difficulties attached to these economic diseases. *A better understanding of the conditions of economic cooperation through a better harmonization of national economic policies is obviously indispensable in this regard, and this is exactly the domain in which a universal organization can be effective.*

Within this general framework, more precise objectives could be defined in General Assembly resolutions or in the Medium-Term Plan of the U.N. and its Introduction (which the Regulations say should "highlight in a coordinated manner the policy orientations of the United Nations System," as noted earlier).

To develop in the U.N. a better definition of objectives in the economic and social areas and deal with problems of finance and development in relation to the political and sociological environment does not mean that the U.N. should take on the functions of any of the agencies of its system—IMF, World Bank, FAO, UNIDO, and the like. This means that the U.N. should better fulfill its role of coordinating the policies applied by all these agencies. It also means that the definition of program orientations should be precise enough to render coherent all the activities of these agencies.

Finally, it can be said that the credibility of the world organization depends on the nature of the objectives it will define. *First*, it is a problem of formulation and style—abandoning unrealistic and excessively ambitious wording in plans and resolutions, adopting a practical and relatively modest approach, identifying the domains in which it seems reasonable to expect some progress, and defining in these domains the possible next "steps."

Second, it should be realized that the attainment of substantive objectives is linked to the progress made on the institutional front. The possibility of organizing the framework of the world organization, requiring meetings of high-level representatives of the West, the East, and the South to discuss questions of common interest, is a difficult and serious undertaking; and when achieved, it represents by itself an important progress because it changes the nature of relations among nations. Consequently, the *process of institutional reform at the world level—as at the European level—should become an integral part of the objectives of the Organization itself.*

As in the case of the EEC, a list of possible U.N. objectives should represent *a strategy for change* and combine *substantive targets*— such as control of fluctuations of exchange rates and commodity prices, the conditions facilitating the stability needed for the economic development of all countries, and the establishment of a global watch of international migrations—with *institutional targets*—such as the progressive development of high-level global consultations on identified issues and the transformation of the U.N. system (including the Bretton Woods institutions) into a more coherent institution. Defining such objectives would be a difficult departure from traditional habits, but it is the condition of any further progress.

The Search for a Common Approach at the Intergovernmental Level

The main institutional difference between the European Community and the U.N. system is that the European Community has a "center" of decisions and negotiations in which member states are represented at a credible level of responsibility.

Establishing a "center" in the U.N. system—i.e., a compact intergovernmental body comparable to the European Community Council of Ministers—requires either a profound restructuring of the existing intergovernmental machinery or the creation of something new.

Restructuring and revitalization have been very popular in the U.N. in the past decade. A restructuring operation in 1975–77, which led to General Assembly resolution 32/197, attempted to revitalize the Economic and Social Council and the General Assembly in economic and social matters. A number of decisions have been taken to obtain a better distribution of work between ECOSOC and the General Assembly by organizing special sessions of ECOSOC, but none of these decisions has been implemented.

In the years that followed, "revitalization of ECOSOC" has become a regular agenda item of ECOSOC itself. This has allowed delegations to propose a number of excellent ideas, some of which have even been partially implemented, notably by developing the biennialization of some items of the agenda. However, nothing has really been improved by these minor changes.

In 1986 the Group of 18 report again addressed this problem and, in its first chapter, made eight recommendations. The most notable of these bore on the reinforcement of the Committee on Conferences, the reduction of the number of meetings, the rationalization of the agenda of the General Assembly, the reduction of the number of resolutions, and the launching of a thorough study of the intergovernmental machinery dealing with economic and social questions (recommendation #8). The length of this last recommendation and the precise definition of the objectives of this study, which the General Assembly in resolution 41/213 entrusted to the Economic and Social Council itself, shows that the Group has acknowledged the seriousness of the situation in this regard.

It remains to be seen whether this new undertaking will be more successful than the previous ones. If the "careful and in-depth study" recommended by the Group of 18 is made with enough precision and in a spirit of constructive criticism, it will certainly bring to light the following: overlaps between the mandates and the agendas of a number of committees, the absence of any results obtained by some other bodies, the uselessness of many reports requested from the Secretariat, the absence of a calendar of operations facilitating the examination of the relevant parts of the Medium-Term Plan by the competent organs, the overlap of the two decision-making processes for defining the program (the approval of the Medium-Term Plan, on the one hand, and the vote of resolutions, on the other), the repetition of the same resolutions year after year, the absence of a logical distribution of work among intergovernmental committees and expert groups, and the absence of a rationale for determining the membership of the various committees.

It will mainly show that there is no well-thought-out distribution of work among ECOSOC, the General Assembly (Second and Third Committees), and UNCTAD or coordination of their activities—and, indeed, that there is often full duplication or triplication of their general debates. It will also show that there is no link between the activities of the Regional Economic Commissions and the various central organs and no center able to utilize the work prepared by the whole machinery, where member states could really take decisions or start negotiations.

Such a study could lead to recommendations for a streamlining of the existing machinery (for example, by doing away with the least-useful committees, such as the committee on Natural Resources and the meeting of experts on the U.N. program of Public Administration); getting rid of the overlaps between the agendas of the various committees dealing with science and technology and with technical and economic cooperation between developing countries; or revising the type of general reports sent to ECOSOC (for example, the World Economic Survey), UNCTAD (for example, the Trade and Development Report), as well as revising the documentation prepared for the Committee on the International Development Strategy—thus beginning the move toward a better distribution of work among UNCTAD, ECOSOC, and the General Assembly.

But very few such recommendations seem to have a chance of being formulated, much less enacted. The experience of the past demonstrates that it is nearly impossible to do away with an existing body. The experiment just made by the Group of 18 concerning the intergovernmental machinery dealing with program and budget matters has shown the size of the obstacles to reshuffling. Despite the fact that the logical approach to the problem of programming and budgeting [is] a merger between the existing subsidiary body dealing with financial and budgetary matters (the Advisory Committee on Administrative and Budgetary Questions) and the existing body dealing with programmatic aspects of the budget (Committee for Program and Coordination), it is impossible to envisage agreement to such a plan. The resistance of delegations to any modification of the existing committees is even greater than the resistance in the Secretariat to any change in its practice or methods of work.

Consequently, *there is no great hope of finding a solution to the existing deficiencies of the intergovernmental machinery by means of any proposal to delete, merge, or reshuffle, particularly because the main problem is the overlap of the activities of the three main bodies— the General Assembly, ECOSOC, and UNCTAD.*

Indeed, *the only solution to the problem is a paradoxical one: It is to create something new,* i.e., the "center" that does not exist at present (a council and commission inspired by the model of the European Community). Objections to this approach—that it would complicate instead of simplify the existing system—are not valid.

There is an obvious need for a center able to fulfill the functions of synthesis, identification, and distribution of work to other bodies. The defining of better answers to the problems of interdependence must become a collective global undertaking, more satisfactory than the present system, which is only partially achieved through the various meetings of the major Western powers (for example, on stabilization of exchange rates or on the debt problem) and fails to include the socialist world, the smaller developed Western countries, and the whole developing world. Such an organ would permit, through various organized channels of representation, all interested member states to participate in the identification, discussion, and definition of solutions to problems concerning the whole international community.

The identification by the Commission in a practical and precise manner of such world problems and of the ways in which it would seem possible to make a reasonable step in the direction of their progressive solution would orient the work of the Council. Such steps might include the harmonization of national policies on population, on rules concerning international migrations, and on support given to some agricultural products; on trade, budgetary, monetary, industrial, environmental, and social policies; and on the possibility of developing joint ventures in science and technology or health. The Council would have a central role (and far more real authority than the General Assembly or the general conferences of the specialized agencies) for defining the pace at which progress is possible.

To be useful, such a center should meet at the highest level—at the ministerial level as often as possible, and regularly at the ambassadorial one. This means that the countries that send representatives to such a body to deal with economic and social matters should appoint ambassadors who have direct access to the economic ministries.

The membership of this body should be limited to a small number of participants. Here, again, the example of the European Community— its Council of Ministers—should be considered, but the transposition at the world level is not possible without devising a system of representation of small and medium-size countries. The type of representation adopted for such a council could result from the following principles: The major countries should have one seat and be represented by their own ministers; the smaller ones should find a way to be represented collectively, through a system of representation preferably on a regional basis.

Criteria for the definition of "major countries" and "smaller" ones should be adopted—this might be, for the major ones, a GNP greater than 2.5 percent of the World Product and, for countries not meeting this criteria, a population of more than 100 million.[19] Once such a center was established, it would begin to give directives to the other bodies and, over a period of time, would be in a position to obtain a useful reshuffling of the existing machinery.

Another way of establishing such a center could be—if the "taboo" on touching the present Charter could be shaken—to return to the initial Charter as adopted in 1945—that is, to do away with the amendments to article 61 that entered into force on August 31, 1965, and September 24, 1973 (the first one enlarging the membership of the ECOSOC from 18 to 27, the second enlarging it to 54). This unfortunate enlargement is one of the main reasons why ECOSOC has been deprived of any prestige, credibility, and decision-making power. The return to the initial membership of 18, if combined with a resolution organizing a system of regional representation (as explained above), could be an elegant way to create the type of "council" we have just described.

Identification of Issues and Intellectual Leadership

The illusion that it is possible at the world level to rely upon an individual to exercise intellectual leadership is still quite prevalent. The naive dream of a great leader able to develop a "vision" of the future of the world and to translate it into the definition of "priorities" that all member states would adopt still plays a role in the conception of possible reforms of the United Nations. Such a hope obviously inspired the creation in 1977 of the post of Director-General of Development charged with coordinating the activities of the whole system in the economic and social sectors.

But experience has shown that neither the Secretary-General nor the Director-General is in a position to exercise any leadership in this field, not only because the Charter and the resolutions fail to give to them the necessary powers, but also because it is just impossible for an individual to fulfill such a function without the full cooperation of all the executive heads of the various agencies of the U.N. system and a system for facilitating the cooperation of member states in this endeavor.

To cope with the complexity of the various problems, only a collective leadership can be envisaged. In this regard, the experience of the Commission of the European Community has shown that it was possible to give such a mandate to a group of competent people. The EEC Commission, composed of distinguished persons chosen by governments on the basis of their competence, was given strong guarantees of independence in carrying out its functions in the interest of the organization. It has the responsibility for seeking out the community view, studying compromise solutions, making recommendations, and executing the budget. But the adoption of such a formula at the world level would present serious difficulties.

First, it would be difficult at this level to develop a "community view.'' It would be more reasonable to speak of an endeavor to identify problems, analyze their many aspects and differing interpretations, and, through discussion and negotiation among member states, try to develop the possibility for convergence and common ground. Second, the creation of such a commission would imply structural changes in the present U.N. system. As we have seen above, the existing decentralization was deliberately engineered in 1945 and seems to be in contradiction with the very idea of a commission.

The structure of the agencies—each with its own executive board, general conference, and budget adopted by their intergovernmental organs without any supervision of the U.N. General Assembly—guarantees their complete independence. The Directors-General of these agencies are accountable only to their executive boards; and they are, within the framework of the constitution of their organization, in charge of one sector. Consequently, they attribute more importance to the sector for which they are responsible than to the connection between this sector and other sectors. Finally, they are so busy with the problems proper to their agencies that they cannot find time for participating in a Commission dealing with more general questions.

For these reasons, all attempts made—in the present setting—to establish an intellectual basis for cooperation have failed. This failure means that, if things remain as they are, the U.N. system will not be able to face the two main categories of world problems, i.e., the problems of development of the Third World and the problems of economic and social interdependence, both of which require an integrated approach. But the knowledge and the capacity to deal with the global issues existing in the main economic and social sectors—money, education, industry, trade, agriculture, etc.—are now addressed in these sectoral agencies, in their secretariats, and by their executive heads. Because it is impossible to organize a common international leadership and a commission without using these agencies, the problem of establishing an intellectual leadership—a capacity for identifying the main issues and of making proposals to the Council—is inevitably linked to the problem of a profound reform of the U.N. system. For such a reform to allow the constitution of a commission, the main changes should be:

• *Budgetary reform:* The Commission and the Council should be in a position to have an overview of the budget of the agencies. Article 17, paragraph 3 of the Charter, which states that ''The General Assembly should examine the administrative budget of the specialized agencies with a view to making recommendations to the agencies concerned," should be applied, and a resolution should extend these powers to the Commission and to the Council. The constitution of the agencies should be modified in order to transfer budgetary powers to these central organs and the existing agreements between the U.N. and the agencies modified accordingly.

A consolidated summary of the budget of these agencies should be established by the Commission and submitted for the approval of the Council before being elaborated in detail by the executive boards of the agencies. This proposal is the only way to counteract the drawbacks of the decentralization of the U.N. system. No doubt it will be resisted, but it is the only measure that could in the future help to solve the problem of "coordination."

• *The mandate given to the Commission should give to this new body important powers:*

1. Within the U.N. budget the Commission should have its own budget and a central secretariat.[20] All the economic and social departments of the U.N. should be at the service of the Commission. They should be reinforced and reorganized and their interdisciplinary capacity developed. Particular consideration should be given to the possibility of developing a centralized economic and social information system and of putting the most modern electronic equipment at the disposal of the Commission to supply it with all the data it would need.

2. The Commission should be given the mandate of identifying the global issues on which the various intergovernmental bodies of the U.N.—mainly the General Assembly, the Council, and the central development board (mentioned in "Development of Joint Activities" below)—should consult.

This type of work should be conceived inside the framework of the reformulated global economic and social objectives of the U.N., as suggested in "Definition of Common Objectives" above. The Commission would be in charge of proposing to the Council the type of incremental steps that its members believed would be acceptable to the Council and lead to a better harmonization of national economic and social policies. The Commission would, of course, draw upon the work done by the secretariats of the U.N. and the agencies and by all intergovernmental and expert bodies.

3. The Commission should also receive the mandate of preparing the consolidated U.N. system budget mentioned above and of giving advice to the member states on the use of all extrabudgetary funds.

4. The Commission should define the types of studies it will need to

fulfill its mandate and recommend the necessary changes in the structure of the services, the type of cooperation requested from the agencies, and the possibilities of utilizing outside research centers when necessary.[21]

• *The membership of the Commission should be as compact as possible:* If, as seems logical, the Commission would be composed of the heads of the main agencies and either the Secretary-General of the U.N. or his representative (such as the Director-General), this would entail very important changes in the present mode of designating these executive heads (and the Director-General) and defining their responsibilities, i.e., their statute.

Transforming the heads of the main agencies and the Director-General into "commissioners" would mean upgrading their present statute. Instead of being responsible for their sector alone, their main duty would now be to cooperate with the other members in identifying global issues. This entails several important modifications of the present situation:

1. The commissioners would be nominated by the "Council," where negotiations on geographical distribution and on the choice of competent personalities would take place, and they would be confirmed by the General Assembly.

2. Each commissioner would be in charge of one of the main agencies but would be assisted in day-to-day operations by one or two deputies. (To allow them the time necessary for participating in the sessions of the Commission, the agenda and the dates of these sessions would have to be defined by them upon the request of the Council.)

3. If the Commission were composed, as seems logical, of the heads of the main agencies, it would include the executive heads of GATT, IBRD, IMF, IAEA, ILO, FAO, WHO, UNESCO, and UNIDO. UNCTAD, despite the fact that its budget is included in the budget of the U.N. could be added. The U.N. should be represented by the Director-General, who normally should be the Chairman of the Commission. Minor technical agencies dealing with telecommunications, post, transport, and meteorology could be represented collectively by one commissioner, and the same type of representation is envisaged for all technical cooperation programs (UNDP, UNICEF, WFP, UNFPA).

Such a composition would consequently lead to the appointment of 13 commissioners. This would leave room for appointing 3-to-5 additional members, who could be elected as commissioners without direct responsibilities in a secretariat of one agency. These members could thus give all their time to the functioning of the Commission and assist its president in the preparation of its work. Their presence would create an element of flexibility in the new institution and facilitate further reorganization of the U.N. system. This would also help to get a satisfactory geographical distribution among the commissioners.

Development of Joint Activities

Development of "joint activities of member states could be more systematically organized and should be used as a method for developing "friendly relations among nations," which is one of the major objectives of the Charter.

Careful studies would obviously show that it is possible to find domains in which governments would cooperate. In fields like health, space, science and technology, and industry, important "joint ventures" could help to create the climate of confidence that is badly needed. Here again the European Community has shown the way by developing within the Community system (Common Agricultural Policy, European Development Fund) and outside it (the European Center for Nuclear Research [CERN], Arianespace, Airbus Industry, Espirit, Eureka) joint ventures for all the members of the Community or only for a few of them—and even at times in association with non-member states.

To reach such an objective in the U.N., the development of such mechanisms could be one of the specific tasks given to the Commission, as discussed above, or it could be entrusted to the "subcommission" specializing in the search for and launching of such ventures.

For the already existing joint activities in the field of technical assistance, a reorganization seems indispensable. It is obviously very difficult to undertake such a thing because of strong vested interests in the present fragmentation of existing structures. A first step might be the establishment of a single executive board ("central development board") for all the existing programs affiliated with the U.N. This step has already been envisaged several times: Already recommended in resolution 32/197, it has again been recommended as a directive for study in the Group of 18 report on the intergovernmental machinery. In any event, a complete revision of the objectives, structures, and methods of the multilateral aid distributed by the U.N. system is absolutely indispensable.

A Strategy for Change

The "vision for change" necessary to facilitate a common definition of a new and more efficient world organization developed in the previous chapter could not be adopted overnight, of course. Time is needed to determine whether it corresponds to the political conceptions of peoples and governments, and time is needed to begin to implement it.

The process to be followed for reaching the necessary changes cannot be forecast precisely because political and economic events can influence it in many ways. It is possible that at some moment in the near future the emergence of new world problems and the aggravation of some existing ones will demonstrate that it is not possible to hesitate any longer. The time will be ripe for profound reform and for consultations at the highest level on this question.

It is also possible that the pressure of the constraints described above will increase progressively; in this case, the process of change could also be progressive. In any event, *the inclusion in a plan of reform of the definition of a strategy for change, including a step-by-step approach (as in the example of the European Community), is indispensable for conferring on it an important degree of credibility.*

Such a strategy might contain the following elements:

• *A clear conception of the new type of world organization that is needed:* This means a definition of the types of reasonable objectives that could be assigned to it and the type of institutional framework able to help reach these objectives. The previous section of this chapter—"A Vision for Change"—provided suggestions in this regard.

• *A precise identification of the obstacles to change:* Such obstacles are enormous. First, there is no real hope that the U.N. will have the capacity to reform itself.[22] All the constraints that have hampered any serious change are still there: the structural decentralization of the U.N. system, which forbids any interagency coordination, particularly between the Bretton Woods institutions and the rest of the system; the resistance of the Secretariat to any innovation; the specialization of the Secretary-General in political matters, which prevents him from giving sufficient attention to managerial and economic problems; the pressure brought by the bureaucracies of the ministries of foreign affairs of all countries to place their nationals in high-level posts regardless of the individual's qualifications; and the reluctance of delegations to consider any prospect of change.

But the main obstacle still remains the lack of importance attributed to the world organization by governments and public opinion. Despite existing frustrations, despite acknowledgement of increasing interdependence, the view of the majority of governments is that the main problems can still be solved through channels other than the United Nations. Despite the general feeling that something should be done to improve the Organization's efficiency, the intellectual confusion about the type of useful role an improved world organization could play has not yet dissipated.

• *A step-by-step approach to the process of change:* To overcome such obstacles, a step-by-step approach to institutional change should accompany the refinement of the vision for the future. Such steps should meet several requirements. They should be meaningful enough to indicate that the process of change has effectively begun; be taken in the directions that offer the least resistance; attract the interest of some member states because they offer new possibilities for solving some of their problems; and create opportunity for further changes.

It should be added that the experience of the process of change in international organization in general, and the U.N. in particular, shows that it is always easier to create new organs or institutions than it is to reshuffle the existing ones.

If one bears in mind these criteria, it seems possible to list some of the steps that could be taken separately to help build the new world organization whose economic and social sectors are suggested in "A Vision for Change."

1. The first step would be to make better use of the existing tools, particularly the Introduction to the Medium-Term Plan of the U.N. If a reasonable approach to the objectives of the U.N. and of the U.N. system for the period of the next plan were to be defined in this Introduction, it would offer to member states their first opportunity to think seriously about reform.

2. Regarding institutional change, the creation of a "council" of the type defined in the subsection "Search for a Common Approach at the Intergovernmental Level" of "A Vision for Change," seems easier to consider than the creation of the Commission. It would imply long and difficult negotiations over representation of small and medium-sized countries, but it would focus the discussion on the main questions of interest to all countries: the relationship between the type of issues that all countries agree to discuss seriously in the U.N. and the type of institutions in which such debates can take place.

3. As far as the Commission is concerned, it would probably be easier to begin by creating a small body of 3-to-5 commissioners composed of independent, competent personalities (to include the Director-General, elevated to the rank of Chairman of the Commission). This embryo of the larger Commission, which could later include

the heads of the main agencies, could represent a useful first step in the right direction and permit the development of an experimental phase. In a more general way it can be assumed that the creation of institutions "on an experimental basis" could facilitate the process of change in the U.N.

4. The consideration of a progressive budgetary reform by applying firmly Article 17, paragraph 3 of the Charter to all the agencies of the U.N. system, excluding the Bretton Woods institutions, could also be a useful step for facilitating an overall view by member states of the activities of the U.N. system.

5. Finally, a systematic research of all opportunities for increasing the working relationship between the U.N. and the Bretton Woods institutions (for example, the establishment of common studies on the world economy and cooperation in the study of various concrete issues, such as the debt problem, commodities, and the situation in Africa) could be undertaken to begin filling the gap between these two categories of world organizations.

Many other steps could be imagined. But if a process of change in the U.N. has any chance to develop in the years to come, it will be the result of a combination of efforts: overcoming the existing and continuing crisis: patient development of a new conceptual approach, mainly in the economic and social sectors; and discussions on the possibility of some institutional changes.

Notes

1. Harold K. Jacobson, *Networks of Interdependence: International Organizations and the Global Political System* (New York: Alfred A. Knopf, 2nd ed., 1984). Also *Yearbook of International Organizations,* prepared by the Union of International Associations (Robert Fenaux, Secretary-General, and Anthony Judge, Assistant Secretary-General).

2. A monograph by David Mitrany, "A Working Peace System" (The Royal Institute of International Affairs. (London: Oxford University Press, June 1943) is the most widely known text on "functionalism." Among those connected with this school of thought are its precursors, such as Leonard Woolf, Norman Angel, Robert Cecil, G. D. H. Cole, and some contemporaries, such as Ernst Haas (*Beyond the Nation State* [Stanford University Press, 1964]), A. J. R. Groom, Joseph Nye, Patrick Sewell, and Paul Taylor.

The author of this chapter shares the idea underlying functionalism, inasmuch as he believes that the development of economic, technical, and cultural relations is the best way to build peace in the long run. Conversely, he does not share the much narrower theory of "sectoral" functions, which advocates collaboration between specialists in each sector and which, when applied to development, is at variance with the integrated and interdisciplinary nature of the problems in this domain.

3. OECD: Organization for Economic Cooperation and Development; established September 30, 1961, Paris. Successor of OEEC: Organization for European Economic Cooperation set up April 1948 (24 member states—developed countries)

EEC: European Economic Community, established January 1, 1958, Brussels (12 member countries—Western Europe)

CMEA: Council for Mutual Economic Assistance, Established January 1949 (10 member states—socialist countries).

4. The date of the first oil crisis.

5. One of the most recent examples of this phenomenon is the decision taken by the French government in 1984 to give up the ''Keynesian'' policy orientations adopted in 1982 and to come back to an economic policy in conformity with policies followed by the major Western countries.

On the other hand, the forces at work are such that in some fields governments are losing control and even abdicating from this control voluntarily—as in the deregulation of financial markets.

6. This is only a trend—but it is developing rapidly. What is at stake in the negotiations on arms control between the U.S. and the USSR is the whole concept of the national defense policy of each party. Success or failure of such negotiations has a tremendous impact on these national policies. The same can be said about discussions between the U.S. and Japan or Europe about the level of interest rates, budgetary policies, or agricultural policies.

7. The Cancun (Mexico) summit involved 14 developing countries and 8 industrialized states.

8. Report of the Group of High-Level Intergovernmental Experts to Review the Efficiency of the Administrative and Financial Functioning of the United Nations, General Assembly Official Records, 41st Session, supplement #49 [A/41/49], August 1986.

9. See Rafael Salas, *Reflections on Population* (New York: Peregamon Press, 1985).

10. See Joint Inspection Unit report on ''Reporting to the Economic and Social Council'' (A/39/281/E/1984/I) of May 31, 1984. Remarks made here on these reports on the world situation do not mean that they are useless or bad; together with the Bank and the Fund reports and some other world surveys they present interesting information. But they are not read by the delegations to the Economic and Social Council, to whom they are directed. The question is: What types of studies would better facilitate the identification of issues to be discussed usefully by member states?

11. The word ''research'' in this context does not have the same meaning as in a purely academic environment. Rather, it means policy planning and analysis, identification of issues, etc. It has to be recognized that the processes

of multilateral diplomacy are so complex that it is hard to do useful "research" on the subject from the outside. Making a proper use of outside experts would be a complex undertaking, because it requires a close association with the evolution of thinking inside the Organization. But such an association with various centers in the world is not impossible and would create a better understanding of the issues at stake inside and outside the U.N.

12. Report of the Group of High-Level Intergovernmental Experts to Review the Efficiency of the Administrative and Financial Functioning of the United Nations, General Assembly Official Records, 41st Session, Supplement #49 [A/41/49], August 1986, p. 4.

13. These remarks on the level of representation do not mean that things would improve automatically if ministers were sent as representatives. The level of representation is indeed conditioned by three factors:
• the importance that member states attach to a question put on the agenda
• the quality of preparation of the discussions on this item
• the level of expectation that discussions in the intergovernmental body concerned will have an influence on a possible solution.

The last factor is obviously linked to the composition of the intergovernmental body and to the economic and political importance of the states (or group of states) that are partners in these discussions. A compact body is always more prestigious than a large one.

14. Joint Inspection Unit Report, REP/84/7, entitled "Reporting to the Economic and Social Council" (U.N. document A/39/281, E/1984/81 of May 31, 1984).

15. Report of the JIU, "Some Reflections on Reform of the United Nations" (A/40/988, December 6, 1985, paragraphs 25–32).

16. A/40/988, paragraphs 17–19 and 89–104.

17. The economic and social objectives of the Charter, as stated in the Foreword and in Article I:

Foreword: to promote social progress and better standards of life in larger freedom

. . . to employ international machinery for the promotion of the economic and social advancement of all peoples.

Article I, Paragraph 3: To achieve international cooperation in solving international problems of an economic, social, cultural or humanitarian character . . . .

18. Among the best examples of unrealistic formulation is the following quotation from paragraph 12 of the latest International Development Strategy, which recommends that governments of member states "end without delay colonialism, imperialism, neocolonialism, interference in internal affairs, apartheid, racial discrimination, hegemony, expansionism and all forms of foreign aggression and occupation, which constitute major obstacles to the economic emancipation and development of the development countries." Other examples can be found in paragraphs 44 to 54 of A/40/988.

19. These criteria are given as examples. The figure for population could also be a percentage: 100 million is approximately 2 percent of the world population. For more details and the list of countries that meet the criteria indicated, see A/40/88, paragraphs 181 to 185 and footnote 63.

20. The merging of the Office of the Director-General (DIEC) and of the Department of International Economic and Social Affairs (DIESA) could be a first step in the right direction. Even if at present the head of DIESA is under the authority of the Director-General, a more interdisciplinary and better integrated secretariat appears to be desirable for allowing the Director-General to fulfill the functions—as envisaged here—of Chairman of the Commission.

21. The changes entailed by the creation of a commission are no doubt far-reaching, and any proposal in this direction will provoke serious opposition in many quarters.

The decentralization of the U.N. system, and in particular the complete separation of the Bretton Woods institutions from the U.N., was voluntarily organized in 1945. The situation of the world in 1987 is completely different, and today this institutional decentralization is not only obsolete but harmful.

For all countries, the foreign policy of the ministries of finance and economy have to be integrated with the foreign policies of the ministries of foreign affairs, and this necessary integration should be reflected at the world level.

But it is impossible now to build something entirely new without taking into account the existence of the "system" (even if, as Robert Jackson said some 20 years ago, it is indeed a "non-system"). The agencies are a part of the international landscape, and they should be maintained; they are in many respects useful.

But a complete reshuffling of the system is now becoming indispensable: The necessity of coordination and even of integration of their programs is obvious, and experience has amply demonstrated that without a change in the institutional framework, no coordination is possible. The process of change in this matter is likely to take time. It is linked with interdependence, on the one hand (particularly for the relationship between the IMF and the rest of the system), and with the role and methods of multilateral aid, on the other hand (particularly for the relationship between programs and agencies dealing with some aspects of development aid).

On the present evolution of ideas and methods concerning development assistance, see R. H. Carey (OECD), "Official financing and growth oriented structural adjustment," a paper prepared for the symposium on "growth oriented adjustment programs" (Washington, D.C., February 25-27, 1987). The following extract has particular relevance for the problems discussed in the present paper:

Against this background, what we are witnessing is not just a rearrangement of the pattern of financial flows, but an important new phase in the forty-year record of development cooperation and official financing.

What, fundamentally, is new?

First, a diverse range of actors is being called upon to respond to a large number of specific country situations *with a degree of rapidity, flexibility and coherence not previously a notable feature of development financing processes.*

Second, the nature of current development problems demands a *programme approach* to the delivery of development assistance and finance, rather than a *policy approach.* In more technical economic terms, there is a general equilibrium problem involving the use of all resources in the recipient economy, and development assistance and other financing agencies cannot divorce themselves from that overall context.

Flexibility and programme approaches have by no means been absent from the development cooperation scene. Major changes in the allocation of aid, both geographically and sectorally, have taken place, while programme aid has a long history. It would nevertheless not be inaccurate to characterize the development assistance process, both bilateral and multilateral, as having evolved mainly along incremental and project lines. It is also fair to say that *the concept of policy-based lending,* in any broad, concerted form at least, *has not been a part of the "culture" of development cooperation.* Even on a discreet, partial equilibrium basis. On the whole, *the development cooperation industry has been prepared to leave it to the IMF to take the general equilibrium approach,* focused on key macroeconomic prices and other variables, having itself neither the orientation nor the competence to handle this difficult task.

22. This does not mean that efforts that are made inside the U.N. are useless. On the contrary, as this author states in "Planning, Programming, Budgeting and Evaluation in the U.N.," some progress is possible from inside. Although it falls short of obtaining decisive reforms, it facilitates the progress of ideas about change. Any effort to restructure the Secretariat and the intergovernmental machinery, or to modify the conception of the U.N. Medium-Term Plan and of its Introduction, will also contribute to the evolution of ideas on the type of United Nations that the world needs. But it is not from inside that a decisive impulse for reform will come.

CHAPTER 9

THE ROLE OF THE U.N. IN DISASTER MANAGEMENT

Prince Sadruddin Aga Khan

The purpose of this inquiry is to determine how the United Nations can redeploy and use more efficiently the existing resources at its disposal to ensure more effective disaster management. Success in improving disaster management would benefit not only those vulnerable to disasters but also those willing to provide assistance to the victims. It would improve the credibility of the United Nations by building upon the already universal consensus that effective disaster management is much to be desired.

Theoretically, the U.N. system possesses the institutional and material capacity to rise to the challenge posed by disasters. Its response, however, is seldom seen as speedy or adequate. Often late on the scene, rarely visible to the public, and beset by problems of internal coordination, the U.N. has suffered a loss of credibility on many occasions.

It is commonly accepted that the United Nations is in a unique position to play a leading role in enabling its member states to respond effectively to disasters. Its ability to perform that leading role, however, has been severely compromised by certain handicaps common to the U.N. system as a whole. These include the politicization of its agencies, changing attitudes toward the relevance and capability of the system by member governments, creeping bureaucratization, the insufficient number of experts within the Secretariat, and decreasing staff morale.

This chapter will not dwell on the malaise that is having a debilitating effect on the system except insofar as it directly affects the U.N.'s ability to respond to disasters.

Our starting point is the fact that the number of emergenices, disasters, and disaster victims continues to rise and that the frequency and complexity of such occurrences, and the damage they cause, will only increase in the coming years.

Emergencies and disasters often result from and always highlight long-term processes that tear the sinews of society: ecological degradation, rapid urbanization, and population growth and demographic distortions, not to mention the impoverishment of large numbers of people. Indeed, the security and geo-political impact of these processes, made dramatically evident during and after disasters, has been demonstrated again and again—for example, by the cylcone in what is now Bangladesh in 1971, the droughts in Ethiopia in 1974 and 1983, and the continuing crisis in Mozambique.

These considerations call for a review of developmental policies and practices. More immediately, they require action by the communities vulnerable to such disasters, by the international community, and by governments in disaster-prone regions. It is they who are in the best position to prevent, prepare for, and respond to disasters.

This chapter will look at the role the U.N. could and should play in improving all aspects of disaster management: prevention, preparedness, response, and recovery. It will look at the scope and limits of the U.N. role and make recommendations about the concrete steps that could be taken in the short and medium term to achieve a more effective disaster-response capability.

Disasters: Definitions and Dimensions

"Man-made and "Natural". There is persistent confusion about the distinction between man-made and natural disasters. The line between them has become increasingly blurred. This is largely because it is often economic development, or lack of it, that makes great numbers of people vulnerable to disasters—for example, the people who live in poorly constructed or badly sited buildings when an earthquake strikes and the peasants who tend ecologically degraded land in a period of drought. Disasters are in large measure man-made, and nearly all can be prepared for; the damage they cause can be contained, if not prevented.

Disasters and Emergencies. A useful distinction between disasters and emergencies was made in the "Report to the Secretary-General on incorporation of OEOA's experiences and capacities into the permanent structure of the U.N."

> The term "disaster" is most often used to describe sudden catastrophic occurrences, limited in time and place, which produce significant losses of and threats to human life. These occur primarily as a result of such natural phenomena as earthquakes, tidal waves, typhoons, floods, etc. The term "emergency" generally has a broader connotation and includes man-made occurrences, such as armed conflicts (both externally and internally provoked), as well as large-scale structural emergencies resulting in part from failures and imbalances in economic and social development and long-range ecological deterioration.[1]

To this general definition may be added the increasingly threatening category of relatively new man-made disasters that have simultaneous elements of "disaster" and "emergency," e.g., nuclear and industrial disasters.

Classifications. For the purposes of this inquiry, it is helpful to identify four broad categories of disasters and emergencies:

1. *The sudden elemental*—for example, such disasters as earthquakes, floods, tidal waves, volcanoes, and landslides. Like some extended disasters, these are prompted by climatic and geological forces, but they are distinguishable from other types of disasters because they are instantaneous occurrences. With adequate monitoring, some of them are predictable, though there is usually little warning that they are about to occur. Man-made errors contribute to the damage they cause.

2. *The foreseeable*—for example, famines and epidemics. These emergency situations have complex roots in the interaction of climatic and human activity over extended periods—a vicious circle that affects ever larger number of people. Because the recurrence of such phenomena can be anticipated more often than not and because an emergency situation develops over time, there are opportunities, not always seized, to contain the damage.

3. *The deliberate*—emergency situations and disasters that are the result of wars between states, civil wars, guerrilla warfare, and insurgency activity. They affect increasing numbers of civilians and turn communities and whole populations into displaced persons and refugees. The easy availability of sophisticated weapons and the emergence of organized terrorism increase the possibility of disparate forms of sabotage that leave large numbers vulnerable.

4. *The accidental*—for example, emergencies and disasters caused by industrial and nuclear accidents. Both international legislation and institutional mechanisms are lacking in this relatively new field, which is likely to expand dramatically as new technologies create new risks and existing facilities age and deteriorate.

Clearly, some emergency and disaster situations contain several elements of these four categories—witness the current situation in Mozambique, where floods and drought have combined with gradual ecological degradation, deliberate economic sabotage, and persistent armed conflict. The result is a situation in which the health and lives of at least 3.5 million people, including 1 million displaced people, are in jeopardy.

Whether a particular occurrence constitutes a disaster that warrants an international effort to deal with its consequences has to be judged in relation to the local resources available for this purpose. Other factors, such as the area's accessibility and the local authorities' experience in handling the situation, must also be considered. Attempts to quantify disasters in terms of persons killed or rendered homeless, or in terms of damage to the environment or to property, seldom yield satisfactory results, since they do not take sufficient account of the local context. In terms of number of casualties, what may be considered a major disaster in a developed country may be viewed as a familiar occurrence in the developing world. Similarly, what may have only a negligible economic impact in a developed country can have a devastating effect on a developing one.

Disaster Management. There are three phases of disaster management:

1. *Predisaster,* with its two closely linked components, prevention and preparedness. *Prevention* involves efforts to prevent disasters from occurring at all and to ensure that certain emergency situations— for example, those arising from typhoons or droughts—do not turn into disasters. It is increasingly being recognized that effective prevention is contingent upon appropriate development. *Preparedness,* on the other hand, involves taking steps to ensure that as much as possible has been done to minimize damage in the event of a disaster and to ensure a swift response when one occurs.

2. *Immediate disaster response.* This is the phase immediately following a disaster—the period in which the greatest human suffering and loss of life occurs. Whether or not such suffering will be contained depends upon the ability of the government of the affected country to respond effectively.

3. *Postdisaster*. This phase follows the immediate response and involves rehabilitation of affected people, damaged economies, and environments. An important aspect of postdisaster work is the collection and analysis of information and of experiences gained so that future preparedness and response may be strengthened.

Increases in the Number and Variety of Disasters

More Disasters

The number of victims of disasters in all four of the classifications above is steadily increasing. Although reliable statistics are difficult to compile, estimates by the Office for Foreign Disaster Assistance (OFDA) suggest that between the 1960s and the 1970s the number of people killed by drought increased more than twentyfold; by earthquakes more than sevenfold; by cyclones threefold; by floods twofold; and in civil strife almost a hundredfold. During the period 1970–81, more than a million people were reported to have died in sudden natural disasters, with estimated material damage in excess of U.S. $46 billion.[2] These trends have, by and large, continued into the 1980s. There are also indications that in the 1980s the figures for the number of persons killed and the damage caused by industrial and nuclear accidents are likely to surpass considerably those of previous decades.

New Variants

Within the four classifications of disasters—the sudden elemental, the foreseeable, the deliberate, and the accidental—there are new variants that are likely to become more familiar as the bimillennium approaches:

Accidental: "New" Industrial Disasters. Industrial disasters are not a new phenomenon, but the increasing scale and complexity of industrial plants and processes, the widening range of dangerous mass-produced products, and increasing population density, particularly around industrial complexes, have added new dimensions to the potential risks involved. The integrity of ecological systems, the health of local as well as distant populations, and the inheritance of future generations are more and more being made conditional upon the safety of certain industrial processes, such as in the nuclear, pharmaceutical, and pesticide industries.

The nuclear industry provides the most striking example of this. The production, storage, and disposal of radioactive substances, whether for civil or military purposes, engenders risks that have yet to be fully assessed and understood, let alone overcome. Still largely unaddressed is the problem of decommissioning nuclear plants—a problem to be seen not only in terms of the threat to life and to the environment but also in terms of the profound psychological impact upon society, particularly upon mothers and children, of even such risks as low-level radiation.

Accidental: Genetic Disasters. Another variant of disaster that technological progress has made more likely is the genetic one. Man is shaping and refining the genetic composition of animals and of agricultural products in the interest of productivity as well as of profit. Genetic resources and genetic variety are being squandered before their potential is understood.

This genetic erosion is resulting in an animal and vegetable "regime" worldwide that is increasingly dependent upon artificial inputs and artificial methods of production and therefore increasingly vulnerable to disasters. These have already resulted in crop failures; imported strains of wheat, for example, often have no resistance when there is even a marginal alteration of the conditions in which they were introduced. Such crop failures, as well as epidemics and hitherto unknown or undiagnosed biological complications, are likely to occur in the coming decades. These, coupled with disasters that could result from experimentation and manufacture of biological and chemical weapons, constitute a new threat to future generations.

Deliberate: New Variants of Armed Conflict. The proliferation of armed conflicts around the globe since World War II has spawned a variety of new risks. The availability of lethal weapons on the open market, and the inability of states to control their sale or use, increase the possibility of wounding and killing innocent people, not only directly but indirectly—as with the poisoning of urban water supplies and the bombing of factories containing lethal substances. Nuclear plants present a particular hazard in this context; even the "safest" is vulnerable to sabotage or missile attack.

As the means, methods, and objectives of combatants become more varied, the dangers mount. The inevitable result is that ever larger numbers of people, particularly civilians, are vulnerable to disaster. The fact that there are active or latent internal armed conflicts in over 40 countries at present gives some indication of the potential hazard to vast populations.

Accidental and Deliberate: Disasters in Uncontrolled Areas. Disasters that occur in areas where authority is either unrecognized or ineffective pose particular problems. This includes politically contested areas, but also remote and inaccessible regions beyond government writ. The dangers faced by, and the well-being of, indigenous peoples in these areas can be neglected through either ignorance or prejudice.

In none of the four classifications has adequate thought been given to disaster management or action, whether prevention and preparedness strategies or relief. International legislation is similarly absent or weak on all four counts. These disasters highlight major rents in the international humanitarian net. The United Nations does not currently address them in a systematic or coherent manner.

Gaps and Weaknesses in Disaster Management

The problems faced by the U.N. in responding to disasters have been catalogued comprehensively and repeatedly. They include non-existent or inadequate warning systems, absence of information on goods and services locally available in a disaster-struck area, and poor transportation and communications infrastructures. They also include a number of major obstacles to the provision of assistance: bureaucratic hurdles relating to the movement and delivery of goods, whether by road, rail, sea, or air; passport and visa requirements for relief personnel; foreign exchange and fiscal regulations; and restrictions on the movement and communications systems of relief organizations. In the absence of reliable and authoritative information and under pressure to act, it is not surprising that donors often respond inappropriately. More often than not, the nature of relief depends on what the donors can readily supply rather than on the real needs of affected populations.

These points were made explicit by the U.N. Secretary-General in his report to ECOSOC in the context of the East Pakistan crisis in 1971. A decade-and-a-half later, they remain valid when disaster strikes.

The Affected Countries

Governments of affected countries bear the primary responsibility for disaster management and response. Most have done little to enhance their own disaster-response capabilities. It is also disturbing that countries where disaster strikes most often are among those least prepared to respond.

Political Will. Too often, governments concerned with internal political stability and socio-economic factors have chosen to avoid mobilizing national and international relief efforts out of reluctance to acknowledge that a disaster or emergency situation exists or out of reluctance to admit to the international community that outside assistance is required. More commonly, they may for a variety of reasons decline to listen or give sufficient support to the individuals and bodies, governmental or nongovernmental, that warn of impending crisis and appeal for action. Early-warning systems are of no avail if they do not provoke an appropriate response.

On occasion, lack of interest in disaster management at the top undermines the national organizations that are undertaking prevention and preparedness measures. In other instances, existing disaster mechanisms are swept aside when political credibility is perceived to be at stake.

Disaster Management. It is more often the case that governments, lacking disaster-management skills and infrastructure, cannot deal with emergency situations or respond adequately to disasters. Administrative unpreparedness compounds logistical and communications constraints. Officials are not sufficiently experienced or coordinated to be able to assess accurately the scale of crises. They do not know what food, matériel, and personnel are locally available. They cannot determine early enough what type of assistance is required from donors. They are not in a position to decline unnecessary donor assistance. They are unable to ensure the efficient reception, storage, or distribution of relief.

Consequently, the effectiveness of assistance provided by donors is compromised. U.N. bodies and nongovernmental organizations (NGOs) in the field lack a focal point for their concerns, their reports, and their operations. Unnecessary confusion, antagonism, and duplication of effort result.

Donors outside the country cannot hope to provide a coordinated response if their embassies, the field offices of NGOs, and the U.N. agencies are at odds. Indeed, such confusion breeds distrust and dismay. It may lead to unreasonable demands by donors wanting to ensure that the assistance they have provided is reaching victims. This can cause misunderstandings and exaggerated press reports, which have a negative effect on the relief operations.

Without a disaster-management infrastructure, the experience gained during emergencies and disasters is dissipated and not used to promote prevention and preparedness. Without such an infrastructure, the basic signs that usually precede emergencies (whether meteorological, environmental, nutritional, economic, or social) are not monitored, not heeded, or both. Without such an infrastructure, it is difficult to generate the political will to maintain emergency food and equipment or to take advance preparedness measures with targeted groups—for example, urban planners, slum dwellers, and construction workers.

As presently administered, disaster relief is often justly criticized as quick-fix therapy—a process of throwing money at problems while neglecting their root causes. It also suffers from being ill-adapted to local conditions.

The greatest single asset in disaster management is, in fact, the intimate knowledge that people have of their own environment, but there has been little effort to use this major instrument either to enable people to provide effective immediate response or to help them return to normal life. As it is, local knowledge plays only a negligible part in prevention or preparedness and may be swamped by ad hoc relief responses.

To ignore the local dimension is to assure that the population will be increasingly vulnerable to disasters. This is all the more regrettable in light of evidence that local knowledge about emergencies and disasters can provide valuable information that will help to decrease the community's vulnerability.

Donor Countries

Official Development Policies. It is now being recognized that much of the aid and development funded and undertaken by industrialized countries is actually contributing to the magnitude and accelerating frequency of disasters. The World Bank, for example, has recently signaled its awareness that some of its projects have not promoted economic development that is sustainable or of a socially and ecologically desirable kind. Most governments of developed countries are much slower in recognizing this. It is often the case, however, that aid and development policies will have more to do with the commercial and political priorities of donors than with the needs of the people they are intended to benefit.

Attitudes Toward Disasters. Such development practices inevitably affect official attitudes toward disaster management and assistance, with the result that the scale and form of donor government response is too often dictated by domestic economic and political considerations more than by the actual needs of disaster-struck areas and populations.

At its most cynical, donor action is prompted by the perception that the donor government stands to gain strategic or political advantages from providing emergency assistance to a country to which it normally gives no development assistance. Humanitarian considerations take a back seat.

Even when—as is often the case—donor response is powered by and reflects the global humanitarian consensus, rooted in compassion and good will, it is rarely translated into the type of assistance that is really appropriate to the occasion.

Too often, and unwittingly, the consequence of this "donor-determined" response has been to complicate emergency and disaster situations, to burden the recipient affected governments, to undermine local economies, and to decrease the ability of victims to recover. The World Health Organization (WHO) Interregional Meeting on Health, Emergency Preparedness and Response in Geneva, in April 1987, noted for example, that

> [T]he health assistance provided by the international community following the recent disasters in Latin America mainly comprised personnel that lacked specific functions and in some cases specialized experience in disaster management and often required local support and infrastructure to be effective; . . . with the exception of personnel from countries in close geographical proximity, this medical assistance arrived after local health services in the affected country had provided the medical assistance; . . . the activities of many unsolicited voluntary groups, without international recognition, arrived without co-ordination to provide medical assistance, creating logistic and financial problems for the affected country. . . .

The recent earthquake in El Salvador is a case in point. Forty-two rescue teams arrived in the country within days, many uninvited, inappropriately equipped, unaware of each others' activities, and unable to speak Spanish. Accommodation, transportation, communications, provisions, and other facilities had to be found by a host government whose administration and resources were already under severe pressure.

The Media and Public Opinion. The power of the media to prompt international response to emergency situations has been demonstrated

repeatedly. The most notable example was the BBC film of the Ethio-
pian famine in October 1984 and the "Band Aid" and "Live Aid"
phenomena that followed. Public pressure can compel governments to
respond to an emergency appeal or a disaster.

Often, however, the pressure is such that governments will wish to
be seen to "do something" promptly, even in the absence of authoritative information about the crisis and about what is needed. This too
rarely leads to an appropriate response.

The media can determine attitudes toward aid—positive and negative. Dramatic reporting and images, if unaccompanied by accurate
information and explanation, contribute greatly to popular misunderstanding of the causes of disasters and, in turn, to inappropriate
responses. They can also help or hamper relief operations, depending
upon how responsible the reporting is. In the absence of accurate
information on either the dynamics of disasters or, more immediately,
on the provision and distribution of relief in a particular situation, the
likelihood of responsible reporting is itself diminished.

Nongovernmental Organizations. NGOs have a particularly important role to play in disaster management and response. Their contribution in the field is justly recognized as invaluable, and often decisive,
in providing relief and in prodding the U.N. agencies and governments
to take action. They pioneer or spearhead relief operations and serve
as vital catalytic agents for international response.

At home, the NGO's access to the media, especially in times of
crisis, gives them a special role in determining popular perceptions of
both the unfolding and the underlying causes of disasters. These
contacts, when combined with the NGOs' popular constituencies, their
closeness to the grass-roots, and their activities as political lobbyists,
have given NGOs the moral lead over the intergovernmental system in
prompting donor response to crises.

The Multilateral System

The United Nations. Each of the major agencies regularly involved
in emergency situations, such as the Food and Agriculture Organization and the World Food Programme (FAO/WFP), the United Nations
Development Programme (UNDP), the Office of the United Nations
High Commissioner for Refugees (UNHCR), the United Nations Children's Fund (UNICEF), and the World Health Organization (WHO),
has evolved mechanisms for dealing with them. This is equally true of
agencies outside the U.N. system, such as the International Committee

of the Red Cross and the League of Red Cross Societies. Broadly, these involve, in varying degrees, measures of preparation (early warning mechanisms, contingency plans, training), response (needs assessment and operations planning systems), and reconstruction/ recovery, including evaluation.

Experience shows, however, that in emergency situations the effectiveness of these measures is compromised by lack of adequate coordination between agencies, both at the headquarters level and at the field level. This is especially true in complex emergency situations, aspects of which fall outside the mandate of a particular organization. Competition for responsibility, for press coverage, for governmental attention, and for resources directs time and energy away from efforts to cooperate, communicate, and coordinate.

United Nations Disaster Relief Co-ordinator's Office (UNDRO). UNDRO's mandate and the U.N. General Assembly resolutions relating to it envisage its main role as that of central focal point of information—whether at the field, national, or international levels— from and to all the bodies responding to disasters.

UNDRO has had difficulty in fully performing this function for a number of reasons. The U.S. Council of Foreign Relations "Disaster!" report put it succinctly:

> (i) Large, established agencies with their own money, resources, policies and priorities are indisposed to be coordinated by anyone or any agency not in a position to help or hurt them; (ii) local authorities in a disaster area are indisposed to be coordinated by a newcomer, whether flown in for that purpose or not; (iii) agency and NGO representatives and donor country ambassadors are indisposed to be co-ordinated by the relatively unknown headquarters officers normally dispatched by UNDRO to disaster spots to assist the resident representative.[3]

UNDRO has insufficient leverage with its big U.N. sister organizations or with other groups to exercise a coordinating role. This may be due in part to a misunderstanding of UNDRO's objectives and to a lack of clear guidelines for other agencies as to their own mandates in a disaster. Whatever the case, UNDRO lacks the financial and human resources to sustain the role it is mandated to fulfill.

1. *UNDRO's background:* The primary objective of UNDRO, established in 1971, was to coordinate response to sudden natural disasters. Its handful of staff, given herculean tasks, never managed to come to terms with them. From the outset UNDRO encountered impediments

familiar to other parts of the U.N.—politicization, bureaucratization, and the need to justify its existence to other, often suspicious, members of the U.N. family.

UNDRO has the dubious distinction of being the object of continuous critical evaluation throughout a 16-year history. The best known of these evaluations—and one from which it has never quite recovered—was that carried out by the Joint Inspection Unit (JIU) in 1980.[4] The JIU recommended that UNDRO be answerable to the UNDP governing body in order to improve its ability to command respect and to coordinate activities in the field. Subsequent evaluations have included the so-called "Davidson Report"[5] and the "Goundry Report."[6]

Although the inference of these reports is that UNDRO is unable to fulfill its mandate, they have had little impact on changing UNDRO's operations other than to cause UNDRO executives to expend considerable energy in lobbying member governments and other agencies to safeguard its position. However, as UNDRO has no governing council, one may legitimately ask how else UNDRO can act to defend and promote its interests.

2. *Communication and coordination:* UNDRO's information-management capability is outdated, even by the standards of other U.N. agencies. It lacks the capacity to digest information that may be provided to it—whether on preparedness measures, early-warning data, situation reports, needs assessments, transportation and delivery details, or storage and distribution measures. (It frequently does not receive all the relevant information in a timely manner; and when it does, it often lacks the technical capacity to absorb, analyze, and disseminate it in a useful way.)

UNDRO's links to its representatives in the field, to other U.N. bodies and NGOs, and to donor governments and governments in countries vulnerable to disasters are inadequate. Because of its shortcomings when it comes to monitoring disaster-management programs and the activities of other bodies, its ability to communicate information received during an emergency or once a disaster has struck is limited. Its ability to edit and disseminate information and experiences gained during disasters is similarly impaired. These factors seriously affect its role and credibility as a coordinating body.

3. *Leadership role:* UNDRO's ability to exercise a leading role in the field during a crisis is undermined by this communications weakness. It is further compromised by a lack of support from other U.N. bodies and from the Secretary-General. It has been suggested that UNDRO be designated "lead agency" in complex emergency situa-

tions, aspects of which fall outside the specific mandate of any one U.N. body. But this would be difficult until UNDRO is able to fulfill a useful communications role.

4. *Expectations and reality:* With a staff of 54, including 6 "Prevention and Support Services" officers and 12 "Relief Co-ordination and Preparedness" officers, UNDRO is not in a position to fulfill its wide-ranging mandate. By and large, the staff, which consists of generalists rather than specialists, would benefit from greater field experience. The yawning gap between UNDRO's capability and the expectations for it does little to help the staff's morale or to secure the office's credibility.

Of the dozen relief officers, several have lacked experience and training in disaster management when they joined UNDRO. Current U.N. recruitment procedures make rectification of this situation improbable. For reasons familiar in any large bureaucracy, proven unsuitability for the job does not necessarily result in removal or replacement.

UNDRO's limited relief staff is not effectively complemented by UNDRO representatives in the field, the UNDP Resident Representatives. The heavy and diverse duties of Resident Representatives leave them with little time to concentrate on UNDRO's objectives, particularly those relating to preparedness. Many have little or no experience of disasters. To designate the Resident Representative the Special Representative of the Secretary-General may only add to the problems he or she faces, not only in terms of the jealousies and rivalries it may generate but also, for example, in terms of the sudden invasion of personnel and the constant bombardment of instructions by the major U.N. agencies. In such a case, concerned ministries and NGOs on the spot would also be expecting advice and attention from the Resident Representative.

When it comes to prevention and preparedness, UNDRO is involved in a number of worthy projects around the world. Undoubtedly, all of them can be justified in terms of UNDRO's mandate, but to the outsider there often seems to be little rationale for these activities in the overall context.

UNDRO suffers from lack of funds that might enable it to supplement and reinforce the work of its small staff. It is unable, for example, to hire a sufficient number of consultants both before and during disasters or to pay for regular visits to the Resident Representatives with a view to making them more aware of UNDRO's concerns.

UNDRO's record in other areas, such as raising funds in emergency situations, has been similarly patchy. Nor has it made great inroads in the formidable task of standardizing the format in which donors, transporters, and recipients provide information—a means of ensuring the rapid flow of accurate and useful information.

UNDRO is being called upon to respond to an increasing number of sudden natural disasters, performing its coordinating role with varying degrees of success. However, rarely has it established itself as the main coordinator of relief operations, the one to which donors, recipients, humanitarian bodies, and the media turn for direction.

Often the net result is that UNDRO has been left on the sidelines in disaster and emergency situations. This was particularly apparent in the African crisis of 1984–85. As the "Report to the Secretary-General on Incorporating OEOA's Experience . . . Into the United Nations" stated:

> [I]t would clearly be better for the United Nations not to have a permanent organization rather than to have an organization with mandated responsibilities but without the capacities and credibility to discharge them effectively. . . . If the mandate is not linked effectively with the capacity to respond, there can be a heavy cost in terms of human lives as well as in terms of the credibility of the United Nations.[7]

Other Bodies. The potential role of regional organizations in promoting disaster-management strategies is often overlooked. A systematic analysis of the contribution that such organizations as the Association of South East Asian Nations (ASEAN), the European Economic Community (EEC), the Organization of African Unity (OAU), and the Organization of American States (OAS) could make in all three stages of disaster needs to be undertaken. Similarly, UNDRO's relationship with some of the major international NGOs with vast field experience, such as the League of Red Cross and Crescent Societies, OXFAM, and CARE, must be strengthened.

What Next?

The objective of the U.N.'s efforts to ensure sound disaster management is, first, to assist member governments in strengthening their own disaster-management capabilities and, second, to enable the international community to lend effective support to efforts at meeting humanitarian needs—before, during, and after disasters—when the governments concerned are unable to do so. The U.N. is in a unique position to undertake the task of strengthening governments' role, both in terms of its global humanitarian mandate and in a practical sense.

There has been a proliferation of studies in the 1980s as to how these goals can be achieved. They range in scope from reviews of development policies to the means of improving disaster training, communications, and logistics arrangements in affected countries. These reports show that it is no longer the knowledge that is lacking in disaster management but, rather, the political, legal, and practical means and the personnel to implement it.

A small U.N. body cannot undertake singlehandedly the task of improving governments' and the international community's disaster-management capability. However, a small body could have an impact out of all proportion to its size and resources if it had won respect for its ability to act as a catalyst that enables all the parties involved in disaster management to fulfill the desired objective.

There are two ways in which a U.N. disaster unit could have such an impact—first, by providing leadership in promoting disaster management overall, and particularly during emergencies and disasters; and, second, by providing authoritative and accurate information on all aspects of disaster management to all the relevant parties. Upon carrying out these tasks will depend its success in coordination, both at the headquarters and field levels.

Where does UNDRO fit into the scheme of things?

There are at least four options to be considered regarding the future of the Disaster Relief Co-ordinator's Office: maintain the status quo; dissolve UNDRO; integrate UNDRO into UNDP; and restructure UNDRO.

1. *Maintain the status quo:* This course of action would be inappropriate for evident reasons. UNDRO's lack of leverage with other U.N. bodies and its limited staff and funding prevent it from fulfilling its mandate. As the frequency and scale of disasters increase, the effectiveness of UNDRO will continue to decline. Moreover, UNDRO's inability to fulfill its mandate can only have a further adverse effect on the international perception of the U.N.'s capability as a whole.

2. *Dissolve UNDRO:* The need that led to the establishment of UNDRO is more urgent today than ever before. Clearly, the U.N. system has a responsibility to meet that need. If UNDRO, or a body with a similar mandate, did not already exist, it would have to be created.

The dissolution of UNDRO would make sense only if its mandate could be met more effectively by other U.N. bodies. Such is not the case, and to argue that another agency might readily assume its mandate is both unrealistic and impractical: The accumulated experience, expertise, and contacts built up by UNDRO would be dissipated.

Furthermore, to follow up even legitimate criticism of UNDRO by dissolving the office would be to set a politically inexpedient precedent for other U.N. bodies in a similar position. In the present climate, such a move is more likely to weaken than to strengthen the international humanitarian network.

3. *Integrate UNDRO into UNDP:* Several reasons are advanced for pursuing this course of action. It has been suggested that the funding problems of UNDRO might be solved by its integration into UNDP. Other advantages cited are that the U.N. budget would be relieved; that UNDRO's field capability, in particular the potential contribution of UNDP resident representatives in disaster situations, would be enhanced; that UNDRO's leverage with other U.N. bodies would be greater; and that its access to the Secretary-General would be improved.

The fact is that UNDRO and its staff of 54 account for a minuscule proportion of the U.N.'s budget; and, in any event, there is no guarantee that UNDRO's merger into UNDP might be met by a proportionate increase in funding for UNDP from the U.N. or elsewhere. This would not further the U.N.'s disaster-management capability.

True, the UNDP resident representative could play a much greater role in disasters to good and useful purpose, particularly in prevention. That part of the prevention role now undertaken by UNDRO might well be integrated into the developmental activities of the U.N., including UNDP.

Still, the merger of UNDP and UNDRO would unavoidably create friction and dissension as new levels of organizational authority were established and existing ones adjusted. Energy that should be focused on meeting humanitarian needs would be expended on problems of internal cohesion.

A UNDP disaster unit's leverage with other U.N. bodies would not necessarily be greater than UNDRO's leverage today and might even be less. Interagency rivalry, both at headquarters and in the field, would likely be more, not less, intense, UNDP being a far more formidable competitor than UNDRO. There is also no reason to believe that the problems encountered in gaining access to the U.N. leadership would be resolved by a UNDP disaster unit; they would merely take on a new character.

Regardless of the attitude of UNDP's current leadership toward such an idea, it is doubtful that the merging of a small organization into a larger one would in itself resolve the problems encountered when disaster strikes.

4. *Restructure UNDRO:* Improvement in the U.N.'s disaster-management capability is more likely to be met by strengthening, reforming, and refining available resources of UNDRO than by starting from scratch. UNDRO's experience must be consolidated; the lessons it has learned must be disseminated and acted upon, not diluted by further institutional rearrangements.

UNDRO Restructured

If UNDRO is to fulfill its task, it needs to be restructured in a more practical way. This should be consistent with the goals of the United Nations in improving disaster management: to strengthen member states' disaster-management and response capability and to complement and supplement this by bringing the skills and resources of the international community to bear when nations facing disaster situations are incapable of rendering effective humanitarian assistance on their own.

A basic requirement is realism about what UNDRO can achieve. It must be recognized, for example, that governments and humanitarian organizations, both within the U.N. and without, are not well disposed to taking direction from a small organization with limited financial and human resources and a minimum local presence.

Given these constraints and its present resources, UNDRO's task is twofold. First, it should facilitate the rapid dissemination of accurate information about disasters in a practical and usable format to the international community. UNDRO, as the primary information source, would then be able to provide leadership to the international community, and act as interim lead agent in responding to disasters until such time as larger bodies are in a position to undertake relief activities or, where necessary, another entity is designated lead agency. Second, UNDRO should service the wide field of organizations in positions of responsibility in disaster management by making available state-of-the-art knowledge and expertise on all aspects of disaster management.

By positioning itself as an available and reliable international resource both before and when disasters strike, UNDRO will earn greater authority through merit.

Communication. To fulfill these two roles—leading the international response to disasters and servicing other larger bodies involved in disaster management—a substantial improvement in UNDRO's technical capacity to gather and communicate relevant information is needed.

UNDRO should develop a central repository of data relating to all phases of disaster management, with the objective of serving as a source and switchboard of information in several key fields. This would entail:

- "mapping" those areas and groups most vulnerable to disasters worldwide
- anticipating the requirements of such vulnerable groups. Indeed, as Randolph Kent's recent study on the international management of disasters has stated:

> [T]here is no reason to assume that one could not know with a good degree of specificity the sorts of assistance that a particular type of disaster, striking a particular vulnerable group, would demand.[8]

- maintaining an up-to-date register on the location and availability of experts in the U.N. system and elsewhere whose skills could be called upon at short notice, by prearrangement, in the event of a disaster
- providing information on the location and availability of emergency matériel for use in disaster situations
- storing accurate and usable records of previous relief operations for use as quick reference or as a resource in longer-term disaster-management planning
- providing up-to-date information on disaster-management programs (and other programs with disaster-management aspects, e.g., in the field of education or medicine) being undertaken by governments, regional bodies, NGOs, and other organizations worldwide
- monitoring major development programs with an eye to their effect on increasing or diminishing the vulnerability of populations to disasters. In effect, this could provide the basis for a "development early-warning" system.

This central repository of data relating to all phases of disaster management should be available to all governments and organizations involved in the disaster-response operation.

There is no technical reason why UNDRO should not share a computer database via satellite with all its potential partners in disaster management. UNICEF, for example, which already has this capability, is able to plug into a wide range of internally compiled and publicly available data—for example, the international press agencies, meteorological services, airline guides, shipping services—through its Electronic Information Network and the Telecommunications Co-operative Network.

UNDRO needs to take advantage of this new technology immediately. Its use of these facilities should be complemented by efforts to encourage other bodies in disaster management to achieve compatibility with the very system UNDRO uses. A high priority would be to familiarize UNDRO's field representatives and their principal government contacts with the system. The costs involved would be relatively minor, and it would not be difficult to find commercial donors of the necessary hardware. The cost of communication by satellite-linked computer networks can be cheaper than telephone or telex, while offering greater flexibility and reliability.

By these means UNDRO's usefulness both to governments in affected countries and to the international community would be greatly enhanced before, during, and after disasters.

Early Warning. The U.N.'s credibility as an organization capable of responding to disasters depends not only upon its access to the right information but upon its ability to prompt suitable action at the appropriate time. The U.N. leadership needs to be kept fully informed of situations around the world if it is to lend direct and speedy support to disaster-response efforts and to alert the media and public to what is happening.

Current arrangements for keeping the U.N. leadership informed need to be improved. The relationship of the Co-ordinator to the Secretary-General should be strengthened.

Under existing arrangements, the UNDRO Co-ordinator may report directly to the Secretary-General and as frequently as seems necessary. Insufficient use is made of this special relationship. The authority and effectiveness of the UNDRO Co-ordinator in his dealings with governments, international relief agencies, and other officials in disaster situations would be enhanced if it was clear that he was acting on behalf of the Secretary-General.

The UNDRO Liaison officer in New York has an important role in facilitating the line of communication between the UNDRO Co-ordinator and the Secretary-General. However, it would be better if this officer were to be accountable only to the UNDRO Co-ordinator rather than, as at present, to both the UNDRO Co-ordinator and the Director of the Office of Research and the Collection of Information.

The Co-ordinator's direct line to the Secretary-General should not be weakened by recent institutional rearrangements in New York. For example, when the Office for Research and the Collection of Information was created in March 1987, it was asked "to provide early warning of developing situations requiring the Secretary-General's attention," among other tasks.[9] Close links between UNDRO and the new office should be encouraged but should not undermine the direct line of authority between the UNDRO Co-ordinator and the Secretary-General.

In addition, it has recently been decided that the responsibility for "mobilizing the international community and promoting a co-ordinated response to disaster by the United Nations system" should be entrusted to the Director-General for Development and International Economic Cooperation.[10] Part of his/her task is to ensure that the Secretary-General is "kept fully informed on potential and existing disaster situations so as to be in a position to take appropriate action."

While the stated aim of this arrangement is "not to duplicate but to streamline and complement existing arrangements," it is not yet clear how the Director-General's duties will dovetail with those of the Office for Research and the Collection of Information or those of the UNDRO Co-ordinator in maintaining a direct line of communication with the Secretary-General.

The Co-ordinator must ensure that UNDRO has an adequate liaison with the Secretariat in New York as well as with the leadership of various specialized agencies. The present arrangement, according to which the UNDRO liaison officer is responsible both to the UNDRO Co-ordinator and to the Under-Secretary-General for Special Political Affairs, does not appear to further this objective. The creation in March 1987 of an Office for Research and the Collection of Information (whose responsibilities include early warning and monitoring of potential emergency situations) has further confused the picture.

UNDRO and Disaster Response. The enhanced status of the Co-ordinator should be complemented by further arrangements both at U.N. headquarters and in the field, with the aim of improving UNDRO's ability to respond to disasters.

One important step in this direction would be a reconfirmation and formalization by the Secretary-General of UNDRO's role as automatic *interim* lead agency when a disaster occurs, and an acknowledgement of this fact by the major U.N. humanitarian agencies. UNDRO's role as de facto *lead* agency was touched upon in General Assembly resolution 36/225, "Strengthening the capacity of the U.N. System to respond to natural disasters and other disaster situations." This resolution states that the Secretary-General will designate a lead agency from the U.N. system once the details of a disaster situation have been assessed by UNDRO. The resolution names UNDRO as one of the entities among which the Secretary-General can chose in designating a lead agency. It would be better if UNDRO were to confine itself to the role of automatic interim lead agency and not allow itself to be drafted into undertaking lengthy relief operations.

As interim lead agency in a disaster, UNDRO would be the first on the scene; would provide rapid initial assessment of the damage; and, through its enhanced communications capability, would have access to a worldwide electronic network that permits it to locate and activate resources and skills relevant to the particular disaster situation.

It has been suggested that arrangements for the secondment of skilled personnel at short notice be accompanied by the creation of the post of Co-ordinator of a panel of consultants—senior experts with field experience who could be called upon by the Co-ordinator to lead UNDRO's operations in disaster situations. This would enable UNDRO to assemble quickly a particular configuration of talents under appropriate field leadership to reflect the nature of the disaster situation.

It has also been suggested that UNDRO have its base in New York to bring it closer to the Secretary-General. Modern communications, properly used, obviate this need. There are clear geographical advantages to being based in Europe and to being located in the "humanitarian community" in Geneva. A good case, however, can be made for providing UNDRO in Geneva with better facilities.

UNDRO's Service Component. Using its communications ability, UNDRO should serve as a clearinghouse for information about the technical services, training courses, and other prevention measures that are necessary, planned, or under way around the world. It could actively promote prevention measures and programs with governments, U.N. bodies, NGOs, and others, but it need not take on more than a supervisory role in implementing them. UNDRO's value in this area was apparent when, for example, it helped to establish the Asian Disaster Preparedness Center in Bangkok. The Center, in turn, has done useful work in training national staff in disaster management.

UNDRO's specific objective in helping governments deal with humanitarian crises and improve their disaster-management capability will also require rendering assistance to governments in establishing the necessary infrastructure. This is as important after—and, indeed, prior to—an emergency as during one. Emergencies often provide the opportunity for consolidating temporary arrangements and securing permanent disaster-preparedness mechanisms.

The UNDP Resrep, in exercising his duties as the Resident Coordinator, is in the best position to undertake this. However, at present the Resrep has only an indirect link with the Secretary-General, even in disaster situations—one that goes through the UNDP Administrator, who, in turn, goes through the office of Development and International Economic Co-operation.

If the Resreps' authority in disaster situations is to be enhanced, their responsibilities as Resident Co-ordinator must be given greater priority and their link with the Secretary-General through the UNDRO Co-ordinator must be formalized and strengthened.

One step in this direction would be to provide the Resreps with the technical means to fulfill their role as Resident Co-ordinator and to receive and relay accurate information and needs assessments. UNDRO's credibility and performance as a whole depends upon the accuracy of the assessments it receives from the field.

Clearly, Resident Representatives and their staffs would also benefit from further training both in disaster management and in the techniques of information management. Not least of all, Resident Representatives may need assurances of direct support in terms of authority, funds, and staff in emergency situations in order to increase their standing with governments and other players.

Finally it is extremely important that UNDRO's own staff have field experience and a field orientation. Indeed, in situations in which UNDRO has had this advantage, it has played a useful and constructive role in emergencies. Its work in recent months in Lebanon is a case in point.

Code of Conduct. In keeping with its service role and with the objective of strengthening member states' disaster-management capability, UNDRO should promote the elaboration of a special legal, administrative, financial, and operational Code of Conduct for the management of disasters. The cornerstone of the code would be the increasingly recognized principle that during a disaster, and for the limited period of the emergency, humanitarian criteria should prevail over any political or sovereignty constraints.

It may be difficult to expect governments to abide by humanitarian principles when political interests are at stake. However, a humanitarian Code of Conduct for disaster situations, helpful in tempering political considerations when these obstruct humanitarian relief efforts, would be an obvious asset. Its value in minimizing the obstacles to relief would extend to such areas as passport, visa, and working-permit requirements; customs, fiscal, and insurance considerations; foreign exchange regulations; communications restrictions; and the security and safety of relief personnel. It could also help tackle the impediments to the rapid transportation, transit, accountability, and security of relief supplies in both the donor and receiving countries.

UNDRO's leadership should help this Code gain acceptance by aiding efforts to consolidate existing legal norms and practices, nationally and regionally, and by promoting the concept in the international community.

Credibility. There is a growing consensus, more visible at the grass roots than at the higher levels of policy-making, that humanitarian action should be undertaken without regard for the politics, race, color, or creed of its beneficiaries. Building on this consensus, U.N. action should be more visible to both recipient and donor communities.

It is necessary to develop an effective media strategy that, on the one hand, serves to warn local people and decision-makers of impending disasters and, on the other, lays the basis for accurate, long-term information on the causes of disasters. The credibility of the U.N. (and its constituent agencies) depends as much on the public perception and media coverage of its action as on the speed and effectiveness with which it is taken.

UNDRO must have close contact with the media and, just as important, with key NGOs in donor countries. The NGOs' relationship with the media is crucial in generating action: Taking a professional approach to the matter, they have developed personal contacts with leading editors, journalists, and media organizations. UNDRO should not hesitate to do the same or to play the "media game" by taking key journalists "into its confidence" and providing them with first-hand information, thereby ensuring the widest and most accurate coverage of events.

UNDRO's Relationship With Donors. During a disaster period, UNDRO needs rapid access to emergency funds, these to be provided according to formulae agreed to in advance by donors and recipient authorities. Funds are more useful and practical than are supplies in a disaster situation, not least of all because cash is immediately accommodated by local economies and permits the purchase of locally or regionally available commodities. UNDRO, with the support of the Secretary-General, should bolster existing arrangements—the UNDRO Trust Fund—with donor countries to ensure that sufficient funds are available to permit immediate response. The support of some of the major donors, such as the United States and Japan, must be regained or strengthened.

The aim of improved communications between UNDRO and donor governments should be to place UNDRO in a position of some authority when it comes to eliciting emergency aid and to discouraging "junk aid." UNDRO's authority in emergency situations should be such that the priorities it establishes on the basis of accurate assessment of need will override those of existing bilateral arrangements.

UNDRO must also update and refine its methods of securing the release of funds and assistance from donors, since bureaucratic delays can hold up even pledged aid for critical periods. UNDRO should detail an officer to simplify, standardize, and reduce the mountains of paperwork involved.

Conclusions

1. The objective of the U.N.'s disaster management efforts should be first, to assist member governments in strengthening their own disaster-management capabilities, particularly preparedness; and, second, to enable the international community to lend effective support to efforts at meeting humanitarian needs when disasters strike if the governments concerned are unable to do so.

There are two ways in which a U.N. disaster unit can achieve these goals: by providing leadership in promoting disaster management overall, particularly during emergencies and disasters; and by providing authoritative and accurate information on all aspects of disaster management to all the relevant parties.

2. UNDRO is in the best position to undertake this mission. But it needs to be restructured if it is to fulfill both its service role in assisting member states and other bodies and its leadership role as the primary source of quickly available skill and information on all aspects of disaster management.

3. In order to fulfill these roles, the information and communications capacity of UNDRO must be rapidly improved; UNDRO should obtain the appropriate technology and the skills to exploit it. This improvement is a prerequisite both to reaffirming its position as a focal point

for governments and all the organizations involved in disaster management and to ensuring its own and the U.N.'s credibility.

Using its communications ability, UNDRO should serve as a "clearinghouse" of information on the technical services, training courses, and other prevention measures that are necessary, planned, or under way around the world. It could actively promote prevention measures and programs with governments, other U.N. bodies, NGOs, and still others, but it need not take on more than a supervisory role in implementing them.

When disaster strikes, UNDRO's role would be to provide a rapid initial assessment of the damage based on the advice and information available from the local government, the Resrep, U.N. bodies, and NGO's already in the field rather than undertaking its own independent assessments; and then, through its communications capability, to set in motion a worldwide electronic network that would locate and activate resources and skills relevant to the particular disaster situation.

4. In light of the above, UNDRO's mandate needs to be reinforced. A much clearer line of authority from the field through the UNDRO Co-ordinator to the Secretary-General is required.

If the Resreps' authority in disaster situations is to be enhanced, their responsibilities as Resident Co-ordinator must be given greater priority and their links with the Secretary-General through the UNDRO Co-ordinator must be strengthened.

One step in this direction would be to provide the Resrep with more relevant training and the technical means to fulfill a role as Resident Co-ordinator and to receive and relay accurate information and needs assessments.

5. The UNDRO Liaison officer in New York has an important role in facilitating the line of communication between the UNDRO Co-ordinator and the Secretary-General. However, it would be better if this officer were to be accountable only to the UNDRO Co-ordinator rather than, as at present, to both the UNDRO Co-ordinator and to the Director of the Office of Research and the Collection of Information.

The Co-ordinator's direct line to the Secretary-General should not be weakened by recent institutional rearrangements in New York.

6. UNDRO's role as "automatic interim lead agency" in providing the immediate response to a disaster must be formally recognized by other agencies in the U.N. system. The other responsibilities in UNDRO's mandate that are of a purely operational nature and that it cannot reasonably be expected to fulfill, such as its role in long-term

relief operations, should be formally transferred to the relevant agency with the appropriate resources.

7. A Code of Conduct for the management of disasters must be elaborated and promoted. The formulation of such a Code will require a systematic approach to disaster management. Its formulation would give practical shape to the series of General Assembly resolutions on UNDRO that have broadened its scope in general terms without offering the specificity to guide it.

8. The emergence of new and more variform disasters has made evident serious gaps in the U.N. system's disaster-management capability. A comprehensive study of these gaps, and specific recommendations for overcoming them, is urgently required.

10. UNDRO must develop a more effective media strategy—one that not only serves to warn local people and decision-makers of impending disasters but also lays the basis for accurate, long-term information on the causes of disasters.

Notes

1. Study entitled "Report of the Working Group on Incorporation of OEOA's Experience and Capacities Into the Permanent Structure of the United Nations." This was attached to an interoffice memorandum from Maurice F. Strong, Under-Secretary-General, OEOA, to the Secretary-General that bears the date September 22, 1986.

2. Figures taken from pp. 34–37 of *Prevention Better Than Cure,* by Gunnar Hagman, published by the Swedish Red Cross, May 1984.

3. *Disaster! The United Nations and International Relief Management,* by Charles A. Schmitz (New York: Council on Foreign Relations, 1987).

4. Study entitled "Evaluation of the Office of the United Nations Disaster Relief Co-ordinator," prepared by the Joint Inspection Unit, JIU/REP/80/11 (October 1980).

5. Annex entitled "International Efforts to Meet Humanitarian Needs in Emergency Situations" attached to ECOSOC Note by the Secretary-General, E/1981/16 (March 9, 1981)—better known as the "Davidson Report" after George F. Davidson, who had been asked to prepare it.

6. Report of the Secretary-General entitled "Strengthening the Capacity of the United Nations System to Respond to Natural Disasters and Other Disaster Situations," ECOSOC document A/38/202—E/1983/94 (June 23, 1983)—better known as the "Goundry Report" after Gordon Goundry, the consultant in its preparation.

7. Ibid.

8. From "The International Management of Disasters: Clarity, Communi-

cations and Co-operation," by Randolph Kent, a document issued by the Washington Program of the Annenberg Schools, 1986.

9. Secretary-General's Bulletin ST/SGB/225 dated March 1, 1987.

10. General Assembly Report of ECOSOC A/42/657 dated October 15, 1987, "Report of the Secretary-General on the implementation of General Assembly resolution 41/201."

CHAPTER 10

LEADERSHIP AT THE U.N.: THE ROLES OF THE SECRETARY-GENERAL AND THE MEMBER STATES

First Panel Report

Whether the U.N. will emerge from its present deep financial and political crisis as a stronger organization with a new vitality or as an aging body of declining relevance will depend upon three critical factors. The first of these is *vision*—the ability (or inability) of the U.N.'s member governments to discern, agree upon, and articulate the kind of organization they want and are willing to support for the remainder of this century and into the next. The second factor is *leadership*, both in sparking the evolution of that vision and in ensuring implementation of the programmatic goals which flow from it. The third factor is *the means to produce and express consensus* regarding what specific goals, activities, and programs the U.N. should undertake.

None of these factors should be treated in isolation. The success of any one depends upon the contribution of the other two. All depend upon involvement of the U.N.'s member states as much as on that of its Secretary-General. It is up to the international community to define a vision of the U.N.'s role that is both compelling and at the same time attractive to a balanced majority of its members. Yet it is the nature of collective bodies like the U.N. General Assembly to give direction by following or not following, by revising or redirecting proposals, rather than by offering initiatives of its own. Consequently, developing a common vision requires a catalyst to discern its constituent parts, to help bring them together in a coherent whole, and then to cultivate, provoke, and inspire a dialogue among member states aimed at converting that vision into specific organizational goals. Once those goals have been delineated, leadership is once again needed to ensure that they are effectively pursued. It is to the Office of the Secretary-General that the international community looks for such leadership.

The emergence of a compelling and common vision of the U.N.'s role requires the Secretary-General to serve as a catalyst. The effectiveness of this programmatic leadership, however, depends upon the willingness of members to reach and express consensus about what practical form the U.N.'s role should take.

This report, which is the Panel's first, addresses these interrelated responsibilities of the U.N.'s member states and its Secretary-General. It proposes a number of modest but essential first steps designed to facilitate the development of consensus with regard to the role of the Organization and to strengthen the ability of the Secretary-General and the Secretariat to translate that consensus into effective performance.

This report is divided into two sections. The first examines the nature of the Secretary-General's responsibility—and, by extension, that of the Secretary-General's office—for providing intellectual and administrative leadership. The second part discusses the responsibilities of member states: to define the type of U.N. role they would be willing to support; to develop a consensus means for expressing that vision; and to provide the Secretary-General with the mandate to manage the U.N. in such a way as to make its performance much more effective.

In releasing its recommendations in these two areas, the Panel wishes to align itself with a consensus now emerging in the international community with regard to both of them.

First, it is widely recognized that Secretaries-General have traditionally given far less attention to managerial tasks than to responsibilities in the political and security area. But it is now generally accepted that the role of the Secretary-General's office is an evolving one and that its programmatic and administrative aspects should be given greater emphasis than in the past. Indeed, the proposals for extensive economies and rationalizations in the program budget presented by the Secretary-General in the spring of 1986 demonstrate that greater importance is now being given by the Office of the Secretary-General to administrative matters, and the Panel would like to encourage more efforts in this direction.

Second, leadership from the Secretary-General cannot succeed unless it is matched by more explicit, coherent, and broadly based direction from member states. This can best be accomplished by the creation of an improved means for achieving general agreement on the program and budget. There is growing international support for the establishment of an intergovernmental body of limited size that would advise the General Assembly on the level and content of the program budget and take its decisions by consensus. This concept is also supported by the Panel.

The Role of the Secretary-General

Changes in the Secretary-General's Role

The choice of a Secretary-General and the nature of his (or her) subsequent performance as chief executive of the U.N. are keys to any effort to make the Organization work better. The role of the Secretary-General has become more critical over the years for several reasons:

• The expansion of the responsibilities of the U.N. has far outstripped anything imagined by its founders. The U.N. has become a major service delivery institution, as well as a forum and deliberative body.

• The increasing complexity and costs of operating the U.N. have made the role of the U.N.'s chief administrative officer more critical in terms of shaping its program, budget, and management.

• Intractable East-West and North-South divisions have repeatedly frustrated the consensus-building process in the U.N.'s deliberative and political organs, increasing the already considerable importance attached to initiatives on a wide range of political and security matters by the Office of the Secretary-General.

• These divisions have prevented the emergence of a consensus on a forward-looking vision for the world body, contributing to a sense of drift and uncertainty.

• In an era when the U.N.'s credibility is sagging in nearly every region of the world, the role of the Secretary-General in projecting the U.N.'s image and vision has become increasingly critical to the future of the Organization.

The role of the Secretary-General can be modified without amending the Charter, since the responsibilities of the office have been defined more by custom, personality, and political pressures than by statutory restraints. As the authority and credibility of the U.N.'s legislative and judicial branches have ebbed, the potential role of the Secretary-General has grown in significance. At its best, the Office of the Secretary-General can perform as a dynamic and catalytic element in the process of institutional evolution, both spurring the consensus-building process and implementing its results.

There is some tension, however, between the need for dynamic leadership and the political realities of a broad-based collective institution in which power flows from individual sovereign member states. This dilemma is most clearly seen in the process by which the Secretary-General is chosen: In exercising their veto in the selection process, the permanent members can try to shape the kind of U.N. they want and will permit. In practice, however, each Secretary-General has managed, to one degree or another, to stretch his political, if not managerial, limits.

Constitutional Issues

The broad political and managerial powers of the Office of the Secretary-General have evolved in an uneven manner. Paradoxically, his political responsibilities, which are defined modestly in Articles 98, 99, and 100, have grown extensively, while his responsibilities as chief administrative officer have atrophied despite a more explicit constitutional writ.[1]

Again and again the inability of the U.N.'s political organs to fulfill their collective security tasks has required the Secretary-General to step into the breach. There are several justifications for this practice:

• the status of the Secretary-General as a separate organ of the U.N. co-equal with the other bodies established by the Charter[2]

• his responsibility, therefore, to speak for the Organization on behalf of the "collectivity of the member states" when he believes the United Nations to be in danger[3]

• his duty to act as "catalyst" and "inspirer"[4] when member states are at loggerheads on major issues

• his obligation to act occasionally without explicit guidance from member states "in order to help in filling any vacuum that may appear in the systems which the Charter and traditional diplomacy provide for the safeguarding of peace and security."[5]

While some Secretaries-General have been more assertive than others, all have recognized that repeated blockages in the U.N.'s collective security arrangements risk immobilizing the Organization in the face of serious threats to international peace and security. Each has been willing to take initiatives in order to prevent such a situation. Yet successive Secretaries-General have been much more cautious in interpreting their roles as chief executive officer and as principal spokesperson for the multilateral agenda. While the consequences of administrative failure are not as immediate or as dramatic as failures in collective security, over time they can be deeply debilitating, even incapacitating, for the Organization as a whole.

What Is at Stake

A number of factors underline the need for a new approach to the Secretary-General's role in the administrative and programmatic field, matching the dynamism he has shown in exerting political leadership:

Administrative issues: The first of these factors is the relationship between the Secretary-General, on the one hand, and the member states and Secretariat staff, on the other, with regard to administrative matters. The Secretary-General's powers as the U.N.'s chief executive are strongly anchored in Articles 7, 97, 98, 100, and 101 of the Charter.[6] Yet over the course of many years, Secretaries-General have actually lost ground to a variety of challengers in carrying out their Charter responsibilities as chief administrative officer. This is particularly noticeable in the personnel area, where governments attempt to influence routine personnel decisions, either by lobbying for or against recruitment or promotion of a particular individual or by second-guessing the execution of management policy. It has also been true in relationships with the staff, who in many instances have amassed such powers and rights as to make them co-managers, capable of curtailing the Secretary-General's freedom of action.[7] Over the years too many of the Secretaries-Generals' top appointments have reflected political considerations as much as management ability or loyalty to the Secretary-General; and too often this has created autonomous power centers within the Secretariat capable of stymieing or at least impeding the executive's efforts to set policy.

Such examples might suggest that Secretaries-General have lost the authority to manage as a result of repeated battles with other claimants. In fact, the Secretary-General's prerogatives usually have been ceded after very little struggle, and sometimes not asserted at all. For example, Secretaries-General rarely present their own policies on recruitment and promotion, something that would make it easier for their delegated officers to withstand outside influence.

Thus, the heart of the problem is not the inroads that staff and member states have been able to make (after all, employees everywhere try to shape the policies that affect them, and political pressures are a fact of life in any national or international organization) but the fact that there has been so little resistance to such pressures. Moreover, there seems little question that these pressures have grown over the years and that they intensify when a Secretary-General is considering a second term. While a single-term rule would jeopardize such valuable assets as a Secretary-General's experience in office and the international trust that he can be expected to earn, these assets need to be balanced against the kind of pressures described above. One compromise might be to adopt a one-term rule while extending the term from the present five years to a maximum of seven years.

Program effectiveness: The second troubling factor involves the joint responsibility of the Secretary-General and member governments for ensuring the effectiveness of U.N. programs. The collective nature of decision-making on the U.N.'s program budget, as well as the variety of sectors and programs covered by it, makes it difficult to shape priorities in a coherent manner and to maintain the quality of U.N. programs. While ultimate authority in this area rests with member states, as a practical matter the sheer size and diversity of the activities funded by the regular budget mean that for the most part "legislative" direction consists of responding to a set of broad strategic choices proposed by the Secretary-General.

To prevent a dangerous vacuum from developing, Secretaries-General could adopt a more expansive view of their powers as chief executive—not by usurping member states' prerogatives, but by taking initiatives that would compel more explicit policy guidance. Vehicles for such a role already exist. They include a regulation requiring the Secretary-General to set forth his priorities for the Organization over a six-year period (in the Introduction to the Medium-Term Plan) and another directing him to indicate which of the U.N.'s ongoing programs should be reinforced and which phased out—a judgment to be based not just on the abstract "importance of the objective to member states" but also on "the Organization's capacity to achieve it, and the real effectiveness and usefulness of the results."[8]

Neither of these mandates has ever been satisfactorily implemented, in part because the structure of the Office of the Secretary-General does not enable him to have a substantive impact on future priorities or on the reallocation of existing resources. For example, in 1978 the United Nations established a new senior post of Director-General for Development and International Cooperation, designed to ensure "effective leadership" and "coherence, coordination and efficient management" in the economic and social fields. But the position has never had the stature or organizational authority necessary to fill such a role.[9] Priority-setting, of course, would require Secretaries-General to take positions that occasionally would bring them into conflict with different member states. This is something most holders of the office have been reluctant to do, given the priority they attach to saving their political capital for critical security issues.

In the short run, a more assertive approach would be more controversial than a reactive one; but if accompanied by careful and politically astute salesmanship, it need not alienate any group of member states. Moreover, if, as recommended in the second part of this report, there is greater intergovernmental involvement at the beginning of and throughout the planning and budget process by means of a program and budget committee, then a more assertive role by the Secretary-General's office would carry less risk of controversy. Indeed, it would be essential to the effective functioning of such a committee. One extremely important result would be that the U.N. could identify more effectively the core of programs on which there was the widest degree of consensus.

Leadership in the economic and social sphere: The third factor relates to the degree of intellectual leadership that the Secretary-General or those who speak for him are able to bring to bear on global economic and social debates. Since so many newly independent countries joined the world organization in the 1950s and 1960s, shaping the climate of North-South relations has become a part of the U.N.'s political mandate—second in importance only to its global security role. In those years and through much of the last decade, the Organization played an influential part both in setting the terms of the international economic and social policy agenda, particularly its North-South axis, and in promoting changes in the structure and management of the international economy.[10] Unfortunately, that formative role has become largely a thing of the past. Because U.N. intergovernmental forums treat economic issues in a manner that tends to be less substantive, more ideological, and more rigidly dependent on the group system than do other venues, they are less and less regarded—by developing and developed countries alike—as places for serious discussion.

Ironically, there is today a greater convergence at the global level in thinking about economic philosophy and about the goals and means of international economic management than has existed at any other point in the postwar period.[11] In fact, the next several years could well produce a reshaping of many of the methods and institutions of international economic cooperation that have developed over the last four decades. Yet, without fundamental changes, the U.N. will be less and less able to affect this debate or to play a role in the arrangements that emerge from it.

Ultimately, the member states themselves will determine the relevance of U.N. economic forums to the major issues of the day. Although there are obvious limits to the extent to which a Secretary-General, with his many other responsibilities, can exercise intellectual leadership in the economic field, there are a number of indirect ways for him to exert a stronger influence. A useful step would be the creation of a much closer working partnership between the Secretary-General and the Director-General, in which the latter would be regarded as the Secretary-General's authoritative spokesman. Also useful would be the creation of a very small, highly qualified secretariat, under the direct supervision of the Director-General, to provide objective and impartial support to all sides of an economic negotiation.

The Secretary-General also needs more effective means for promoting the coordination of those U.N. activities in the economic and social field that are closely interrelated. The meetings of executive heads that currently take place through the Advisory Committee for Coordination are too general in subject matter and have too diverse a group of participants to provide meaningful oversight of U.N. activities in this area. Consequently, to provide a better basis for coordination at the policy level, the Secretary-General should co-convene with the President of the World Bank and the Managing Director of the International Monetary Fund an annual gathering of the executive heads of the major U.N. agencies devoted to economic and social activities. The object of such a U.N. system summit would be to examine, in a unified and intersectoral way, two or three important common policy issues in the economic and social fields and to agree to a general outline for a more coordinated approach to them.

Finally, complementing the Secretary-General's duties as a coordinator and programmatic leader is his responsibility—or that of his representative—to act as the focal point of a U.N. "global watch," addressing the General Assembly whenever it is necessary to focus world attention on emerging issues with global implications. While the idea of such a U.N. "early-warning" system spearheaded by the Secretary-General is not new, it is one that has not been acted upon with the frequency or given the visibility it deserves.

Elements of a New Role

To cope effectively with the challenges to the world body described above, the responsibilities of the Office of the Secretary-General would have to be stretched well beyond what has, through tradition and practice, come to be accepted as their normal sphere. The election process, too, would have to adjust its focus. In addition to the customary attention to such qualities as integrity, political acceptability, and negotiating acumen, this conception of the office would raise the importance of duties less widely valued—or even welcomed—by member states in the past:

• *Programmatic leadership*: To develop the momentum and sense of direction the world body now lacks, a Secretary-General should act as a forceful and inspiring programmatic leader with a clear conception not only of the U.N. of today but also of where he would like it to go.

• *Vigorous management*: No single trait is more effective when asserted—or leaves a greater void when it is not—than the will to manage.

• *Intellectual guidance*: The Secretary-General and his deputies should help define realistic and imaginative tasks for the U.N., especially regarding international economic cooperation.

• *Presenting the U.N. to the world*: In an era of mass media and global communications, the Secretary-General should be both the U.N.'s most powerful image maker and the world's most prominent spokesperson for multilateral approaches to global problem-solving.

Constraints

The Secretary-General and a small personal staff cannot possibly exercise effective oversight over the myriad departmental activities funded by the U.N.'s regular budget. Yet under the current structure there is no one to whom the Secretary-General can delegate this responsibility. The post of Director-General was not intended to be that of a deputy and has not evolved into one. Nor is there any senior cabinet or executive council to ease the burden. Consequently, more than 30 Under-Secretaries-General, each responsible for some facet of the Organization's work, report to the Secretary-General directly, making overall supervision impossible and resulting in a large measure of autonomy in operational and administrative terms.

Greater activism on the part of Secretaries-General would also encounter political and psychological obstacles along the lines described earlier. Nevertheless, the potential gains for the reputation and smooth functioning of the Organization could be well worth the effort. There are risks in encouraging assertiveness by the Office of the Secretary-General, but the dangers to the very life of the world body inherent in maintaining the present path are reflected in the depth of the current political and financial crisis.

Whether these risks are worth undertaking depends on the degree to which a Secretary-General feels confident of having received a mandate from the member states to assert the powers of chief executive officer energetically and creatively. Based on past experience, any Secretary-General would have to question whether the member states really want an effective United Nations led by a strong and independent Secretary-General. If they do, then the obstacles and constraints, while presenting difficulties, would certainly be surmountable. If not, then the undertaking would be impossible, even foolhardy. It is to be hoped that the severity of the current crisis and the damage it has done to the institution—and therefore to the stake which the member states have in its survival—will cause some fundamental rethinking in national capitals about their commitment to the Organization and about their interests in seeing it run efficiently.

If member states do indeed want to make the Organization work better, which obstacles and constraints facing the Secretary-General are intractable and which are subject to change? The exercise of powers by the Secretary-General faces certain legal, financial, and staff constraints that define the outer limits of what is possible. Yet, as noted above, these limitations have rarely been tested, except in the security realm, and allow considerable latitude. The greatest inhibitions, on the other hand, stem from custom, psychology, and expectations. Things are not done because they have not been done before, or because there is insufficient will to probe limits that in some cases may exist simply because they have never been tested. The law of anticipatory reactions has affected all of the occupants of the 38th floor at one point or another, encouraging a trend toward self-regulated behavior.

Seldom are executives in any organization eager to take the risk of breaking the mold set by their predecessors. Yet one of the characteristics of leadership is to go beyond the limits of tradition and custom, seeking to redefine the parameters of what is possible. The political and psychological pressures, after all, need not always go in one direction. While lacking economic and military power, the Secretary-General does command an unusually visible pulpit from which to seek to shape both public and official opinion around the world. If a Secretary-General begins with a true mandate for leadership and carefully husbands this precious resource even while redefining the management role of the office, it is conceivable that this could begin to reshape the conditions under which the office operates, especially in the realm of administration and management.

Recommendations

Nothing is more far-reaching or has greater significance for the efficiency and effectiveness of U.N. performance than the choice of Secretary-General and the support this official is given by member states. Few things, however, are less susceptible to influence by means of policy recommendations. Yet if the will to manage and the mandate to do so *are* present, there are a number of modifications—in organizational structure, in delegated authorities, in relations with member states, and in still other areas—that would help to make more effective management possible. Because some of these changes can be identified immediately, while others flow more naturally from an analysis of detailed administrative and structural issues beyond the scope of this report, the Panel has decided to issue its recommendations in two stages.

The proposals offered here represent the first stage and are, in the Panel's opinion, so essential to more effective U.N. leadership that their implementation is desirable no matter what changes in organization and management structure may eventually be recommended. Elsewhere in this volume the Panel deals directly with the issues of organizational and administrative structure in the U.N. proper and the organs subordinate to the General Assembly and ECOSOC (U.N. group), and presents a number of more detailed recommendations designed to reinforce management and leadership.

Responsibilities of the Secretary-General:
   1. In view of the enormous demands upon the Secretary-General's time and the great energy and personal resources that must be

devoted to diplomacy in the political and security area, it is necessary that the Secretary-General make explicit and binding delegations of authority to capable individuals with executive responsibility for: planning and development of the program budget; financial and administrative policy, with particular emphasis on the personnel area; and coordination of related activities of the U.N. proper and the U.N. group.

2. Complementing the Secretary-General's responsibilities as a programmatic leader are his responsibilities as the initiator and focal point of a "global watch" function. It should be the Secretary-General's task to address the General Assembly whenever necessary to focus world attention on emerging issues that require a multilateral response at the regional or global level.

3. As head of the U.N. system, the Secretary-General should co-convene, with the President of the World Bank and the Managing Director of the IMF, an annual gathering of the executive heads of the major U.N. agencies devoted to economic and social activities. The object of such a U.N. summit would be to examine, in a unified and intersectoral way, two or three important common policy issues in the economic and social area and to agree to a general outline for a more coordinated approach to them.

Other Organizational and Structural Changes:

1. To establish a coherent administrative structure of manageable proportions, responsibility for the departmental activities funded by the U.N.'s regular budget should be coordinated in a small management committee chaired by the Secretary-General and including among its members the Under-Secretary-General for Administration and Management and the Director-General.

2. The management committee should meet on a weekly basis to assist the Secretary-General in the formulation of decisions on any matter in the programmatic and administrative area that he chooses to place before it. Ultimate decision-making power should remain with the Secretary-General.

Term of the Secretary-General:

1. Effective as of the next election, Secretaries-General should be elected for a single term not to exceed seven years.

2. The terms of the Director-General and of all Under-Secretaries-General and Assistant Secretaries-General whom the Secretary-General appoints in his own capacity should coincide with that of

the Secretary-General, although any of these officers could be reappointed.

The Role of Member States

Development of the Program Budget

It is widely agreed that better means need to be found for clarifying U.N. goals, for setting its priorities, and for formulating its specific programs to reflect those priorities. This would make it less likely that any member state would do anything—deliberate or not—that would cause harm to the world body. This will require a more sustained dialogue, commencing at an earlier stage in the planning and budgeting process, among member states themselves and between them and the Secretary-General. To foster such a dialogue, and in a sense to systematize it, a procedure for planning, programming, budgeting, and evaluation has been established over the last decade. The process, to work properly, requires intellectual leadership from the Secretary-General and overall policy direction from member states. Its functioning also depends on a set of rules and regulations dealing with planning, programming, budgeting, and evaluation.

Unfortunately, these regulations, particularly those regarding the delineation of relative priorities, have not been fully implemented. As a consequence, inadequate attention has been given to the fact that different programs often have very different degrees of international support. Yet it is clearly essential to distinguish between the effort to build consensus, a process that relies chiefly upon the exchange of views and occasionally negotiation, and the effort to convert consensus into useful results, which involves the attempt to organize common strategies and joint actions among all member states. Both of these are appropriate functions of the U.N., but without a distinction of this kind it is very difficult to design feasible programs with reasonable objectives or to evaluate their results properly.

The U.N., by its very nature, strives to promote consensus on subjects where deep political divisions have long existed. In some of these areas it has been able to spur enough agreement to allow the adoption of action programs to address the underlying political, economic, social, or humanitarian problems. On many other subjects, though, it has been impossible for the U.N., or for many other groups or bodies, to bridge intractable political differences. In the latter cases, the U.N.'s deliberative function may continue to be valuable, but it raises false expectations and misunderstandings when the U.N. tries to undertake action programs that go beyond the degree of consensus that actually exists. In order to place greater emphasis on this point in the design of the U.N.'s activities, the Rules and Regulations governing the formulation of the program budget should be refined in the following ways:

1. For those areas where consensus exists—such as humanitarian activities, technical cooperation, and agreed research programs—it is both possible and desirable to define objectives more precisely. In particular, all objectives should be time-limited and spelled out with precision, and the human and material resources necessary to carry them out should be carefully calculated.

2. For those areas where a consensus must be developed—such as negotiations on commodities, disarmament, or the development of international law—a reappraisal of the nature of the U.N.'s contribution is needed. Both publics and governments need a better sense of what the U.N. can and cannot be expected to accomplish and what its comparative advantages and disadvantages are in addressing different kinds of international problems. For example, what types of studies and reports are needed to identify emerging global problems and the potential U.N. role in alleviating them? And what kinds of negotiations are needed before the U.N. can put in place effective programs in these areas?

The disciplined application of these two points would enhance the effectiveness of the U.N. planning, programming, and budgetary process and, over time, would help to bring its program mandates into line with its actual capabilities. This, in turn, would lead to more realistic expectations and fairer evaluations of U.N. performance. It would dampen the tendency of the U.N. to overreach itself in terms of taking on tasks it does not have the resources to carry out adequately. These points should be taken into account in the preparation of the Introduction to the Medium-Term Plan, as well as in the launching of the "global watch" discussed earlier in this report. In undertaking such important studies and assessments, it would be useful for the U.N. to call upon the experience and knowledge of the best research centers in the world.

Budgetary Decision-making

An improved means for reaching broad agreement on budgetary matters is also needed. Under existing arrangements, both the program implications and the budgetary effects of resolutions are never considered in the same place at the same time. The budget side of any new undertaking is reviewed by the Advisory Committee for Administrative and Budgetary Questions (ACABQ), which then recommends adjustments in expenditure—usually downward—based upon an analysis from an efficiency point of view. Recommendations of the ACABQ are then accepted or rejected by the U.N.'s Fifth Committee, a body whose authority extends no further than the financial aspects of programs. Decisions related to program are handled through a parallel process, carried out by a Committee for Program and Coordination (CPC) and the six other substantive committees of the General Assembly. Unfortunately, the program track and the budget track never intersect in such a way as to provide for a joint examination of program goals and program capabilities.

The present financial crisis and the feelings of the largest contributors that they have had an inadequate voice in the budget decision-making process are putting these matters in a new light. In fact, deliberations that have taken place in recent months have succeeded in moving the international community toward acceptance of several key principles:

• the need for a new procedure involving member states in the determination of the level and content of the program budget at an early stage in order to ensure their full input

• the need for revising and strengthening the Committee for Program and Coordination (CPC) so that it can carry out this task, and the need for ensuring that programs and their financial implications are examined at the same time and in the same place

• the desirability of the CPC continuing to work on a consensus basis

• the usefulness of preserving the present functions of the Advisory Committee on Administrative and Budgetary Questions, which provides a careful review of the U.N. budget by competent experts.

The deliberations among member states regarding the suggestion—endorsed by this Panel—that the revised and strengthened CPC should operate by consensus revolve around two issues. The first is how this procedure would relate to the current responsibilities and authority of the General Assembly on budgetary matters. The second is how the principle of consensus should be interpreted in practice.

Regarding the first point, it should be stressed that the revised and strengthened CPC would retain its current advisory character, serving as a subsidiary intergovernmental body to the General Assembly and its Fifth Committee. It would report its recommendations through the Fifth Committee to the General Assembly, which would retain its full authority and responsibilities under the Charter for the ultimate determination of the budget and program of the Organization. Its objective, as those of the CPC at present, would be to facilitate the work of the General Assembly rather than to usurp its authority in any way or to undermine the provisions of the Charter.

Regarding the second point, the Panel is conscious of the very positive role that consensus procedures have played in many cultures around the world, in regional bodies, and in the U.N. itself. Consensus rules have been very helpful over the years in narrowing differences and facilitating intergovernmental agreements in many U.N. bodies, including the General Assembly itself, which continues to adopt most resolutions by consensus. In the view of the Panel, consensus does not necessarily mean unanimity on every item. The spirit of consensus is one of give-and-take until agreement is broad enough to assure that no one member will block the overall package even if it is concerned about some individual elements of it. Consensus cannot operate properly if individual countries—large or small—seek to abuse the spirit of consensus by "vetoing" item after item. At the same time, the Panel recognizes the risks to the financial integrity of the U.N. if the present trend continues in which the budgets of the institution fail to attract the support of major donors.

The reports of the revised CPC to the Assembly, moreover, would present recommendations only when a consensus had been reached. If no consensus was possible, this would be indicated in the report, which would summarize the positions of different delegations or groups of delegations. It also should be recalled that the consensus rule within the group would simply reflect the traditional, and largely successful, practice of the CPC.

If the role of the revised CPC and the principle of consensus are explained in this way, then the understandable apprehensions expressed in some quarters about the proposed steps should be substantially relieved. It is, after all, in the interests of all member states, large and small, to make such a process work. In recent months a number of alternatives to the consensus procedure have been discussed. All of these, however, would represent a failure of the strengthened procedures—and the positive spirit of cooperation they would embody.

Several other positive features of consensus should also be emphasized. First of all, as the budget crisis of 1986 demonstrates, it is certainly desirable for a consensus to exist on the program and budget, if the U.N. is to function smoothly. Second, a committee of limited membership—elected for three years as government representatives, with due regard for their expertise on these issues—could greatly facilitate the emergence of a consensus within the General Assembly itself.

Recommendations

1. To enable member states to exercise the necessary intergovernmental leadership throughout the planning and decision-making process on the U.N. budget, the Committee for Program and Coordination should be revised, strengthened, and renamed the Committee for Program, Budget and Coordination. The new Committee for Program, Budget and Coordination should advise the General Assembly and the Fifth Committee on the size, composition, and priorities of the U.N. program budget and Medium-Term Plan and should take its decisions by consensus.

2. A clear distinction should be made between programs aimed at the search for consensus and those aimed at converting existing consensus into useful results. This distinction should be applied in the design of the Medium-Term Plan and in the definition of programs.

3. For programs dealing with joint management in the areas of limited consensus, time-limited objectives should be established and followed.

4. In order to strengthen the U.N. global watch function and to promote consensus-building, the process of identifying problems that the U.N. could usefully address should be better organized by (i) use of the Introduction to the Medium-Term Plan to pinpoint those emerging issues requiring collective response in which a U.N. role is feasible; (ii) adoption of regulations describing the type of global watch studies to be conducted, the means for deciding upon them, and the calendar for their preparation and review by member states; (iii) establishment of a list of international centers of research and expertise which, in addition to relevant U.N. system secretariats, could usefully contribute to a global watch function.

Notes

1. Article 7 of the Charter of the United Nations:

1. There are established as the principal organs of the United Nations: a General Assembly, a Security Council, an Economic and Social Council, a Trusteeship Council, an International Court of Justice, and a Secretariat.
2. Such subsidiary organs as may be found necessary may be established in accordance with the present Charter.

Article 97 of the Charter of the United Nations:

The Secretariat shall comprise a Secretary-General and such staff as the Organization may require. The Secretary-General shall be appointed by the General Assembly upon the recommendation of the Security Council.

Article 98 of the Charter of the United Nations:

The Secretary-General shall act in that capacity in all meetings of the General Assembly, of the Security Council, and of the Trusteeship Council, and shall perform such other functions as are entrusted to him by these organs. The Secretary-General shall make an annual report to the General Assembly on the work of the Organization.

Article 99 of the Charter of the United Nations:

The Secretary-General may bring to the attention of the Security Council any matter which in his opinion may threaten the maintenance of international peace and security.

Article 100 of the Charter of the United Nations:

1. In the performance of their duties, the Secretary-General and the staff shall not seek or receive instructions from any government or from any other authority external to the Organization. They shall refrain from any action which might reflect on their position as international officials responsible only to the Organization.
2. Each Member of the United Nations undertakes to respect the exclusively international character of the responsibilities of the Secretary-General and the staff and not to seek to influence them in the discharge of their responsibilities.

Article 101 of the Charter of the United Nations:

1. The staff shall be appointed by the Secretary-General under regulations established by the General Assembly.
2. Appropriate staffs shall be permanently assigned to the Economic and Social Council, the Trusteeship Council, and, as required, to other organs of the United Nations. These staffs shall form a part of the Secretariat.
3. The paramount consideration in the employment of the staff and in determination of the conditions of service shall be the necessity of securing the highest standards of efficiency, competence, and integrity. Due regard shall be paid to the importance of recruiting staff on as wide a geographical basis as possible.

2. For a contemporary defense of the Secretary-General's independence and responsibilities as a "principal organ" see Javier Pérez de Cuéllar, "The Role of the Secretary-General," a lecture delivered at Oxford University on May 13, 1986, U.N. Doc. SG/SM/3870.

3. Andrew W. Cordier and Wilder Foote, eds., *Public Papers of the Secretaries-General of the United Nations*, Vol. 1: Trygvie Lie (New York: Columbia University Press, 1969), p. 124. Reprinted in Thomas M. Franck, *Nation Against Nation*, (New York: Oxford University Press, 1985), p. 120.

4. Remarks by Dag Hammarskjöld, cited in Brian Urquhart, *Hammarskjold* (New York: Alfred Knopf, 1972), p. 15.

5. Remarks by Dag Hammarskjöld to the General Assembly, September 26, 1957. Cited in Franck, p. 121.

6. Thus Article 97 makes him the chief administrative officer of the Organization, a status that the U.N.'s Preparatory Commission interpreted as involving both "preparing the ground for the decisions of the organs and of executing them in cooperation with members." Article 98, in keeping with the expansive view implied by the Preparatory Commission's gloss, directs the Secretary-General to "make an annual report to the General Assembly on the work of the Organization" and invites the General Assembly and the Security Council to go beyond the authority implicit in Article 97 by "entrusting" to him "other functions." In Article 98 the Secretary-General is charged with appointing the Secretariat, a power that, when combined with the Secretariat's status under Article 7 as a "principal organ of the United Nations," appears to give the Secretary-General an autonomy that is equivalent in some respects to that of the other principal bodies. Finally, Article 100 reproduces the League of Nations' regulations on the independence, impartiality, and international responsibility of the Secretariat, but goes one step further by prohibiting the Secretary-General and staff from seeking or receiving instructions from any government. [Dag Hammarskjöld, "The International Civil Service in Law and Fact," a lecture delivered at Oxford University on May 30, 1961. U.N. Press Release SG/1035, May 29, 1961.]

7. For example, the principle of equal representation for staff and management is a rule that is followed for virtually all internal bodies having oversight over personnel matters. Thus such things as the appointment and promotion machinery have a 50–50 staff/management composition, as does the Joint Advisory Committee, whose recommendations to the Secretary-General on personnel policy and general questions of staff welfare are usually adopted.

8. Regulations and Rules Governing Program Planning, U.N. Doc. ST/SGB/204, June 1984, published pursuant to General Assembly resolutions 37/234 and 38/227.

9. General Assembly resolution 32/197. Restructuring of the economic and social sectors of the United Nations system.

10. Examples of the U.N.'s influence abound. They include establishment of the International Development Association and the concept of concession-

ary financing for development, the Generalized System of Preferences, the IMF's Compensatory Financing Facility, addition of Part IV of GATT, etc. While the record in this area during the 1970s was much less significant, the U.N. nonetheless affected the terms of the policy dialogue between North and South, and put onto the international agenda such subjects as commodity stabilization and the codes of conduct for business practices and technology transfer that would otherwise be absent.

11. This is evident on such issues as the dependence of a healthy trading system upon a more harmonious and disciplined monetary regime, the injuriousness to trade and global economic growth of exchange rate volatility, the dependence of developing countries on both public and private sources of financing, the dangers to the world trade and monetary system of an approach to debt repayment that impedes growth and a resumption of investment, the important potential contributions to development of both the private and the public sector, and on other key issues.

CHAPTER 11

U.N. PERSONNEL POLICY ISSUES
Peter Fromuth and Ruth Raymond

The Challenge and the Constraints

Many of the characteristics that make the U.N. unique as a world organization also impose conditions that made the task of human resource management particularly challenging. Although the United Nations shares a number of qualities with other large organizations, its unique human, political, and cultural environment creates certain problems of administration that are not widely understood. Like a national diplomatic service, the U.N. staff is expatriate, composed of people working in countries other than their own. But unlike a national diplomatic service, the U.N. staff lacks the "glue" of a common culture, language, political perspective, and work habits. Like a multinational company, the United Nations has to deliver services—and even actual products on occasion—to a variety of "consumers" in different locales around the world. But unlike an international business, the U.N. has to "deliver" with a workforce reflecting many different ethoses, habits, and traditions and, to extend the analogy, with a Board of Directors that is often deeply divided on very basic matters of policy. As in other international organizations, the U.N. staff must be truly representative of its members. Yet the U.N. lacks the cohesiveness conferred, for example, by the World Health Organization's limited and concrete mission or by the distinct geographical focus of the Organization of American States or a regional development bank.

In short, the very features that distinguish the U.N. as an organiza-

213

tion—the comprehensiveness of its global mission, the universality of its membership, the multicultural character of its staff—are those that make the task of personnel management particularly difficult and challenging. This point is emphasized not to justify the current personnel situation at the U.N., which is widely perceived to be a troubled one, but to stress that it is important to view the personnel issues in the context of this unique environment.

No single aspect of this environment plays a more important role than the attitude and behavior of the U.N.'s member governments, whose constructive assistance is the key to an efficient Secretariat. Yet few member states are willing to subordinate their political interests to such less pressing matters as personnel policy. While considerable attention is paid to some specifics of employment—levels of remuneration, geographical representation, the treatment of women, the grading of senior posts, expenditures on consultants, the independence and integrity of the Secretariat—there is very little interest in ensuring administrative efficiency. Indeed, in the area of recruitment and promotion, member states are more often than not an obstacle to efficiency by virtue of their continuing pressure upon the Secretary-General and his assistants to provide jobs and promotions for candidates of their own choosing, regardless of qualifications.

Behind such an approach to personnel lies an even deeper problem: the member countries' generally low level of interest in the output of most of the U.N.'s programs. Thus, even with widespread agreement that the existing personnel system is deeply flawed—and that their own actions may contribute to the problem—many, if not most, countries will have to be convinced that those flaws carry a heavy price in the program outputs that are important to them before they bend to the task of bringing about significant improvements. They will be convinced of this when they have a much sharper and clearer definition of the U.N.'s role in its various fields of activity and are more willing to take that role seriously. It is the purpose of the final report of the U.N. Management and Decision-Making Project to help catalyze this change in thinking and behavior—a long-term process. For the short term, however, it is necessary to take all available steps so that the current flaws in the personnel system do not become magnified.

The recommendations contained in this chapter are offered for consideration in the short and medium term and are therefore founded on the premise that proposals rooted in a careful appraisal of the nature and intensity of political and other constraints may serve, at the very least, to extend the realm of the possible. Specifically, it is assumed here that there is little to be gained by increasing the formal powers of the Secretary-General, since this would increase his visibility as a target of political pressure while only marginally affecting his ability to resist it. Instead, it might actually be easier to strengthen the independence of the personnel function by deflecting attention from the Secretary-General and his key managers. This approach would free the Secretary-General from involvement in the most routine personnel matters, through explicit delegation of authority and regulations designed to increase the objectivity of recruitment, staff evaluations, promotions, and terminations. At the same time, it would put a premium on the Secretary-General's leadership in fundamental issues of personnel policy.

Improving U.N. personnel management will require the identification of approaches appropriate to the unusual mix of institutional characteristics that makes the United Nations virtually sui generis among international organizations. There is, however, another set of conditions resulting from the institutional politics and culture of the U.N. that presents its own obstacles to reform. The most formidable of these constraints is the highly politicized environment that is now the background for most personnel decisions. As the situation was described in a staff report: "Politicization of the Secretariat has spread from the original notion whereby political appointments were limited to the D-2 level and above, into every level and aspect of work, thereby undermining the overall technical and managerial competence of the staff."[1]

Politicization takes a wide variety of forms. There is, for example, the requirement of some countries that their citizens serve only on the basis of short-term "secondments," that they relinquish part of their salaries to their governments,[2] and that their recruitment by the U.N. be limited to a prescribed list of candidates.

Although such actions clearly violate the independence of the U.N. Secretariat, a number of other forms of political interference are also very damaging. One of these is the tradition of considering certain posts, offices, or divisions the domain of particular member states or groups of member states—a situation that makes concepts of efficiency in workforce management and fairness in career development impossible to apply.[3] Even more injurious is the nearly universal propensity of member states to try to influence the outcome of personnel decisions. Though especially egregious in the recruitment area, in recent years this lobbying has also focused on promotions and has even gone so far as to include the marks given a staff member on evaluation reports.

Another complicating factor is the nature of the legislative/executive relationship, which has led to an increasing involvement by the General Assembly in administrative matters. In a recent speech on the role of the Secretary-General, Javier Pérez de Cuéllar commented:

> It is ironic and unfortunate that, while there has been a dramatic rise in the Secretary-General's political responsibilities, his powers in the administrative field have steadily eroded over the years . . . the distribution of functions between the legislative and executive, so essential to sound management, tends to be blurred when increasingly detailed directives about management policy are issued by the General Assembly.[4]

While the Assembly clearly has an important role in the setting of broad policy goals, on a number of issues it has adopted a "command and compliance" approach to reaching them. Thus, for example, the Office of Personnel Services (OPS) is directed to implement the goal of equitable geographical distribution—obviously an essential characteristic of any global organization—but to do so in such a way as to impose serious obstacles to the speed and efficiency of U.N. recruitment.[5] Other, less well-intentioned, Assembly policies have had a sharply counterproductive effect. For example, a resolution of the 1980 session gave legislative sanction to the practice of reserving certain fixed-term posts for nationals of the same country.[6] In another action, the General Assembly directed the Secretary-General to give staff members with five-year fixed-term contracts at the U.N. "every reasonable consideration for a career appointment."[7]—a decision which, by implying that U.N. professionals were, under normal circumstances, to be given a permanent contract after a given period, increases the obstacles to a merit-based approach to employee management.

Finally, no really significant improvement in personnel matters is likely to take place without a fundamental change in the attitude of the U.N.'s top leadership. One of the reasons why the last 15 years have seen the Assembly wander so far into detailed policy-making in personnel matters—and, indeed, across the entire range of management issues—is that Secretaries-General have not sufficiently asserted their administrative prerogatives under Chapter 15 of the U.N. Charter. Articles 97 and 101 of Chapter 15 give to the Secretary-General exclusively the powers of chief executive officer—powers that must be defended against challenges, not just by member states acting as "micro-managers" or as lobbyists, but by the various staff associations and other competing sources of influence in the Organization's decentralized management structure as well. In the words of one former senior U.N. official, "job lobbying is a bit like an appetite that grows the more you are willing to feed it. Deny it meals, and the clamor to be fed will go away."

One of the reasons why the U.N. has found it difficult to resist overtures by foreign ministers or ambassadors on behalf of their nationals is the fear that refusal may cause dissatisfaction that will ricochet—resulting in the denial of financial assistance to some extra-budgetary program, for example. But it would appear that the Secretariat's fears about spillover have been exaggerated. Another important prerogative of the Secretary-General, in which, again, too much is ceded to others, is the power of appointment at the senior level. Because political considerations are permitted to play so great a role, unqualified individuals are frequently appointed to key administrative posts.

Role of the Secretariat

It is impossible to examine the conditions under which United Nations employees are currently managed without some basic understanding of the nature and role of the U.N. Secretariat. Members of the Secretariat are international civil servants, differing from national civil servants—in theory, at least—by virtue of their impartiality; their international loyalty, which supercedes but does not replace national loyalty; and their allegiance to the interests of the international organization.[8]

The United Nations Secretariat has 11,964 employees, of which 3,873 are classified as "professional" and 8,091 are considered in the "General Service" category.[9] The General Service consists of staff engaged in semi-professional, clerical, secretarial, and maintenance work. These individuals are, for the most part, recruited locally and are not required to have a university-level degree. A duty station may have anywhere from five to ten General Service grades, including extended General Service levels.

Professional staff positions require a university-level degree or equivalent experience and training. Professional staff are recruited globally and are, for the most part, subject to balanced nationality distribution. The professional staff consists of five grades (P-1 through P-5), two categories of directors (D-1 and D-2), and two upper grades (Assistant Secretary-General and Under-Secretary-General). All U.N. posts in the professional category have been classified according to 14 occupational groupings—finance, economics, administration, legal, political affairs, etc.

According to Article 101 of the U.N. Charter, the paramount consideration in the employment of staff shall be the "necessity of securing the highest standard of efficiency, competence, and integrity," with due regard for "the importance of recruiting the staff on as wide a geographical basis as possible."[10]

A profile of the U.N. professional staff reveals the preference of the Organization for recruiting older males with previous experience. Only 14 percent of all professionals are under the age of 35, the average age of recruitment is over 40, and 36 percent of the staff are over 50 years old.

One effect of this tendency has been a thickening of the Organization's waistline. For example, in 1984, 46 percent of the U.N.'s employees fell into the P-4 or P-5 category, as opposed to 41 percent in 1975 (see Table I).

The professional segment of the Secretariat is 83 percent male; most of the female employees are to be found at the lower grade levels. For example, as of January 1987 women held only three of the 105 D-2 posts and only four of the 74 upper-grade posts.[11]

Although meeting the minimum standards, the level of education achieved by the average staff member at the professional level is not high. Only 13 percent have received a doctorate in their field. In fact, less than half hold more than a first university degree.

The responsibilities of the U.N. Secretariat originally consisted mainly of servicing the U.N.'s policy-making organs. However, the Secretariat's responsibilities have tended to broaden as the size and diversity of the U.N.'s operational and programmatic activities have increased. A professional staff member might manage peacekeeping operations; organize international conferences and provide analysis of problems of worldwide concern; survey world economic and social trends; prepare studies on such subjects as human rights, disarmament, and development; interpret speeches; translate documents; or provide the media with information about the United Nations.

In the U.N. system, career appointments, normally following a two-to-five-year probationary period, are permanent, with the retirement

Table I

U.N. ONLY—GRADE DISTRIBUTION
(1970–85)

Year	P-1	P-2	P-3	P-4	P-5	D-1	D-2	UG	
1970	133	560	811	711	403	184	67	25	2894
%	4.6	19.4	28	24.6	13.9	6.4	2.3	.8	100%
1975	98	609	977	903	497	219	76	35	3414
%	2.9	17.8	28.6	26.5	14.6	6.4	2.2	1	100%
1976	109	619	982	922	526	225	87	41	3511
%	3.1	17.6	28	26.3	15	6.4	2.5	1.2	100%
1977	95	612	1029	914	520	232	81	43	3526
%	2.7	17.4	29.2	25.9	14.7	6.6	2.3	1.2	100%
1978	80	636	1080	1023	578	237	85	52	3771
%	2.1	16.9	28.6	27.1	15.3	6.3	2.3	1.4	100%
1979	59	574	1098	1048	588	257	86	51	3761
%	1.5	15.3	29.2	27.9	15.6	6.8	2.3	1.4	100%
1980	54	542	1148	1050	610	263	90	57	3814
%	1.4	14.1	30	27.3	15.9	6.9	2.3	1.5	100%
1981	57	602	1146	1123	664	274	97	56	4019
%	1.4	15	28.5	28	16.5	6.8	2.4	1.4	100%
1982	54	596	1161	1136	702	262	95	55	4063
%	1.3	14.7	28.6	28	17.3	6.5	2.3	1.3	100%
1983	44	637	1145	1173	733	252	61	59	4144
%	1.1	15.4	27.6	28.3	17.7	6.1	2.4	1.4	100%
1984	50	628	1155	1192	762	274	105	61	4227
%	1.2	14.9	27.3	28.2	18	6.5	2.5	1.4	100%
1985	36	634	1089	1030	661	256	102	65	3873
%	.9	16.4	28.4	26.5	17	6.6	2.6	1.6	100%*

*1985 figures reflect the transformation of UNIDO, formerly a component of the U.N. group, into a specialized agency. The consequent separation of the UNIDO staff resulted in the reduction of overall U.N. staff figures by approximately 350 (mostly at the P-4 and P-5 levels). 1985 staff figures, therefore, are somewhat misleading in any discussion of "grade creep," and for that reason, 1984 figures have been used for purposes of comparison.

age fixed at 60 years. Non-career appointments, variously called fixed-term, short-term, or temporary appointments, may be granted for a period not exceeding five years. The fixed-term contract does not carry a guarantee of renewal or of conversion to any other type of appointment. Nevertheless, fixed-term contracts are routinely rolled over several times, and even more routinely converted into probationary contracts and then into career appointments.

Table II-a

Percentage Change in Grade Distribution (1970–1984)

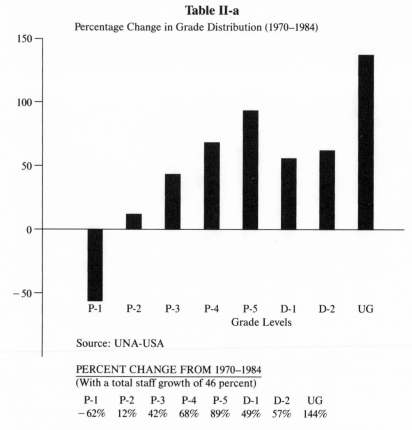

Source: UNA-USA

PERCENT CHANGE FROM 1970–1984
(With a total staff growth of 46 percent)

P-1	P-2	P-3	P-4	P-5	D-1	D-2	UG
−62%	12%	42%	68%	89%	49%	57%	144%

Pay, Pensions, and the ICSC

Salaries

Much of member states' criticism in recent years has focused on the level of U.N. staff pay and benefits. While practices relating to the determination of salaries and pensions certainly deserve closer scrutiny, governmental preoccupation with these questions should not be allowed to divert attention away from issues—such as recruitment and staff management—that are more closely linked to U.N. efficiency and performance.

The most frequently voiced complaints about U.N. salaries are that they are too high and are tax free. In fact, there seems to be little basis for either contention. The base pay of the U.N. staff and its agencies

Table II-b

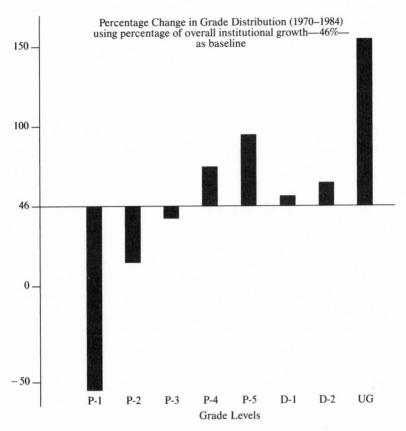

Percentage Change in Grade Distribution (1970–1984)
using percentage of overall institutional growth—46%—
as baseline

is fixed by the General Assembly. U.N. net salaries at the professional levels are compared with the net salaries of the U.S. Civil Service, referred to as the "comparator" service.[12] The ratios resulting from this comparison reveal the extent to which U.N. salaries are higher than those of the U.S. Civil Service, taken as 100. (Salaries for the General Service staff, recruited locally, are determined by the "best prevailing local rates"—that is, the most favorable conditions of employment in the locality of the office concerned.) The fundamental rationale for the level of U.N. professional salaries is rooted in the Noblemaire Principle, which dates from the League of Nations. According to this principle, in order to recruit the most highly qualified international civil servants, an international organization must be willing to pay at least as much as the highest-paying national civil

Table III

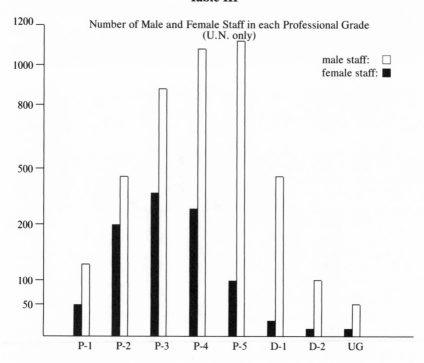

Number of Male and Female Staff in each Professional Grade
(U.N. only)

male staff: ☐
female staff: ■

Grade Level

Source: ACC/1985/Per/R.34
Adapted from Tables 7 & 8

service,[13] which, since the earliest days of the U.N., has been the United States Civil Service.

A post-adjustment is added to (or occasionally subtracted from) base U.N. salary to equalize purchasing power in all duty stations. The cost of living in New York is used as the base for determining the relevant post-adjustment in every other duty station.[14] The base salary and post-adjustment are interdependent; at the U.N., the term "salary" means base salary *plus* post-adjustment.

A slight salary advantage, known as the "margin," is considered necessary to account for certain factors unique to the international civil service. Among these factors are: the limited prospects of promotion to the highest levels in an international civil service, and the additional expenses incurred and sacrifices made by over 90 percent of the U.N. professional staff as a result of their expatriate status. An additional justification for the margin came with recognition that a reasonable premium over the salaries of the highest-paying national civil service might be a means of attracting and retaining the citizens of that particular country. No clear rationale has yet been offered for the way in which the precise amounts assigned to these rather qualitative factors are calculated. The cost-of-living differential between Washington, D.C., home of the main body of the U.S. Civil Service, and New York, is figured into the margin as well and is a more readily quantifiable factor.[15]

Reacting to governmental pressures to keep U.N. salaries more in line with the Noblemaire formulation, the 40th General Assembly in 1985 approved a range of 10–20 percent, with a desirable midpoint of 15 percent, for the margin between net remuneration of officials in the professional and higher categories of the U.N. in New York and officials in comparable positions in the U.S. Federal Civil Service. As a consequence, U.N. New York salaries are now frozen at their current levels until the margin itself falls, due to rising U.S. salaries, from its current level of 20 percent to the preferred level of 15 percent.[16] In fact, the gap has already begun to narrow as a result of a 3 percent pay increase granted to U.S. employees this year.

It is incorrect to say, as is sometimes alleged, that U.N. personnel are not taxed. Although, in general, the salaries of U.N. employees are not taxed directly by their home governments, they *are* taxed indirectly through a staff assessment system, which has as its object the uniform treatment of all U.N. employees. The United Nations passes on the proceeds from these "taxes" to each staff member's home government. Under the Noblemaire Principle, U.S. Civil Service salaries—net after taxes—are compared to U.N. salaries after the application of staff assessment—a form of internal taxation—at the rate applicable to a staff member with a dependent spouse.[17] Included in this amount is the post-adjustment (which is not taxed by the staff assessment); this too is calculated at the rate applicable to a staff member with a dependent spouse.

Nor is U.N. pay out of line with the salaries paid by the major Washington-based international organizations. In fact, the salaries paid by the International Monetary Fund and the World Bank are, in essence, tax free and significantly higher than those of the U.N. at all but the lowest level (see Table IV).[18]

In light of the foregoing, it would appear that the level of U.N. salaries per se is not a basis for concern. However, the method for

Table IV

Comparison of Compensation: U.N., U.S., and Various International Organizations at Midpoint of Grade Level

	United Nations	Grade Equivalency	OAS	Grade Equivalency	IMF	Grade Equivalency	World Bank	Grade Equivalency	United States
P1	$28,568	J	$26,181	E	$28,220	17	$27,290	GS-9	$21,463.50
P2	35,196	K	31,357.50	G	42,710	22	42,570	GS-11 GS-12	25,474.50
P3	43,553	L	37,295.50	H	50,715	23	51,225	GS-12 GS-13	30,075.50 35,384
P4	50,728	M	44,067.50	I	59,135	24	59,685	GS-13 GS-14	35,384 40,337.50
P5	58,468	N	50,517	J	68,600	26	69,215	GS-15 SES-2 SES-4	46,725.50 49,907 53,359
D1	63,085	P	54,556.50	K	76,375	27	74,705	GS-16 SES-1 SES-4 SES-5	49,778.50 48,318 53,359 54,479
D2	69,023	Q	57,060.50	L	80,595	27	80,595	GS-17 GS-18 SES-4 SES-5 SES-6	52,295* 52,295* 53,359 54,479 55,645

Net for single with no dependents after staff assessment plus post-adjustment of 12 months at class 7/ + 2 (multiplier 93) effective January 1, 1985

Net plus 12.2 COLA at midpoint effective January 1, 1986

Net at midpoint effective May 1, 1985

Net at midpoint effective October 1, 1985

Based on published after-tax salary rates effective January 1, 1984 & January 1, 1985 (includes bonuses and special awards where applicable)

*Limited to the ceiling on the rates of pay under the General Schedule determining U.N. salary levels does raise significant questions. For example, a salary-only comparison of the U.S. Civil Service in Washington and U.N. New York gives an incomplete picture at best. Such a comparison completely ignores the relative value of the benefits—health and life insurance, annual leave, dependents' allowance, etc.—available to each service and in most cases more generous to U.N. employees than to their U.S. counterparts.

On the other hand, the U.S. civil servant may take a number of deductions from his taxable income that are not available to the U.N. civil servant. In addition, a small percentage of U.S. civil servants—principally medical staff and engineers—are paid according to a special rate program that provides higher salaries than is provided by the General Schedule scale—the basis for comparison with U.N. salaries. The special rate program, which allows the U.S. government to compete more favorably with private sector employers for individuals who are highly skilled in "shortage" occupations, was a response to the large gap between the salaries suggested by the United States Pay Comparability Act and the General Schedule.[19]

Over 90 percent of the U.N. professional staff receive expatriate entitlements on an as-needed basis, certain of which may contribute to discretionary income. These entitlements[20] are not included in the calculation of net U.N. salary figures. In recent years the General Assembly has shown some interest in calculating the margin between U.N. and U.S. salaries on the basis of a comparison of total compensation, including the non-expatriate benefits available to each service.[21] Some member states have argued that U.N. expatriate entitlements should be included in the calculation of the margin as well.

Such a comparison—which has yet to be endorsed by the General Assembly—raises significant problems of implementation because expatriate service in a national civil service is very different from expatriate service in an international civil service.[22] Nevertheless, if it were possible to make a comparison that took into account expatriate elements of U.N. remuneration, it would reveal that over 90 percent of U.N. professional employees are compensated *twice* for some of their expatriate costs. This results from the combination of expatriate allowances and the margin itself, whose main justification is to provide for the additional expenses incurred by U.N. staff living away from home.

There is some question as to whether salaries of the United States Federal Civil Service continue to be the appropriate measure for determining U.N. remuneration. While U.S. gross salaries remain the world's highest, they are not subject to cost-of-living supplements—as are most national civil services—with the result that U.S. employees living in New York (over 32,000) may in fact bring home considerably less than the employees of other governments serving in New York.

A possible alternative to the present emphasis on U.S. Civil Service salaries at the professional levels and above at the U.N. would establish pay levels on the basis of a comparison with the salary scales of a basket of highly paid permanent missions in New York. Such a comparison, which has been used in the past to determine ASG/USG salaries,[23] would eliminate any distortions caused by the U.N.'s dependence on the system followed by the U.S. Federal Civil Service.

Pensions

The U.N. retirement plan, like the Organization's salary system, has frequently been criticized as being excessively generous. In this case, there may have been some basis for concern.

As of January 1986, pensions paid to 20-year veterans of the U.N. service exceeded pensions paid to 20-year veterans of the U.S. Civil Service by 20 to 30 percent, depending on rank. The annual pensions for the U.N. retiree at that time were $22,547 at the P-3 level, $30,414 at the P-5 level, and $33,495 at the D-2 level.

The rare U.N. pensioner with 35 years of service—the maximum number of years of credible service—received a retirement income which was 95 to 105 percent of that received by a U.S. civil servant with 40 years of service. This amounted, as of January 1986, to a maximum annual pension of $41,207 at the P-3 level, $55,584 at the P-5 level, and $61,215 at the D-2 level (see Annex I).

The U.N. pension plan is based on providing benefits that are reasonable in relation to the emoluments of the staff, which are determined on the basis of the Noblemaire Principle. In many ways the pension systems of the U.N. and the U.S. Federal Service—if not the benefits—are nearly identical.[24] The rate of accumulation of pension entitlement per year of contributory service, for example, is now the same under the two pension systems.[25] In addition, pensions are calculated in an almost identical fashion under both systems.

There are marked differences between the two systems, however, in the definitions and methods used for the determination of pensionable remuneration.[26] As a consequence of these differences, and despite the precepts of the Noblemaire Principle, the U.N. system of pensionable remuneration had led to a situation where U.N. pensions were significantly higher than those of the comparator.

The U.N. has changed its methods of determining pensionable remuneration several times in an effort to reduce the levels of pensions.[27] The scale of pensionable remuneration has been reduced twice in recent years, on 1 January 1985 and on 1 April 1987. The amount of the reductions ranged from 1.3 percent at the P-1 level to 24.2 percent at the USG level. The methodology applied to determine the latest scale of pensionable remuneration used as its starting point a comparison of U.N./New York and United States Civil Service net remuneration. The established margin range for U.N. net remuneration of between 10 and 20 percent above United States net remuneration therefore serves as a constraint on the level of U.N. pensionable remuneration. The extension of a margin to pensionable remuneration has been justified by a number of considerations, including the higher average age at recruitment, shorter careers, more limited opportunity to rise to the highest levels in the U.N. as well as the existence of a mandatory age of separation of 60 in the U.N. as against no mandatory retirement age for U.S. civil servants.

International Civil Service Commission

The International Civil Service Commission (ICSC) was established by the General Assembly in 1974 to regulate and coordinate the United Nations common system of salaries, allowances, and other conditions of service. The United Nations common system is a loose confederation joining the U.N., its specialized agencies (except for the IMF and the World Bank system), and other major U.N. programs and bodies for the purpose both of avoiding disparities in the terms and conditions of employment and of discouraging competition in recruitment. The goal of the common system is the development of a unified and coordinated international civil service with related personnel policies and practices through the application of common personnel standards, methods, and arrangements. Because of the independent nature of the organs of the system, the ICSC plays a largely advisory, rather than managerial, role in this process.[28] The Commission is responsible as a body to the General Assembly, to which it submits an annual report.

From the Commission's inception, its effectiveness in contributing to the development of policy on personnel issues has been limited by a number of factors. According to the Statute of the ICSC, the Commission's 15 members must be "individuals of recognized competence who have had experience of executive responsibility in public administration or related fields, particularly in personnel management.[29] Yet a notable lack of such qualifications among the Commissioners is primarily to blame for the Commission's ineffectuality. The standard of technical competence among Commissioners was higher in the ICSC's early years; more recently, however, members have been drawn primarily from their countries' foreign services, many after serving in the government's delegation to the U.N.

The tendency of the General Assembly to appoint non-experts to the Commission seems to be tied in part to the fact that member states have played too dominant a role in the selection process. The ICSC Statute states that all 15 members—including the Chairman and Vice-Chairman, the only full-time members of the ICSC—are to be chosen by the General Assembly from a list of candidates prepared by the Secretary-General "after appropriate consultations with member states, with the executive heads of other organizations, and with staff representatives."[30]

In recent years, however, the virtual exclusion of the staff and organizations from the consulting process—in direct contravention of the ICSC Statute—has resulted in a far less balanced approach to candidate selection. All of the appointments have been the candidates of member states and have tended to be selected for reasons other than their expertise. Certain of these states, aware of the key role that the ICSC plays in the determination of U.N. expenditures—nearly 80 percent of the Organization's budget goes toward staff salaries and benefits whose levels are greatly influenced by the ICSC—tend to favor candidates who share their budgetary viewpoint regardless of their expertise in the field of personnel management and public administration.

At the same time, the ICSC's potential contribution to matters other than budget—recruitment, advancement, and career development—is not given a high priority by member states when proposing candidates for the ICSC. As a result of the low visibility of personnel issues generally, appointments to the Commission are often doled out to trusted government employees as a reward for loyal service—in other fields of endeavor.

A Commission whose membership consists almost entirely of retired or still-active government officials is necessarily limited in its ability to carry out its mandate. Not only does a Commission so composed often lack expertise and demonstrated skill in modern techniques of personnel management and public administration, it also fails to supply the continuing flow of new ideas and approaches to U.N. personnel issues that was foreseen when the Commission was established. At the same time, a longstanding preoccupation with issues related to pay and benefits—to some degree reflecting the priority given them by member states—has caused the ICSC to pay inadequate attention to other personnel matters.

Another concern stems from the fact that the decisions and recommendations made by the Commission are largely based on positions that are developed by its own secretariat. Since the Commission staff are members of the common system and therefore have the same salary system and set of allowances as other members of the U.N. system, there is at least the potential for some conflict of interest on matters relating to salaries and allowances. The potential for this conflict grows as the ICSC staff is allowed to become more "permanent." A possible alternative to the present system involves the creation of a separate ICSC secretariat with its own system of salaries and allowances. However, such an alternative, although providing greater assurance of staff independence, would be costly and bureaucratically complex. Another alternative involves building a "temporary" character into ICSC staff positions—something that would not only reduce the self-interest factor in the discussions of salary but would also provide the opportunity for bringing in outside experts from government, the private sector, and academia on a short-term basis at the staff level.

Recommendations

1. The ICSC should study the possibility of determining the salary levels of U.N. employees at the professional levels and above based on a basket of average salary rates payable to national civil servants at the ten highest-paid permanent missions in New York.

2. The U.N. should institute a special rate program for "shortage" occupations, similar to that which exists in the U.S. Civil Service, to ensure that recruitment and retention of highly skilled personnel is brought into acceptable range.

3. The General Assembly should adopt the recent recommendations of the ICSC requiring U.N. pensions not to exceed pensions paid to the U.S. Civil Service by a range of more than 10 to 20 percent, with a desirable midpoint of 15 percent.

4. No member state should be permitted to require its citizens in United Nations service to give up any part of their salaries to their government.

5. The selection process for ICSC members should be changed by

amending Article 4(1) of the ICSC Statute so that 50 percent of the membership of the Commission will be selected by the General Assembly on the basis of recommendations by member states; 25 percent on the basis of recommendations by staff representatives; and 25 percent on the basis of recommendations by executive heads of other organizations.

6. The Chairman and Vice-Chairman of the Commission should be appointed directly by the Secretary-General. This would require the amendment of Articles 2(2) and 4(1) of the ICSC Statute.

7. Requirements for membership on the Commission should be changed by amending Article 3(1) of the Statute. The members of the Commission should be appointed in their personal capacity as individuals of recognized competence (a) who have had substantial experience of executive responsibility in administration in the public or private sectors, particularly in the area of personnel management, or (b) who are recognized scholars in the field of administration and pesonnel management.

8. The staff of the ICSC should be recruited from outside the U.N. system on the basis of renewable, fixed-term contracts, or on secondment from the personnel offices of national governments, private firms, universities, or other organizations. Service on the ICSC staff, whether by fixed-term contract or by secondment, should not exceed a total of five years.

Main Personnel Policy Review

Such questions as the role and composition of the ICSC and appropriate levels for pay and pensions are of the most immediate concern to many governments because they can strongly influence the level of the U.N.'s costs. On the other hand, the long-term ability of the U.N. to serve the pressing needs of the world community hinges more directly on such matters as the structure, management, and operations of the personnel system itself. In fact, serious and growing shortcomings in these areas of the personnel system have created a situation that is widely criticized by member governments and even inspires misgivings among the staff itself. At the heart of this situation are the following basic problems:

• the absence of objective, uniform criteria guiding recruitment and management (promotion, termination, training, rotation, etc.) of U.N. employees

• the absence of an administrative environment that is conducive to the application of such criteria

• the lack of clarity about the mission of the Office of Personnel Services (OPS) and too little disposition on the part of the U.N.'s top leadership to ensure that OPS's function is clarified and fulfilled

• the tendency by the member states to give the Secretariat inappropriate and unproductive tasks to fulfill.

This situation has caused an erosion in the collective self-image of the U.N. staff and in the reputation enjoyed by the U.N. Secretariat among numerous member governments and sections of the international press and public as well. Among the consequences of the shortcomings listed above are:

• the considerable number of staff who are not well qualified for the positions they hold or the grade levels at which they are employed. (An advanced university degree for all entering professionals is a "policy objective" of OPS, but the available data reveals that more than half lack such a degree, while 12.5 percent of those at the Under-Secretary or Assistant Secretary-General level do not have Bachelor's degrees.)

• the large number of staff in management positions, including many at the most senior levels, who lack management skills, training, or previous management experience

• the extreme unevenness in the quality of the "outputs" of individual U.N. offices

• the disproportionately small number of women employed in the professional ranks and the extremely low representation of women at the senior levels

• the tendency for political considerations to exert a strong influence on recruitment at the level of P-3 and above

• the insufficient emphasis on fairness and objective, merit-based considerations in some promotions

• the frequent disregard for maintaining minimal standards of efficiency and competence, particularly after an employee has received a permanent contract

• the near impossibility of terminating an employee's service on the basis of unsatisfactory performance

• the generally low morale among the staff, reflecting a feeling that promotion opportunities are not merit-based, and frustration over poor supervision and badly conceived work assignments—a situation that causes some of the U.N.'s most talented employees to leave its service.

This chapter examines in greater detail three of the four areas of concern mentioned above: lack of objective criteria for recruitment and staff management, lack of structures and processes for ensuring that they are applied, and uncertainty regarding the mission of the Office of Personnel Services itself. The fourth issue—the absence of well-defined work assignments—raises basic questions about the way member states establish goals and is addressed in the chapter on U.N. planning, programming, budgeting, and evaluation.

Recruitment

There are effectively two formal recruitment procedures for U.N. professional staff. One, for junior staff, is widely used, while the other, for employees entering at the P-3 level and above, is often disregarded in practive.

Competitive Examinations. The system in place for junior staff (P-1 and P-2 grades) utilizes internal and external competitive examinations for all language posts or posts subject to geographical distribution, which are the majority of career-path positions. Internal examinations are conducted annually in one or more of the U.N.'s 14 occupational groups. These standardized written tests, which contain analytical and essay sections as well as sections specific to the occupational group's skills, are the only avenue through which individuals in the U.N.'s general sevice category can advance to the professional service.[31] In 1985, 534 candidates took the G-to-P examination, and 20 of these (3.7 percent) were promoted. Since they were instituted in 1979, the internal examinations for G-to-P promotion have generally raised the quality of employees entering professional grades through internal promotion.

External examinations, also conducted annually and by occupational group, are held in countries whose nationals are underrepresented in the Secretriat. In 1985, 505 candidates took the external examination, and 51 (10 percent) of these were recruited by the U.N. Like the internal G-to-P test, the national competitive examinations have generally improved the caliber of entering U.N. professionals since their institution in 1981. They have also been an effective means of increasing the percentage of new employees from countries with traditionally low levels of representation on the staff, *without* compromising selection standards.

The success of the external exams in identifying candidates for recruitment indicates that they might be equally useful in the recruitment of candidates at higher levels. An occupation-based exam could be offered to candidates for posts at the P-3 and P-4 level as a means of "weeding out" candidates without the requisite skills for the posts. Obviously, the degree of sophistication and skill required for positions at these levels could not be ascertained conclusively through a basic knowledge test, but it would be a useful first step.

Unfortunately, the competitive exams have not proven an effective mechanism for improving the external recruitment of women. In fact, recruitment of women at the P-1 and P-2 levels has fallen off sharply relative to the recruitment of men since the introduction of competitive examinations at these levels. This is not the result of poor performance on the examinations; indeed, women tend to score as well, if not better, on the tests than male candidates. The problem is that in many parts of the world women are far more likely to present themselves as candidates when they are actively sought out for recruitment than to seek employment by taking a competitive exam. In the case of the G-to-P exam—where identification of women candidates is not an issue—promotion of women to the professional level has been more success-ful.

Finally, despite the obvious benefits of the competitive examination, its actual contribution to the fairness and efficiency of U.N. recruit-ment declines each year as the number of entry posts as a percentage of total positions steadily falls. For example, in the period 1980–81 (when the examination system was implemented) to the 1986–87 biennium, the total percentage of P-1/P-2 posts dropped from 14.7 percent to 13.6 percent.[32]

Formal Recruitment Procedures. At the middle and senior levels—P-3, 4, 5, and D-1—a lengthy, formal set of procedures for recruitment is in place: A job description is prepared by the department where the opening occurs; a vacancy announcement is produced and circulated by the Office of Personnel Services (OPS), which also selects candi-dates from its internal and external rosters who fit the job description, screens the names, and forewards them to the department; and the department then interviews, evaluates, and selects a candidate from among these names as well as those submitted by the U.N. agencies and the governments of member countries. If the candidate is from the outside, the department's selection is reviewed by one of the selection bodies, whose recommendation is submitted for final decision by the Secretary-General. The Appointment and Promotion Board is the reviewing body for candidates at the P-5 and D-1 level; the Appointment and Promotion Committee conducts the review of candidates at the P-3 and P-4 level.[33]

Flaws in the Process. In reality, recruitment varies greatly, depending upon the manager whose section or unit is hiring a new officer, and often bears little resemblance to the seemingly open and rigorous process described above. This is because the formal system is flawed in such fundamental respects that there is a general tendency to circumvent it through the use of ad hoc measures, which often rely heavily on personal contacts.

The most serious of these flaws is the fact that the U.N. has no common, objective, job-specific standards to guide recruitment at the P-3/P-4 level or the more managerial P-5/D-1 level, with the result that the Organization inevitably relies upon haphazard, subjective, highly personalized processes. The absence of such standards has helped create a situation in which the OPS makes only a desultory and superficial contribution to the recruitment process. For example, although OPS maintains rosters of individuals seeking recruitment or (internal) advancement, they are not classified by educational background, work experience, occupational skills, or other relevant categories and tend to be regarded as "dead lists" that are rarely considered in candidate selection. Similarly, without concrete criteria to adhere to, OPS's screening of applications submitted by the entire range of recruitment sources—including missions and foreign ministries—varies with the quality of the recruitment officer, the degree of pressure exerted on behalf of a candidate, etc., and the degree of objectivity he can bring to the list.

Even if such criteria did exist, there would have to be a way to ensure they were being applied. Currently, OPS and the appointment and promotion machinery lack both the credibility and the effective authority to oversee recruitment on behalf of the Organization as a whole.

Among the reasons for this are the following:

• OPS's attempts to implement the General Assembly's policy instructions—particularly on equitable geographical distribution—are often rigid and unresponsive to the needs of a department's particular mission.

• OPS's own staff lacks both professional training in the personnel area and grounding in the specific skills required by the U.N.'s 14 occupational groups.

• OPS has very little effective authority to enforce its actions or policies when they are challenged by other areas of U.N. management, the staff, or interested external parties and rarely exercises what little authority it has.

• Often individuals who sit on the appointment and promotion boards are not competent to make judgments about candidates' technical proficiency and, in some cases, managerial capabilities as well. This machinery is often subject to the same political pressures as the other recruitment decision—making bodies, which, in principle, it should counterbalance.

A "Counter System." For these reasons, and because—as is the case in many large organizations—operational managers are reluctant to share recruitment decisions with personnel managers, the former are inclined to minimize OPS's involvement in the hiring process. As a result, a kind of "counter system" of recruitment has evolved, which, while formally incorporating the steps outlined above, does so primarily as a means of ratifying recruitment decisions already made by the operational managers themselves. Thus, sometimes a manager will select a candidate before a vacancy announcement is circulated. On other occasions the position will be filled by internal transfer arranged between two departments, and OPS will be requested not to circulate a vacancy announcement at all. When hiring is done externally, a common method for circumventing the formal process is to recruit an individual by offering a series of three-month contracts, tailoring a job description to his particular characteristics, and then presenting him as the front-running candidate after he is already effectively installed in the position.

This "counter system," while sometimes enabling enterprising managers to recruit better-qualified people more quickly, has flaws of its own. Like the formal system, it lacks a set of common recruitment criteria and the means of applying them objectively, and it produces its own share of poorly qualified employees. It also depends too heavily on each manager's ability to choose his staff wisely, and often means that his selection is limited to people he already knows personally. In any event, the manipulation or bypassing of the vacancy announcement process greatly limits the pool of qualified candidates—both within and outside the Organization and, consequently, the possibility that the best-suited person will be found. This approach to recruitment often lowers staff morale, since in addition to denying opportunities for career advancement, it fosters the impression that career prospects depend upon personal contacts, patronage, and one's status with various regional or national interest groups within the Secretariat. Finally, the informality of this approach, the highly personalized way in which decisions are made, and the absence of any demonstrably merit-based system of recruitment increases the U.N.'s vulnerability to political pressures from a variety of sources.

Staff Management

As an influence upon staff efficiency, the dynamic side of workforce mangement—accountability and quality control, mobility, career development, the shaping of staff-management relations, and the design of an appropriate grade structure—is second in importance only to recruitment itself.

Evaluations. The purpose of a system of personnel evaluation is threefold: to measure employee performance, to identify candidates for promotion, and to identify nonperformers who may be candidates for termination. At the U.N., evaluations are made of every employee regardless of contract type at three-year intervals. Yet the U.N.'s performance evaluation process, although intended to be the backbone of its quality-control system, is too weak to perform any useful function at all.

The problems begin with the report's design, which tends to elicit highly subjective appraisals or observations of a very general character, asking supervisors to rate employees from A to E in such areas as professional competence, quality of work accomplished, planning and organization of work, etc. Indeed, the only part of the report that is explicitly task-related is the section completed by the employee himself. Since there is no "control" dimension, i.e., comparison of expected achievements against actual achievements, virtually every negative comment is open to challenge.

Compounding the design flaw is the fact that employees dissatisfied with their performance reports can initiate a rebuttal procedure that is lengthy, time-consuming, places the onus of justification on the supervisor rather than the employee, and usually *overturns* the supervisor's recommendations. Not surprisingly, most managers attempt to avoid the rebuttal process by giving high marks irrespective of performance. The result is a severe case of ratings inflation, with over 90 percent of the staff consistently in the "A" category. Since it generally requires two negative evaluations, and thus six years, before action can be taken, managers faced with poor performers tend to overrate them and then seek their transfer to another department.

Promotions. Promotions also suffer from a lack of objective criteria. This is in part because there is no systematic means for ensuring that equally qualified people fill the same or comparable posts within the various occupational groups. In fact, there are no clear across-the-board criteria for advancement in the professional grades, and whether promotions are granted on a rigorous or open-handed basis depends not only on the individual supervisor but on the presence or absence of powerful patrons elsewhere in the Organization or in the mission community. Further aggravating the weaknesses of the U.N.'s promotion procedure is the fact that appointment and promotion bodies for the professional service are not composed along occupational lines and are not competent to make judgments about a candidate's technical proficiency.

Terminations. Terminations are virtually nonexistent once an employee has been granted a permanent contract—a process that can take as little as two years and seldom more than five. Theoretically, managers have several opportunities to use the threat of termination during the period prior to the award of a permanent contract, either by refusing to recommend an extension of a fixed-term contract or by blocking its conversion to probationary status (a preliminary to permanent status). Yet the onus of proof is always on the manager, and the process is so lengthy and cumbersome that few utilize it. Of course, terminations are problematic in any organization, not just the U.N. For example, the U.S. Civil Service has a firing rate of .0065 percent.[34] Still, the issues of accountability and quality control cannot be ignored much longer by the U.N.

Internal Recourse Procedures. There are three categories of recourse procedures open to staff members in the event of an alleged violation of the terms of appointment. The first category provides an informal means of resolving problems through one of the nine "Panels on Discrimination and Other Grievances" that have been established throughout the U.N. system.[35] The functions of the three-to-five member panels are chiefly conciliatory: Members investigate allegations by the staff of unfair or discriminatory treatment and attempt to mediate between the concerned parties or, if this proves impossible, recommend appropriate action to the Assistant Secretary-General for Personnel Services. Despite some criticisms about their efficiency and objectivity, the grievance panels have reached a settlement in a fairly large number of cases.[36]

The second category consists of a number of special procedures to be used in very narrowly defined situations, such as: appeal from decisions of organs in the United Nations Joint Staff Pension Fund (UNJSPF), appeal in cases of service-incurred injury or illness and loss or damage of personal effects, appeal in matters involving sick leave, and the classification of posts, rebuttal of performance evaluation reports, and appeal in matters involving promotions and competitive examinations for promotion to the professional category. In each case the appeal is handled by the relevant board or committee. For example, appeals in cases of service-incurred injury or illness are handled by an Advisory Board on Compensation Claims (ABCC) and appeals in matters involving the classification of posts involve recourse to a Secretariat-wide Classification Appeals and Review Committee. Generally in all such cases, the prescribed procedures must be followed before the matter can be considered under any of the general review procedures.

In the third category of grievance procedures are the various general review procedures that may be invoked in all matters involving administrative measures or decisions. To initiate these procedures requires registering an appeal with the appropriate Joint Appeals Board (JAB). The JABs—established in New York, Nairobi, London, and Geneva— serve an advisory function only, since their recommendations are subject to the final decision of the Secretary-General. The work of the JABs involves many stages and is ponderous, expensive, and subject to excessive delays. For example, each case brought before the JAB in New York takes about two years to complete, with the result that the JAB secretariat in New York can dispose of only about 27 cases per year at an average cost to the Organization of $24,000 per case. The number of appeals submitted to the Board clearly exceeds its capabilities, resulting in a substantial increase in the case backlog. As of March 31, 1986, there were 94 cases pending before the New York JAB, representing a potential cost of over $2,200,000.

Once a Board has submitted its report to the Secretary-General for his decision, the staff member has the right to appeal that decision to the United Nations Administrative Tribunal (UNAT). The decisions of the UNAT, a judicial body established by the General Assembly in 1949, are final, binding on the Secretary-General as well as on the applicant, and subject to review, only in extraordinary cases, by the International Court of Justice.

In general, staff members do not require legal assistance in pursuing the informal or special recourse procedures. However, staff may always be represented before the JAB by another member of the Secretariat; and in matters before the UNAT and the ICJ, they have the further option of retaining outside counsel. The United Nations is generally responsible for meeting legal costs.

Clearly, the right of employees to appeal unfair or discriminatory treatment by the Organization is unassailable. However, in recent years staff members have tended to exercise this right in an immoderate way—in one instance, an employee submitted 20 complaints against administrative decisions.[37] The proliferation of claims may be due in part to the ease with which the process may be triggered and to the fact that none of the procedures detailed above requires a fee to initiate or impose penalties for frivolous claims.

The present multilayered approach to the administration of justice is sluggish and unwieldly. Appeals may take months or even years to process. Staff members are permitted to spend valuable work hours in the counseling process and in the preparation of their claims—an obvious hindrance to the functioning of the Organization. A more efficient and streamlined approach might limit the process to two stages: an informal conciliation effort through the Grievance Panels and binding adjudication by a Claims Tribunal.

Staff Mobility. Another area of workforce management that is obviously critical for an international organization is staff mobility. The U.N. Staff Regulations authorize the Secretary-General to assign staff to "any of the activities or offices of the United Nations" as the Organization's needs require.[38] Rotation could involve movement between posts, organizational units, occupational groups, duty stations, or U.N. agencies and should be integrated with opportunities for career development and, for hardship posts, with a system of incentives.

In fact there has been little effort to associate advancement opportunities or other incentives with staff mobility, and staff members are often reluctant to accept a new posting out of fear that a move away from one of the headquarters' areas will cause them to be overlooked for advancement. In addition to the complications that a rotation system with postings in unfamiliar, far-off countries might create for family reasons, the open-ended aspect of such postings leads staff to fear a permanent exile in these countries. Consequently, management requests for staff relocation are often strenuously resisted. Since relocation is effectively voluntary, such staff mobility as exists at the U.N. is very haphazard and sometimes leaves important but unpopular posts understaffed.

Staff-Management Relations. Another essential ingredient of workforce management is an appropriate system of distributing powers and responsibilities between staff and management. Currently, the staff play a major role in determining a large number of key administrative policy matters. This is partly because of staff representation—in equal numbers with management—on virtually all advisory bodies having to do with personnel issues, and partly because the representatives of the various staff associations have considerable access to and influence with the leadership of the Secretariat. Although there is clearly a need for the staff to be heard fully and fairly on matters affecting the terms of their service at the U.N., the staff's current capacity—both formally and informally—to assume some of the prerogatives and responsibilities of the Secretary-General does not seem in the best interests of the Organization as a whole and weakens the accountability of the Secretary-General to member states.

Recent Attempts at Reform. A significant step toward the correction of many personnel problems discussed in this paper was taken recently by the Office of Personnel Services in the form of a sweeping proposal for a new career development policy.[39] Under the OPS plan, posts would be classified in 14 occupational groups, movements between groups would be mapped along well-defined career paths, both recruitment and promotion would be organized along occupational lines, and the U.N. would develop a more performance-based evaluation system, a more systematic approach to assignment and rotation, and an occupational group-based training program.

Implementation of the OPS plan, however, has been extremely slow. Since changes contemplated in the plan would alter practices and power relationships ingrained in the Secretariat, a strong push from the leadership is needed. This has not occurred. Another impediment is the fact that the member states themselves, although sanctioning the plan in principle, have yet to support certain key elements in practice. For example, an occupational group-based recruitment and promotion system would require governments to relinquish their heavy involvement in these areas—something they appear reluctant to do. Also, while the ideas incorporated in the plan represent an important beginning, they tend to be simple statements of goals with no clear indication of how they could be achieved in terms of structural and procedural changes.

Recommendations

1. No posts, offices, or divisions should be considered as the domain of particular member states or groups of member states.
2. Recruitment should be conducted by occupational group.

3. Competitive examinations should be conducted for all recruitment at P-1, P-2, P-3, and P-4 levels. At the P-3 and P-4 level, the exams will serve a "weeding-out" function, as a means of identifying candidates with the basic competence required for the post.

4. Writing tests, occupation-based oral examinations, and more intensive interviews should be conducted for recruitment at the P-5 and D-1 levels.

5. To accelerate recruitment from underrepresented areas of the globe, rosters should be maintained of all candidates who place in the top 15 percent on the national competitive examinations for U.N. service.

6. No more than 50 percent of those recruited for U.N. service from any single country should serve on the basis of secondment.[40]

7. No country should be permitted to limit U.N. recruitment of its nationals to a prescribed list of candidates.

8. To achieve a greater degree of uniformity in the academic and vocational standards for recruitment and advancement within occupational groups, a unit within OPS should conduct an investigation of the major university and professional training schools within each region so as to determine the relative value of their degrees.

9. The present appointment and promotion machinery at the P-3 and P-4 level should be replaced by two or three bodies whose composition would reflect the distribution of occupational groups in the Secretariat. Two-thirds of the membership of these bodies would be appointed by the Secretary-General, and one-third would be appointed by the Secretary-General on the recommendation of the staff. Appointments should be made with some consideration of geographical distribution.

10. The present appointment and promotion machinery at the P-5 and D-1 level should be replaced by a single board composed of individuals competent to judge managerial skills as well as the technical skills required by the U.N.'s chief occupational groups. Two-thirds of the membership of this body would be appointed by the Secretary-General, and one-third would be appointed by the Secretary-General on the recommendation of the staff. A minority of the members (possibly 20 percent) would be individuals from outside the U.N. with considerable experience in one of the relevant occupations. Appointments would be made with some consideration of geographical distribution.

11. A high-level, independent advisory panel should be established, composed of persons from outside the U.N. with expertise in each

of the U.N.'s occupational areas. Members, who would be appointed by the Secretary-General, might include university heads, foundation heads, former cabinet members, and others of similar stature. For each appointment at the D-2 level and above, the Secretary-General would choose from the panel four or five individuals with appropriate background to serve as a "search and review" committee to provide him with a short list of candidates, both internal and external, for the vacant position.

12. The Secretary-General should create a rated, occupation-based roster system for career development and promotions at P-3, P-4, P-5, and D-1 levels.

13. No "permanent" contracts should be granted before six years.

14. All professional employees should be evaluated annually.

15. Two successive negative ratings should result in a dismissal.

16. The current evaluation form should be replaced with one that measures achievement of specific tasks previously defined and jointly agreed upon by supervisor and employee. A staff member's overall performance should be ranked in one of three broad categories: exceptional (no more than 10 percent could fall into this category), adequate, and substandard.

17. The evaluation "rebuttal" procedure should be replaced by a simple "right of review."

18. The Organization should not automatically assume the legal costs of recourse procedures initiated by staff members. Compensation should be awarded only in the event the applicant's claims are judged to have merit.

19. The Secretary-General should propose, in consultation with the staff associations, a streamlined and simplified procedure for the administration of justice at the U.N.

20. OPS should establish a contract-based system of rotation for professionals, integrated with career development plans. The length of the rotation might vary according to post and occupation. For example, in order to strengthen their independence, managers in the administrative services might be rotated relatively frequently. The duration of the rotation should be stated at the outset.

21. It should be part of the OPS mandate to create occupation-based training programs, participation in which would affect employee ratings on occupation group rosters and would be required for promotion to certain posts. Training should be paid for out of OPS's regular budget. Qualified staff should be given incentives to act as part-time trainers, and member governments should be en-

couraged to provide qualified trainers from their countries on a short-term donation basis.

22. OPS should utilize external consultants to a greater degree, with a corresponding decrease in what are now designated as permanent staff positions.

23. The Secretary-General should propose, in consultation with the staff, a framework for staff-management relations that clearly defines the type and extent of co-management considered to be in the best interests of the Organization and consistent with the Secretary-General's ultimate accountability to member states. Such a framework should indicate when the staff has a right to be informed of decisions, when it must be consulted, and when it may participate in their determination.

The Office of Personnel Services

Contributing to the underlying structural weaknesses of U.N. personnel management is the fact that the current Office of Personnel Services lacks a sense of its role in the general life of the Organization and the specific services it should provide to enhance the efficiency of the U.N.'s operations. The situations already noted in the areas of recruitment and staff management are only a few, if the most serious, of the array of shortcomings.

One looks in vain, for example, for evidence of effective planning for human resource needs—or even recognition that planning is necessary. An obvious planning function would be to analyze and monitor budgetary and programming changes, developments in occupational groups, and so on, in order to forecast the need for future changes in the level and type of staffing. One benefit would be an ability to fill vacancies in less time than the 12 months that are now required.

Another important planning role for OPS is to provide a source of fresh and farsighted thinking about the best way to match the structure and composition of the Secretariat with its actual mission. Currently, a large number of U.N. posts are graded too high for the work that is required. This steady inflation of grades over the last 15 years—known as "grade creep"—has led to the replacement of the traditional bureaucratic pyramid with a diamond-shaped distribution of grade levels. A reduction of recruitment at the P-1 and P-2 levels concurrent with the expansion of the upper grades has resulted in the widening of the Organization's girth. ASG and USG posts have increased by some 144 percent since 1970, and D-1 and D-2 posts have increased by 49 percent and 51 percent respectively, while P-1s have declined by 62 percent.

From the outset, the U.N. has favored the notion of a career-long relationship with its employees, as a means both of attracting the best candidates and of protecting the independence of the Secretariat.[41] Yet in recent years there has been a notable decline in the hiring of young officers on the junior level and an increase in the hiring of more senior-level officers, whose careers are mostly behind them. It is not clear that one or the other approach provides a staff that can take on all of the U.N.'s highly varied tasks and also respond to the need for constantly updated skills. An obvious task for the OPS planners would be to reexamine the U.N.'s approach to contracts in order to propose the ratio of career, fixed-term, and consulting contracts that best fits the needs of the Organization.

Another essential personnel service that is largely neglected is job and career-related training. With the exception of language instruction, provisions for training to improve job performance, whether through academic furloughs, course subsidies, or in-service training by occupational group, are either extremely limited or nonexistent—a situation that contributes to the stagnation of staff skills and lowering of morale.

There are several reasons why the U.N.'s personnel function has never developed a clear mission. Most important is the fact that no such mission has been defined by the Secretary-General, the Under-Secretary-General for Administration and Management, or the Assistant Secretary-General for Personnel Services. Another obstacle is the tendency of the General Assembly to give explicit instructions to OPS on a host of personnel matters, with the almost unavoidable result that OPS often behaves more like an instrument of legislative fiat than of operational efficiency. Yet another obstacle is the fact that delegations of authority on routine personnel matters are imprecise, nonbinding, and often disregarded. In practice, the office of the Secretary-General itself becomes heavily involved in personnel cases, acting as arbiter on issues that should be resolved at much lower levels.

Recommendations

1. The Secretary-General should vigorously defend his duties and prerogatives as chief executive and recognize that his responsibilities under the Charter require him to be an initiative-taker rather than a caretaker in the service of efficient management and to take a lead role in the formulation of personnel policy.

2. To fulfill his official responsibilities in the area of personnel management, the Secretary-General should delegate authority to his Under-Secreatry-General for Administration and Management and to the Assistant Secretary-General for Personnel Matters—authority that is at once explicit and binding.

3. The General Assembly should discontinue its "command and compliance" approach to personnel matters and restrict itself to broad issues of policy.

4. OPS should be given a clear "charter" requiring it to support the recruitment and staff-management needs of "line departments" as well as to conduct human resource planning for the Secretariat as a whole.

5. OPS should have the capability to monitor and analyze data affecting personnel in order to forecast changes and be able to respond quickly.

6. The Secretary-General should adopt a short-term policy that favors recruitment of young candidates at junior levels over recruitment at more senior levels for the purposes of eventually effecting a balance between the two.

7. The Secretary-General should direct OPS to reexamine the ratio of permanent versus fixed-term contracts, with a view to establishing the contractual mix that best serves the operational interests of the Organization.

Notes

1. United Nations Document A/C.5/40/59, November 22, 1985. *Personnel Questions: Views of Staff Representatives of Secretariat.*

2. Soviet bloc countries and the People's Republic of China require their nationals in U.N. service to return a portion of their salaries to the government.

3. See John P. Renninger, *Can the Common System be Maintained? The Role of the International Civil Service Commission* (UNITAR, Policy and Efficacy Studies No. 10, New York, 1986), pp. 70–71; and Anders Carsten Daamsgard, *Staffing an International Secretariat: Principles and Practices* (Copenhagen: Political Studies Press, 1983), pp. 191–205.

4. Delivered at Oxford University, May 13, 1986. U.N. Document SG/SM/3870.

5. For General Assembly directives on equitable geographical distribution and on recruitment of women see, for example, U.N. documents A/35/210 and Annex, A/39/243, A/39/245, and A/37/143.

6. GA/Res/35/210.

7. GA/Res/37/126.

8. This general concept of the international civil servant was specifically applied to the United Nations Secretariat by Secretary-General Dag Hammarskjöld. U.N. PR/SG/1035 of May 29, 1961.

9. U.N. Document No. 5/Add.15, Information Requested by the Group of High-Level Intergovernmental Experts to Review the Efficiency of the Administrative and Financial Functioning of the United Nations, April 2, 1986.

10. To buttress the requirements of the Charter, recent General Assembly resolutions have sought to correct more rapidly the existing imbalance in representation of men and women staff and to emphasize the hiring of a greater percentage of younger candidates at the P-1 and P-2 levels. See, for example, GA/Res/33/143 and GA/Res/35/210.

11. U.N. PR/SG/SM/3447.

12. Comparisons are based on the findings of a 1978 job-equivalency study prepared by the International Civil Service Commission. Federal Civil Service grades GS-9 through GS-18 and Senior Executive Service (SES) grades 1 through 6 on the United States side are measured against comparable jobs in the United Nations at grade levels P-1 through D-2. The matching grades were established with the active cooperation of the U.S. State Department and Office of Personnel Management. A new study, which could change the present determination of grade equivalencies—widely felt to be unsatisfactory—is currently being developed by the ICSC and is expected to be released soon. The establishment of grade equivalencies between United States Federal Civil Service jobs and United Nations jobs at the Assistant Secretary-General and Under-Secretary-General level is even more problematic, owing to the non-comparability of function of an international and national civil servant at the highest level. (Efforts to establish such equivalencies continue. In 1986, the ICSC requested its secretariat to study various methods of comparing ASG/USG positions with positions in the United States Civil Service and to present the results of its findings at its 25th session in 1987.) The salary levels for these grades are currently determined by extrapolation of salaries at grades P-1 to D-2. Member states have been greatly concerned by the breakdown in the application of the Noblemaire Principle—requiring that comparable jobs in the U.N. be measured against those in the comparator—which is implied by the method of salary determination at the ASG/USG levels.

The current salary for an Under-Secretary-General in New York (after staff assessment at the rate applicable to a single staff member with no dependents and including post-adjustment) is $78,965. The salary payable to an Assistant Secretary-General under the same conditions is $72,171. Unlike U.N. professional and director-grade posts, there is only one step at grade levels ASG/USG.

13. League of Nations, Organization of the Secretariat and of the International Labor Office. Report of the Committee of Experts appointed by the League of Nations at its meeting of December 7, 1920 (A.3.21) (Noblemaire Report) 18:

. . . the salaries which we propose are based on those of the highest paid civil service in the world, i.e., those of the British empire. We do not see how any other course could have been followed since, if lower salaries had been offered, it would be impossible to obtain the services of the Britishers of the required standard . . . on the other hand, it would be difficult to pay lower salaries for the same kind of work to members of other nationalities whose work of the kind required by the League is obtainable at lower figures.

14. U.N. salaries payable in New York contain a post-adjustment element, despite the fact that New York is the base of the system. This anomaly has been justified by the fact that, since the cost of living in New York is very high relative to other duty stations, any post-adjustment system that used the current New York cost of living as the base would require negative post-adjustments in all of the duty stations where the cost of living is lower—a bureaucratic complication that the U.N. seeks to avoid. The cost of living in New York in December 1979 is taken as the base for post-adjustment classification purposes.

15. The ICSC has recommended dropping the use of the cost-of-living differential factor in the margin calculation to account for the differences in cost of living between New York and Washington, D.C. The Commission has observed that the real comparison is with the national civil service, and not with Washington, D.C., and that therefore the cost-of-living differential is not relevant.

16. It should be noted that the valuation of the margin depends to a large extent on the components of the method of comparison of U.N. and U.S. remuneration. A modification of any one of these components—selection of U.N. post used as the base for comparison; formula used for the derivation of U.S. taxes; point of comparison, i.e., step in the grade level—could yield an entirely different margin.

In the U.N. the margin is calculated on the basis of a net-to-net salary comparison with a married official without children. Net remuneration of the U.S. Civil Service is calculated on the basis of salary after income taxes. An average amount, which employs both standard and itemized deductions, is used to determine the taxable income and, consequently, the U.S. employee's federal and state tax liabilities (averaged for D.C., Virginia, and Maryland). The margin has traditionally been based on a comparison of U.S. salaries in Washington, D.C., and U.N. salaries.

17. The basic rates of staff assessment are determined by taking account of national income tax rates in the seven headquarter cities, with particular reference to the applicable rates in the comparator countries. All staff assessment monies go into a tax-equalization fund.

At the end of the year, nationals of the four countries that filed reservations to the tax-related provisions of the U.N. Convention on Privileges and Immunities (U.S., Canada, Mexico, Laos) pay taxes to their governments. The tax-equalization fund is used both to reimburse the taxed individuals for these amounts and to compensate the non-taxing governments for failing to collect from their nationals. Tax reimbursement is considered necessary in order to ensure that U.N. staff members from the four countries receive the same remuneration as their colleagues from other countries.

18. IMF and World Bank employees, other than U.S. citizens, generally do not pay income taxes on the salaries they receive. U.S. citizens and others who are taxed by their governments receive a tax allowance based on a system of assumed average deductions for the employee's income level.

19. Under the United States Pay Comparability Act, U.S. Civil Service salaries are based on "comparability" with those paid for equivalent jobs in nongovernmental employment. The salary figures are compiled from surveys conducted by the Bureau of Labor Statistics, among a wide range of occupations. Annual adjustment of Civil Service salaries is made by the President, who may act either to close the gap between government and nongovernment salaries or to implement an "alternative pay plan." Although the President has not acted to close the gap since 1977, under the "alternative pay plan," U.S. civil servants will receive a 3 percent increase in pay in 1986–87.

20. Major U.N. Expatriate Entitlements:

Rental Subsidy: The ICSC establishes a threshold related to emoluments that is linked to the average rents paid in each duty station. In particularly difficult situations, a renter may receive a subsidy of 80 percent of the difference between the rent and the threshold. Unless an exception is granted by the Commission, the normal rent subsidy cannot exceed 40 percent of total rent. The amount of rental subsidy decreases to zero over five years.

Installation Grant: When a staff member is transferred to a new duty station on an assignment of at least one year's duration, an installation grant is paid to cover extra costs incurred in the initial period after arrival. The amount of the grant is linked to the daily subsistence allowance at that duty station— based on an average cost of hotels and meals in the area—and is normally the equivalent of 30 days' allowance for each staff member and half that rate for each dependent. Also, a lump sum is payable for staff relocating to duty stations outside of North America and Europe, at a rate of $600 per person, up to a maximum of $2,400.

Removal Costs: The payment of the cost of removal of household effects to a field duty station is authorized within certain weight and volume limits.

Assignment Allowance: In certain cases, the Secretary-General may find it preferable to pay an assignment allowance rather than to pay for removal. This usually relates to assignments at duty stations in the field for which the costs of removal would be prohibitive. Assignment allowances ranges from $1,200 to $3,600 per year, depending on grade level, and is payable for up to five years. A staff member who is given the assignment-allowance option still has a removal right of up to 1,000 kilos of personal effects.

Education Allowance: The education allowance is available to all internationally recruited staff members residing outside their home country with school-age children (first grade through university). The grant reimburses 75 percent of the cost of education, up to a maximum of $4,500 per child. The cost of board can be included in this figure as well. If the child attends school outside of the duty station, the Organization will pay for one (in certain cases two) trips home each year.

Financial Incentive Supplement: Staff serving at duty stations considered "hardship posts" get some additional entitlements—for example, accelerated home leave and additional trips home under the education grant. Staff may qualify for a financial-incentive supplement of up to $3,600, depending on the difficulty of the post.

Repatriation Grant: The grant is payable to staff members who the Organization must repatriate on separation, normally to their country of origin. The grant is linked to the number of years of service; a staff member may receive up to 28 weeks of pay for each 12 years of service.

Home Leave: Every two years, an expatriate staff member can visit the home country at U.N. expense for a substantial portion of the six-week annual leave period.

21. In its 38th Session, the General Assembly requested the International Civil Service Commission "to inform the General Assembly, on an annual basis, of the margin between the remuneration of the U.N. employees and those of the U.S. federal civil service on this total compensation basis." GA/Res/38/232.

22. For a discussion of this point, see Henri Reymond and Sydney Malick, *International Personnel Policies and Practices* (New York: Praeger, 1985), p. 20.

23. See The Report of the International Civil Service Commission, A/39/39, p. 27.

24. There are two major differences between benefits received under the U.N. and the U.S. pension systems:

a. Under the U.N.'s "two-track" adjustment system, pensioners who retire in the United States have their benefits adjusted in accordance with U.S. CPI. For all other retirees, two amounts are calculated: one by the U.S. CPI, and one by the local CPI. Pensioners have the option of receiving their benefits adjusted by the "local track" to compensate for loss of purchasing power in the event of reductions in the value of the dollar. To qualify for a "local track" adjustment, a pensioner must submit acceptable proof of residence in the country in question.

b. The U.N. pension system contains a provision under which a retiring employee can choose either a full pension or a lump sum, with the pension reduced accordingly. For regular and early retirements, the maximum amount of the lump sum is equal to the actuarial equivalent of one-third of the periodic benefit; for deferred retirement, it is the amount of the participant's own contributions.

25. The current pension entitlement for both the U.S. and U.N. pensions systems is 1.5 percent per year of final pensionable renumeration for the first five years, 1.75 percent for the next five years, and 2 percent per year thereafter. Before 1983, the U.N. rate of accumulation was more generous than the U.S. rate (2 percent per year), causing disproportionate growth in U.N. pensions; however, the present reduced U.N. rates of accumulation should result in the gradual closing of the present yawning gap between U.N. and U.S. pensions.

26. In the U.S. Federal Civil Service, pensionable remuneration is based on gross salaries, which are reviewed every year. The gross salaries of international civil servants—also the basis for pensionable remuneration in the U.N. until January 1, 1985—have not been reviewed since 1975. In the intervening years, U.N. remuneration has been adjusted by means of the post-adjustment mechanism, and a portion of the post-adjustment has been consolidated into base salary from time to time. The basic retirement benefit in both systems is equal to the product of the participant's final average remuneration (best 36 out of the last 60 months) multiplied by his total accumulation. Over the years, the General Assembly has made a number of adjustments to deal with factors of inflation or the devaluation of the U.S. dollar. Prior to January 1, 1985, adjustments in the scale of pensionable remuneration were based on the movement of the weighted average of post-adjustments at headquarters and the main field offices, or by the movement of the U.S. consumer price index.

27. Ironically, the notion of calculating U.N. pensions in accordance with the Noblemaire formulation—proposed in the ICSC's 1986 report to the General Assembly—coincides with the overhaul of the U.S. pension system. The new Federal Employees Retirement System (FERS) has less in common with the U.N. system than did the old Civil Service Retirement System (CSRS); in fact, two of the major components of the new system—social security and the third thrift plan—have no counterparts in the U.N. system.

The inflated levels of the scale of pensionable remuneration date from the system that was in place prior to December 1980, which based the scale of pensionable remuneration on gross salary levels, indexed by the movement of a weighted average of post-adjustments (WAPA) at headquarters and main field offices. The scale also took into account the fact that most employees, on retirement, return to their home countries, in most cases *not* the United States. The rapid fall of the U.S. dollar in relation to European currencies in the 1970s led the United Nations to increase the level of post-adjustments in non-U.S. duty stations in order to equalize purchasing power for all U.N. employees. Because the scale of pensionable remuneration was tied to the level of post-adjustments, the scale was boosted as well, with the result that pension benefits increased. In a notable case of bad timing, a new scale was adopted in January 1981 that tied the determination of pensionable remuneration to the movement of the U.S. consumer price index (CPI) at the precise moment that the U.S. dollar had bottomed out and had begun to strengthen. Had the WAPA-based adjustment been retained, the strengthening of the dollar would have offset the continuing impact of inflation, including inflation in the United States. The new scale was superimposed on the old, already high, levels, with the result that pensionable remuneration and, therefore, pensions grew too fast. The fact that U.S. gross salaries (pensionable remuneration) have not kept up with inflation has only made matters worse.

28. Under the ICSC Statute, the Commission has the power to establish: the methods by which principles for determining the conditions of service of international civil servants shall be applied; the classification of duty stations for the purpose of applying post-adjustments; and job classification standards for all categories of staff in fields of work common to several of the U.N. organizations. In most other important areas of personnel management—salary scales, most allowances and benefits, standards of recruitment, and the development of common staff regulations—the ICSC may only make recommendations to the General Assembly.

29. Charter of the International Civil Service Commission, Article 3.1.

30. Charter of the International Civil Service Commission, Article 4.1.

31. The criteria for entrance into the professional service is slightly less rigorous for internal candidates than for those entering from the outside. External candidates must have completed a first university degree, while internal candidates need only show evidence of some post-high school study. Nevertheless, 80 percent of the staff recruited internally do have a university degree.

32. A/C.5/40/59, p. 11.

33. Both selection bodies consist of six members who are appointed by the Secretary-General after consultation with the appropriate staff representative bodies. A designated official of OPS serves ex officio as a non-voting member on each of the bodies.

34. This rate applies to all Federal Civil Service staff under the General Schedule. It is believed that the inclusion of termination figures for the U.S. Postal Service—an independent establishment with its own pay and benefits schedules—would raise the rate to about 1 percent.

35. Panels sit in New York, Addis Ababa, Baghdad, Bangkok, Geneva, Jerusalem, Nairobi, Santiago, and Vienna.

36. During the period February 4, 1983 to February 4, 1984, 119 cases were submitted to the panels, 74 of which were resolved through conciliation (62 percent). Only four of these cases (3.3 percent) went on to the Joint Appeals Board (St/IT/84/49, July 17, 1984, p. 6).

37. A/41/640, p. 20.

38. U.N. Staff Rules, Regulation 1.2.

39. U.N. document A/C.5/39/11, October 16, 1984: Programme Budget for the Biennium 1984–85, Other Personnel Questions. . . . A System of Career, Development for All Categories of Staff.

40. See Charles M. Lichtenstein, "By Breaking the Rules, Moscow Keeps

a Tight Grip on U.N., " Heritage Foundation Backgrounder, No. 526, July 23, 1986.

41. The career principle was formulated by the U.N. Preparatory Commission in 1945:

Unless members of the staff can be offered assurance of being able to make their careers in the Secretariat, many of the best candidates from all countries will inevitably be kept away. Nor can members of the staff be expected fully to subordinate the special interests of their countries to their international interests if they are merely detached temporarily from national administrations and remain dependent on them for their future [U.N. Document PC/20, 92].

Annex I

Pension benefits of United Nations and United States officials
(United States dollars)

Pension benefits that would be earned by United Nations officials at the end of 20, 25, 30 and 35 (maximum) years of service, using the benefit accumulation formula for those who joined the system on or after 1 January 1983, are shown under part A. Pension benefits of United Nations officials, calculated using the benefit accumulation formula, for those who joined the system prior to 1 January 1983, are shown under part B. Only one benefit accumulation formula applies in the case of United States federal civil service employees. The benefit accumulation formula for United States federal civil service employees and that for United Nations officials who joined the system on or after 1 January 1983 are identical for up to 35 years of contributory service. Pension benefits of United States federal civil service officials calculated at the end of 20, 25, 30 and 35 years of service along with the maximum pension benefits that would be earned are shown under part C. In all cases pension benefits have been calculated on the basis of the current levels of pensionable remuneration at the top step of each grade.

A. For United Nations officials (using new benefit accumulation formula)

Grade	Pensionable Remuneration	20 years (36.25%)	25 years (46.25%)	30 years (56.25%)	35 years (66.25%)
P-1	37,400	13,577	17,297	21,037	24,777
P-2	47,900	17,364	22,154	26,944	31,734
P-3	62,200	22,547	28,767	34,987	41,207
P-4	70,900	25,701	32,791	39,881	46,971
P-5	83,900	30,414	38,804	47,194	55,584
D-1	87,900	31,864	40,654	49,444	58,234
D-2	92,400	33,495	42,735	51,975	61,215
ASG	103,900	37,664	48,054	58,444	62,340[a]/
USG	115,700	41,941	53,511	65,081	69,420[a]/

B. For United Nations officials (using old benefit accumulation formula)

Grade	Pensionable Remuneration	20 years (40%)	25 years (50%)	30 years (60%)	35 years (65%)
P-1	37,400	14,960	18,700	22,440	24,310
P-2	47,900	19,160	23,950	28,740	31,135

P-3	62,200	24,880	31,100	37,320	40,430
P-4	70,900	28,360	35,450	42,540	46,085
P-5	83,900	33,560	41,950	50,340	54,535
D-1	87,900	35,160	43,950	52,740	57,135
D-2	92,400	36,960	46,200	55,440	60,060
ASG	103,900	41,560	51,950	62,340	62,340a/
USG	115,700	46,280	57,850	69,420	69,420a/

C. For United States officials

Grade	Pensionable Remuneration	20 years (36.25%)	25 years (46.25%)	30 years (56.25%)	35 years (66.25%)	Maximum (80%)
GS-9	28,347	10,276	13,110	15,945	18,780	22,678
GS-10	31,211	11,314	14,435	17,556	20,677	24,969
GS-11	34,292	12,431	15,860	19,289	22,718	27,434
GS-12	41,105	14,901	19,011	23,122	27,232	32,884
GS-13	48,876	17,718	22,605	27,499	32,380	39,100
GS-14	57,759	20,938	26,714	32,489	38,265	46,207
GS-15	67,940	24,628	31,422	38,216	45,010	54,352
GS-16	68,700	24,904	31,774	38,644	45,514	54,960
GS-17	68,700	24,904	31,774	38,644	45,514	54,960
GS-18	68,700	24,904	31,774	38,644	45,514	54,960
SES-1	61,296	22,220	28,349	34,479	40,609	49,037
SES-2	63,764	23,114	29,491	35,867	42,244	51,011
SES-3	66,232	24,009	30,632	37,255	43,879	52,986
SES-4	68,700	24,904	31,774	38,644	45,514	54,960
SES-5	70,500	25,556	32,606	39,656	46,706	56,400
SES-6	72,300	26,209	33,439	40,669	47,899	57,840

aIn accordance with General Assembly resolution 40.245 of December 18, 1985, annex.
From ICSC Report to the 41st General Assembly

CHAPTER 12

PLANNING, PROGRAMMING, BUDGETING, AND EVALUATION IN THE U.N.

Maurice Bertrand

U.N. programs and budgets are today an object of controversy. The U.S. government and the other large contributors contend that the level of the U.N. budget is too high and that it finances too many activities that are obsolete or of marginal usefulness, while developing countries believe that a lack of resources keeps programs from reaching their threshold of efficiency.

This controversy is not new: It has been reflected in the debates of the General Assembly since the creation of the U.N., and particularly since the 1960s. But it is less well known, in general, that important efforts have been made by member states to settle these differences of opinion—i.e., to develop procedures and mechanisms for facilitating the establishment of priorities, defining precise and reasonable objectives, monitoring the execution of the programs, evaluating the results obtained, and drawing lessons from these evaluations. Unfortunately, this modern and sophisticated approach has not worked: It has not yet facilitated the estblishment of a broader agreement on the content and level of the budget. The present crisis is additional proof of this failure.

An analysis of why and how the planning, programming, budgeting, and evaluation system was established and why it has not been able to solve the U.N.'s persistent problems may help us to understand better the nature of the present crisis and the reasons for misunderstandings among member states concerning the role the U.N. must play in 1987 and in the next decade.

Such an analysis reveals that the program planning, budgeting, and evaluation system, which has not been yet fully implemented, can be improved at a number of points; and that the process of reform thus undertaken could contribute to a new and more realistic conception of the role of the U.N. in the modern world.

History of the System of Planning, Programming, Budgeting, and Evaluation

In the mid-1960s, the need for a better system of programming was first felt in the U.N. Not surprisingly, this need was expressed on the occasion of a financial crisis. The crisis was due to the events in the Congo from 1960 to 1964.[1] A large deficit occurred when some member states, notably the USSR and France, refused to pay their share of the expenditures of the United Nations Operation in Congo (ONUC),[2] which included civilian operations and an international armed peace force (UNEF).[3]

The financial situation of the U.N. at that stage was the following: The total budget (gross) of the U.N. in 1960 was $65.7 million. This amount doubled from 1960 to 1966, the figures being respectively 71.6 million in 1961, $85.8 million in 1962, $92.8 million in 1963, $102.9 million in 1964, $108.4 million in 1965, and $121 million in 1966.[4]

The budget of the U.N. was at that time presented annually by object of expenditures. It comprised 20 sections (travel, meetings, salaries, building, equipment, printing, field service, etc.) and contained very little programmatic description. Section III on salaries and wages and Section 4 on common staff costs were the most important sections, accounting for approximately 57 to 60 percent of the total budget.[5]

In light of the difficult financial situation, the General Assembly at its 16th Session in 1961 authorized the Secretary-General to sell up to $200 million worth of U.N. bonds to governments, national banks, and approved nonprofit institutions. Final receipts of the bond issue totaled $169,905,679, representing purchases by 64 countries.[6]

The total expenditures authorized for ONUC (including UNEF) for the period July 14, 1960–September 30, 1965, amounted to $392.8 million ($48.5 million in 1960, $120 million in 1961, $120 million in 1962, $83.7 million in 1963, $18.2 million in 1964, $2.4 million in 1965). It is to be noted that in 1961 and 1962 these annual expenditures were significantly larger than was the budget of the U.N. itself.[7]

The amount of the deficit—resulting mainly from unpaid assessed contributions—was not known in 1965. In order to clarify the situation and, in particular, "to obtain information giving a clear and accurate picture of the financial situation of the Organization, including a detailed description of its commitments," and to make "a detailed examination of the procedures for preparing and approving the budgets and a review of the procedures for controlling the execution thereof," the General Assembly, in resolution 2049 (XX) of December 13, 1965, decided to "establish an Ad Hoc Committee of Experts to examine the finances of the U.N. and the specialized agencies consisting of 14 member states."[8] Paragraph 6 of the resolution explicitly mentioned the necessity of examining "the entire range of the budgetary problems of the U.N. and the organizations brought into a relationship with it, notably their administrative and budgetary procedures, the means of comparing and if possible standardizing their budgets, and the financial aspects of their expansion with a view to avoiding needless expenditures, particularly expenditures resulting from duplication." It also mentioned the need for "rationalization and better coordination."

The Ad Hoc Committee, known as the "Committee of 14," issued two reports. The first report (U.N. Document A/6289 of March 28, 1966) concerned the U.N. financial situation as of September 30, 1965.[9] The second (U.N. Document A/6343 of July 19, 1966), which dealt with budget preparation, presentation, and performance; standardization of budget documents and of financial regulations; the budget cycle; program planning and evaluation; and coordination, is a fundamental document insofar as it established the basis of the system of planning, programming, budgeting, and evaluation that has been progressively developed over the past 20 years.

The second report offered numerous recommendations and suggestions concerning the presentation of approximate estimates of the budget one year in advance, uniform budget presentation by the organizations of the U.N. system, reporting on budget performance, standardization of financial regulations, the possibility of establishing a biennial budget cycle, standardization of nomenclature, establishment of an inspection unit, development of planning, programming, and budgeting processes (effective long-term planning in each organization, establishment of a program budget, synchronization of planning and budget cycles in each organization, evaluation process), and reconstitution of a special committee on coordination by the Economic and Social Council.

A reading of the 1966 document raises the question of why it has taken 20 years to implement only partially the solutions that were recommended in the report. In fact, only one recommendation has been implemented: the creation in 1967 of the Joint Inspection Unit (JIU), composed of eight inspectors "chosen among members of national supervision or inspection bodies or from among persons of similar competence in charge of drawing, over their own signature, reports for which they alone would be responsible and in which they should state their findings and propose solutions to problems they have noted." The JIU began its operations on an experimental basis on January 1, 1968.

At about the same time, the Committee on Coordination (referred to in Paragraph 90 of the Report of the Committee of 14), which was created in 1962, was given the name of Committee on Program and Coordination (CPC) by Resolution 17 (XLI) of ECOSOC in 1966. No other recommendation was implemented until the JIU took up the problems of planning, programming, budgeting, and evaluation. Nevertheless, beginning in 1969, a thorough cooperation between JIU, ACABQ,[10] and CPC led to the establishment of the planning and evaluation cycle.

In a 1969 report on "Programming and Budgets in the U.N. Family of Organizations" (U.N. Document A/7822 of December 3, 1969), the JIU recommended the presentation of the U.N. budget by program, the establishment of the program budget for a two-year cycle, the general adoption of medium-term programming, and the establishment of a United Nations programming service. It took three years for these recommendations to be implemented. The U.N. Secretariat and the agency secretariats were resistant to change, but the JIU had the advantage of following up its recommendation by establishing new notes and new reports—assisting the Secretariat, for example, in the preparation of an outline of the new program budget and explaining to delegates the usefulness and the practicality of the new methods.

In fact, some of the specialized agencies had already adopted some form of program budget in the 1950s: WHO, UNESCO (1951); FAO (1952). There were biennial budgets for UNESCO beginning in 1953–54 and for FAO in 1958–59. ILO opted for a biennial program budget in 1971–72. The United Nations finally agreed to adopt a biennial program budget, effective 1974–75.

The agencies' adoption of medium-term plans started a little later—with the exception of WHO, which since 1952 has had a "program of work for a specific period" (of five years). UNESCO established its first Medium-Term Plan for 1971–76 and a second one for 1973–78.

FAO and ILO adopted a plan for the period 1972–77, and ILO followed up with a second plan for 1973–79. The U.N. decided in 1972 to adopt its first Medium-Term Plan for a period of four years (1974–77).

The adoption of the new programming and budgeting tools led to some important changes. The presentation of the Medium-Term Plan was made by "major programs, programs, and subprograms," thus facilitating understanding of the numerous and complex activities of the U.N. The presentation of the budget, although it did not correspond exactly to the list of major programs, permitted a better understanding of the relationship between the various departments and units, the volume of their staff, the level of their resources, and the list of various "program elements" composing the various "subprograms." A biennial program performance report permitted delegations to monitor the execution of the program.

The biennialization of the program budget had an important influence on the rationalization of the work of the General Assembly—or of the Fifth Committee at least. In the budget years, the attention of delegations concentrated on the questions of finance and program; in the off-budget years it became possible to devote more time to a number of other problems, particularly the problems of personnel.

But it soon appeared that the new tools had to be refined and that the Secretariat and the delegations had to be educated in their use.

The years between 1974 (the first year of the Medium-Term Plan and the program budget) and 1984 (the date of publication of the Regulations and Rules concerning program planning, budgeting, and evaluation) saw the evolution of mechanisms and the improvement of procedures for getting the system working. The results of this process are still theoretical and formal and the practice is not yet satisfactory, but important steps have been taken toward the definition of an efficient system. The developments that took place during those years can be summarized as follows:

The interest of delegations in the improvement of the methodology has increased since 1974, particularly in the Committee for Programme and Coordination and in the Fifth Committee. The preparation of four successive Medium-Term Plans (three four-year rolling plans 1976–79, 1978–81, 1980–83, and one six-year, fixed-term plan, 1984–89) and of biennial program budgets has allowed the Secretariat and the delegations to experiment with the proposed methods and to put them gradually into practice. Resolutions of the General Assembly have become progressively more precise concerning the manner in which priorities, objectives, programs, and methods of evaluation should be defined. Successive resolutions on program budgets,[11] on medium-term planning,[12] and on evaluation[13] have refined the methodology to be followed. An important resolution on the restructuring of the economic and social sectors of the U.N. (General Assembly resolution 32/197 of December 20, 1977) described in Parts VI and VII of its annex the role that the CPC should play in planning, programming, evaluation, and coordination; the nature of its cooperation with the JIU; the harmonization of plans and programs within the system; joint planning; etc. General Assembly resolutions 37/234 and 38/227 defined regulations and approved the rules that govern program planning, program aspects of the budget, the monitoring of implementation, and the methods of evaluation.

The important work that has been done so far on program planning, budgeting, and evaluation is a result of the combined activities of the Joint Inspection Unit,[14] the Committee for Programme and Coordination,[15] the Economic and Social Council (which has also taken a number of resolutions on these questions), the Fifth Committee of the General Assembly, and (upon its creations in 1978) the Planning, Programming and Coordinating Office (PPCO) of the Department of International Economic and Social Activities (DIESA).[16] An exceptional contribution was made by the Committee of 25 Experts, convened in 1975, whose report, "A New U.N. Structure for Global Economic Cooperation" (E/AC.62/9 of May 28, 1975), formed the basis for the restructuring operation mandated in resolution 32/197.

The discussion of these problems—for which partial solutions have been found—related to the shape of the tools for program planning and budgeting (Medium-Term Plans and program budgets), priorities, coordination of the programs of the U.N. system, evaluation, and, finally, institutional mechanisms.[17]

The Medium-Term Plan

Because the establishment of a Medium-Term Plan for the U.N. was an entirely new exercise, it was quite natural that delegates and members of the Secretariat raised a number of questions concerning the utility of the plan, the comparability of planning for the U.N. and planning at the national level, the nature of the objectives, etc.

Although there has been important progress, confusion about the role of the new tools has yet to be resolved. The conception of "planning" tends to vary with national or cultural backgrounds, a fact that led some to oppose the Medium-Term Plan. Supporters of the plan stressed the need for clarity, the necessity for defining clearer objectives, the possibility the plan offered for deeper reflection on the role of the Organization, the rationalization of work, etc. The plan's adversaries stressed the impossibility of forecasting the evolution of world problems, the need for flexibility in U.N. activities, and the practical impossibility of planning the majority of the U.N.'s activities, particularly negotiating activities, six-to-eight years in advance (taking into account the period of preparation). Among aspects of planning discussed at length were:

A *"rolling plan"* versus a *"fixed-term plan"*: The supporters of the rolling plan favored preparing a new plan every two years, which would contain a general orientation for a planning period of four to six years (the new plan would also cover part of the period covered by the previous one). Supporters of a fixed-term plan contended that in order to establish clear-cut and time-limited objectives, it is necessary to establish a stable framework for the U.N.'s activities—including a calendar of operations—with the understanding that the objectives and orientations of the plan would be corrected, if necessary, every two years, to take into account new events that might affect the role of the U.N. The fixed-term plan was finally adopted, with a six-year planning period corresponding to three biennial program budgets.

Plan format and subdivisions: The adoption of the notion of "major program"[18] (for example, concerning population, human rights, or drugs) and its division into various "programs" (for example, to analyze world population or to provide technical cooperation in the field of population) and "subprograms" (for example, to produce demographic analyses, demographic projections, or demographic policies) resulted from a number of studies and discussions, notably at the interagency level.[19] This format would allow precise and time-limited objectives to be defined at the subprogram level—in the program budget, subprograms would be divided into "program elements" that are often identical to "outputs" (studies, reports, symposia, etc.).[20]

Format and content of the narratives, identification of problems, description of "strategies," justification of the choice of objectives, definition and conception of objectives (both of the Organization and of the Secretariat), distinction between various types of activities, and the necessity and possibility of making in-depth, preliminary studies. Research on these and other questions allowed the Secretariat and delegates of member states to reach a better understanding of the economic, social, humanitarian, and operational activities of the U.N.

and began to close the gap separating the day-to-day work of document preparation, studies, publications, and meetings from the Organization's final objectives.

The necessity was acknowledged of distinguishing between areas where joint action is made possible by the existence of some level of consensus and those areas where further negotiations are required to establish a common understanding of the issues to be addressed. Nevertheless, this distinction was not taken into account by the plan.

A clear differentiation was made between continuing activities that could not be time-limited because they corresponded to some permanent function of the Organization (for example, the establishment, on a regular basis, of demographic projections or the collection of world statistics) and activities that related to specific objectives (for example, the establishment of an institution for the training of a specific number of specialists).

Because the Secretariat found it difficult to understand this new methodology imposed from above and because there was no training program to help professionals use the new tools, the preparation of the plan was not taken seriously by the units concerned and the first plan they produced did not correspond to the intentions of the legislators. As stated in a report of the JIU published in 1979 after the presentation of the third Medium-Term Plan (1980–83): "anyone who has tried to read these texts must inevitably have been disheartened by the plethora of banalities, by the vague and general wording devoid of any information, by the lack of descriptions of policies and objectives, by the substitutions of lists of outputs for the description of strategies."[21]

The 1979 JIU report made a precise distinction between activities that can be programmed and those that cannot, proposing for the first time a precise methodology for defining "time-limited objectives." The report recommended as well the adoption of in-depth studies, a timetable for the preparation of the Medium-Term Plan, and a new method of presenting policy descriptions for major programs. The JIU underlined the importance of the role of the Introduction to the Medium-Term Plan in the establishment of priorities.

Despite the importance attached to the definition of a better methodology by the Committee for Programme and Coordination and by the General Assembly, and despite the approval by the member states of the main thrust of the JIU's recommendations, these recommendations were implemented only partially—and, indeed, the next Medium-Term Plan was not really any better than the previous one.

The Problem of "Priorities"

The word "priority" is quite popular among delegations. The concentration of efforts on a reduced number of essential activities seems a logical means of addressing the U.N.'s mandate. Prioritization answers the need, generally felt, for the clarification and simplification of the role of the U.N. Unfortunately, priorities are set differently by each member state or group of member states, and even the concept of priority is not absolutely clear. At what level can priorities be set? Is it even possible to establish an order of priorities among peace, justice, human rights, and economic and social development—in other words, among major programs? Does setting of priorities mean the allocation of resources according to the importance of the objectives? These questions are difficult to answer, especially since the costs of programs are mainly related to the type of activities involved (the cost of helping refugees represents $400 million a year, while for human rights the U.N. spends only some $10 million).

An attempt was made by the CPC, taking into account various criteria, to rank major programs according to their importance or success and on this basis to assign a percentage of growth or decrease. This attempt was unsuccessful, despite its modest ambitions, because it was unaccompanied by a more thorough analysis by the Secretariat, by serious evaluations of the results already obtained, and by a firm proposal on priorities from the Secretary-General himself. But an acknowledgement of the need to set priorities did lead to the formulation of Regulation 3.7 on the Introduction to the Medium-Term Plan, which states:

> The plan shall be preceded by an Introduction which will constitute a key integral element in the planning process and shall:
> a. Highlight in a coordinated manner the policy orientations of the United Nations System;
> b. Indicate the medium-term objectives and strategies and trends deduced from mandates which reflect priorities set by intergovernmental organizations;
> c. Contain the Secretary-General's proposals on priorities.

Unfortunately, the only Introduction prepared so far by the Secretariat under these guidelines has neither responded to expectations nor respected the requirement of Regulation 3.7. Nevertheless, it is to be noted that the setting of priorities still remains a permanent preoccupation of delegations. This preoccupation is reflected in the repetitive use of the word in a great many regulations. The matter of priorities was taken up again in the report of the Group of High-Level Intergovernmental Experts to Review the Efficiency of the Administrative and Financial Functioning of the United Nations.[22]

The word "priority" has been so overused that it no longer has any meaning. In fact, this word must be replaced by two concepts: a better system of reflection for the consensus-seeking activities; and a better system of management for the joint activities of member states on which consensus exists.

Format of the Program Budget

Since the beginning of program planning, the program budget has been defined as an "installment of the plan." Resolution 31/99 (XXVIII) of December 18, 1973, states that "the Medium-Term Plan should provide the framework for the biennial program budget." But the respective formats and contents of the Medium-Term Plan and the program budget remain to be defined and their respective roles fully understood. After a number of discussions it was resolved that the Medium-Term Plan would confine itself to major programs, programs, and subprograms, concentrating on narratives describing strategies at these levels—although particularly at the subprogram level—and limiting mention of resources to the number of staff required to execute the programs. The program budget, on the other hand, was to be a very detailed document, enumerating all the program elements of each subprogram and providing not only the precise dollar figures for each but an equally precise account of the staff required for its execution.

In defining the format of the program budgets, particular attention was devoted to the description of program elements and outputs. The list of program elements—by subprogram—corresponds to the plan of work distributed to the units of the secretariats insofar as the completion dates and the primary users of each program element are indicated, and a typology of standard categories of outputs is established and approved. The presentation of the budget (which has improved over the years) has made possible the establishment of a "biennial program performance report," which indicates—to the General Assembly—the extent to which the programs have been implemented and the reasons for nonexecution.

The Role of Evaluation[23]

The evaluation of program results is obviously an essential tool. Most delegations were in favor of the development of such a procedure, but evaluation techniques have taken a long time to develop, and the present stituation remains far from satisfactory. The major problems were as follows:

Allocation of responsibility for evaluation: Many delegates were unable to draw the line between the responsibilities and rights of member states to pass judgment on the results of programs and the responsibilities and duties of the units and the technicians charged with preparing reports and evaluation studies. It was finally determined that only intergovernmental bodies (like CPC) would pass judgment and that evaluation units within the Secretariat, or the Joint Inspection Unit, would prepare reports.

Self-evaluation versus outside independent evaluation: Some delegations considered it necessary for the staff in charge of a program to conduct the evaluation of that program and to derive continual inspiration from the spirit of self-evaluation. Other delegations contended that the need for independent outside evaluation was obvious—and not incompatible with self-analysis.

Nature, size, and location of the units charged with preparing reports of evaluation: It was acknowledged that the amount of work involved in establishing evaluation studies was such that it would be necessary to allocate it not only to specialists inside the departments and units executing the program but also to a central evaluation unit inside the Secretariat and the Joint Inspection Unit. The JIU would be responsible for defining the principles and the methods of analysis and would make some ad hoc evaluation studies.

Difficulty of measuring program impact: The first evaluation studies showed clearly that, while it was relatively easy to monitor the execution of program elements and even to pass judgment on their quality and on the skillfulness of their utilization, it was more difficult to evaluate the impact of programs on national policies, on the advancement of ongoing negotiations, and on the process of development within a country. The definition and measurement of program impact was made more difficult by the fact that, in many cases, the U.N.'s role in the undertaking—as well as the resources involved—was marginal. In fact, evaluation studies have not yet developed to the point of usefulness.

The Relation Between Planning in the U.N. and Planning in the U.N. System

The idea of "joint planning" between the U.N. and the specialized agencies of the U.N. system was a very attractive one, and resolution

32/197 had given particular emphasis to this concept.[24] As indicated in our discussion of the Introduction to the Medium-Term Plan, the hope was to develop the U.N. plan in relation to the plans of the other agencies. Since 1978, DIESA's Programme Planning and Coordination Office (PPCO) has prepared a number of studies comparing the activities of various agencies in a number of fields, and the majority of these studies—called COPAS (cross-organizational program analyses)—have been examined by CPC. The creation of the Coordination Committee on Substantive Questions (CCSQ), bringing together the people in charge of programs in the various agencies, has also allowed the development of a better knowledge of the content of the programs of the various agencies. Nevertheless, the results of all these efforts are still limited and "joint planning" remains an ideal.

The Institutional Mechanisms

Establishing medium-term planning and program budgeting without creating a body empowered to deal with both program and budget has appeared somewhat paradoxical from the very beginning. Each agency in the U.N. system has an executive board that deals with both aspects of the program budget. Even when the executive boards establish subcommittees to deal separately with program and with budgetary matters, they keep the two areas under their control; and when they adopt a program budget, they have a complete picture of the activities of their ogranization. When it comes to the U.N. itself, however, the intergovernmental machinery dealing with these problems is more complex. At the level of the General Assembly, six committees (the First, Special Political, Second, Third, Fourth, and Sixth committees) deal with the definition of the programs, and one committee (the Fifth) deals with administrative and financial matters. The Economic and Social Council also deals with programs involving economic and social activities, as does UNCTAD's Trade and Development Board. In addition, two subsidiary organs of the General Assembly work separately on program and financial aspects of the budget: the Committee for Programme and Coordination (CPC), a 21-member intergovernmental body that deals with program aspects of the budget and the Medium-Term Plan; and the Advisory Committee on Administrative and Budgetary Questions (ACABQ), in principle a committee of 16 experts, that deals with the financial and administrative aspects of the budget.

The establishment of a single committee to deal with program and budget has been proposed ever since the early days of program budgeting. In his comments on the first JIU report on this matter, the Secretary-General mentioned that the examination of the program budget could be made "ideally by a single body" (AC.5/1429). Proposals for creating a subsidiary body of the U.N. by merging ACABQ and CPC or by replacing these committees with a single compact body have been made on several occasions by a number of delegations and by the JIU.[25] But these suggestions have not yet been accepted.

The Establishment of Regulations and Rules Governing Planning and Programming, the Program Aspects of the Budget, the Monitoring of Implementation, and the Methods of Evaluation

The process of codifying the planning, programming, budgeting, and evaluation (PPBE) methodology, gradually defined by the General Assembly over a period of 15–20 years, began with the approval of a recommendation by the JIU in its report 81/7 (A/36/171 of March 1981). General Assembly resolution 36/228 requested the Secretary-General to present proposals "enabling it to adopt official rules and regulations." The actual work of codification resulted from thoroughgoing cooperation between and among CPC, JIU, and the Planning, Programming and Coordination Office in the Secretariat. The Regulations, preceded by a preamble stating their aims, contain six articles (concerning applicability, instruments of integrated management, Medium-Term Plan, program aspects of the budget, monitoring of program implementation, and evaluation). They reflect the current understanding of the U.N.'s practice of planning, programming, and evaluation. But despite their codification, the regulations are widely misunderstood and incorrectly implemented. They fail to achieve their real purpose: to facilitate a better agreement among member states on the content of programs and on the financing of activities of the United Nations.

Lessons to Be Drawn from This Historical Evolution

The lessons one can draw from a history of the program planning, budget, and evaluation cycle depend on the philosophy that inspires one's analysis of U.N. achievements and failures.

Everyone acknowledges—and the present financial and political crisis makes clear—that the system has failed to facilitate a better agreement among member states on the content of programs and the financing of the activities of the U.N. Wordiness, which should have been reduced by the definition of precise objectives, is still flourishing in resolutions as well as in documents prepared by the Secretariat—particularly the Medium-Term Plan. The efficiency of the Secretariat does not seem much improved. Objectives are not defined in a more precise way and are not, as prescribed, time limited. So rare is the use of evaluation studies and so limited the use of program performance reports that these instruments have not made possible a regular improvement of the methods the U.N. applies to its work.

Achievements seem meager: A better understanding of what the U.N. does and of what it might accomplish is developing; a more widespread knowledge of the various activities of the U.N.—and their relative costs and importance—is spreading; delegations have documents that give them a precise overview of all activities; and the process of reflection on possible changes has begun. Specialized committees like the CPC are responsible for facilitating and nurturing this process. It has become possible to identify the fields in which, despite inevitable limitations, the Organization has been useful and has helped member states to make some progress—on population, environment, human rights, international law, law of the sea, the peaceful uses of outer space, etc. In addition, member states have been provided with descriptions of programs dealing with similar issues that are carried out by the various agencies of the U.N. system.

But these achievements still fall short of the real ambitions of the program planning, budgeting, and evaluation system, and a feeling of failure tends to prevail.

According to critics of the program planning, budgeting, and evaluation cycle, the problems facing the U.N. since the very beginning have been purely political—the result mainly of a "lack of political will" and thus impervious to technical solutions. According to this interpretation, sophisticated systems alone cannot help to solve a financial and political crisis. This simplistic conception of the U.N. limits the Organization's role to that of political forum, a meeting place for diplomats. It fails to attribute any real importance to the economic and social programs that are the majority of U.N. programs and, consequently, fails to recognize the necessity of improving their efficiency.

This study supports a totally different analysis. It considers the U.N. in its entirety and not just as a meeting place. It affirms:

• that the General Assembly was right in trying to clarify the nature of U.N. activities and objectives and to define better methods of

reaching agreement on the content of the programs and on the level of the resources
• that the program planning, budgeting, and evaluation system is the only method at the disposal of the international community that might facilitate a better understanding of how the U.N. could play a more useful role in the modern world and help member states to identify and solve their common problems
• that the reasons for the "failure" of the program planning, budgeting, and evaluation system are due to the fact that it has not yet been correctly implemented or even fully developed, and has not been permitted to reach its principal objective, which is to obtain a clear definition of the U.N.'s role at the end of the 20th century.

It is first necessary to acknowledge that the Regulations and Rules guiding the system are not correctly implemented.[26] The main points of the Regulations that have not been correctly implemented are: the use of the Introduction of the Medium-Term Plan as a tool for analyzing the world problems and indicating the U.N.'s main orientations, the establishment of fixed-term objectives, the drafting of understandable strategies for the Medium-Term Plan, the establishment of precise evaluation studies that can provide lessons for the future, and the organization of a calendar of meetings in order to facilitate considera-tion by the different intergovernmental organs of the relevant parts of the plan corresponding to their mandate.

Member states insist on obtaining better implementation of the PPBE regulations while trying to overcome the resistance of the Secretariat. These efforts have certainly to be pursued vigorously. The Secretary-General should be requested to report as soon as possible on the measures he intends to take for the full implementation of the Regula-tions, particularly the preparation of the next Medium-Term Plan; and the General Assembly should establish a procedure for monitoring the implementation of its decisions on this subject.

But this is not enough. In fact, the main advantage of the PPBE system is that it has begun to shed some light on the manner in which the usefulness of the U.N. could be increased. But to achieve this purpose fully, the reasons for the resistance of the Secretariat have to be analyzed and understood and the lacunae in the Regulations identi-fied and filled in.

The resistance of the U.N.'s Secretariat to the new system can be explained as the usual attitude of bureaucracies toward change. It is never easy or pleasant to have to modify one's methods of work, to have to explain clearly one's objectives and policies, to be monitored and evaluated, or to be obliged to take on more responsibilities.

In a more general way, it is also more convenient and comfortable to stick to a traditional explanation of the U.N.'s situation than to try to find a new and more accurate one—for example, to give an idealized image of the institution's role in the areas of peace, development, or human rights and to attribute the defeat of this ideal to the vicious policies of a state or group of states rather than try to define the kind of changes that would permit the U.N. to cope with the real political, economic, and social problems of the world. It is always easier to indulge in wordiness than to make serious and realistic analyses. It is always more pleasant to state grandiose objectives to be implemented at some indefinite date than to state modest and precise goals and try to reach them by an assigned date.

The process of education toward realism, precision, and modesty of approach that was built into the PPBE process has not had time yet to develop or to bear results.

But it is obviously not only a question of time: The present Regulations and Rules are unclear on some important points, due in part to the tendency to subject very different types of activities to the same methodology. In fact, experience shows clearly that some gaps remain. The first and the most important is the absence of a distinction between the two main types of activities of the U.N., i.e., *the search for a better consensus in a number of fields, on the one hand, and the joint management of activities on which some consensus exists, on the other hand.*

The importance of this distinction can be understood only if one considers that the whole purpose of the PPBE system is to offer an opportunity for reflection and definition of the best possible and reasonable objectives for the U.N. and the best possible strategies for reaching them. There is no doubt that the authors of the Regulations were aware of these needs. The preamble of the Regulations and Rules clearly states that the main objectives of the PPBE cycle are:

> to afford an opportunity for reflection before the choices among the various types of action possible are made in the light of all existing conditions
> to associate in this reflection all participants in the Organization's actions, especially member states and the Secretariat
> to assess what is feasible and derive from this assessment objectives which are both feasible and politically acceptable to member states as a whole.

But such a formulation, despite its appeal as a collective intellectual endeavor, seems to suggest that all activities should be subjected to the same type of analysis, as if the types of problems existing in the areas where some consensus is present were the same as those in areas that require consensus-seeking.

What led to the confusion of the authors of the Regulations and Rules on this important point is obviously the comparison, rather unconsciously, between planning at the national level and planning in an intergovernmental organization like the United Nations.

At the national level, the purpose of a plan is to identify the sectors or types of investment that will receive preferential treatment and to define objectives accordingly. Planning in this case is done in a context of national consensus, and even in very poor countries with limited resources, planners can achieve reasonably concrete objectives.

Not only are constraints different in an international organization like the U.N., but the purposes of planning are different as well, both in the areas where limited consensus exists and in those where the search for consensus has yet to be completed.

Areas of Limited Consensus

In areas where a limited amount of consensus must be converted into useful results, the main constraint is the enormous gap that exists between the ambitious goals indicated in the mandates and the very limited resources allocated for reaching them. This situation is well known and has been described in a number of critical studies.[27] The objectives of programs and subprograms are often formulated in such terms as "overcoming the bottlenecks and constraints facing the developing countries," "identifying critical issues confronting developing countries and fostering and promoting cooperation and coordination regarding those issues of global interest," and "strengthening and enlarging mutual cooperation at the sub-regional, regional and inter-regional levels." But the manpower resources for reaching these "objectives" are, in the majority of cases, two or three professionals. It is therefore not surprising that the output of these programs frequently consists of a few publications of no great consequence, occasional meetings unrelated to the problems of the countries concerned, and occasional interpretations and ineffectual projects.

Among the broad areas where there is only limited consensus at the U.N. are those involving assistance in defining and implementing national policies, organization of international cooperation in a particular sector, collection and dissemination of information, and dissemination of norms approved by the General Assembly.

The degree of consensus in these areas varies. It is higher for the collection and dissemination of world and national statistics than for natural resources or science and technology. The level of consensus can be measured by the adequacy of the resources allocated to the pursuit of objectives. In the majority of cases, the gap between needs and resources remains enormous. Obviously, the units in charge of the various programs may take an easy way out by choosing to indulge in wordiness, stating ambitious and even unattainable objectives, and pursuing them from plan to plan and from budget to budget, with the obvious advantage of guaranteeing a long life to the unit itself. Delegations are accustomed to these practices and understand too well that it is not the fault of the unit if the outputs are inadequate.

If the regulation requesting precise and time-limited objectives has not yet been executed, it is because no serious attempt has been made to change the existing routine. To obtain a result of this importance, it would be necessary to define a typology of time-limited objectives for subprograms, to render compulsory its use for defining the content of the programs, and to organize some training for professionals who will put it into practice. This is perfectly possible. Examples of types of time-limited objectives can be given easily. A 1979 JIU report [28] offered the following examples:

• preparation of a series of descriptive studies relating to a specific field
• establishment of an information system
• setting of a target level or stage to be reached in research in a particular field
• establishment of an institutionalized research system
• establishment of an intergovernmental research program
• training of a specific number of specialists to be available to member states for implementation of a policy
• setting the level of information for a specific subject, for an audience defined by composition and quantified order of magnitude
• construction of a network of multipurpose institutions for use by member states to facilitate their implementation of a plan in a particular field
• development of an instrument for cooperation in a regional area
• definition, in consultation with a number of governments, of "concentration areas" for technical cooperation programs and establishment within the areas thus defined of specific social objectives.

It is not easy to determine which time-limited objectives are most in keeping with the general orientation of the programs and apt to be implemented in the allotted time and with the limited resources that are available.

For example, it is obviously easier to divide the major program on Public Administration into a six-subprogram structure that merely breaks down the program under headings as perpetual as the program itself[29] than to propose a two-subprogram structure that defines such precise, time-limited objectives as:

• creation, over a five-year period, of a set of manuals (or handbooks) covering the various branches of public administration (with a supplementary target number of copies to be sold in various languages)
• establishment, over a four-year period, of a standard methodology for analysis of public administration problems.

The search for time-limited and precise objectives is obviously difficult, but if member states want realism, efficiency, and a more modest approach to prevail in the U.N., the regulations should be completed on this very important point and training should be organized along these lines.

Areas of Consensus-Seeking

In the areas of consensus-seeking—that is, where there is room for exploration of problems, discussions, and (possibly at certain stages) negotiations, it is clearly pointless to establish time-limited objectives or to fix a date for the completion of a convention. In the quest for peace, the development of international law, the adoption of conventions on human rights, the exploration of a common approach to international trade and the price of commodities, to world population, global migrations, and economic and social relations in general and the North-South dialogue in particular, it is obvious that suitable reflection cannot take place or strategies be defined at the program or subprogram level.

The primary task here should be to identify those problems the U.N. can help to solve—by making a contribution to mutual understanding and by defining how best to go about exploring their resolution. The process of identification that has been used thus far in the U.N. for this purpose has not been a systematic one. It relies mainly upon initiatives taken by delegations or by individuals in the Secretariat. The existing programs of research, discussions, and negotiations in the

U.N.—such as those concerning the Law of the Sea, transnational corporations, and commodities—have been established on personal initiative rather than by a rational process. The exercises in collective research and discussion—like the ritual discussions every year on the "World Economic Survey" and the decennial "International Development Strategies"—have remained formal and have not led to a real identification of problems on which the U.N. could usefully conduct research and negotiations.

The main objectives of the Medium-Term Plan in the areas of consensus-seeking should be to try to rationalize and to improve this process and to organize a kind of global watch for the U.N. This was obviously the purpose for creation of the Introduction to the Medium-Term Plan. Yet we have seen that no use has been made of the opportunity the Introduction affords. Here again, experience reveals the necessity not only of reiterating the need for a useful Introduction but of further reforming and developing the whole process of preliminary reflection, in order *to obtain a better system for identifying global problems that it will be useful for the U.N. to try to tackle.* To this end, the Regulations should describe more precisely:

- the type of preliminary studies that are necessary for this identification
- the methods for establishing them
- the calendar for preparation and examination of these studies.

In particular, *serious consideration should be given to (a) replacing the traditional studies that are ritually presented to the Economic and Social Council or to the Trade and Development Board—and even the International Development Strategies—with studies that are more oriented toward identifying world problems,* and (b) entrusting such studies to the best centers of research and reflection, rather than relying on the Secretariat alone to prepare them.

Evaluation

A good system of evaluation should be an integral part of a system for identifying world problems that it is useful for the U.N. to tackle. But the functioning of such a system requires the recruitment of competent people in the relevant fields, not to mention a greater allocation of resources. Independent evaluations should be developed, for example, by allocating the necessary manpower to the Joint Inspection Unit. Special sessions of the Committee for Program and Coordination should also be devoted to the examination of evaluation studies.

Calendar of Preparation of the Medium-Term Plan

Were the Medium-Term Plan to become the main policy directive of the Organization, as required by the Regulations, it seems obvious that it should serve as a framework for all the decisions taken by intergovernmental and expert organs. This implies that these organs should be fully associated with the process of preparation. Such is not the case at present, despite the existence of Regulation 3.12, which states that "the chapters of the proposed Medium-Term Plan shall be reviewed by the relevant sectoral, functional, and regional intergovernmental bodies, if possible during the regular cycle of their meetings prior to their review by the Committee for Programme and Coordination, the Economic and Social Council and the General Assembly." The existing calendar of preparation has never allowed interested organs to receive a draft of the relevant parts of the proposed Medium-Term Plan in timely fashion.

The calendar has to be reorganized carefully, and the process of preparation, which occurs every six years, should start sufficiently in advance of that period to permit delegations in all intergovernmental and expert committees to be actively engaged in defining the objectives of the Organization. The present overlap between resolutions defining mandates, on the one hand, and the Medium-Term Plan, on the other, should be eliminated. *The preparation of the relevant parts of the Medium-Term Plan by the various intergovernmental organs, and their approval by the central organs, should replace the use of resolutions for taking decisions and defining mandates.*

Procedures for Preparation of the Program Budget and the Restructuring of the Intergovernmental Machinery

The creation of a single committee to deal with both the definition of the program content and the allocation of resources has now become *a political problem.*[30] To the logical argument in favor of such a committee (see the discussion of "The Institutional Mechanisms" and "The Establishment of Regulations and Rules" early in this chapter) is now added the necessity of finding a way to facilitate the building of consensus on the level and content of the program budget, which is at the heart of the present crisis.

In this regard, the report of the Group of 18 High-Level Intergovernmental Experts to Review the Efficiency of the Administrative and Financial Functions of the United Nations shows that, on this point, important progress has been made, even if a final agreement is not yet possible. After having acknowledged the importance of the present Regulations and Rules governing the planning cycle, and having recommended that they be strictly applied by the intergovernmental organs concerned and by the Secretariat, the Group considered it "necessary to rectify the deficiency of the present planning and budget mechanisms," explaining that "the present methodology of the preparation of the program budget does not allow for the participation of members in the process of definition of the program budget. *A procedure must therefore be developed which makes it possible for member states to exercise at the very beginning of the planning and budget process, as well as throughout the whole process, the necessary intergovernmental leadership, particularly regarding the setting of priorities within the resources likely to be available."*

In fact, this procedure would imply the presentation by the Secretary-General, in the spring of the non-budget year, of an *"outline of the program budget"* for the next biennium, based on the Medium-Term Plan, with an indication of the resources that the Secretary-General expects to be available.

The study and discussion of this outline should allow the Committee for Programme and Budget *to try to reach a consensus* and, on this basis, *to give advice* to the General Assembly.

The function, powers, and composition of such a committee were the subject of intensive negotiations in the Group—and in the General Assembly. The "major contributors," who pay more than 80 percent of the budget, argued from the outset that there should be a way to ensure that their views regarding the amount and content of the budget are taken into account, since the two-thirds majority required to pass on the budget (Article 18, paragraph 2 of the Charter) is readily formed by other member states. They requested the creation of a compact Committee of Programme and Budget, which would be authorized by the General Assembly to decide on budgetary matters. Decisions would be made either by consensus or by vote; in the latter case the composition of the committee would be such as to give major contributors a "blocking minority."

The opposing argument was that there was no reason to modify the current decision-making methods with regard to the budget—based on the provisions of Articles 17 and 18 of the Charter—and that the new procedure of examination of an outline of the program budget a year in advance could be used within the present setting of auxiliary bodies: the CPC and ACABQ.

Ultimately, the members of the Group of 18 offered three competing proposals to reinforce the present intergovernmental machinery dealing with budget and program. The *first* of these solutions gives to a renewed CPC of 21 members the responsibility for advising the General Assembly on the content and the level of resources of the budget. Here, the CPC would be renamed Committee for Programme, Budget and Coordination. It would examine the Medium-Term Plan and would receive—in the spring of the non-budget year—an outline of the program budget for the next biennium, as prepared by the Secretary-General. Its members would be elected on the basis of expert capacity, but the committee would keep its intergovernmental character.

The *second* solution reinforces the CPC in the consideration of the program aspects of the budget and of the Medium-Term Plan without giving to it a right to advise the General Assembly on the level of the budget. The second solution, like the first, would request the presentation of an outline of the program budget, and it recommends setting the same requirements for the appointment of the members of the CPC. The ACABQ would remain unchanged.

The *third* solution entrusts the function of advising the General Assembly on the budget and the program to a single committee that has the right to determine the overall limit of the future budget. The CPC and ACABQ would be replaced by this single committee.

The three solutions recommend the presentation of an outline budget in advance and a stronger cooperation between the delegations and the Secretariat in the preparation of the budget and program. The first two solutions recommend a reinforcement of the CPC. The first and the third favor a single committee dealing with both programming and budget.

This brief analysis shows that differences were limited, particularly between the two first proposals. In fact, the first solution was a *compromise* between the initial positions of the two groups of negotiators.

On December 19, 1986, the General Assembly finally adopted a *fourth* solution. The Committee for Programme and Coordination will receive the outline of the program budget presented by the Secretary-General one year in advance and will "submit its conclusions and recommendations" to the General Assembly. It will "continue its existing practice of reaching decisions by consensus" (A/Res/41/213).

But it is stressed that the General Assembly will continue to take its final decision on the program budget "according to the provisions of the Charter" (Articles 17 and 18). The system for appointing members of the CPC is not changed.

Despite interpretations given by some delegations that the U.N. budget would henceforth be established "by consensus," there is no provision of this kind in the resolution. The CPC presents a report which—as has always been the case in the past—may reflect divergent views of its members—if they have not succeeded in establishing a consensus. One may wish that the new formula will facilitate the establishment of such a consensus in the future, but very much depends on the goodwill of all delegations.

Furthermore, the problems that arise from the present deficiencies of the intergovernmental U.N. structure will not be solved simply by a change in the budgetary process. The obstacles that have hampered the development of the planning, programming, budgeting, and evaluation system have clearly shown their durability.

We have enough data on the problem posed by the structure of the intergovernmental machinery of the U.N. to understand that the creation of such a committee would be only *a first step*. The difficulties of developing the planning, programming, budgeting, and evaluation (PPBE) system within the present intergovernmental structure have helped to reveal the deficiencies of that structure. Particularly in the economic and social fields, the intergovernmental machinery is too complicated, needlessly divided along various lines without having direct communication (General Assembly, ECOSOC, UNCTAD), and was not conceived to facilitate either the discussions and negotiations among all categories of member states or joint management in areas where some consensus exists. A thorough study of the possibility of a restructuring is badly needed. A recommendation made by the Group of 18 in this regard (Recommendation 8 of its report) has been approved by resolution 41/213, and this study has been entrusted to the Economic and Social Council.

Recommendations and Conclusions

The development of the planning, programming, and evaluation cycle continues to play an important role in the present process of reflection on the U.N. It has not only shown that a process of change is possible but allows the identification of direction for future changes that will help to improve significantly the efficiency and effectiveness of the United Nations.

The process of reform has been slow, but it has been continuous. As the first section of this chapter shows, some ideas have been adopted relatively rapidly (for example, the creation of the program budget and the Medium-Term Plan, the performance reports, standardization of nomenclature), while some have been favorably considered without being implemented (evaluation, joint planning, use of the Introduction of the Medium-Term Plan). Others, like the creation of a single committee on program and budget, are still waiting for adoption. And still other new ideas are emerging.

Since the pace of reform in the U.N. could accelerate as a result of the present crisis, it is necessary to formulate precise recommendations for improvement in the planning, programming, and budgeting area. But it is also necessary to understand that *only if the changes recommended are clearly understood and implemented will they help to redefine the role of the U.N. in the modern world.*

Recommendations that flow from the present analysis are the following:

1. Full implementation of the existing Regulations and Rules Governing Program Planning, the Program Aspects of the Budget, the Monitoring of Implementation and the Methods of Evaluation by the Secretariat should be vigorously requested by member states and a reporting and monitoring system should be organized by the General Assembly.

Improvement of the present Regulations and Rules (Recommendations 2, 3, 4, and 6) and the existing practices (Recommendations 5, 7, 8, 9) should be obtained through the following recommendations:

2. A clear distinction should be made between programs aimed at the search for consensus and those aimed at converting existing consensus into useful results. This distinction should be taken into account in the design of the Medium-Term Plan and the definition of programs.

3. For programs dealing with joint management in the areas of limited consensus, time-limited objectives should be established and followed.

4. In order to strengthen the U.N. global watch function and to promote consensus-building, the process of identifying problems that the U.N. could usefully address should be better organized by (a) use of the Introduction to the Medium-Term Plan to pinpoint

those emerging issues requiring collective response in which a U.N. role is feasible; (b) adoption of regulations describing the type of global watch studies to be conducted, the means for deciding upon them, and the calendar for their preparation and review by member states; and (c) establishment of a list of international centers of research and expertise that, in addition to relevant secretariats of the U.N. system, could contribute to a global watch function.

5. The necessary resources should be allocated to establish a workforce of a reasonable size for preparing evaluation studies. Independent evaluation should be developed, for example, by allocating the necessary manpower to the Joint Inspection Unit.

6. The calendar for the preparation of the Medium-Term Plan should be organized in order to permit all intergovernmental and expert bodies to participate in the preparation of the relevant parts of the Medium-Term Plan. Approval of the Medium-Term Plan should replace the usual process of definition of mandates through resolutions.

7. The study of the restructuring of the intergovernmental machinery dealing with economic and social problems should be undertaken with a view toward the creation of a system that goes beyond the mere passage of resolutions and has a real effect on the outcome of the problems with which they are concerned.

Apparently, there is a long way to go before these recommendations can be adopted and implemented. The main obstacle to overcome is a conceptual one—the illusion that there is enough consensus in the international community to allow the U.N. a central role in the international system. The fading of this illusion has not yet given way to a new conception of the world organization. This same illusion has fostered an exaggerated belief in the ability of the Organization to maintain peace and security and to "achieve international cooperation in solving international problems of an economic, social, cultural, or humanitarian character" (U.N. Charter, Article 1.3).

Forty years of experience have shown how misconceived a role this was. The failure to succeed at it has given rise to various attitudes, the most popular being that the U.N. has been reduced to a political forum and that the lack of political will has restricted its ability to produce results. Some ideas of reform are now developing; however, they are, in general, limited to the idea that better management would improve the Organization's efficiency.

Yet it has not yet been acknowledged that the whole conception of the U.N. has to be changed and that the basic concepts on which it has been built have to be reconsidered, including its capacity to maintain peace and to solve development problems.

The essential problem in the present world—which is characterized by a growing acknowledgement of the interdependence of member states—is to find a system for building progressively better consensus on questions of common interest. The Charter has assumed that the initial level of consensus was high, and its articles have built the institution on the basis of this assumption.

Such an assumption, unfortunately, cannot be made. The level of support for the world organization is and always has been very low, as is clearly shown by the permanent financial difficulties of the Organization and by the reluctance of member states to pay their assessed contributions or to accept their growth.

A new conception has to take the place of the old—one *based on the idea that the low level of existing consensus can, with patience, be elevated over time.*

The development of the PPBE system could help in this endeavor by showing that the quest for peace requires, first, a patient and inevitably lengthy search for a better consensus on the nature and on the solution of world problems; and, second, an attempt to convert, as much as possible, the consensus gained through this search into modest but useful results. If this understanding of the role of the U.N. were adopted, it would be easier to implement the recommendations listed above and to make real progress toward a new and more efficient United Nations.[31]

Notes

1. Disorders and mutiny after the proclamation of independence of the Republic of Congo (and the capital, Leopoldville, renamed Kinshasa) on July 1, 1966, led to a mass exodus of Belgian administrators and technicians. On July 12, Congolese leaders requested military assistance from the U.N. and asked the U.N. to put an end to the secession of the province of Katanga. The Security Council authorized Secretary-General Dag Hammarskjöld to provide military and technical assistance to the Congo. The Secretary-General's response was to set up ONUC (the acronym derived from the French formulation, Opérations des Nations Unis aux Congo).

Among the major events in the Congo from 1960 to 1964 (when the U.N. military force was withdrawn):

July-August 1960: withdrawal of the Belgian troops and their replacement by the U.N. military force.

August 1960: entry of U.N. forces into Katanga—the first contingent led by Dag Hammarskjöld himself—and the refusal of Prime Minister Patrice Lumumba to cooperate with the Secretary-General

a constitutional crisis in the Congo, resulting in the replacement of Mr. Lumumba by Mr. Ileo and the taking of power by Colonel Joesph Mobutu

January 1961: murder of Patrice Lumumba

February 1961: refusal of USSR to recognize Dag Hammarskjöld as Secretary-General

formation of the national unity government of Mr. Adoula

secession of Katanga under the leadership of Mr. Tshombe; intervention of ONUC to round up mercenaries in Elizabethville; and attack on U.N. forces by the Katangese "gendarmerie"

September 17, 1961: death of Dag Hammarskjöld and seven U.N. staff members in the crash of an aircraft en route to Ndola in northern Rhodesia

November 1961: appointment of U Thant as acting Secretary-General

August 1962: proposal by the new Secretary-General of a plan of national reconciliation

February 4, 1963: end of secession of Katanga

June 30, 1964: withdrawal of U.N. forces

November 1964: the "Stanleyville operation" by Belgian paracommandos carried by U.S. aircraft.

2. The military arm of ONUC—the U.N. Emergency Force (UNEF)—was made up of contingents from states other than the great powers and reached a maximum strength of about 20,000 soldiers. It was the second UNEF: The acronym was used for the first time in 1956 for the force sent to the Suez Canal and the Sinai Peninsula.

3. The Assembly took the position that the expenses involved in ONUC for 1960 were "expenses of the Organization" within the meaning of Article 17, paragraph 2 of the Charter and that, therefore, member states had binding legal obligations to pay their assessed shares. This view was upheld by a majority opinion of the International Court of Justice handed down on July 20, 1962.

The Assembly subsequently decided that the extraordinary expenses of ONUC were essentially different in nature from those covered by the Organization's regular budget, and that, therefore, a different procedure for meeting them was required. The Assembly noted in this connection that the five permanent members of the Security Council had a special responsibility for contributing to the cost of peacekeeping operations. Accordingly, the Assembly devised a special formula under which developing nations were given a substantial reduction on their assessments, with the difference to be made up by voluntary contributions from the developed countries. Twenty-six countries were subsequently designated as "developed" by the Assembly, but a number of these countries did not contribute to the peacekeeping operations.

The Assembly later appealed to members in arrears to make their payments, without prejudice to their respective political positions, and set up machinery and guidelines for special methods of financing peacekeeping operations that involved heavy expenditures, such as those for the Congo and the Middle East *(Everyone's United Nations, March 1968 edition).*

4. *Ibid.,* p. 476.

5. In 1960, the number of staff was 4,215 (1,731 professionals; 2,484 general services and local level staff). In 1966 it reached 5,651 (2,245 professionals; 3,406 general services and local level staff). See U.N. Document A/6289, Add. 2 of May 31, 1966.

6. The bonds, issued for a 25-year period, bear an annual interest rate of 2 percent. Between 1963 and 1987 interest charges and principal were to be paid in annual installments averaging $8.7 million; in 1988, 1989, and 1990, would come final installments of $2.5 million, $0.9 million, and $0.06 million respectively.

7. A financial report issued by the Secretary-General in 1966 showed that the actual cash expenses incurred by ONUC by September 1965 totalled $337.4 million, with unliquidated obligations amounting to $30.8 million.

8. In 1965 there were 118 U.N. member states.

9. This report notes that "according to the Committee judgment of the difference between the current obligations and the currently available assets which can be secured to meet them," there would be an estimated $52–73.4 million "deficit for which voluntary contributions were originally requested."

10. The Advisory Committee on Administrative and Budgetary Questions (ACABQ) since its inception has been the body of experts that deals with budgetary and administrative problems in cooperation with the Fifth Committee of the General Assembly.

11. Resolutions on the program budget: 3043 (XXVII) of 1972, 3534 (XXX) of December 17, 1975, 32/210 and 32/211 of December 21, 1977, 33/203 of January 29, 1979.

12. Resolutions on the Medium-Term Plan: 3199 (XXVIII) of December 18, 1973; 31/93 of December 14, 1976; 33/48 of December 19, 1978; 34/224 of December 20, 1980; 37/234 of 1983; 38/227 of 1984.

13. Resolutions on evaluation:

Resolution of the Economic and Social Council 222A (IX) of August 15, 1949, paragraph 6.a, Resolution 1042 (XXXVIII) of 1964, Resolution 1092 (XXXIX) of 1964, Resolution 1263 (XLIII) of 1967, Resolution 1364 (XLV) of 1968. General Assembly resolution 32/206, 33/118, 35/9 and other resolutions dealing with Medium-Term Plans and budgets already quoted.

14. During this period the JIU has established the following reports and notes on these matters:

JIU/REP/69/7—Report on Programming and Budget of the United Nations
JIU/NOTE/70/2—Interagency cooperation in programming
JIU/NOTE/70/3—Presentation of an outline program budget for the United Nations

JIU/REP/74/1—Report on Medium-Term Planning in the U.N. system
JIU/NOTE/75/1—Harmonization of program budget presentation
Comments on the report of the group of experts on the structure of the
U.N. system (E/AC/62/9)
JIU/REP/76/19—Reports on country programming as an instrument for
coordination and cooperation at the country level
A/28—Note on the concept of objective in international organizations in
the context of Medium-Term Plans and program budgets
JIU/REP/78/1—Report on programming and evaluation in the United
Nations
September 1978—tentative mock-up of a presentation of a program in the
Medium-Term Plan
JIU/REP/79/5—Medium-Term Planning in the United Nations
JIU/REP/81/7—Report on the Setting of Priorities and the Identification
of Obsolete Activities at the U.N.
JIU/REP/82/10—Report on the Elaboration of Regulations for the Plan-
ning, Programming and Evaluation Cycle of the United Nations
JIU/REP/83/6—Second Report on the Elaboration of Regulations on the
Planning, Programming and Evaluation Cycle of the United Nations.
In addition: Evaluation of the U.N. System (1977), Glossary of Evaluation
Terms (1978), Initial Guidelines for Internal Evaluation Systems (1979),
Status of Internal Evaluation in the U.N. System (1981), Second Report on
Evaluation of the U.N. System (1982).

15. In its annual reports throughout this period, CPC has regularly studied
problems of methodology and has described and commented upon the various
experiments made in evaluation, planning, and comparison of programs of the
U.N. with those of other agencies (cross-organizational program analyses, or
COPAS).

16. It should be noted that after having been involved in the discussion of
the establishment of the first program budget, the ACABQ has not participated
in the establishment of this methodology.

17. This chapter does not deal with programming at the country level of
operational activities. Despite the fact that it is closely related with the
planning and programming activities of the U.N. and of the agencies of the
U.N. system, "country programming" has been dealt with separately, particularly by the governing council of UNDP, ECOSOC, and the Second Committee of the General Assembly.

18. The 24 "major programs" of the last Medium-Term Plan (1984–89):

Political and Security Council Affairs; Special Political Affairs and Special
Missions; International Justice and International Law; Trusteeship and Decol-
onization; Disaster Relief; Human Rights; International Drug Control; Inter-
national Protection and Assistance to Refugees; Information; Development
Questions and Policies; Energy; Environment; Food and Agriculture; Human
Settlements; Industrial Development; International Trade and Financing of

Development; Natural Resources; Population; Public Administration and Finance; Science and Technology; Social Development and Humanitarian Affairs; Statistics; Transnational Corporations; and Transport, Communications and Tourism.

19. The official definitions of these notions:

Major program: A major program consists of all activities, regardless of organizational location, conducted by the United Nations in one of the sectors listed in the Medium-Term Plan, e.g., all work on transport conducted by the United Nations. The major program on transport consists of the work in the sector conducted by the United Nations Conference on Trade and Development, the Department of International, Economic and Social Affairs, and the Regional Commissions.

Program: A program consists of the activities within a major program undertaken by a department, office, or division, e.g., work in the Economic and Social Commission for Asia and the Pacific on transport in Asia and the Pacific.

Subprogram: A subprogram consists of all activities within a program aimed at achieving one or a few closely related objectives as set out in the Medium-Term Plan, e.g., work in the Economic Commission for Europe directed toward traffic facilities in Europe.

Program element: A program element consists of activities within a subprogram, addressing specific and well-circumscribed subject matter, and is usually designed to produce one or a few final outputs per biennium, such as a publication, a meeting, or services of an advisory nature, e.g., within the traffic facilitation program in the Economic Commission for Europe, review of the implementation of the Convention on International Intermodal Transport.

Final output: In the United Nations a final output is a product or service delivered by the Secretariat to users external to the secretariats of the organizations of the United Nations system. All Secretariat work needed to generate the final output is intermediate activity.

Delivery of output: An output is delivered when the service is completed or when the products resulting from a program activity are made available to intended primary user(s): e.g., in the case of services to a session of an intergovernmental meeting, when the final report of the session has been circulated to member states; in the case of a report or a technical publication when these have been circulated to member states, interested governments, or other primary users; in the case of a sales publication, when it is placed on sale; in the case of a technical assistance project, when the final report following completion of the project has been received by the recipient country; in the case of a grant, when the recipient has received the final payment; and in the case of a fellowship, when the recipient has completed the course of study.

Source: glossary of programming terms published as an annex of ST/SGB/204 of June 14, 1984.

20. The list of standard categories is given in Rule 104: "Substantive services of intergovernmental meetings, including support of negotiations, report to intergovernmental bodies, peacekeeping and humanitarian operations, technical publications, public information service, technical cooperative projects including advisory services, financial contributions including grants and fellowship, other final outputs."

21. U.N. Document A/34/84 of March 26, 1979, "Medium-Term Planning in the United Nations" (JIU/REP/79/5).

22. U.N. Document A/41/49. The group made these remarks on the subject of priorities:

The criteria for the setting of relative priorities are set out in the Secretary-General's bulletin entitled Regulations and Rules Governing Program Planning, the Program Aspects of the Budget, the Monitoring of Implementation and the Methods of Evaluation (ST/SGB/204). These Regulations and Rules devote special attention to the application of priorities at all levels. Regulation 3.15, relating to the Medium-Term Plan, states that the establishment of priorities among both substantive programs and common services shall form an integral part of the general planning . . . process." The determining criteria are defined as being based on the importance of the objective to member states, the Organization's capacity to achieve it and the real effectiveness and usefulness of the results. Regulation 3.16 defines the process according to which intergovernmental bodies formulate recommendations on priorities among the subprograms in their field of competence. The idea of priority is taken even further in Regulation 3.17, which calls for the establishment of priorities by the General Assembly among the subprograms, and in Regulation 4.6 relating to the program budget, which requests the Secretary-General to identify "program elements of high and low priority."

These criteria are by and large satisfactory. The problems experienced regarding the setting of priorities are primarily related to the lack of application of these criteria by the intergovernmental machinery and the Secretariat.

23. As defined by Regulation 6.1, the purpose of evaluation is:

to determine as systematically and objectively as possible the relevance, efficiency, effectiveness and impact of the Organization's activities in relation to their objectives;

to enable the Secretariat and member states to engage in systematic reflections with a view to increasing the effectiveness of the main programs of the Organization by altering their content and, if necessary, reviewing their objectives [ST/SGB/204, pp. 22–23].

24. See resolution 32/197, Annex, paragraphs 43 and 52.

25. Recommendation 15 of JIU Report A/36/171 of April 10, 1981: "Explo-

ration of the possibilities of establishing in the the United Nations a single intergovernmental committee to review plans, programs and budgets."

26. Two reports of the JIU—JIU/REP/82/10 of September 1982 and JIU/ REP/83/6 of April 1983—give an account of the problems found and of the discussions that took place about the establishment of Regulations and Rules. See also Report of the Secretary-General (A/38/126) and the Annual Reports of CPC during the years 1981, '82, '83, and '84. The Regulations and Rules have yet to be published in the same form as the Personnel or the Financial regulations, despite the insistence of the CPC that this be done. They can be found in a bulletin of the Secretary-General (ST/SGB/204 of June 14, 1984).

27. See in particular A/34/84 of March 26, 1979, A/36/171 of April 10, 1981, JIU/REP/82/10 of September 1982, and JIU/REP/85/9.

28. JIU/REP/79/5, "Medium-Term Planning in the United Nations," paragraph 60.

29. The six subprograms in 1978–81:

Trends and development
Reform of public administration and management of development
Institutional and management techniques
Budgeting and financial management
Mobilization of financial resources
Public enterprises

The manpower at the disposal of these programs for this period was 29 professionals and the situation is the same today (see, for more detail, JIU/ REP A/34/84, paragraphs 64 and 65 and annex VI presenting a tentative mock-up of a presentation of a program in the Medium-Term Plan).

30. For a description of many of the issues underlying the current debate over U.N. financial decision-making and the scale of assessments, see the chapter by Frederick K. Lister, *"Fairness and Accountability in U.N. Financial Decision-Making"*.

31. See the chapter by Peter Fromuth, *"The U.N. at 40: The Problems and the Opportunities,"* p. 12. See also JIU Report A/40/988 of December 6, 1985, *"Some Reflections on Reform of the United Nations,"* paragraphs 65–75.

CHAPTER 13

FAIRNESS AND ACCOUNTABILITY IN U.N. FINANCIAL DECISION-MAKING

Frederick K. Lister

This study has a limited scope. It does not deal with the underlying political and economic issues that nearly everybody agrees brought on the U.N.'s present financial crisis. Rather, it is addressed mainly to the way that financial decision-making has been working in two sensitive areas, which seems to be directly responsible for the uneasy relationship between many of the main contributors and the rest of the membership. These areas are the rules and practices that surround the formulation, negotiation, and voting of the program budget on the one hand and the scale of assessments on the other. It is hoped that if these rules and practices can be made more acceptable to all concerned, the U.N. will be able to carry on its search for ways of solving controversial substantive issues and, equally important, maintain the many noncontroversial services it provides to member states. The study concludes with a number of options and ideas that might help to relieve the various financial tensions that have now reached the crisis stage.

The Problem of Financial Decision-Making in the U.N.

At first glance, the principal voting system of the U.N. appears simple and straightforward. It provides that each member state shall have one and only one vote, and that decisions will be taken by a simple or two-thirds majority of those present and voting "yea" or "nay." The national parliaments of most democratic countries have long followed similar procedures, and these have, in general, worked tolerably well.

But when it comes to voting, there is one all-important difference between national parliaments and U.N. bodies: National parliaments are composed of members whose constituencies are of roughly the same order of magnitude, whereas the U.N.'s constituencies—its member states—run the gamut from countries with hundreds of millions of people to mini-states, some of which have populations smaller than that of Yonkers, New York. Differences in population are large; for example, the population of China is some 25,688 times that of St. Christopher-Nevis.[1] Thus, on the basis of population—the basis used in most democratic countries—the large states are grossly underrepresented. Furthermore, if capacity to pay or to help implement decisions (which are important to the U.N.'s ability to function effectively day-by-day) are taken as the criteria, the potential of the various member states differs not just a little but a lot.

Those who set up the U.N. were well aware of these anomalies. The rules of procedure of the General Assembly and other U.N. bodies do not in fact require or encourage voting. In general, most chairmen and presiding officers seek to avoid voting, making every effort to arrive at decisions by consensus or "without objection." Recognition of the limitations of the one-state/one vote system is surely one reason why, with the exception of the Security Council, which has its own, very different procedures, U.N. bodies were given only the power to make recommendations to states and not the power to take decisions that would be binding on them.

One category of decision-making in particular was exempted from the rule that the General Assembly could recommend but not decide. This was the category of financial decisions, whereby the Assembly assesses member states and determines how the common funds are to be spent. For obvious reasons, it was not deemed practical or fair to allow each member state to decide on its own how much or how little it wished to contribute toward the U.N.'s expenses. At the same time, it was not anticipated that the Organization would become involved in so many different activities and that its expenses would reach their present level. Also, when the Charter was adopted, the states that became the U.N.'s main contributors did not doubt that their combined influence would suffice to ensure that the level and use of U.N. funds would be controlled in a manner satisfactory to them.[2]

As will be seen below, these expectations were too optimistic. The fact that the U.N.'s member states hold sharply differing views on many political and economic issues makes it likely that they will differ just as strongly over what actions the Organization should or should not take with regard to such issues. Nor should it be surprising that members outvoted in such circumstances will sometimes resist paying for activities that they have staunchly opposed.

Evan Luard, writing in 1979, concluded:

> It seems safe to predict that conflicts about the level and type of expenditure within the U.N. will become more frequent and fierce in the future. . . . They could become perhaps the central issue of international government.[3]

The U.N.'s Mounting Financial Crisis

Every year since 1976 the General Assembly has had on its agenda an item entitled "Financial Emergency of the United Nations."[4] This refers to the increasing level of unpaid assessments, which rose from $120.9 million in 1976 to an estimated $504 million by January 1, 1986. Of this sum, $242 million represents unpaid contributions to the U.N. regular budget, while the rest consists of unpaid contributions to the separate accounts of the peacekeeping forces. It is the regular budget withholdings in particular that now threaten the U.N.'s financial viability.

While the sums involved may not seem very large (especially when compared to the U.S. budget deficit), the U.N. has no power to borrow. As a consequence, the combination of the slowness with which member governments pay their annual assessments and the relatively low ($100 million) limit on the U.N.'s working capital fund has been creating increasingly serious cash flow problems for the Organization. For many years now, the U.N. controller has had to scrape to meet the payroll and to discharge urgent bills in certain months of the year.

The U.N.'s cash flow problem has arisen partly from a natural tendency of governments to postpone making payments and partly from the refusal of some governments to pay for certain activities for reasons of principle. Under the U.N. financial rules, contributions to the regular budget are payable in full within 30 days of the receipt of the Secretary-General's letter requesting them. In 1985 this letter was sent on January 10, but by the end of June only 35.5 percent of the 1985 contributions had been paid and, by the end of September, only 53.6 percent. At that time, 54 members also owed $68.2 million of previous assessments.

It is important to distinguish the different reasons for nonpayment. Some members simply neglect to pay; others do not have (or claim not to have) the means to pay; and still others oppose the undertaking of certain activities so strongly that they refuse to pay for their share of the costs involved.

For most member states, the payment of U.N. dues means parting with foreign exchange. Those facing foreign exchange shortages tend to postpone payment as long as they can. Nonetheless, most of them could probably pay more promptly if they had to; indeed, in 1986, because of the crisis, a number of members sent in their payments earlier than usual. In exceptional cases, however, a country's heavy foreign exchange indebtedness may present a real obstacle to timely payment or to payment at any time.

A much more serious problem for the U.N., however, is the refusal of some governments to pay for regular budget activities approved by the General Assembly or the Security Council that they do not support and/or feel were incurred improperly. In this group are 17 member governments, including ten socialist countries, three developing countries, and four Western developed countries.[5] Four of the five permanent members of the Security Council are among these withholders. Some of these same countries and nine others[6] also withhold payments from major peacekeeping forces, such as the second Middle East U.N. Emergency Force of 1973, the U.N. Disengagement Observer Force (UNDOF), and the U.N. Interim Force in Lebanon (UNIFIL).

In effect, all of these countries are ignoring Article 17 of the Charter, which provides that "expenses of the Organization shall be borne by the members as apportioned by the General Assembly." In 1962 the International Court of Justice handed down an Advisory Opinion which found that even expenditures for peacekeeping forces constituted "expenses of the Organization within the meaning of Article 17."[7] Though not obliged to do so, the Assembly by a considerable majority "accepted" this opinion. Two years later, however, it refused to invoke the sanction that would have denied the Soviet Union (whose payments were two years in arrears) its vote in the Assembly, even though such a sanction would seem to flow from the language of Article 19, which provides that any exemption from the rule set in

Article 17, must rest on the Assembly's finding that "failure to pay is due to conditions beyond the control of the Members."[8] During the 1964 session of the Assembly there was no voting because the U.S. threatened to challenge the USSR's right to vote. In 1965, however, the U.S. representative withdrew this threat while stating that the United States "reserves the same option to make exceptions [to the principle of collective financing] if, in our view, strong and compelling reasons exist for doing so."[9]

While the Assembly may have acted prudently in refusing to deny the Soviet Union its vote, this confrontation and the way in which it was eventually resolved undermined the mandatory nature of Article 17.

It is into this murky situation that several pieces of United States legislation brought new and very serious complications. One was the Kassebaum Amendment, which reduced U.S. payments to the U.N.'s regular budget from the 25 percent required by the scale of assessments to 20 percent. Still other legislation, including the Gramm-Rudman-Hollings Act, involved additional across-the-board reductions that further cut U.S. payments to less than 15 percent of the total U.N. assessment of member states.

The sharing of the U.N.'s costs is defined by a "scale of assessments" that is worked out by a Committee on Contributions and approved in accordance with Article 17;[10] there are few more difficult negotiations that the Organization has to undertake. Until recently and despite the fact that many members have felt that they were being overassessed, none has withheld payments on this basis. If member states were henceforth to decide unilaterally to reduce the rates assigned to them, obviously the financial emergency of the U.N. would be compounded. Meanwhile, the Organization, already in a very tight situation, is confronted with a 10 percent or more shortfall in its receipts for 1986.

While the U.N.'s financial emergency has many underlying causes, one of them deserves special attention. With ever-increasing frequency, many of the main contributors and the bulk of the U.N.'s membership have found themselves on opposite sides in the U.N.'s financial decision-making.[11] The former seek to hold the line on regular budget expenditures, while the latter believe that program needs should determine the level of expenditures rather than the other way around. Outvoted in the tallies, some of the main contributors have been applying a number of financial pressures that pinch because of the U.N.'s dependency on their payments. These include keeping the

Working Capital Fund from rising at the same rate as the budget level, delaying their payments until later in the budget year, and withholding payments for activities they do not support.

Over the years a number of steps have been taken to deal with U.N. financial problems. In 1961 a $200 million bond issue (of which $30 million was never subscribed) was agreed upon to cover unpaid expenses of the first Middle East U.N. Emergency Force and of the Congo peacekeeping force. In 1965 a Special Account for Voluntary Contributions was opened, which now has pledges and contributions of $77 million. The Working Capital Fund *has* been increased from $20 million to $100 million. Also, unspent funds, instead of being returned to governments at the end of a fiscal year, have been left temporarily with the Controller in order to reduce cash flow problems.

But these measures have permitted the U.N. just to squeak by. The most recent steps taken by the U.S. government, by far the U.N.'s largest contributor (and traditionally the one that in times of financial stringency helped to keep it financially afloat), threaten to bring about a situation in which the U.N. will no longer be able to pay its bills. Clearly, the time has come to bring about a better working relationship between the main contributors and the rest of the membership. Particularly urgent is the need to find a modus vivendi between the U.N. and its biggest contributor, the United States, whose unpaid contributions will now probably increase at a rate of more than $100 million per year.[12]

At its last session the General Assembly acted, albeit somewhat reluctantly, to meet main-contributor concerns. By its resolution 40/237 it constituted a Group of High-Level Intergovernmental Experts with the mandate to conduct "a thorough review of the administrative and financial matters of the U.N." and to identify measures for "further improving the efficiency of the administrative and financial functioning of the U.N." The members of the Group have met, and their report is now available. But it is still too early to know whether the Group's recommendations will be adopted by the General Assembly and what effect they will have on the serious financial crisis toward which the U.N. is now headed. The prospect of its running out of money in October or November 1986 brought the Assembly back into session in May 1986, at which time it approved a package of savings for fiscal 1986 amounting to $60 million. But these stopgap measures will only delay the crisis several months, and the outlook for 1987 remains very bleak indeed.

The U.N.'s System for Budgetary Decision-Making

There are really two separate systems governing the way in which the U.N. appropriates funds. One is the formal voting system. The other is a series of informal practices and unwritten rules by which the U.N.'s 159 member states seek a consensus that includes both the 15 main contributors and the 144 other members. Not surprisingly, this simultaneous use of two systems, the second of which is informal and nowhere clearly defined, is confusing and has led to tensions and financial instability.

The formal system treats financial decision-making in the same way it treats decision-making on other subjects. That is to say, whatever a member's rate of assessment, it has one vote in the Fifth (Administrative and Budgetary) Committee and the General Assembly. Decisions designated as "important"—financial decisions among them—are taken by a simple majority in the Committee and by a two-thirds majority in the plenary Assembly. However, financial decisions differ from other kinds of decisions in one important respect: They are supposed to be binding on member states and thus have the character of a tax (with the inevitable unpopularity of taxes). All member states may at times resent this obligation to pay; as already shown, a number of small and middle-sized contributors are among those refusing to pay for certain U.N. activities. However, the main contributors tend to be particularly sensitive to the size of the bill and to the purposes for which they are providing the funds.

In this connection, it is of interest that at the time of the Dumbarton Oaks deliberations in 1944, the first draft of what became the U.N. Charter contained a special voting procedure for budgetary appropriations, whereby voting rights would have been proportional to each member's assessment rate. However, this provision was dropped, partly as a friendly gesture to smaller states but mainly in the belief that the principal contributors would have sufficient influence over the appropriations process without it.[13]

In the early years of the U.N. this was by and large the case. Yet as the international community (and the U.N.'s membership) doubled and tripled in size, and as the Organization became involved in a widening spectrum of activities not foreseen in 1944, a number of the main contributors became increasingly uneasy over the gradual decline of their influence in financial decision-making.

At the same time, the desirability of reaching a consensus including main contributors and other members on the overall level of the regular budget and on the amounts to be spent for each U.N. activity had always been recognized. The Secretary-General, the Advisory Committee on Administrative and Budgetary Questions (ACABQ) and the Fifth Committee have traditionally each played a key role in the efforts (in recent years none too successful) to bring about such a consensus. The main contributors play a proportionately greater role in this "second system."

In drawing up successive budgets for the Organization, the Secretary-General must calculate the costs involved in carrying out the many activities that the U.N.'s intergovernmental bodies have approved. At the same time, he tries to ensure that the total budget does not exceed what member states, and particularly the main contributors, are prepared to pay. This tends to be a well-nigh impossible task, for government representatives who sit in U.N. program organs generally call for more and more to be done while other government representatives who sit in U.N. financial bodies generally object to paying the higher costs. Since the organs that can approve new activities are numerous and often out of touch with the financial constraints, and since the Assembly's control over program expansion is far from complete, it is not easy to find a generally acceptable balance between the funds needed to carry out all the activities that have been approved and the amount of money that member states are willing to provide.

In order to find such a balance, the Secretary-General must bear in mind the views of a wide cross-section of member states. Naturally, the concerns of the larger contributors occupy a special place in such discussions, but he also has to be sensitive to the desire of smaller countries that sufficient resources be provided for activities that are important to them. In this process, the aim is not to negotiate a consensus on any particular growth rate or level of expenditure. It is, rather, to feel out the membership in order to reach a realistic target figure on which the Secretariat's program planning can proceed. In other words, in reaching this notional budget ceiling (usually expressed as a "real" growth rate), he must first make a judgment about what most member states, including most large contributors, would be willing to support. The problem then is to squeeze what the various intergovernmental bodies have asked the Secretariat to do within these budgetary "outer limits."

Members of the ACABQ may be consulted individually on what these limits should be, but the Committee as such is not consulted. It is, however, informed of the proposed growth rate when it begins its review of the Secretary-General's program budget. The Committee has no substantive role in deciding what should or should not be done. The work program has already been established by the various intergovernmental bodies having program-making powers. The Secretary-General has proposed what, in his opinion, are the minimum resources that will be required to implement the work program these bodies have jointly evolved. The ACABQ's role is to review each component to ensure that it will in fact be carried out as efficiently as possible and at minimum cost. In this capacity, the Committee usually proposes modest reductions under some or most of the budget headings. Here it acts on the basis of decisions formulated by its chairman reflecting the "weight of opinion" that would generally constitute a consensus or near-consensus among the members.

From the first years of the U.N., a key element surrounding the adoption of the regular budget was the Fifth Committee's customary acceptance of almost all of the Advisory Committee's proposed reductions of the Secretary-General's budget estimates. The Fifth Committee could and sometimes did reject such reductions, but it was long understood both by members of the Committee and by the Secretariat that they would normally be allowed to stand. While in the main these reductions were merely designed to ensure optimum output at minimum cost, they occasionally impinged discreetly on the realm of program policy, particularly on matters of concern to the main contributors. For example, a program may be carried out rapidly or slowly, and the immediate costs of a controversial activity will be less (and probably arouse less opposition) if it is carried out in stages.

As already stated, the Fifth Committee occasionally rejects the recommendations it receives from the Advisory Committee, but almost always in respect to minor rather than major matters. For instance, it has often not accepted the Advisory Committee's negative recommendations on the Secretary-General's proposals to upgrade posts (especially senior posts) and to spend money on recruitment missions.

At the same time, the Advisory Committee's mandate does not enable it to help very much in resolving the opposing views of member states on politically sensitive expenditures, such as those for controversial conferences (e.g., Conference on Alliance between Israel and South Africa) or for Secretariat units established for the purpose of conducting controversial activities (e.g., Division for Palestinian Rights). When the Fifth Committee pushes such expenditures through by means of bloc voting, it reveals a serious gap in the informal system that was designed to avert this kind of confrontation between main contributors and the rest of the U.N. membership. Over the years, the number of such politically sensitive expenditures (which all too often provoke withholding of funds) has been on the increase. The seriousness of the current financial crisis suggests that the informal system must in some way be extended to deal with this kind of problem. Perhaps the time has come to consider giving the informal system a more formal basis.

It should be added that the regular budget controls only a fraction of the total expenditures associated with the U.N. As much as 70 percent of the U.N.'s outlays are funded by other means. For example, the various peacekeeping forces, such as the U.N. Emergency Forces in the Middle East and in Lebanon, usually have their own separate budgets and scales of assessments. In addition, most of the U.N.'s humanitarian and development activities in member countries are financed by voluntary contributions. The main voluntary funds, which depend almost entirely on their ability to attract financial support, are UNICEF, the U.N. Development Programme, the World Food Programme, the Office of the High Commissioner for Refugees, the Palestine Refugee Agency (UNRWA), and the U.N. Funds for Population Activities and Drug Abuse Control.

As a general rule, the peacekeeping forces have enjoyed a higher degree of support among the main contributors (in spite of their relatively high costs) than does the regular budget.[14] Many large and middle-sized contributors have also given quite generously to the U.N.'s voluntary programs, with most members matching increases in their assessed contributions with similar (and sometimes even greater) increases in their voluntary ones.

Main Issues of Budgetary Decision-Making

A major issue, at least for many main contributors, has been the substantial increase in U.N. regular budget levels. Table I gives the figures for the last seven biennia (the U.N. works in two-year periods), including the current 1986–87 biennium. The table shows for each biennium the Secretary-General's original budget proposals, the ACABQ's recommendations, the General Assembly's original and final appropriations, and in each case the nominal growth rate in dollars from one biennium to the next.

Distinguishing real budgetary growth from nominal growth is problematic, since U.N. expenditures are made in several countries, each of which has its own fluctuating rate of inflation and its own shifting

Table I

Rate of Increase in Net Regular Budget Appropriations
1974–87, in Millions of U.S. Dollars

Biennium	S.G.'s Original Budget Proposals		ACABQ's Recommendations		General Assembly's Orig. Appropriations		General Assembly's Final Appropriations	
	Amount	% Increase over previous Biennium (nominal)	Amount	% Increase over previous Biennium (nominal)	Amount	% Increase over previous Biennium (nominal)	Amount	% Increase over previous Biennium (nominal)
1974–75	431		420		448		512	
1976–77	620	43.9	606	44.3	629	40.4	654	27.7
1978–79	775	25.0	749	23.6	812	29.1	899	37.5
1980–81	993	28.1	969	29.4	1026	26.4	1095	21.8
1982–83	1251	26.0	1208	24.7	1222	19.1	1213	10.8
1984–85	1311	4.8	1305	8.0	1303	6.6	1314	8.3
1986–87	1416	8.0	1400	7.3	1345	3.2		

Sources: Secretary-General's Proposed Program Budgets; ACABQ's reports to the General Assembly; General Assembly resolutions.

rates of exchange with the dollar. Also, capital and other non-recurrent expenditures differ, sometimes substantially, from one biennium to the next.[15] For example, though U.N. expenditures did grow at a rather rapid pace in the mid and late 1970s, it has to be borne in mind that this was also a period of peak inflation in most of the countries where the U.N. had its main offices. Nonetheless, much of that increase must still be attributed to a high rate of real program growth. Since the 1982–83 biennium, however, the growth rate of the regular budget in terms of current dollars has been considerably reduced; in 1984–85, for example, the final appropriation was $3 million less than the Secretary-General's original proposals. Thus, while the issue of the regular budget level is still raised by several contributors, it has clearly lost some of its former urgency.

Nonetheless, the regular budget still has problems in winning the support of many larger contributors (see the figures in Table II). This is probably not only because of the budget's overall size but also because of opposition to some of the activities for which it provides resources. For example, the U.S. representative stated in the Fifth Committee in 1985 that the budget continued to finance many inappropriate programs, support of which the Congress had prohibited.[16]

Each biennial budget is voted on by the General Assembly on three occasions, normally during three successive Decembers: the year before it goes into effect, and at the end of its first and second years.[17] Table II shows that each budget enjoyed more support in the initial voting than in the second and third votes. This was because many larger contributors abstained on the initial estimates but registered their opposition to the supplementary appropriations with which they were presented at the end of the first and second years. It is also significant that none of the last four budgets was able at any stage to gain the positive support of governments whose combined assessment accounted for more than 24 percent of the total, and that on one occasion the figure fell below 14 percent. It should have been regarded as ominous that the combined assessments of those voting against the budget at times rose as high as 78 percent, and was never any lower than 64 percent figure for second and third votes. This is in sharp contrast to earlier years, when most large contributors supported the regular budget and, on the occasions when their objections were not met, were content merely to abstain.

It is perhaps equally noteworthy that in more recent times the regular budget has continued to be heavily supported by the much larger

Table II

Budgetary Voting in the U.N. (1979–86)

(Percentages indicate the combined assessments of the members involved)

| | 1980–81 Budget | | | 1982–83 Budget | | | 1984–85 Budget | | | 1985–86 Budget |
| | 1979 | 1980 | 1981 | 1981 | 1982 | 1983 | 1983 | 1984 | 1985 | 1985 |
		As Revised			As Revised			As Revised		
In Favor	23.16	17.36	20.81	24.06	13.79	17.11	20.08	17.14	18.38	19.96
Against	16.91	78.73	74.22	64.54	64.27	64.27	15.51	67.39	64.03	40.73
Abstaining	59.14	3.91	4.76	11.20	21.80	18.47	64.27	15.35	17.47	39.20
Absent	0.79	—	0.21	0.20	0.14	0.15	0.14	0.12	0.12	0.11
Total Not Voting in Favor	76.84	82.64	79.19	75.94	86.21	82.89	79.92	82.86	81.62	80.04

number of smaller contributors and has always been adopted by margins far in excess of the two-thirds majority required.

As indicated earlier, there has been much wider support for the various peacekeeping forces. In recent votes on the budgets for these forces, members paying for at least 70 percent of U.N. expenses voted in their favor, and in some cases the figure reached nearly 85 percent. Despite this high level of support, the failure of the second largest contributor and some other countries to support and pay for certain peacekeeping operations has created the financial problem described earlier—and may even limit the extent to which such forces can be called upon in future crises. The importance of securing a consensus in U.N. financial decision-making that includes at least the several largest contributors is highlighted by this situation.

One of the perennial issues facing international organizations is the extent to which it is feasible to insist upon members paying for activities they strongly oppose and may sometimes even regard as inimical to their national interests. U.N. peacekeeping forces are, not surprisingly, sometimes regarded in this light by states that have taken sides in the disputes concerned. But activities under the regular budget have also inspired strong opposition, whether on the ground that they are inherently objectionable or that they do not belong in the regular budget. These include payments for the U.N. Memorial Cemetery in Korea, the Secretariat Division for Palestinian Rights, the Preparatory Commission on the Law of the Sea, and the Conferences on the Situation in Kampuchea (Cambodia) and on Alliance between Israel and South Africa. In these and some other cases, certain member states have said that they do not consider themselves bound to pay their shares of the costs. Some member states have also argued that they should not be required, under the regular budget, to make payments on the U.N. bond issue or to pay for the regular program of technical assistance. However, in addition to these relatively few activities for which funds are actually withheld, there are many more that members oppose with less insistence, either as being unnecessary or better carried out elsewhere.

The Kassebaum Amendment raises the question of how the General Assembly should take its financial decisions. It asks that in this area either there should be weighted voting on the basis of each member's rate of assessment or that the U.S.'s rate should be reduced. So far, no other member has spoken in favor of the first alternative, and it is clear that there is little prospect of securing sufficient support for weighted voting—which would require amendment of the Charter—in the near or medium term.[18] But this lack of support does not necessarily imply that other large contributors are pleased with the way the present system has been evolving. Indeed, as already indicated, the informal procedures whereby the large contributors and the other members balance their respective budgetary concerns have been breaking down. The way in which the U.N. reaches its financial decisions has become an issue—and one on which there is an urgent need for frank discussions and innovative ideas. There is reason to believe, for example, that the U.S. would be ready to consider suggestions about ways in which the main objectives of the Kassebaum Amendment would be attained through devices other than weighted voting.

Finally, there is the issue of the effectiveness of central review and control over what the U.N. does or does not decide to do. At present, the power to initiate and in effect authorize program activities is shared among a rather large number of intergovernmental organs: These include the five regional commissions and the various functional commissions and many committees of the Economic and Social Council, the governing bodies of the United Nations Conference on Trade and Development (UNCTAD) and the United Nations Environment Programme (UNEP), the International Law Commission, the Outer Space Committee, the Committee of 24 on Decolonization, and many similar bodies.

In some cases, program proposals are submitted for formal approval to more senior bodies; in some cases not. In some cases such proposals are accompanied by statements of financial implications; in some cases the Secretariat rather blithely undertakes to carry them out "within its existing resources." Eventually, all adopted proposals are consolidated in the biennial program budget, where they tend to be lost in the mass of program detail in small print.

While the Committee for Program and Coordination and the ACABQ attempt to oversee and guide the complex evolution of the U.N.'s widening spectrum of program activities, it is beyond their present capacity to do so in any meaningful way. Clearly, the Fifth Committee and the Assembly are in no position to do what is beyond the capacity of their two subsidiary bodies set up for that purpose. The budget estimates they approve merely set a cap on overall expenditures and on the expenditures for each program and subprogram. Since all of the many activities approved cannot be carried out effectively with the resources allocated to them, there is a good deal of uncertainty as to which of them will in fact be pursued and with what degree of diligence. The latitude that this leaves to lower-level intergovernmental organs and to Secretariat officials may have certain advantages, but it increases the difficulty of setting central priorities and of allocating limited financial resources in a rational way. This great dispersion of programming power prevents the Assembly from taking full charge of the directions in which the U.N. is moving—a situation that concerns (or should concern) all the U.N.'s members, whether big or small.[19]

Assessments

We may now turn from the appropriation of funds to the U.N.'s procedures for determining how these costs should be allocated among the various member states. As already noted, U.N. assessment is a form of taxation whereby governments find themselves in the unfamiliar role of payer rather than receiver. And it is now quite clear that they dislike being taxed just as much as do private individuals and corporations. Like taxpayers generally, they usually seek to minimize their assessment rates and tend to use whatever arguments and devices they can to do so. This nautrally complicates life for the 18-member expert Committee on Contributions, which is the General Assembly's arm for negotiating an agreed scale of assessments to finance the U.N.'s expenditures. What would have seemed, given the quite modest sums involved, to be a routine technical function has turned out to be a highly political one. Those responsible for shepherding tax bills through national legislatures would hardly be surprised by this.

In order to see what the present assessment situation is like, the various member states may be ranked by the size of their assessments as large, middle-sized, and small contributors. For this purpose, large contributors are defined as those assessed at 1 percent or more, small contributors as those assessed at 0.09 percent or less, and middle-level contributors as those paying less than 1 percent but more than 0.09 percent. Table III summarizes the results of such a ranking, utilizing the scale of assessments approved by the General Assembly for the years 1986–88.

Table III shows that the 15 main contributors (less than a tenth of the member states) provide nearly 85 percent of the U.N.'s assessed income, and that the 50 main and middle-sized contributors together (less than a third of the member states) carry more than 98 percent of the assessment burden. This means that the remaining 107 members provide a little less than 2 percent of the U.N.'s costs. The disparity is

Table III

U.N. Scale of Assessments for 1986–88

I. *Main Contributors* (paying 1% or more)

Country	% Assessed	Cumulative % Total
1. United States	25.00	25.00
2. USSR*	11.82	36.82
3. Japan	10.84	47.66
4. Fed. Rep. Germany	8.26	55.92
5. France	6.37	62.29
6. United Kingdom	4.86	67.15
7. Italy	3.79	70.94
8. Canada	3.06	74.00
9. Spain	2.03	76.03
10. Netherlands	1.74	77.77
11. Australia	1.66	79.43
12. Brazil	1.40	80.83
13. German Dem. Republic	1.33	82.16
14. Sweden	1.25	83.41
15. Belgium	1.18	84.59

II. *Middle-Level Contributors* (35 countries paying between 0.99% and 0.10% each)	13.51	98.10
III. *Small Contributors* (107 countries paying between 0.09% and 0.01% each)	1.92	100.02

*Includes the Byelorussian and Ukrainian SSRs
Source: General Assembly resolution 40/248, December 18, 1985

attributable to the fact that most of the latter are small countries (in some cases mini-states), and that many of them are very poor and face chronic shortages of foreign exchange. The differential between the largest and smallest contributor (25 percent and 0.01 percent) is nevertheless a rather wide one, i.e., 2,500 times.

A second way of viewing the scale of assessments is in terms of the U.N.'s main political groups. The following listing is based on recent scales of assessment provided in the most recent report of the Committee on Contributions:

Group	1978–79	1980–82	1983–85	1986–88
A. Group of 77*	7.87%	8.98	9.34	9.67
(of which OPEC)	1.90	2.89	3.30	3.63
B. OECD countries	68.39	71.81	73.66	74.00

C. Countries with centrally planned economies	17.58	16.91	15.51	14.87
D. China	5.50	1.62	0.88	0.79

---

*Includes Romania and Yugoslavia
Source: U.N. Document A/40/11, p. 14

It will be seen that almost three-quarters of the U.N.'s costs are now borne by the OECD countries, about a seventh by the countries with centrally planned economies (i.e., the USSR and its COMECON allies), and the remaining tenth by the developing countries. Over recent years the main change has been in the share of China and the Socialist countries, which has dropped from 23 percent to the present 16 percent, with the difference picked up by the OECD and OPEC countries.[20]

The starting-point and principal criterion for determining the size of each member's assessment has always been its aggregate national income. The U.N. has also always had a graduated system designed to ensure that poorer countries were assessed at a lower rate. It works this way: All members whose per capita income is below a fixed ceiling are assessed only on their "qualifying income," which declines more than proportionally as their per capita income falls below the ceiling. In addition, only part of this "qualifying income" is subject to assessment, and a gradient determines what proportion of this lesser amount is also exempt. As the steepness of this gradient has steadily risen, the assessment rates for most developing countries have dropped substantially.

To calculate the proportion of a country's national income that is exempt, one must multiply the percentage by which its per capita national income falls short of the ceiling by the gradient. For example, in 1985, India's per capita income of $185 was 92 percent short of the $2,100 ceiling. This 92 percent difference, when multiplied by the 85 percent gradient, produces an exemption level of 78 percent. Thus, only 22 percent of India's national income was counted in calculating its assessment rate. Since 1946, under these arrangements, India's assessment rate has fallen from 4.09 percent to 0.35 percent, Indonesia's from 0.60 percent to 0.14 percent, Argentina's from 1.94 percent to 0.62 percent, and Pakistan's from 0.70 percent to 0.06 percent. Seventy-eight members (about half of the membership) are required to pay only 0.01 percent each (or $65,814 in 1985) under the U.N.'s regular budget.

In 1985 two further adjustments to the scale of assessments were considered by the Committee on Contributions. Countries with high levels of external indebtedness won special treatment. For purposes of calculating their assessment, their aggregate national incomes were further lowered by a proportion (between 2.5 and 10 percent) of their external indebtedness. The second proposal involved the redistribution among more affluent countries of the assessment forgone by low-income countries. Developing countries with per capita income higher than the ceiling sought to be relieved from sharing in this additional burden, notwithstanding the fact that this would give differential treatment to developed and developing countries in the same per capita income brackets. Although no decision was taken on this second proposal, the assessment rates of four such countries were slightly reduced.

From time to time there have been complaints that rates of assessment are not based on the "real capacity of member states to pay," but the Committee on Contributions has failed to find any more acceptable indicator than national income. Among the indicators that have been considered are manufacturing as a percentage of GNP; per capita energy consumption; life expectancy at birth; the literacy rate; per capita daily calorie intake; commercial vehicles in use; external debt levels; and terms of trade. However, none of these, either singly or in combination, has commended itself to the Committee.

It should be added that there are special assessment scales for some extrabudgetary expenditures, such as those for the peacekeeping forces. According to the principles followed in setting up these scales, low-income countries not involved in the dispute should in fairness contribute only minimally to the costs of such forces, and that the five permanent members of the Security Council, who bear a special responsibility for these matters, should be assessed accordingly.

Over time, the scale of assessments for the regular budget has become a focal point for increasing disagreement among member states. The last two scales of assessment have been adopted even with members responsible for paying nearly three-quarters of the U.N.'s costs abstaining or voting against them. Those with grievances, real or imaginary, have also included a number of small and middle-sized contributors that did not receive satisfaction in the long and difficult negotiations that preceded the voting.

Brief Analysis of the Major Issues

Foremost among the questions confronting the U.N. with regard to the scale of assessments are: (1) What should be the highest and lowest possible assessments? (2) Is the present system operating fairly for those members that are neither at the top nor at the bottom of the scale?

The United States assessment has always been higher than that of any other member, although the percentage it pays has been lowered, in stages, from 39.89 percent in the early years of the Organization's existence to the present 25 percent. Today the U.S., with about 28 percent of global national income, pays a little less than would be its share of U.N. expenses if that indicator were strictly applied; and unlike other developed countries, the United States is not called upon to bear any of the redistributed burden of low-income developing countries. As already mentioned, the United States appears less interested in having its rate of assessment reduced than in achieving some change in the U.N.'s procedures for financial decision-making.

At the same time, the Secretary-General and some other members, such as Sweden, have felt that 25 percent is too high a ceiling and provides the country paying that percentage with too ready a means of applying pressure on the Organization.[21] It has been suggested that the top assessment be considerably reduced, perhaps even to 10 percent. But a 10 percent ceiling would require middle-sized and large contributors other than the United States, the USSR, and Japan to accept much higher assessments, which they have so far seemed reluctant to do.[22]

Much less attention has been directed to the assessment floor level of 0.01 percent, though recently the question has been raised whether it is not a little on the low side and whether too many members—as noted, now almost half the U.N.'s membership—are being assessed at that minimal rate. In informal comments, the Secretary-General expressed the view that some countries whose assessments are "very, very low" ought to pay more.[23] The present floor assessment (now only $65,800 per annum) does seem almost a token amount, especially for such middle-sized member states as Sri Lanka and Sudan. It is also true that members of this group tend to be less concerned over regular-budget levels.

Somewhat similar questions arise about the way the present system operates for members that are slightly higher up on the scale. Almost everybody would agree that low-income countries should pay at much lower rates than high-income ones, but has the rise in the gradient from 40 to 85 percent and a further exemption for external indebtedness carried matters too far? Would the developing countries not be in a stronger position to justify their major influence in the Organization's decision-making if they contributed somewhat more than they now do toward the costs it incurs?

A final matter of special concern is the overcomplexity of the present system for calculating rates of assessment. The methodology for the reduction and redistribution of assessments is not easy even for the informed outsider to understand. It is even harder to explain the U.N.'s system of fixing assessments to governmental bodies called upon to appropriate its funds. The addition of a new indicator, such as external indebtedness, and the proposed differential treatment of developed and developing countries in the same per capita income brackets, further complicates matters. Finally, there are serious technical problems in ensuring the true comparability of national income statistics when some rates of exchange with the dollar are set arbitrarily (as in the case of centrally planned economies) and not by market forces.[24]

The desirability of simplifying the present system for determining the scale of assessments and making it fair—in appearance as well as in reality—seems obvious.

Fairness and Accountability in the U.N.'s Financial Decision-Making: Some of the Options

The gravity of the U.N.'s current financial crisis underscores the urgency of its need to find some better way of arriving at its key financial decisions. For example, the present practice whereby it now repeatedly adopts program budgets and scales of assessment that lack the support of member states responsible for paying as much as four-fifths of their costs is undermining the U.N.'s financial viability. Unless this problem is recognized and addressed, it seems likely that some time next year the Organization will find itself in a state of financial breakdown, unable to meet its obligations or to pay its staff.

Should matters be allowed to drift that far, it will not be easy to find a way out. The economies that could be made readily have already been made. A very large part of the remaining outlays represent staff costs; and because of separation entitlements, any discharge of staff temporarily increases rather than reduces such outlays.

Fortunately, there are many ways to break through the present impasse. In this concluding section, a number of options are offered for consideration. Most of them are not mutually exclusive and could be combined in various ways to make up a "package."

The following considerations might guide this search for solutions for the U.N.'s pressing financial problems and at the same time place the Organization on a sounder financial footing for the long term:

• The present cash-flow crisis provides a not-to-be-lost opportunity to work out financial rules and practices (which would, inter alia, deal with the problem of political objections to certain controversial items) on the basis of which all contributors, whether large, middle-sized, or small, would be willing to pay in full their U.N. assessments.[25]

• The fact that the U.N.'s 159 member states have widely varying capacities to provide it with financial resources and equally widely varying contributions to make toward the carrying out of its decisions needs to be adequately reflected in whatever new rules and practices are adopted for financial decision-making.

• Financial decisions should be taken by consensus or by broad agreement that would include a sufficient number of the main contributors.

• Because of the great difficulties and delays that would probably be involved in any revision of the U.N. Charter, any new rules should be of the sort that can be implemented within the existing provisions of the Charter.

Some clarification may be in order regarding the third of these considerations, calling for financial decision-making on the basis of consensus or broad agreement among the membership. At the recent meetings of the Group of 18, some members from developing countries held that the Charter provided that all types of decisions, including financial ones, were to be made on the basis of simple and two-thirds majorities, and that this could not be called into question.[26] At the same time, some members from developed countries held that, according to the spirit of the Charter, important financial decisions should be made on the basis of consensus and that some such interpretation was a necessary element in solving the U.N.'s current financial crisis. The Group of 18 was unable to resolve this issue, but it is assumed that efforts to reach a mutually acceptable compromise on this subject will continue.[27] Some of the options outlined below indicate approaches that might prove useful starting points for further negotiations.

For the sake of convenience, the options are divided into three groups:

• those involving appropriations (Options 1–5)
• those involving assessments (Options 6–11)
• those involving the reallocation of U.N. activities between those

to be financed by assessment and those to be financed by voluntary contributions (Options 12–14).

Appropriations

Two main issues arise under this heading: how money should be appropriated and how that money should be allocated among competing programs and activities. Under the system of informal practices and unwritten rules, described earlier, these issues used to be resolved jointly by the Secretary-General, the ACABQ, and the Fifth Committee. But, as we have seen, there is a tendency now for the Fifth Committee to take important financial decisions—such as the adoption of the biennial program budget—without the concurrence of most of the main contributors. Also, in some cases, confrontations between the main blocs of members over expenditures for certain controversial activities have been settled by voting rather than by negotiation.

The present financial crisis thus stems largely from the Assembly's recent tendency to appropriate funds at levels and for purposes that do not have wide enough support among the main contributors. In these circumstances, two courses are possible: to seek new informal agreements on how the Fifth Committee (and, of course, the plenary Assembly) will proceed in its financial decision-making; and/or to strengthen the formal machinery for dealing with these kinds of problems. The following are a few of the options that might be explored under these two headings.

Tightening up informal procedures:

Option 1. Experience has shown how risky it is for the U.N. to try to make governments pay for activities that they strongly oppose. Financial and political prudence suggest that decisions calling for substantial expenditures should not be taken unless they are supported by members that, in combination, will pay most of the expenses they will entail. To avoid future financial crises, it might be agreed (by resolutions, by gentlemen's agreement, or other means)[28] that the Fifth Committee would approve any measure requiring substantial expenditures only when it commanded the support of votes of member states that together pay "x" percent of the total U.N. assessment. The actual size of "x" would be the subject of negotiation, as would the question whether the shares paid by abstainers would be included with, or excluded from, the percentage required. The percentage chosen for "x" would reflect a balance between the need for stability (which would suggest a higher figure) and the exercise of undue influence by the largest contributors (which would suggest a lower figure). By way of example: As shown in Table III, if "x" were 30 percent, the seven largest contributors, voting together, could bar an appropriation. If "x" were 40 percent, 50 percent, or 60 percent, the number of states exercising such combined influence would be five, four, and three, respectively. It may be borne in mind that the largest contributors rarely vote as a bloc; but when they do so on a major financial decision, the U.N. might be well-advised to proceed cautiously. Adjustments in the scale of assessments could be made to reduce what may be perceived as undue influence by the main contributors resulting from any such arrangements.

Formal measures:

Informal procedures of this kind would give large contributors much greater power to block activities they strongly opposed, and would thus considerably reduce (but probably not eliminate) withholding for cause. It is also true that informal practices tend to break down in the long run. There are a number of formal measures that might be considered to bring about a better balance of the interests of all member states in the U.N.'s program budgeting process. Among the objectives would be to stimulate main-contributor interest in regular-budget activities by giving them a greater voice in determining what those activities should be.

Option 2—Enlargement of the Advisory Committee's Mandate. The Advisory Committee's mandate might be extended by giving it the additional function of reviewing and approving the U.N.'s program budget in all its financial aspects—subject, of course, to the Assembly's final endorsement. The purpose of this review would be to ensure that every program budget approved by it would be consonant with the U.N.'s financial stability. If it were felt that this new function, which would sometimes involve the Committee in policy-type judgments, required that it become an intergovernmental organ, it should never-theless remain a body of experts appointed by name by the General Assembly in order to preserve its present character.

Option 3—New Program and Budget Committee. An alternative option would be to establish an entirely new intergovernmental body to review and approve the U.N.'s program budget in all its aspects—subject, again, to the Assembly's final endorsement. Such a body might be composed of specified ratios of large, middle-sized, and small contributors (for example, a third of each), with a total membership in the range of 21 to 27. In order to ensure that decisions on appropria-tions enjoy a sufficient preponderance of support, they might be made to require the affirmative votes of a large proportion of the members of the Committee and of each of the three groups of members. The ACABQ and/or the Committee for Program and Coordination might or might not be retained under this option. Should one or both be retained, they should report to the Assembly through the Program and Budget Committee.

Options 2 and 3 would probably need to be accompanied by an understanding among U.N. members that the Assembly would not *ordinarily* overrule lower-level decisions designed to safeguard the U.N.'s financial stability.

Option 4—Revival of the Idea of a Planning Estimate for the Regular Budget. In December 1967 the Assembly adopted a resolution[29] asking the Secretary-General, taking into account all the actions of the program-formulating bodies, to submit planning estimates to guide the preparation of his future budgets. Under the terms of the resolution, the ACABQ would review the Secretary-General's estimates and transmit it with the Committee's recommendations to the Assembly for that body's final approval. At the same time, the resolution envisaged a separate procedure for dealing with "unforeseen and extraordinary" expenses. France, the U.K., the USSR, and the United States had sponsored and actively pressed for the adoption of the resolution. This was at least partly in response to a request from Secretary-General U Thant for guidance from the Assembly on the total resources that member states were prepared to make available. It was understood that the planning estimate would not be a binding ceiling but was a necessary part of the U.N.'s evolving procedures for long-term planning and priority-setting. Nevertheless, in the years that followed, the setting of any planning estimate was postponed, and with the introduction of biennial budgeting, the idea was quietly dropped.

As an additional means of providing a basis for priority-setting and controlling expenditures, the concept of the planning estimate might be revived and modified as necessary to meet the requirements of biennial budgeting. The ACABQ (whether reconstituted or not) or a new Program and Budget Committee might be given a major role in determining the level of the planning estimate—subject, of course, to its final approval by the General Assembly.

Option 5—Expanded Role for the Secretary-General. As part of a process of tighter budgetary control, the Secretary-General would need to take more far-reaching initiatives in preparing the program budget. For example, when not all activities authorized by one or another of the U.N.'s many intergovernmental bodies can be adequately financed within an agreed budgetary planning estimate, the Secretary-General might be expected to come forward with his suggestions as to which activities should be postponed or dropped. He might also be asked to go one step further and include in his program budget only those activities that could be financed and staffed in such a way as to permit them to have the intended impact.

Assessments

Many of the foregoing options might be accompanied by changes in the U.N.'s scale of assessments; and, in any event, the procedures by which individual assessments are established might benefit from some adjustment and simplification.

Option 6—Lowering the Highest Amount Any Member Must Pay. As already indicated, the Secretary-General and the Swedish government have suggested that this ceiling might be dropped to 10 percent. This suggestion presents the practical problems of finding members willing to assume the additional financial burden and also raises the issue of fairness in burden-sharing. It might also lead to a substantial diminishment of U.S. influence (and interest) in the world organization. Should it nonetheless be concluded that, on balance, some reduction in the ceiling is justified, the reduction would probably have to be made gradually. One possibility would be to reduce the ceiling by a small amount—say, 1 to 2 percent—in each of five successive assessment periods. Somewhat more rapid reductions might be envisaged in combination with Option 1. The Committee on Contributions—or, perhaps better, a small ad hoc advisory committee created for this purpose— should review and report to the Assembly by 1988 (when the next scale of assessments will be adopted) on the possibilities inherent in this approach.

Option 7—Raising the Minimum Amount Any Member May Pay. One of many possibilities would be to raise the floor level in slow stages to, say, 0.05 percent (now $329,000), which is still much less than the cost of maintaining a small mission in New York. Exceptions might still be made for some of the smaller least-developed countries.

Option 8—Simplified Graduated Scale of Assessments. The present system of gradients and per capita income ceilings (now further complicated by the new indicator of external indebtedness) is a hodgepodge of accretions over the years. Perhaps the time has come to replace it with a graduated scale of assessments similar to that of most national income tax systems. Thus, higher per capita income would be assessed at progressively higher rates so that wealthier countries would be charged proportionately more. This would make it easier to explain the rationale of the system to the governments and peoples of developed countries that pay for most of the U.N.'s expenses.

Option 9—Modified Decision-Making for the Scale of Assessments. In the interest of the U.N.'s financial stability it is only prudent to ensure that the scale of assessments is acceptable to a sufficient number of the main contributors as well as to the great majority of the U.N.'s other members. To ensure this, it might be decided (by resolution, gentlemen's agreement, or some other means) that when a revised scale of assessment could not be adopted by consensus in the Assembly, its approval would require the affirmative votes of members that together are assessed "x" percent of the aggregate assessment. Again, the figure to be assigned to "x" would have to be negotiated, but prudence would suggest that it be in the same range of 30–60 percent.

Option 10—Interest Charge on Late Payments. One step that might be taken to encourage greater promptness by member states in paying their dues would be to impose a mild penalty on defaulters. For example, after the second monthly reminder, the sum due might start drawing interest at a pre-agreed rate.

Option 11—Screening of the Scale of Assessments. If Options 2 or 3 were adopted, it might be provided that any revised scale of assessments would require the preliminary approval of the reconstituted ACABQ or the Program and Budget Committee before its adoption by the General Assembly.

Scope of the Regular Budget

From the earliest days of the U.N., member states have held differing views as to which activities should be financed through assessment and which through voluntary contributions. The Charter is vague on the question of what expenses the U.N.'s budget should include; and, as already noted, a large proportion of its expenditures are now being financed by special accounts and voluntary contributions—in particular, those for technical assistance and humanitarian activities. But there has been no consistency in this: For example, the $36 million "regular program of technical cooperation," as well as $32 million of the High Commissioner for Refugees' expenditures and $10 million of UNRWA's, form part of the regular budget for 1986–87. Furthermore, there would be nothing to prevent any other activities that lack the requisite degree of support among member states from being transferred over to the voluntary-contribution segment of the U.N.'s activities. If it were deemed desirable to proceed still further in this direction, most of the so-called "program activities" might also be financed on a voluntary basis, leaving mainly administrative, capital, and internal servicing expenses within the regular budget.[30] It should be kept in mind in this connection that any such removal of activities from the scope of the regular budget constitutes a departure from the principle of common financing of the U.N.'s work and might switch out of the regular budget a number of activities that still give the Organization a positive image in many developed countries. The following options are among the many that might be contemplated in this connection:

Option 12—Exclusion of Controversial Activities From the Regular Budget. It might be agreed that activities strongly opposed by member states that together pay "x" percent of the global U.N. assessment would no longer be financed by assessed payments but by voluntary contributions. This time "x" percent probably should not be more than 50 percent and, to be on the safe side, lower.

Option 13—Establishment of Consistency of Approach. It might be agreed that henceforth *all* activities involving technical cooperation or humanitarian concerns would be financed by voluntary contributions alone.

Option 14—Contraction of Scope of the Regular Budget. It might be agreed that the scope of the regular budget should be limited to administrative, capital, and internal servicing expenses, which would include substantive and other services required by the General Assembly, the Security Council, and other U.N. intergovernmental bodies, including the preparation of documentation and the provision of the expertise that they require to carry on their work. Alternatively, certain important, generally agreed-upon global activities of the Secretariat, such as widely used publications and studies and the expenses of expert groups, might also be retained within the regular budget. In either instance, other activities could continue, but only if there were member states willing to underwrite their cost.

The U.N.'s financial stability would be greatly enhanced by a final option that does not fall in any of the foregoing three groups:

Option 15. One element of any new understanding on financial procedures among member states might be the replenishment and increase in size of the Working Capital Fund, which is now less than 25 percent of the annual regular budget. If member states cannot be persuaded to take such a step, one could pursue the alternative of seeking contributions to the Fund on a voluntary basis from those member states that do see the need for the U.N. to have an adequate financial cushion.

The foregoing options show the many widely differing approaches that might be utilized in addressing the U.N.'s financial crisis. If none of these prove widely acceptable, others could certainly be devised. What still seems wanting is a sufficient appreciation on the part of governments of how grave that crisis has become and a readiness to work together to find ways of putting the U.N.'s financial decision-making on a more viable basis. If governments really do set store by what the Organization does and is capable of doing, as their representatives proclaimed at the U.N.'s 40th anniversary celebration, there is no time to be lost. For they alone are in a position to undertake and carry through the negotiating effort required to ensure the Organization's survival as an effective instrument for international cooperation.

Notes

1. Even in the U.S. Senate, where representation is by state rather than population, the comparable figure is 59:1; and in most legislative bodies the differential would be less than 2:1.

2. Ruth E. Russell, *A History of the United Nations Charter* (Washington, D.C.: Brookings Institution, 1958), passim.

3. Evan Luard, *The United Nations: How It Works and What It Does* (New York: Saint Martin's Press, 1979), p. 124.

4. In fact, its financial problems date back to the early 1960s.

5. Bulgaria, Byelorussian SSR, China, Czechoslovakia, Kampuchea, France, German Democratic Republic, Hungary, Israel, Mongolia, Poland, Romania, South Africa, Urkrainian SSR, Soviet Union, United States, and Vietnam.

6. Algeria, Benin, Cuba, Democratic Yemen, Iraq, Laos, Libya, Syria, Yemen.

7. Advisory Opinion of July 20, 1962, certain expenses of the U.N. (Article 17, paragraph 2 of the Charter), *ICJ Reports 1962,* p. 185.

8. The Soviet Union argued that neither the International Court nor the General Assembly could authoritatively interpret the obligations of member states under the U.N. Charter.

9. Evan Luard, *op cit.,* pp. 122–24; Leland M. Goodrich, *The United Nations in a Changing World* (New York: Columbia University Press, 1974), pp. 155–56; and Thomas M. Franck, *Nation Against Nation* (New York: Oxford University Press, 1985), pp. 84–87.

10. The next revision will be undertaken in 1988.

11. Only in 1978 did main contributors other than the Soviet Union begin to vote against the regular budget.

12. This figure is based on the best available information but may increase or decrease substantially as the result of future congressional action.

13. Russell, pp. 367, 378, 426.

14. The main exception has been the USSR, which has sometimes withheld its assesed payments for such forces. But recently the United States has also been re-examining its financial support of UNIFIL.

15. The U.N. uses the concept of "non-recurrent costs" for such expenses as world conferences and new construction or maintenance. These are excluded from its computation of real growth on the ground that their inclusion would distort the overall impression of budget growth. In standard budgetary practice, however, the term "real growth" describes the increase in expenditures after discounting for inflation and other uncontrollable costs, such as currency fluctuation. The foregoing figures in Table I lump together ongoing program costs and non-recurrent costs.

16. A/C.5/40/SR.70, p. 32.

17. The second and third votes provide supplementary appropriations of funds for the biennium concerned, in some cases ex post facto.

18. Before coming into force, amendments must be approved and ratified by two-thirds of the U.N. members, including all five permanent members of the Security Council.

19. This problem is described in greater detail in the JIU reports of Inspector Maurice Bertrand and in Luard, pp. 129–32.

20. The share of China has dropped because national income figures for that country, only recently available, showed that it had been greatly overassessed. The share of the socialist countries has dropped because the national income of OECD and OPEC countries has risen much more rapidly.

21. *New York Times,* April 29, 1986.

22. A total of 17.76 percent of the global assessment would have to be redistributed presumably mostly among the 12 other main contributors, whose willingness to participate in such a scheme would be a prerequisite to its success. In fact, in a memorandum of March 14, 1986, the 12 states of the European Community indicated that they would not make up the difference.

23. *New York Times,* April 29, 1986.

24. Although no option is offered below to deal with this last problem, its importance is obvious, and efforts should be made to resolve it.

25. In the case of the United States, any such arrangement should have the concurrence of the Congress.

26. The "Group of 18 High-Level Intergovernmental Experts to Review the Efficiency of the Administrative and Financial Functions of the United Nations" met from January through August of 1986.

27. Although the report of the Group of 18 was not conclusive on this issue, on December 19, 1986, the General Assembly adopted a reform of its bud-

getary decision-making procedure (described on page 277–78) that moves in the direction of a solution. Since it is unclear whether this reform will be sufficient, the options explored in Chapter 13 continue to have relevance.

28. The adoption of "self-denying ordinances" has a long history in international organizations. For example, the League of Nations long followed a "convention" whereby its budget, once approved in committee, would not be subject to the unanimity rule of the plenary Assembly (Luard, p. 115).

29. The vote was 84–0, with 2 abstentions.

30. "Program activities" supportive of the intergovernmental organs should probably continue to be financed jointly.

CHAPTER 14

TELLING THE WORLD: A PROPOSAL FOR THE IMPROVEMENT OF THE U.N. DEPARTMENT OF PUBLIC INFORMATION

Ruth D. Raymond

If the United Nations is to further the ambitious goals set forth in its Charter, it must have the support not only of member governments but of its ultimate constituents—all the peoples of the world. The better informed its constituents are about the Organization's aims and activities and the realities with which it must cope, the more likely they are to lend the necessary support.

In the view of the General Assembly of 1946, which established an Office of Public Information (now the Department of Public Information [DPI],) the U.N.'s informational materials would serve primarily as educational tools—a means of "promo[ting] to the greatest extent possible an informed understanding of the work and purposes of the United Nations among the peoples of the world." More recently it has become apparent that some of these products must also serve a public relations function—a means of promoting the United Nations and its successes at a time when support for the Organization has fallen off. Experience has also taught that, given the diversity of DPI's constituency, its various outputs will have the appropriate effect only if they are targeted to specific audiences. One such audience is composed of policy-makers and opinion-shapers in member countries, whose influence in garnering wide support for the work of the United Nations is essential to its success.

Today's public is more likely to be apathetic to or even negative about the U.N. than 40 years ago, having little actual knowledge of the Organization's activities and readily accepting information that is often distorted. As a result, many people have come to perceive the U.N. as nothing more than a political battleground, where any attempt to further even the most laudable goals is hampered by endless bickering and by a hopelessly bloated bureaucracy. They know little of the U.N.'s humanitarian and development activities, which account for 75 percent of the Organization's budget,[1] and still less about the important contributions the U.N. has been making in these fields from 1945 to the present.

The products of the Department of Public Information must be uniquely suited to serve a number of purposes. They must be educational tools, as required by General Assembly Resolution 13(1), which instructs DPI to "promote to the greatest extent possible an informed understanding of the work and purposes of the United Nations among the peoples of the world." At the same time, they should serve a public relations function. While promotion of the United Nations as an institution has become more difficult in recent years as public support of the Organization has fallen off, promotion of the U.N.'s successes should form an important part of any public information strategy. A related issue concerns the target audiences for DPI's information products. While the number of audiences that the department ultimately hopes to reach is large and quite diverse—"the peoples of the world"—DPI's products will be most helpful as public relations tools if they are targeted toward specific priority audiences, such as those that can influence existing support and mobilize additional forms of support for the Organization: primarily policy-makers and opinion-shapers in member countries.

Perhaps the most important function of the Department of Public Information's products should be the active promotion of the United Nations' goals. This is a step beyond the simple information function envisioned by the General Assembly when it established the department in 1946. At that time, support for the U.N. and its goals was nearly universal and any attempts by DPI to adopt a policy of sustained advocacy would have amounted to preaching to the converted. This is no longer the case, however, and, as a result, promotion of the Organization and its policies by DPI has become both appropriate and necessary.

The media, of course, must take some of the blame for the woeful underpublication of U.N. activities. Today, for example, the U.S. public receives less information about the United Nations from the media than at any other time in the Organization's history, and only one major U.S. newspaper—*The New York Times*—has a full-time staff correspondent at the U.N. To some extent it is the nature of the U.N.'s activities that is responsible for the inadequate coverage they receive— even when it comes to the Organization's very significant successes in the area of decolonization, human rights, and economic development, and in its services to refugees and children. Advances in these areas, though substantial, are incremental and cumulative and thus seldom produce the kind of dramatic headlines that ensure newspaper sales. Inflammatory resolutions adopted by the General Assembly make far better copy.

But the roots of the underpublication of U.N. activities go much deeper. As one long-time U.N. correspondent put it, the public has always received just as much coverage of the U.N. as it has wanted. With the dashing of the world's high expectations, the U.N. has lost prestige and, consequently, the interest of the press.

When the Organization was front-page news and journalists aggressively sought out stories on their own, it was enough for DPI to provide them with typewriters and press releases. The fading of the U.N.'s political promise has changed all that, but DPI has not yet learned how to sell the U.N.'s story to a less responsive press. As one U.N. correspondent put it, "the mountain doesn't come to Mohammed anymore."

In addition to tending to the needs of the U.N. press corps, promotion of the Organization is accomplished through pamphlets, books, movies, and radio and TV features. These information products— appearing in the 1986–87 program budget as 240 different items— afford the U.N. its greatest opportunity for communicating its successes in terms that the public will find both compelling and easy to understand. Yet it is clear that these products rarely live up to such a standard. Too often DPI's output can be characterized as production for production's sake, and as serving the political needs and demands of delegates more than they do a public information function. At best, these outputs preach to the converted; at worst, they are so stilted or circumspect that they fall short of minimum standards of competence.

The uniqueness of the United Nations as an institution imposes certain requirements on its information function. Its Department of Public Information must be able to identify national information needs and respond quickly to opportunities for promoting the U.N. throughout the world—all while taking into account the geographical, linguistic, cultural, and political differences among the nations it is attempting to reach. The highly centralized structure of the department makes such flexibility nearly impossible.

A more fundamental problem is the lack of an overall strategy to guide and inform the U.N.'s information and communication activities. An important part of such a strategy would be the identification of particular "target audiences," their priority concerns, and the most effective means of reaching these audiences. This approach would permit the DPI staff to rationalize its information activities, to develop a more systematic approach to the dissemination of its information outputs, and to measure the impact of the department's activities and products against specific strategic objectives.

At the same time, improvements in outputs have little value if the product fails to reach the intended audience. DPI has done little to develop its distribution capabilities. For example, although there are 68 United Nations Information Centres (UNICs) located throughout the world and an extensive network of nongovernmental organizations affiliated with the U.N., DPI has made few efforts to use these resources creatively to improve the distribution of U.N. information resources.

It is in attempting to fulfill its function as promoter of the U.N.'s goals that DPI will face its greatest challenge: walking the narrow line between promotion and propaganda. Since the 1970s, DPI's mandate has been papered over with layer upon layer of General Assembly resolutions requiring DPI to give priority to certain areas of U.N. involvement, including some—the new world orders, for example— that do not enjoy the support of all member states.[2] As a result, DPI has been forced to follow two conflicting mandates: on the one hand, to disseminate information about and promote the work of the U.N. in all its infinite variety and, on the other hand, to "orient its work mainly" toward certain objectives that may not, in fact, have the support of the entire membership.

Having imposed contrary mandates on the department, the General Assembly has left DPI confused about its purpose and has seriously limited its ability to function successfully as a public relations/public information service. The quality of the department's output is evidence of this. DPI's information products are often characterized as unreadable, unusable, and outdated at the time of release. Significant production delays plague even the Organization's most important ongoing publications—a delay of four years in the case of the *U.N. Yearbook.*

General Assembly resolution 13(1), which established the department in 1946, prohibits it from engaging in "propaganda." Yet from the point of view of some member states, the active promotion of objectives they do not support serves just such a purpose.[3] Although promotion of the U.N.'s goals should form an important part of DPI's information strategy, the department must be sensitive to the fact that its products will continue to be labeled as propaganda and alienate an important minority so long as the General Assembly promulgates resolutions that require the department to advocate the majority's views on contentious issues. In such cases, the department should not only carefully set out the issues that have led the majority to seek a particular objective but should also include a fair discussion of the minority position. Sensitivity to the views of the minority can help to blunt—if not do away with—the criticism leveled at the department by these member states.

U.N. Information in Perspective

Concepts of the Information Function

Some of the problems that plague DPI are structural. The most intractable ones, however, grow out of the very nature of the United Nations—a body whose members represent widely varying cultures, backgrounds, political ideologies, and economic and social philosophies. The divergence of views that stands in the way of consensus among Western, Soviet-bloc, and developing countries on many political and economic matters that come before the General Assembly also stands in the way of agreement about how the public should be informed. As one or another of these sometimes irreconcilable philosophies about the proper place and purpose of the information function became the majority view, it was incorporated in DPI's mandate. The result is a department caught between opposing strictures.

How member states view the proper role and function of the U.N. Department of Public Information is closely related to their view of the role and function of the media in society. The Western nations are committed to the free flow of information. The media in these countries are relatively free of government interference—a condition that allows them to serve as an independent monitor of the state's activities.

The media model for much of the developing world is based upon a far different view of the role of the press in society. Here the media are expected to play an activist role in development by demonstrating support for basic government policies and, in most cases, for the regime itself. In such countries, news is regarded not only as information but as a means of guiding social development. A similar, if more rigorous, model is followed by most of the Soviet-bloc countries and by some others as well. Here the media are servants of the state and actors in achieving state goals. This model is not only intolerant of any dissent from government policies but requires the press to serve as a constant propagandist and progovernment agitator. The role of the press under the "communist" model, said Malaysian Prime Minister Datuk Seri Mahathir Mohamad in a speech to ASEAN journalists, is "to act as an instrument of revelation, not information."[4]

With postwar decolonization, a new majority emerged in the General Assembly, one whose presence transformed the Assembly and altered the approach to disseminating information. Although most member states would agree that the main goal of DPI is to provide information about the U.N.'s goals and achievements in language that is clear and in forms that make it accessible to its audience, they are often unable to agree on the specific function of DPI's products: whether a pure information function, reporting the activities and decisions of the U.N. in a dispassionate way, or that of "instrument of revelation," actively promoting all of the U.N.'s policies and objectives.

The Evolution of DPI's Mandate

DPI's mandate has evolved over the years, reflecting the growing ideological rift among member states on the media function. The legislative authority for what was originally called the Office of Public Information (OPI) lies in General Assembly Resolution 13(1) adopted by the General Assembly on February 13, 1946, which calls upon the U.N.'s public information arm to "promote to the greatest extent possible an informed understanding of the work and purposes of the United Nations among the peoples of the world." In the early days, OPI (renamed the Department of Public Information in 1978) fulfilled its mandate chiefly by describing the activities of the nascent Organization and announcing its decisions in the areas of peace, international security, and humanitarian affairs.

The rapid decolonization that took place in the 1960s led to an expansion of OPI's role and the beginning of a philosophical shift in its information function. A General Assembly radically different from the one that adopted resolution 13(1) in 1946 increasingly called upon OPI to address new concerns in its publications and radio and audio-visual programs—concerns that expressed the priorities of the developing world: decolonization, disarmament, development, the new world orders, and the struggle against apartheid, among other forms of racial discrimination.

Communications issues have played an important role in the discussions of United Nations bodies since the introduction by the Soviet Union of the controversial "Draft Declaration on the Role of the Mass Media" at a general conference of UNESCO in 1974.[5] At the center of these discussions has been the call by Third World nations for a New World Information and Communications Order (NWICO). The decade-old debate on NWICO emerged from a perception by the developing world of a marked imbalance in the international flow of news. These nations claim that the developed world—which owns over 90 percent of the world's communications facilities, including the four dominant news agencies—effectively controls the world press. Third World representatives contend—with some justification—that the news reported by the West reflects only Western preferences and needs: Insufficient coverage is given to Third World needs and achievements, and, all too often, its problems and failings are emphasized or dealt with in an unsympathetic way. Debate over the definition and implementation of NWICO has been extensive and difficult. Western governments have balked at the concept of an "order" regulating the media and have contended that UNESCO discussions have helped to promote acceptance of greater government control of the press, including the licensing of journalists.

Despite strong Western opposition, interest in the idea of a New World Information and Communication Order spread quickly in the General Assembly. By the late 1970s resolutions had begun to acknowledge the "potential of the field of communication . . . to further enhance the economic and social progress of developing countries" and the "essential role of information in the implementation of international decisions concerning economic and social development."[6] In 1978 the General Assembly responded to UNESCO's call for a NWICO by affirming "the need to establish a new, more just, and more effective world information and communication order, intended to strengthen international peace and understanding and based on the free circulation and wider and better-balanced dissemination of information."[7]

The same Assembly resolution established an intergovernmental committee—the Committee to Review the United Nations Public Information Policies and Objectives on Information (renamed the Committee on Information in 1979)—to oversee U.N. information activities and acknowledge that DPI, through the dissemination of information, had an important role to play "in the implementation of international decisions concerning economic and social development needs of the developing world." The General Assembly's instructions to this end remained somewhat vague, although reference to the importance of information as a way of creating support for specific policies began to appear in resolutions on disarmament and decolonization at this time.[8]

In 1980 the General Assembly instructed DPI for the first time to "orient its work specifically towards dissemination of information mainly on problems concerning international peace and security, disarmament, peace-keeping, and peace-making operations, decolonization, the promotion of human rights, the struggle against racial discrimination, the integration of women in the struggle for peace and development, the establishment of a new international economic order, and the establishment of a new world information and communication order."[9] Special attention was to be given to the U.N.'s activities against apartheid and to the work of the U.N. Council for Namibia. Subsequent instructions to the department by the General Assembly have contained similar language.[10]

The involvement of the General Assembly in public information affairs is not limited to the passage of general resolutions requiring DPI to promote certain political objectives, however. Its instructions to the department are often specific and detailed—a resolution a few years ago, for example, required the department to initiate radio broadcasts in French/Creole and Dutch/Papiemento.[11] These resolutions, which often reflect the political needs of member states, limit the department's ability to make strategic decisions based on a professional assessment of national information needs, the relevance of material for a particular audience, and the U.N.'s need, as an institution, to cultivate the support of important or disaffected member states.

Conflicting Mandates

The U.N.'s Department of Public Information has been given the task of walking the line between two contrary mandates: on the one hand, to inform the people of the world of the work of the U.N. in a balanced and objective fashion and, on the other, to "orient its work mainly" toward certain areas of U.N. involvement that do not, in fact, enjoy the support of the entire membership. DPI's difficulties are rooted in philosophical differences among member states concerning the extent to which "information" should move beyond the factual reporting of events and trends and act as advocate for certain international norms. The department's original mandate—to ensure that people in all parts of the world receive the fullest possible information about the United Nations—reflects the strong influence of the Western, "free-press" nations, which call on DPI to mobilize public opinion in support of various specific objectives.

While promotion of the Organization's goals is, and should be, an important objective of its public information work, the question arises as to whether it is appropriate for the United Nations to use its Department of Public Information to advocate positions on certain issues, when such positions may be objectionable to a large minority of states. One alternative that has been proposed gives responsibility for the promotion of the U.N.'s more contentious objectives to the special units within the Secretariat that are specifically concerned with these issues—for example, the Centre against Apartheid and the Office of the Commissioner for Namibia. Many of these units have subdivisions that perform some information functions.

But such a "pass the buck" approach is shortsighted and even dangerous. The removal of promotional activities for "non-consensus objectives" to the units whose raison d'être" is the achievement of these objectives virtually assures an advocacy approach in treating such issues and would hardly be acceptable to member states holding the minority position. Moreover, the general public will not differentiate between publications of the United Nations Department of Public Information and those of other United Nations units, thus opening the DPI to additional charges of propagandizing. At the same time, the dispersion of the U.N.'s public information activities among other Secretariat units—already requiring resources of nearly $11 million[12]— makes coordination of the Organization's total information activities very difficult and causes some duplication of effort. If these units— which are usually substantive departments—were to take on additional information activities, it would almost certainly make matters worse. Furthermore, any restriction on the type of information issues to be handled by DPI could seriously limit the department's ability to play a dynamic, responsive role in the dissemination of U.N. information.

The United Nations is a public service organization whose continued existence depends on the support it receives from member governments. For this reason, the Organization's information department must take account of *all* member states in carrying out its mandate and not just those that form a parliamentary majority. DPI's mandate, as clearly set out in resolution 13(1), is to promote an informed understanding of both the purposes and the work of the U.N. To generate support for the Organization requires systematic and sustained advocacy, and this must form an important part of the department's information strategy. To promote an understanding of the work of the Organization—its particular program goals and priorities—requires even greater sensitivity to the views of *all* the U.N.'s constituents. General Assembly resolutions directing DPI to advocate the majority's view on contentious issues will continue to alienate a minority of important member states, leaving the department open to charges of propagandizing, in direct contravention of 13(1). In such cases, the department should take care to set out the issues that have led the majority to seek a particular object and to include a fair discussion of the minority position.

The Committee on Information (COI)

The Committee on Information (COI) was established by the General Assembly in 1978 to review United Nations public information policies and activities and to report to the General Assembly—through the Special Political Committee—on the policies and activities of the public information services of the United Nations system, giving particular attention to activities in the economic and social sphere.[13] In its resolution 34/182 of December 18, 1979, the General Assembly requested the Committee on Information to:

1. "continue to examine the U.N. public information policies and activities in the light of the evolution of international relations, particularly during the last two decades, and of the imperatives of the establishment of the new international economic order and of a new world information and communication order"

2. "evaluate and follow up on the efforts made and the progress achieved by the U.N. in the field of information and communication"

3. "promote the establishment of a new, more just and more effective world information and communication order intended to strengthen peace and international understanding and based on the free circulation and wider and better balanced dissemination of information and to make recommendations thereon to the General Assembly."

The committee—an intergovernmental group consisting of 70 member states—holds two meetings each year: a two-day organizational session in March and a three-week substantive session in June.[14] The overwhelming proportion of the COI's discussions concern the political aspects of information. This is largely due to the fact that the debate on the New World Information and Communication Order, which originated in UNESCO, has now moved almost entirely into COI.[15] For example, at the 1986 substantive session of the committee, four full days were given over to general debate largely focusing on NWICO and other political themes, while only two days were reserved for discussion of 17 different aspects of the U.N.'s public information activities.[16]

As COI has paid increasing attention to the political aspects of information, the omnibus information resolutions it submits to the Special Political Committee have increasingly concentrated on ideological issues. In the case of COI's 1986 set of recommendations, more than 25 percent were directly related to the New World Information and Communication Order. It was intended that the Committee on Information arrive at its recommendations by consensus, but lack of Western support for the positions taken by the COI majority has prevented this since 1982.

When the COI, meeting in substantive session, does turn to the nonpolitical aspects of U.N. information activities, it disregards the limitations of time and concentrates on the fine details of DPI's work. Items on the agenda of the 1986 substantive meeting included: discussion of a report on the prices charged member states and the media for U.N. video tapes, audio tapes, and news photos; review of DPI's distribution of its photo materials; and review of a report on the strengthening and expansion of the Middle East/Arabic unit.[17]

It is no more appropriate for the COI to concern itself with the specifics of DPI's work than it is for the General Assembly to do so. Like the Assembly, COI is an intergovernmental group, and most of its members lack expertise in the field of public information. Resolutions of the General Assembly and of the Committee on Information that seek to direct the daily work of departmental units bind DPI to the political agenda of two inexpert bodies and restrict its ability to make decisions based on the needs of its constituents.

The Committee on Information has proven more of a hindrance than a help to the U.N.'s Department of Public Information. COI's involvement in DPI's daily affairs is obstructive, as is its attempt to stress the political aspects of information. Furthermore, COI duplicates the work of the General Assembly, which, through the Special Political Committee, oversees DPI's information activities. The General Assembly itself would serve the Organization's interests better if it focused on broad questions of departmental management and programming rather than on the daily particulars of running DPI or the political aspects of information.

The Committee on Information should be dissolved. In its place, a high-level independent panel should be established to advise the General Assembly on questions relating to information and communication. The panel, to be appointed by the Secretary-General, would be composed of approximately ten men and women from outside the U.N. with considerable experience in the areas of public information, media, communications, and public relations.

Administrative and Structural Issues*

The United Nations Department of Public Information is divided by function into four major parts: Press and Publications, Radio and Visual Services, External Relations, and Economic and Social Information. As the principal U.N. body engaged in public information activities, DPI produces and distributes pamphlets, books and journals; broadcasts and distributes taped radio programs around the world; provides TV news coverage of U.N. events; sponsors or produces films about the U.N.; and provides a variety of services to the press and representatives of NGOs. Through its External Relations Division, DPI also administers a total of 68 Information Centres—the department's "branch offices"—throughout the world.

Recommendation 37(1) of the Group of High-Level Intergovernmental Experts—adopted by the General Assembly—calls for a

> thorough review of the functions and working methods as well as of the policies of the Department of Public Information (DPI) . . . conducted with a view to bringing its role and policies up to date in order to improve the capacity and ability of the Department to provide information on United Nations activities as approved by the inter-governmental bodies. To this end, the working methods of the Department should be rational-

---

*During the course of 1987–1988 Under-Secretary-General Sevigny conducted a major restructuring of DPI at the request of the Secretary-General. Many of the functional and structural changes which emerged from that restructuring appear to address issues raised in the following pages and elsewhere in this chapter.

ized, in order that the funds allocated to that department should, to a larger extent than hitherto, be used for programme activities.[18]

This is an important step, and long overdue. Not all of DPI's problems stem from the confusion over its proper function described in previous sections. It suffers from many of the problems that plague other U.N. departments: personnel that are unqualified for their posts, wastage, uneven outputs, and overlapping functions.[19] One major constraint on the department's effectiveness, for example, is the lack of a mechanism for the coordination of news dissemination. Each day U.N. news reaches the public through press releases and radio and TV spots, yet there is no means of ensuring that the information released by various divisions within the Department of Public Information is nonduplicative and, more important, noncontradictory. Most news agencies operating in a variety of media rely on a central news desk to coordinate the sharing of resources and a rational allocation of responsibilities. DPI needs a similar central authority to coordinate the allocation of its news products. A daily meeting of producers and news editors—the so-called "product managers"—would be a simple way of ensuring that those with the responsibility for news dissemination in every division are kept abreast of the activities of their colleagues.

Another major problem has arisen from the budgetary constraints on the Department of Public Information: Although the activities of the U.N., and therefore its public information needs, have grown increasingly complex over the past 41 years, DPI's budget has steadily decreased as a proportion of U.N. spending. In 1950, DPI's budget was 11.8 percent of the total U.N. budget; in 1960, 7.1 percent; in 1970, 4.7 percent; in 1980, 3.7 percent; and in 1985, 2 percent. The result has been that DPI's four divisions, which have increased in size and complexity over the same period, must compete for shares of an ever-shrinking pie. For example, ten new Information Centres have been established since 1979—all of these at the request of member states and mandated by General Assembly resolutions—without the appropriation of additional funds, with the result that each time a new center has been established, the operational resources for all of the centers must be divided into smaller portions.

Press and Publications Division (PPD)

The Press and Publications Division, with a staff of 92 (51 professionals) and a budget of $10.7 million in 1986, is the major publisher of

United Nations materials for various audiences throughout the world. The division consists of Press Services, which is responsible for all news coverage activities; and Publications Services, which handles information in depth. The PPD publishes thousands of press releases and briefing notes every year, holds over 100 press conferences, and publishes all of the U.N.'s major periodicals, pamphlets, and reference books.

PPD is one of the most widely criticized of DPI's divisions, in part because it is an active promoter—through its publications—of majority views that alienate an important minority of member states. The division's greatest failing, however, is its tendency to view the recipients of its information products as an undifferentiated mass that is best served by a centralized decision-making structure. It does not take sufficiently into account the fact that "the people of the world" is made up of many different groups of individuals who are separated not only by language but by a multitude of cultural variables as well. Each audience group has its own specific information needs that may not overlap with the information needs of another audience. Certain developing countries, for example, will have little need for basic information on decolonization—having experienced it first hand—but may have a very great need for information on population control or economic and social development.

When the products of the PPD are underutilized or less than effective, the problem can often be traced directly to DPI's current structure. The highly centralized nature of the department has restricted PPD's ability to tailor its information products to the specific needs and interests of its audiences. Instead, the division's information activities are reduced to cursory coverage of the Organization's every activity or to the sort of promotion of majority positions on certain political issues that may leave the department open to charges of propagandizing.

Press Services: It is unquestionably in the best interests of DPI to encourage extensive independent coverage of the U.N.'s activities by the press, which, after all, provides the Organization with its most direct access to the "peoples of the world." Yet the U.N. press corps has contended that the Press Services unit is not always responsive to its particular needs, and relations between the United Nations Correspondents Association (UNCA) and the unit are strained.

DPI, for its part, has contended that a lack of professionalism among many in the press corps is responsible for the quality of coverage the U.N. receives. If such were the case, a review of the current U.N.

press-accreditation policy would certainly be in order. But however one assesses the quality of the press corps, DPI's attitude toward the press must be characterized as reticent at best. This may be the department's defensive reaction to the media's increasing criticism of the U.N., or it may be due to the fact that all too few at the highest levels of DPI have had a journalism background and, thus, have little familiarity with needs and attitudes of the press. (It should be noted that the new Under-Secretary-General for Public Information, Thérèse Paquet-Sévigny, has significant professional experience in the field.[20]) All information officers, whether serving at headquarters or in Information Centres abroad, should be required to have considerable experience in the field of information.

The most visible contact between DPI and the press corps takes place at a daily press briefing and question-and-answer period, held by the Spokesman for the Secretary-General to review each day's events. The Office of the Spokesman is the key liaison between the United Nations and the press corps and, as such, is in constant communication with the media: releasing official news, arranging interviews, and providing background. Yet despite the obvious advantages to DPI of cultivating a friendly and cooperative relationship with the media, there is no doubt that, at times, the department has taken a defensive position vis-à-vis the press.[21] In addition, Press Services has, on several occasions, passed up excellent opportunities to communicate a U.N. success story to the media[22] or has relayed the story in such a passive way—distributing press releases rather than trying to "sell" the story and actively encourage media interest—that the press corps has not picked it up. Unfortunately, the effect of these lapses has been to further weaken an already lackluster treatment of the U.N. by the media.

United Nations press officers prepare thousands of press releases each year in English and French.[23] These press releases distill proceedings, speeches, and votes held in open meetings of the General Assembly, the Security Council, and the Assembly's principal committees. Each meeting is generally covered by a team of two press officers, who take turns preparing summaries or paraphrasing the speeches of delegates while the meeting is going on. Some of the meeting rooms have word-processing equipment that relays the press officers' notes to the editors and proofreaders automatically; but in most cases the officers must write out their stories by hand and pass them, page by page, to a messenger, who then runs them upstairs to be edited and checked for errors, typed, proofread, and mimeographed. Four hundred copies of each press release are run off within an hour of the end of the meeting for distribution to the press (600 copies in the case of a meeting of the Security Council or a statement of the Secretary-General). An additional 75 copies are run off for distribution to United Nations Information Centres, and the Department of Conference Services prepares another 800 for distribution to delegations. The English-language section of the press unit also publishes biographical notes, statements of the Secretary-General, statements of appointments, and reissues press releases from local Information Centres.

Correspondents describe the English press releases as generally accurate and well-balanced. However, they contend that, because English is the *lingua franca* of the international media, the French releases are unnecessary and serve only to satisfy the political concerns of certain delegations. In addition, the French press releases are considered to be of generally inferior quality, with the result that even the French news agencies—of which there are only five[24]—tend to favor the English-language releases.

Like DPI's other divisions, Press Services has been affected by the U.N.'s budgetary constraints: Coverage of U.N. events has been cut by nearly a third over the past year.[25] The reduction of coverage has been carried out in a somewhat arbitrary fashion, with little consideration of such matters as news value. The result has been that some important U.N. sessions receive no coverage at all or are covered only in French and therefore unusable for most correspondents. At the same time, some highly technical meetings—which rarely produce news of interest to the daily press—receive complete and thorough coverage.

A further problem stems from the cutback on summary meeting records previously produced by the Department of Conference Services. U.N. press releases have increased in length and detail to fill the void, mostly in order to appease delegates, whose speeches are often quoted at length. Yet, it is clearly not the function of a press release to describe U.N. meetings in great detail or to provide delegates with the means of proving to their governments their active participation in U.N. processes.

There is a clear need to be more selective in the daily coverage of U.N. activities by the press unit. To this end, DPI should solicit the views of the U.N. press corps and selected media users outside of the U.N. and monitor the actual use of DPI releases in the world press. Coverage of U.N. meetings should be restricted to those determined to be of substantial interest and demonstrated utility to the daily press.

Round-up press releases or feature articles would seem a better way to publicize technical meetings, but only when their reports have been released and only if their achievements warrant an effort to attract public attention. DPI's Press Services must also play a more active role in obtaining media coverage of the U.N. Press Services, as well as the Office of the Spokesman for the Secretary-General, should be in constant contact with members of the news media—including the non-U.N. press corps—feeding them good stories, rather than relying too heavily on passive press releases. In addition, the media should be given reasonable advance warning when an important consensus decision by a U.N. body is anticipated; and, whenever possible, the vote should be timed in such a way as to allow the press to meet deadlines. No matter how important the issue, decisions taken in the evening—as in the case of the consensus decision on the budgetary mechanism—or on the weekend will fail to receive proper coverage.

Publications Services: Information in depth includes books, pamphlets, and periodicals, most of which are concerned with the promotion of the U.N.'s so-called "priority concerns": disarmament, the new world orders, peacekeeping, apartheid, etc. DPI's publications range from weighty reference books like the *U.N. Yearbook* to pocket-sized leaflets that provide at-a-glance facts and figures on U.N. operations. Some of these publications are hardy perennials—for example, reprints of such basic documents as the Charter of the United Nations and the Declaration of Human Rights in 70 languages. Other yearly publications—*Image and Reality*, and *Objective: Justice*—describe the Organization's structure and some of its enduring activities. These are updated frequently and serve as useful general resource materials for legislators, journalists, representatives of nongovernmental organizations (NGOs), and students.

As with all of DPI's outputs, the subject matter of DPI's publications is determined by General Assembly resolutions and corresponds to requests by NGOs and missions. These subjects must be noted when PPD submits its budget to DPI's Planning, Programming, and Evaluation Unit (PPEU) for approval. PPEU compares publications proposals from each of DPI's divisions to ensure that there is no overlap. However, given the snail's pace of the U.N. budgeting process—proposals may be submitted to PPEU as many as four years before a publication actually rolls off the press—PPD may stray rather far from its projected publications list, thus greatly increasing the possibility of duplication. Even more likely is a duplication of the publications of other U.N. departments whose budgets are not screened by PPEU.

The *U.N. Chronicle*, the principal periodical issued by the Press and Publications Division[26] (with an English language circulation of 13,750 and a paid subscription of 7,292)[27] attempts to cover every major session of the main organs of the U.N. in just four issues each year and to present the views of governments on major issues before the Organization. In trying to do so much, the *Chronicle* has spread itself far too thin. Given the breadth of the periodical's coverage, its tiny staff (three writers and one editor—halved as a result of the financial crisis) is unable to do any original work and is forced to rely on dry press releases and official documents. As a result, the *Chronicle* is tedious reading indeed. The question may also be raised whether there is a need for the kind of coverage supplied by the *Chronicle*. Readers interested in archival descriptions of the U.N.'s activities have many other sources: press releases, the weekly *News Digest*, and the *U.N. Yearbook*, for example (although, as noted, the Yearbook is published only after significant delays).

The *Chronicle* has identified students and educators, NGOs, media leaders, and diplomats as its principal audience. In another form, the *Chronicle* has the potential to serve these readers better, and perhaps even to enlarge its audience. The *Chronicle*—and the U.N.—could profit from a magazine approach that offered a mix of feature and news stories oriented toward the information needs of its audiences. Feature stories—perhaps written by freelance journalists to take some of the burden off of the *Chronicle's* small staff—could examine broad areas of United Nations involvement. These would be accompanied by punchy news stories that detail the U.N.'s activities in these areas.

PPD's failure to view its audience as a world of disparate groups separated by linguistic and other differences, combined with the lack of any systematic method for assessing the impact of its publications, militates against the rationalization of U.N. information activities and the improvement of DPI's effectiveness overall. To ensure the effectiveness of the United Nations publications service, no publication should go into production until:

- the target audience has been identified;
- the best vehicle for approaching a particular audience has been determined, taking into account such variables as language, culture, income level, education, occupation, and fields of interest
- the impact of the output can be measured against its strategic objective: to stimulate the support and involvement of a broad range of partners and allies in the activities of the Organization. (To reduce

costs, such impact studies could be conducted on a national level through the U.N.'s extensive network of nongovernmental organizations.)

External Relations Division: United Nations Information Centres (UNICs)

In 1946 the Preparatory Commission on the United Nations recommended that the General Assembly create "branch offices" for its public information service, since "the development of improved world opinion and intelligent support depends as much on the establishment of a wide and well-organized network of information distributing centres as an adequate and efficient public information service at Headquarters." Resolution 13(1) itself recommended the earliest possible establishment of branch offices "to ensure that people in all parts of the world receive as full information as possible about the United Nations."

Within a year Information Centres had been established in ten countries—Brazil, China, Czechoslovakia, Denmark, France, India, Mexico, Switzerland, the United Kingdom, and the United States. By mid-1986, 68 centers had been established worldwide—most of them at the initiative of member states. The centers are supposed to maintain up-to-date reference libraries of U.N. publications and documentation in order to respond to public inquiries. DPI material—cabled or sent by diplomatic pouch from Headquarters—is translated by the centers, which work closely with the local media, information offices, educational authorities, and nongovernmental organizations. The centers are also supposed to keep Headquarters apprised of local U.N. activities, which in turn are published by DPI.

Throughout the U.N.'s history, Secretaries-General and the General Assembly have stressed the need to strengthen the functioning of the Information Centres. Nevertheless, they are generally acknowledged to be ineffective. There are a number of structural reasons for this:

Information Centres have been established on an ad hoc basis at the request of member states, with the result that there is no logical pattern to their placement. There is a high concentration of centers in some areas (Africa, Western Europe) and relatively few centers in others (Eastern Europe, the Americas). The highest concentration of centers is in developing countries, where the social and economic work of the United Nations is already well known, while there are comparatively few centers in major contributor countries, where the U.N.'s work is not known firsthand but the need for support and understanding of the Organization's activities is great.

Staff at U.N. Information Centres generally consists of one expatriate professional on the P-5 or D-1 level and several local general service staff, who act as information or reference assistants, messengers, etc. However, the size of a center's staff frequently has little relation to the size of the territory it must service. This may have ludicrous consequences, as in the case of the Information Centre in Dakar, Senegal, where one professional and four general service staff must serve the information needs of seven countries.

The resources allocated to the Information Centres are woefully inadequate for their needs. Sixty-eight UNICs received a total of $19.1 million in 1984–85, about a third of DPI's total budget. In addition, the funds are allocated to the various centers with little consideration to the size of the territory to be covered, the differences in costs-of-living between countries, and whether the host government is paying some of the costs of the center.

Nearly 80 percent of the budget of the UNICs goes toward staff costs, with only 2 percent allocated for travel expenses. This makes it impossible for a center that covers several countries, or even one large country, to have a real impact outside of the city in which it is located.

According to General Assembly resolution 2897 of 1971, the Secretary-General is requested to "appoint to the United Nations Information Centres highly qualified professionals in the field of public information." This is not often the case; in fact, many of the centers that share quarters with UNDP offices are headed by a UNDP resident representative, whose expertise is in a field other than that of information.[28]

Many of these problems can be resolved in a fairly straightforward manner: for example, by forming regional or subregional information offices or by enforcing the requirement that all information officers have professional experience in the field. But the reallocation of funds and the redeployment of information services alone is not sufficient to improve the effectiveness of the Information Centres. The Department of Public Information will never be a powerful and persuasive source of information about the United Nations until it learns how to respond to the information needs of its priority audiences: the policy-makers in member states and those who can be called upon to develop future support for the U.N.'s activities. DPI's tendency to centralize the distribution of its information products has placed serious restrictions on the functioning of its "branch offices."

United Nations Information Centres are completely dependent on headquarters for their information resources. They are passive receivers of DPI's products, rarely initiating their own information activities. In the first six months of 1986, for example, the total public outreach of 68 Information Centers was a mere 19 NGO briefings, 31 publications—most of them simply translations of materials sent from headquarters—and 35 press conferences.[29] The Information Centres themselves cannot be faulted, since they do not have the resources, the expertise, or the authority to operate independently of the Secretariat.

Any attempt by DPI to adopt a more systematic approach to the dissemination of information must begin with an assessment of the kinds of decisions that should be made centrally and those that should be taken closer to the audience—on a national or regional level. DPI's first order of business, however, is to identify its priority audiences and its strategic objectives. It must then develop a plan for meeting these objectives, one that is as well tailored as possible to the information needs of the targeted audience, taking into consideration such factors as culture, income levels, fields of employment, etc. Special attention should be given to the possibility of enhanced collaboration with NGOs and local universities. The local UNICs could be an invaluable tool in identifying opportunities for specialized information activities on a national or regional level.

Another important issue concerns the manner in which information is sent to the centers and the criteria for determining the sort of information that is most appropriate for each center's use. Currently, centers receive information in an ad hoc fashion from all of the divisions of DPI as well as from other U.N. agencies. Every center receives cables from Headquartes each day that describe meetings of the Security Council, sessions of the General Assembly, and contain the text of statements by the Secretary-General. Multiple copies of every major U.N. publication are also pouched to the centers—at significant expense—along with still other materials that the information support section of the External Relations Division (ERD) considers relevant to a particular center's interests. There is no coordination in sending information to the centers and duplications are frequent. Even so, materials pouched to the centers may take weeks to arrive, rendering them outdated and useless. ERD has proven time and again that it is unable to meet the specific information needs of 68 very different regions. Former information officers are full of stories about large shipments of irrelevant materials that reached their centers.

DPI has begun to experiment with a computer system—the Division of Economic and Social Information (DESI) Electronic Information Network (DEIN)—that could be installed, at minimal cost, in Information Centres abroad. The program is a promising one and would have the double benefit of substantially reducing the costs and delays involved in sending information by pouch or cable and of allowing Information Centres to determine for themselves the types of information they require.

The department should go even further, however. Information Centres should be greatly enlarged and strengthened; serious consideration should be given to reorganizing them along regional or at least subregional lines, in keeping with the recommendation of the Group of 18; and they should be given the resources adequate to serving their regions. A decentralized information system, if it is to be strong, will probably require a greater percentage of DPI's budget than the 30 percent that is now alloted to the UNICs. Obviously, any reduction in the number of UNICs will mean a proportionate increase in the resources than can be applied to the remaining centers.

At the same time, the department should examine ways to respond better to the information needs of its "branch offices," perhaps by producing high-quality prototypes for recopying or raw information— facts and figures—for translation and adaptation by the individual centers. The decentralized production of some information products should result in a reduction of materials produced in final form at headquarters. In that case, increased costs to the centres would be offset by decreasing production costs at Headquarters. General information products—such as *Basic Facts,* the *Yearbook,* etc.—would continue to be produced at Headquarters.

The decentralization of some information activities raises the question of control. The department's longstanding policy of avoiding the appointment of center directors who are nationals of the host country helps to insulate UNIC directors from local political pressures. DPI already keeps a close watch on each Information Centre, which must report biennially on its activities. The balance of information products—prepared by the UNICs from DPI prototypes—could be similarly monitored on a spot basis through a database like DEIN.

Finally, DPI should investigate the possibility of the co-production of information materials by UNICs and national NGOs, as a way both to reduce costs and to involve NGOs more fully in the work of the U.N. Co-produced materials would be monitored in the same way as information products produced by the Information Centres themselves. The United Nations Development Programme (UNDP) has had some success with this approach.

Division of Economic and Social Information (DESI)

The U.N. founded a Center for Economic and Social Information (CESI) in the 1960s as the Organization was rapidly expanding its role in the economic and social fields. CESI was administered through voluntary contributions until 1974, when it became a division—the department's smallest—of DPI. The Division of Economic and Social Information (DESI) has a 1986–87 budget of $2.5 million and employs a total of 16 professionals and 24 general service staff.

The mandate of DESI is to produce thematic information on the U.N.'s economic and social activities. Many of the division's information materials relate to the international conferences convened by the United Nations and to special observances mandated by the General Assembly. The division also acts as secretariat for the Joint U.N. Information Committee (JUNIC), which has the responsibility for coordinating the information activities of all of the organizations of the United Nations system.

DESI's small size and the comparatively limited range of issues for which it is responsible have combined to make the division one of DPI's most flexible units. Unlike the other divisions, which are separated by function, DESI has the full spectrum of information products at its disposal. The division has produced (or co-produced) radio and TV programs, books, pamphlets, press releases, and movies. It is also, in some ways, the department's most creative division. The experimental DESI Electronic Information Network was fully conceived by DESI, is administered by DESI, and is completely financed by external funds raised by DESI. DEIN aims to become a full-fledged externally oriented communication and information network, linking NGOs, media, educational institutions, government, and other "redisseminators" and users worldwide with DPI, the Information Centres, and other JUNIC members through electronic mail, bulletin boards, and user-searchable full-text data bases. In addition, two of the U.N. system's most successful interagency projects—*Development Forum*[30] and the Non-Governmental Liaison Services (NGLS)[31]—are coordinated through the division. DESI has also arranged a series of successful training programs at the U.N. for young journalists from developing countries.

The division, however, is hardly trouble free. As the "new kid on the block," DESI is treated with suspicion and some resentment by DPI's more established divisions, which find it difficult to relate to the unique subject-orientation of DESI's mandate. This resentment has often produced calls for its dissolution. The second-class status of DESI within DPI, while undeserved, has serious consequences. There is far too little effort to coordinate research between DESI and other divisions or to ensure that there is no duplication of efforts (except through the faulty PPEU mechanism described above). Because the Publications Service produces materials on some of the themes that fall under DESI's mandate—economic and social development, women's issues, and the new world orders—the potential for duplication is high.

Like the other divisions, DESI should concentrate more of its efforts on responding to the information requests of its audiences than on producing large numbers of finished information products. At the same time, the U.N. has a great need for interesting feature stories that cover the U.N.'s many activities in the economic and social spheres. The thematic nature of DESI's function makes this division a logical source for such stories. DESI's very successful *Development Forum* already employs a feature-oriented approach, publishing a wide range of feature articles on development issues, often written by freelance journalists. DESI should utilize a similar approach in its other publications that concentrate on econmic and social themes. The articles in these publications should—whenever possible—be prepared by freelance journalists in response to particular subject requests from the field.

Radio and Visual Services Division (RVS)

Radio and Visual Services—DPI's largest division—has provided a generally effective means of disseminating information about the United Nations on a global scale. The division carries out this function in two ways: through the preparation of "news nuggets"—daily radio and TV coverage of U.N. news in a form suitable for adaptation and redissemination by broadcasters; and through the production of feature materials—radio, television, and film—that seek to inform the world of the "work and purposes" of the United Nations. (Outside TV correspondents gain access to U.N. camera crews and facilities on a fee basis.) Radio Services, which employs 50 professionals and 30 in general service posts, has a budget of $11.2 million for 1986–87. Visual

Services, with 38 professional and 32 general service staff, has a budget of $13.9 million for 1986–87.

In 1985, U.N. Radio taped over 2,000 hours of programs, ranging from weekly news magazines to daily summaries of U.N. news. The U.N. has the facilities to broadcast these programs—89 in all—in 18 languages. A 1985 study, prepared at the request of the Committee on Programme and Coordination and the Committee on Information, reported that in 1984 about 7,967 reels and 3,841 cassettes containing U.N. taped radio programs were sent each month to 1,156 recipients, on request, in 160 different countries—approximately 142,000 tapes every year. Eighty-two percent of the recipients were broadcast organizations, 8 percent nongovernmental organizations and educational institutions, 4 percent government agencies, and the remaining 6 percent United Nations Information Centres. Sixty-six percent of the recipients reported receiving the tapes regularly and in a timely fashion.[32] Although it is much more difficult to ascertain the use that is made of these radio programs, RVS has conducted marketing surveys throughout the world in an attempt to gauge the needs of its listening public.

The United States began providing radio transmission services to the United Natins in 1946, in what was seen as a temporary arrangement, until the Organization could obtain its own transmitter. The U.N. initially contracted directly with the Voice of America (VOA) licensees operating the transmitters. Later, RVS negotiated annual leasing contracts with the U.S. Information Agency (USIA) for these services. In April 1985, VOA officials advised the U.N. that it planned to recalculate the rate charged for its transmission services—then $30 per broadcast hour—to reflect their actual cost to VOA. The new rate of $179 per broadcast hour represented an increase of almost 500 percent over the 1985 rate, and the financially strapped U.N. radio services unit called a temporary halt to its broadcasts in January 1986. (Reportedly, VOA's decision to increase its fees was prompted as much by its assessment of the U.N. broadcasts as anti-Western as by its desire to cut its losses.)

U.N. TV covers virtually all General Assembly and Security Council sessions, as well as major events at Headquarters and at U.N. conferences worldwide. DPI sends out about a thousand weekly news packages on tape or film every year. These include news magazines in Arabic, Chinese, French, and Spanish as well as "World Chronicle," a series of weekly interviews with key U.N. officials conducted by members of the U.N. Press Corps.

The visual services unit has made too little effort to measure the impact of its product or the effectiveness of its programming mix. The unit would do well to undertake marketing surveys, similar to those conducted by the radio unit, to evaluate its television products. The surveys, which could be conducted through the Information Centres, should attempt to measure audience demand to determine the most effective programming mix between news coverage and feature programming.

Because of the tremendous expense involved in the production of films and video features, DPI's film unit is limited to one or two new films each year. There is a definite demand for its products—some of which have won awards—among school groups, NGOs, and UNICS, and an excellent distribution channel is in place. But the unit simply does not have the budgetary resources to meet the demand for timely and topical films. Many of its circulating films are badly out of date: Over half of the 146 films listed in the 1986–87 Film and Video catalogue are over ten years old.

The Radio and Visual Services Division has, nevertheless, proven its resilience when hit by major budget cuts. To trim costs, Visual Services is experimenting with co-production—with individual countries, independent producers, and other U.N. agencies. For example, the TV series "Agenda for a Small Planet" was organized as a cooperative venture between DPI, the Canadian International Development Agency (CIDA), and television organizations in a number of countries, the BBC among them. Participants finance and produce their own films and, in return, obtain the rights to broadcast the other films on their own networks. The 1979 disarmament film *Boom,* which won a Cannes Film Festival Special Jury Prize, was co-produced with Czech animator Bretislav Pojar. These sorts of creative arrangements for maintaining—or expanding—production despite a restricted budget should be encouraged. The division should also encourage participation by NGOs in these projects, either as co-producers or as sponsors.

The decentralized approach to the dissemination of information proposed in previous sections is also to be recommended for the Radio and Visual Services Division. While, in most cases, individual UNICs will not have the resources or the facilities for radio or film production, they can provide valuable assistance in the cultivation of relationships with potential co-producers and sponsors. And because the development of these products often requires a close working relationship between producers that cannot easily be sustained from Headquarters, there are still other advantages to operating close to the marketplace.

The UNICs should be encouraged to develop a network of potential sponsors, drawn from national and regional broadcast agencies, local governments, and nongovernmental agencies. (As with other information materials prepared away from Headquarters, such RVS products should be monitored by Headquarters—on a spot basis—to ensure balance and fairness.) The centers should also be responsible for the constant updating of the user list for RVS products, keeping abreast of user needs and, when appropriate, promoting certain information products.

A proposal to separate Radio and Visual Services into two distinct divisions is contained in the Secretary-General's proposed program budget for the 1986–87 biennium. The split has been justified by the large size of the present division and, reportedly, would not involve any additional cost (although requiring the creation of an additional post at the D-2 level). Division personnel have expressed the fear that the split would reduce the division's flexibility—its greatest strength—and will inhibit resource-sharing and career mobility between divisions. The split, which was to become effective as of January 1987, has been postponed, and the issue appears to be something of a dead letter. If the plan is revived by the new Under-Secretary-General for Public Information, however, it should be made a matter of priority to ensure that the two divisions' flexibility is retained at all costs.

Objectivity Of Information Products

U.N. information products are supposed to present a balanced view of every issue, yet there is no formal mechanism to ensure that this is the case. The Under-Secretary-General has, in the past, issued several directives to the DPI staff emphasizing the importance of objectivity in the department's information products. One of these directives, which amounts to guidelines for the production of information materials, encourages staff members to consult with the relevant U.N. departments in preparing publications to ensure their accuracy. Another encourages the staff to present controversial views as one set of opinions and to balance them with opposing views. DPI's guidelines appear to receive little recognition in practice, however, and many staff members seem to be unaware of their existence.

In actuality, the content of each information product is usually determined by its creator, with little input from the relevant substantive department. Ultimately, then, the objectivity of U.N. information activities depends upon DPI staff members. Like all U.N. employees, they are international civil servants who are required to be impartial in the exercise of their duties and to put the interests of the Organization before national loyalties.[33] Yet the inability of member states to agree on the proper role of the information function inevitably produces situations in which some U.N. information products are labeled propagandist by some member states. Thus over the years Western members—the "free press nations"—have been particularly vehement in criticism of what they consider DPI's tendency to proselytize for political positions they themselves oppose.[34]

So long as the Department of Public Information is required to promote the decisions of the General Assembly and other U.N. organs, so long as those decisions lack consensus, the full and fair treatment of minority views will be vital to universal public confidence in the fairness of the United Nations. The imposition of a formal mechanism for ensuring the fair and balanced treatment of issues might serve to ease criticism and allegations of propaganda by those member states who often find themselves in the minority position. While careful monitoring of every information output is probably unnecessary (and is likely to cause considerable delays in production), spot checks of information outputs should be conducted by an independent panel of experts in the field of information. When appropriate, representatives of the relevant substantive department should be permitted to take part in the discussions of the panel.

Recommendations

1. In promoting the priority concerns of the United Nations, the Department of Public Information must be sensitive to the views of all of its constituents and not just those of the majority. The department should be careful to present clearly the minority position in its information products, especially when they concern divisive issues.
2. In its capacity as overseer of the Department of Public Information's activities, the General Assembly should take care to focus on broad questions of departmental management rather than on the daily particulars of running DPI or the political aspects of information.
3. The Committee on Information should be dissolved. In its place, a high-level independent panel should be established to advise the General Assembly on questions relating to information and communication. The panel, to be appointed by the Secretary-General,

would be composed of approximately ten men and women from outside the United Nations with considerable experience in the areas of public information, media, communications, and public relations.

4. DPI should solicit the views of the U.N. press corps and selected media users outside of the U.N. on the usefulness of their press releases and monitor the actual use of the releases in the world press. Coverage of U.N. meetings should be restricted to those determined to be of substantial interest and utility to a significant number of the daily press.

5. Press Service and the Office of the Spokesman for the Secretary-General should actively encourage media interest whenever possible—including that of the non-U.N. press corps.

6. The media should be given reasonable advance warning when an important decision by a U.N. body is anticipated; and, whenever possible, the vote should be timed in such a way as to allow the press to meet its deadlines.

7. The *U.N. Chronicle* should publish a mix of feature and news stories oriented toward the information needs of its audiences. Feature stories—perhaps written by freelance journalists to take some of the burden off of the *Chronicle's* small staff—could examine broad areas of U.N. involvement. These would be accompanied by punchy news stories that detail the U.N.'s activities in these areas.

8. No publication should go into production until the target audience has been identified; the best means for approaching a particular audience has been determined, taking into account such factors as culture, income level, education, occupation, and field of interest; and the impact of such an output can be measured against its strategic objectives.

9. All information officers, whether serving at Headquarters or in Information Centres abroad, should be required to have considerable experience in the field of information.

10. The United Nations should develop an information strategy that has as its principal object the enhancement of public support for United Nations activities. An important part of this strategy would be the identification of particular "target audiences" (notably opinion-shapers and decision-makers), the priority concerns of these audiences, and the effective means of reaching them.

11. DPI should examine ways to respond better to the information needs of the United Nations Information Centres, perhaps by producing high-quality prototypes or raw information—facts and figures—for translation and adaptation by the individual centers.

12. Efforts should be made to strengthen the relationship between NGOs and Information Centres and to use NGOs creatively to improve the distribution of U.N. information products.

13. Serious consideration should be given to reorganizing United Nations Information Centres along regional or at least subregional lines, and they should be given the resources adequate to serving their regions.

14. The co-production of U.N. information materials by NGOs, individual countries, independent producers, or other U.N. agencies should be encouraged. In addition, the U.N. Information Centres should work actively to develop a network of potential sponsors for the products of the Radio and Visual Services Division. The centers should also be responsible for the constant updating of user lists, keeping abreast of user needs and, when appropriate, promoting certain information products.

15. DESI should utilize a feature-oriented approach in its publications on economic and social issues. The articles in these publications should—whenever possible—be prepared by freelance journalists in response to particular subject requests from the field.

16. The Visual Services unit should undertake marketing surveys, similar to those conducted by the radio unit, to evaluate its television products. The surveys, which could be conducted through the Information Centres, should attempt to measure audience demand to determine the most effective programming mix between news coverage and feature programming.

17. A daily meeting of producers and news editors should be held at Headquarters to ensure that those with the responsibility for disseminating news concerning the United Nations are kept abreast of the activities of their colleagues.

18. To ensure that all U.N. issues are covered in a fair and balanced manner by high-quality products adapted to the needs and interests of their intended audiences, spot checks of information outputs—including those produced by the UNICs—should be conducted by an independent panel of experts in the field of information. When appropriate, representatives of the relevant substantive departments should be permitted to take part in the discussions of the panel.

Notes

1. Maurice Bertrand, "The U.N. in Profile: How Its Resources Are Distributed," Chapter 15.

2. See, for example, A/Res/35/201, A/Res/36/149, A/Res/37/94, A/Res/38/82, A/Res/39/98, A/Res/40/164/, A/Res/41/68.

3. Two widely publicized reports—by the Heritage Foundation and the United States General Accounting Office (GAO)—charged that a great number of DPI's information products contain elements of anti-Western propaganda. DPI responded that the two reports contained numerous errors of fact and logic and that, in the case of the GAO report, the methodology badly skewed the results of the research. Nonetheless, the papers conclusions had harmful repercussions in Washington. The GAO report, in particular, prompted an amendment by Representative Patrick Swindall (R-Ga.) that reduced the 1986 United States contribution to the U.N. regular budget by $7.57 million—that portion of the contribution ordinarily designated for DPI.

4. Quoted in *Far Eastern Economic Review,* October 10, 1985.

5. See UNESCO 18C/35.

6. A/Res/33/115C.

7. See A/Res/33/115B.

8. See, for example, A/Res/33/45, A/Res/33/71G, A/Res/34/92F, and A/Res/35/95.

9. A/Res/35/201.

10. See A/Res/36/149, A/Res/37/94, A/Res/38/82, A/Res/39/98, A/Res/40/164, and A/Res/41/68.

11. See A/Res/38/82.

12. See U.N. Document A/40/7, p. 121.

13. See A/Res/33/115.

14. Due to the financial crisis, meetings of the committee in 1986 were shortened; the planning session lasted just one day and the substantive session lasted two weeks.

15. Prompted by the withdrawal of the United States and Britain, UNESCO has itself begun to take a far less controversial stand on information issues than it has in recent years and is now concentrating on practical ways to build communications infrastructures in the Third World.

16. This included evaluation and follow-up on the efforts made and progress achieved by the U.N. system in the fields of information and communication and the adoption of the committee's report to the General Assembly at its 41st Session.

17. U.N. Document A/SPC/41/L.41.

18. Report of the Group of High-Level Intergovernmental Experts to Review the Effectiveness of the Administrative and Financial Functioning of the United Nations, Supplement No. 49 (A/41/49).

19. Peter Fromuth and Ruth Raymond, "U.N. Personnel Policy Issues," pp. 33–34.

20. Prior to coming to the U.N., Madame Paquet-Sévigny was Vice-President for Communications at CBC/Radio Canada. Under-Secretary-General Sévigny is also a former President of BCP Limitée, a private Montreal-based

communications company. From 1952 to 1961, Sévigny held a number of journalistic, research, and public relations posts with *La Tribune* in Sherbrooke, Laval University in Quebec, the University of Montreal, and the monthly *l'Actualité*.

21. DPI's initial response to ABC's decision to air the controversial miniseries "Amerika" in February 1987 is a case in point. Rather than use the opportunity to launch a publicity campaign emphasizing the very positive contributions of the U.N. peacekeeping forces—depicted in the film as Gestapo-like troops who enforce a brutal Soveit regime—the department's first reaction was to threaten to sue ABC for the unauthorized use of the U.N. symbol. Subsequently, the department took a softer line.

22. Some recent occasions on which the U.N. Press Services missed opportunities to publicize positive U.N. stories:

• The General Assembly's landmark compromise vote on the budgetary decision-making process on Friday, December 19, 1986, was barely acknowledged by the department, which merely set out a few press releases on the racks at dinner-time on the night of the vote. The U.S. Mission, by comparison, held a full-scale press conference on Saturday morning.

• President Reagan's endorsement—by personal phone call to Secretary-General Pérez de Cuéllar—of the General Assembly's compromise vote on the budgetary decision-making process was widely publicized by the White House but received no coverage at all by the United Nations.

• The historic consensus vote by the General Assembly against terrorism in 1985 received only minimal coverage in the press due to the U.N.'s passive transmittal of the story to the media.

• The very active and positive role played by the United Nations during the African emergency received little recognition because it was not adequately publicized by the U.N.

• In January 1985, Secretary-General Pérez de Cuéllar convened the first meeting of the President of the Republic of Cyprus and the Turkish-Cypriot leader to be held in five years. Fuzzy coverage by DPI obscured the very hard work of the Secretary-General and, when the talks broke down after three days, the U.N. got the blame.

• In March 1987 the Secretary-General announced significant structural modification in the political function of the Secretariat. These modifications, which were taken to give effect to recommendations of the Group of 18 and of the international panel of the United Nations Association of the USA's Management and Decision-Making Project, include the elimination of some posts and will have the effect of streamlining the function. DPI did little to publicize this important step toward reform.

23. In the first six months of 1986, for example, DPI published a total of 2,186 press releases: 1,318 in English and 868 in French.

24. Agence France Presse, Medias France Intercontinents (radio), Radio France Internationale (radio), France Soir, and Marches Tropicaux et Méditerranéens.

25. In the first six months of 1986, DPI published a total of 2,186 press releases, down from 3,239 in the same period in 1985.

26. The *Chronicle* was published ten times a year until 1985, when budgetary restrictions forced the division to cut back to a quarterly production schedule.

27. The *Chronicle* is also published in French, Spanish, Arabic, Chinese, and Russian.

28. Twenty Information Centres (or just slightly less than a third of the total) are currently headed by UNDP resident representatives. It should be noted that the Secretary-General recently moved to consolidate Information Centres with the offices of UNDP resident representatives, whenever possible as a means of improving the cost-effectiveness and efficiency of both operations (see A/42/234). Such consolidation is certainly to be encouraged as long as the officer in charge of the UNIC has substantial experience in the field of information.

29. United Nations Planning, Programming, and Evaluation Unit Report, September 16, 1986.

30. *Development Forum,* co-published by DESI and U.N. University, is funded by contributions by organizations of the U.N. system and governments. The periodical, which has a circulation of 50,000 in three languages, is concerned with the continuing debate on economic and social issues. It also describes the activities carried out in these areas throughout the U.N. system. *Development Business, Development Forum's* business issue, contains procurement notes and other material of special interest to businessmen, consultants, contractors, and suppliers regarding internationally financed development projects of the World Bank, UNDP, and the regional development banks. *Development Business* (circulation 4,000) also seeks to familiarize the international business community with the requirements for international economic cooperation.

31. The Non-Governmental Liaison Services, based in New York and Geneva, works with NGOs in industrialized countries that are concerned with development issues. NGLS also collaborates with NGOs on their own development activities and assists development-related U.N. offices and agencies in their relations with NGOs. NGLS conducts briefings, organizes meetings and seminars, and produces educational materials on a variety of development-related topics.

32. See U.N. Document A/AC.198/99.

33. This general concept of the international civil servant was specifically applied to the United Nations Secretariat by Secretary-General Dag Hammarskjöld (U.N. PR/SG/1035 of May 29, 1961).

34. Two recent examples are contained in the reports by the Heritage Foundation and the United States General Accounting Office cited above. These accused the department of promoting anti-Western, anti-free market, and anti-democratic values through biased reporting of events. The GAO

report was particularly critical of the topical radio program "Radio Perspectives," which, it held, opposed United States interests most of the time. As noted, the GAO report's methodology appears to have been quite flawed: for example, reported quotes by governmental representatives or intergovernmental bodies expressing views "contrary to U.S. policies and/or interests" were often wrongly attributed to DPI. Two of the Radio and Visual Services Division's recent feature films have also been the targets of Western criticism. A 1985 film, *Being Young,* which juxtaposed an impoverished black American youth with a successful Soviet pole-vaulter, was regarded by some U.S. viewers as being unfairly biased. Some British viewers objected to the same film for its sympathetic portrayal of an Irish youth in war-torn Northern Ireland. A film to promote the International Year of Shelter for the Homeless will not include scenes filmed at two New York-based shelters because of objections raised by the United States Mission to the United Nations.

CHAPTER 15

THE U.N. IN PROFILE: HOW ITS RESOURCES ARE DISTRIBUTED

Maurice Bertrand

Financial problems are at the heart of the political crisis of the U.N. today. The main contributors to the budget, particularly the U.S. government, are concerned by the fact that their influence does not correspond to the level of their contributions. At the same time, they continue to offer in the way of voluntary contributions—mainly for humanitarian activities and for technical assistance—sums that are far greater than their assessed contributions to the regular budget.

In these circumstances it seems particularly important to have a clear picture of the manner in which the various types of U.N. activities are financed, their relative costs, and their nature and purpose. Although books and documents provide numerous descriptions of the institutional setting, it is not easy to understand what the U.N. is doing or to have a clear picture of its resources and expenditures.

First, the documents containing the data are numerous, not easy to find, and incomplete. Second, the U.N. deals with a tremendous number of subjects, and the types of activities corresponding to the programs vary greatly. Finally, although some of the U.N.'s activities are similar to those of national services, some others—notably in the economic and social sector—are of a very specific nature, and their relation with the objectives is difficult to grasp.

This chapter endeavors to overcome these deficiencies by giving a concise and clear presentation of the distribution of U.N. resources among its main activities.

Table I

Distribution of U.N. Resources (U.N. Proper, Budgetary & Extrabudgetary) 1984–85, 1986–87 in millions of U.S. $

Activities	Budgetary		% of Budgetary		Extrabudgetary		% of Extrabudgetary		Total		% of Total	
	84–85	86–87	84–85	86–87	84–85	86–87	84–85	86–87	84–85	86–87	84–85	86–87
1. Humanitarian[a]												
UNHCR	28.4	32.2			820	801			848.4	833.2		
UNWRA	9.6	10.7			481.9	571.3			491.5	582		
Kampuchea	—	—			33.2	40.1			33.2	40.1		
SUBTOTAL	38	42.9	2.7	2.9	1335.1	1412.4	63.2	62.8	1373.1	1455.3	39.4	39.1
2. Forum of Negotiations[b] and Information												
Conference Scvs.	266.6	279.1			1.4	1.6			268	280.7		
OSSECS	3.6	4.3			—	—			3.6	4.2		
Public Information	70.1	76.4			6.5	5.8			76.6	82.2		
SUBTOTAL	340.3	359.7	24.9	24.5	7.9	7.4	0.3	0.3	348.3	367.1	10	9.8
3. Administration[c]												
Personnel, Finances, Gen. Scvs.	303.4	337			24.4	26.2			327.8	363.2		
Other Admin. Exps.	37	28.7			—	—			37	28.7		
SUBTOTAL	340.4	365.7	24.9	24.9	24.4	26.2	1.1	1.1	364.8	391.9	10.4	10.5
4. Economic and Social Programs[d]												
Gen. Direction	12.2	11.7			—	—			12.2	11.7		
Human Rights	10.3	9.4			0.7	1			11	10.4		
DIESA	50	55.8			8.3	7.5			58.3	62.3		
DTCD	18.1	20			242.3	275.2			260.4	295.2		
UNCTAD	51.7	51.9			21.7	19.4			72.8	71.4		
International Trade Center	7.8	8.1			—	—			7.8	8.1		
Human Settlement	8.8	10.4			43	43.4			51.8	53.5		
Science and Technology	4	4.4			—	—			4	4.4		
UNEP	9.9	11.4			78.5	84.3			88.4	95.7		
Transnational Corporations	9.8	10.8			3.7	4.1			13.5	14.9		
Disaster Relief	4.8	5.2			2.4	3			7.2	8.2		
Drug Control	5.4	5.6			27.4	37.7			32.8	43.3		
Regional Economic Commissions	174	199			88.7	42.6			265.3	291.6		
UNIDO	74.2	77.9			190.8	199.5			265.1	279.4		
Reg. Programs of Tech. Cooperation	32.9	36.6			—	—			32.9	36.6		
SUBTOTAL	474	517.8	34.6	35.3	706.9	775.2	33.5	34.4	1180.9	1293	33.9	34.8

	Regular Budget 1984–85	1986–87	% 84–85	% 86–87	Extra-budgetary 1984–85	1986–87	% 84–85	% 86–87	Total 1984–85	1986–87	% 84–85	% 86–87
5. Legal Activities[e]												
International Court of Justice	9	8.5										
International Law	15	16.6										
SUBTOTAL	24	25.1	1.7	1.7			1.2	—	16	17.5	0.4	0.4
6. Political Activities[f] Collective Security, Disarmament Trusteeship, Decolonization Overall Policy	150	152.8	10.9	10.4	32.2		1.5		191.3	197.9	5.5	5.3
EXPENDITURES TOTAL NET [g]	1366.8	1463	100	100	2109.8	2249.6	100	100	3476.6	3712.6	100	100
Staff Assessment	244.7	279.7							244.7	279.7		
TOTAL GROSS	1611.5	1742.8			2109.8	2249.6			3721.4	3992.4		
Income (Revenue & Staff Assessments)[h]	301.4	327.1										
TOTAL NET BUDGET	1310.2	1415.7										
Peace-keeping Operations[i] (in 1984–85)									309.3			
TOTAL UN Proper 1984–85									4030.7			

[a] Humanitarian activities are described on pp. 360–363
UNHCR: U.N. High Commissioner for Refugees
UNRWA: U.N. Relief and Works Agency for Palestinian Refugees

[b] See pp. 363–364
OSSECS: Office of Secretariat Services for Economic and Social Affairs

[c] Administration, pp. 365–366

[d] Economic and Social Programs, pp. 366–377; Extrabudgetary activities are described on pp. 372, 377
DIESA: Department of International Economic and Social Affairs
DTCD: Department of Technical Cooperation for Development
UNCTAD: U.N. Conference on Trade and Development
UNIDO: U.N. Industrial Development Organization. Although an independent agency since the beginning of 1986, its resources are still included in the U.N. budget for 1986–87.
UNEP: U.N. Environment Program

[e] Legal Activities, pp. 378–379

[f] Political Activities: pp. 379–380

[g] Expenditures Total Net: The difference between net and gross figures is due to the existence of the staff assessment, which is deducted from the salaries paid to U.N. civil servants. Net figures do not include staff assessment, which appears in the U.N. budget first as an expenditure, then as an income item.

[h] Revenue-producing activities include various reimbursements, bank interest, sales of used equipment, sales of postage stamps, sales of publications, etc.

[i] Some peacekeeping operations—Military Observer Group in India and Pakistan (UNMOGIP), U.N. Supply Depot in Pisa, Truce Supervision Organization (UNTSO)—are partially financed in the regular budget by assessed contributions. But three peacekeeping forces are financed outside the budget by special contributions:

U.N. Interim Force in Lebanon (UNIFIL)	$182.5
U.N. Disengagement Observer Force (UNDOF)	70.8
U.N. Force in Cyprus (UNFICYP)	56.0
	$309.3

Our inquiry is confined to the U.N. proper, that is, to the activities mentioned in the U.N. program budget (with the exception of the resources of three peacekeeping operations). It will not describe in detail the activities of main programs associated with the U.N. or those having separate budgets—UNDP, UNICEF, UNFPA, WFP—or those of the specialized agencies of the U.N. system. The main expenditures of those independent entities are indicated in order to situate the U.N. proper inside the U.N. system.[1]

General Distribution of U.N. Resources

There are several categories of U.N. resources:

The assessed contributions to the U.N. budget: The scale of assessments is calculated by a formula that takes into account the absolute level of national income and the per capita national income of each member state (with the exception of the U.S. contribution, which is limited to 25 percent). The total net amount was $1,366 million in 1984–85, $1,463 million in 1986–87.[2]

The special contributions to the three peacekeeping operations: These are not financed through the budget. The special contributions amounted to $309.3 million in 1984–85.

The voluntary contributions: These are either given to trust funds, pledged for specific purposes, or channeled to the U.N. through the United Nations Development Programme (UNDP), and amounted to $2,109 million in 1984–85 and $2,249 million in 1986–87.

The income from revenue-producing activities and staff assessment: $301 million in 1984–85; $327 million in 1986–87.

Total resources (including peacekeeping operations) were $4,030 million in 1984–85, of which $1,611 (40 percent) were budgetary funds. The distribution of these resources among the various functions and programs is shown in Table I for the bienniums 1984–85 and 1986–87 in millions of U.S. dollars.

The distribution of the total resources as described in the program budget (not including peacekeeping operations) shows that the U.N. is mainly an economic and social organization, with heavy emphasis on humanitarian and operational activities in the field of development. In fact, 75 percent of the U.N.'s resources are used in these fields. Political and legal activities represent less than 6 percent. The remaining 20 percent is used for the support of the forum of discussion and negotiation and for general administration.

The budgetary resources provided by assessed contributions to the U.N.'s regular budget are used for the economic and social programs, the forum of discussions, and the administrative expenditures. Extrabudgetary resources, greater than the budgetary, are distributed between humanitarian activities (65 percent) and technical cooperation (35 percent). Finally, the financing of peacekeeping operations (partially voluntary, partially calculated according to a special scale of assessments) represents 7.6 percent of the total amount of resources available to the U.N.[3]

The humanitarian and operational character of the U.N. would appear even more striking when one considers the resources of the entities directly related to it. For example, programs like UNDP, UNICEF, WFP, and UNFPA, which are partially humanitarian and mainly operational, had resources amounting, for the biennium 1984–85, to an amount close to $4 billion.[4]

U.N. Development Programme (UNDP)	$1,525.4
Other contributions to UNDP and its trust funds	79.9
U.N. Children's Fund (UNICEF)	634.1
U.N. Fund for Population Activities (UNFPA)	259.4
World Food Programme (WFP)	1,473.0
Total	$3,971.8

It is not possible, however, to add this amount to the resources of the U.N. proper, if one wants to calculate the costs of the activity of the U.N. and its affiliates. The resources of UNDP (and partially those of UNFPA) are distributed to "executive agencies" like the specialized agencies and the U.N. itself (extrabudgetary resources for technical cooperation quoted above for the U.N. proper are in large part UNDP funds). The magnitude of the expenditures of the four programs listed above can be estimated by taking into account for UNDP only the amount of its administrative budget ($232 million), which includes projects executed by UNDP itself through its office of program execution, thereby reducing the total to roughly $2,600 million.

When this amount is added to the expenditures of the U.N. proper, the total is $6,630 million for 1984–85, of which $1,611 million is budgetary, bringing the percentages of budgetary and extrabudgetary contributions to roughly 26 percent and 74 percent, respectively.

The expenditures of the other organizations of the U.N. system

(FAO, ILO, WHO, UNESCO, IAEA, ICAO, UPU, ITU, IMO, WMO, WIPO) for the same period amount to $4,009 million, of which $2,093 million are assessed contributions and $1,916 million voluntary contributions. The major part of these voluntary contributions is used for operational activities and more than half are UNDP funds. The relative importance of these expenditures of the U.N. proper and its direct affiliates in the U.N. system is shown by the following percentages:

U.N. Proper	$ 4,030 million	37.9% of Total	together
U.N. Affiliates[5]	$ 2,600 million	24.4% of Total	62.3%
Other Organizations of the U.N. System	$ 4,009 million	37.6% of Total	
Total	$10,639 million	99.9%	

The U.N. is not only the centerpiece of a system that devotes the bulk of its resources to humanitarian and operational activities but is itself the main component of the system.[6]

Description of the Type of Activities by Main Function

1. HUMANITARIAN ACTIVITIES
($1.373 billion in 1984–85; $1.455 billion in 1986–87, mainly from voluntary contributions. (See Table I, 1)

Although all humanitarian activities have common features, there are three areas of concentration:

- supply of food, shelter, medical care (mainly in case of emergency)

- legal protection (mainly in the case of refugees)

- prolonged assistance for education, employment development in case of long-term, difficult situations.

U.N. High Commissioner for Refugees. The bulk of humanitarian assistance is devoted to refugees. The main organ for this purpose is the High Commissioner for Refugees, established in 1950. The budget of UNHCR, approximately $850 million for the biennium, is mainly financed through voluntary contributions from member states and some private sources; only a very small part—$28 million, included in the U.N. budget—is financed by assessed contributions.

UNHCR has a staff of 1,076, which includes 399 professionals, 21 national officers, and 429 in the general services category. It negotiates with governments to promote the adoption of necessary legislative and administrative measures and the application of the standards laid down in international instruments, disseminates information on principles of international protection, provides material assistance in an important number of locations, facilitates the movement of refugees to countries of permanent asylum, helps to secure socio-economic protection for refugees to facilitate their integration in the new country, and monitors implementation of projects.

The legal status, rights, and duties of refugees have been defined specifically in two international instruments: the 1951 Convention and the 1967 Protocol relating to the status of refugees. These also contain provisions dealing with a variety of matters that concern the day-to-day life of the refugee, such as the right to work, public assistance, and social security. In many of these matters, refugees are to receive the same treatment as nationals of their country of residence.

In extending international protection to refugees, UNHCR also seeks to facilitate their voluntary repatriation in cases in which this is a feasible solution.

Material assistance enables refugees or displaced persons to achieve permanent solutions to their problems, whether it be through voluntary repatriation, settlement in the country of first asylum, or migration to another country. Material assistance measures vary widely according to need. Integration through rural settlement is the approach commonly adopted for refugees of rural background who cannot hope for repatriation for some time. In Africa, for instance, UNHCR helps refugees to settle on the land through the establishment of new rural communities or through strengthening the infrastructure in areas where the refugees can be absorbed spontaneously into the local population.)

Assistance in voluntary repatriation may involve a large-scale transportation and resettlement operation (as in the case of former refugees from Zimbabwe and Nicaragua) or may simply entail the payment of travel expenses for individuals.

In instances where massive resettlement is necessary, as in the case of the Indochinese refugees, UNHCR's role has been to negotiate with prospective host governments to encourage the admission of displaced persons.

UNHCR has for many years helped to organize:

• special resettlement schemes for handicapped refugees who cannot qualify under normal immigration criteria because of physical or social handicaps

• the reunion of families separated by circumstances beyond their control, enabling them to make a new life together

• counseling services to help individual refugees find the most appropriate solutions to their problems.

The main intergovernmental organ of UNHCR is the 40-member Executive Committee of the High Commissioner Program. Its reports are submitted to the General Assembly.

U.N. Relief and Works Agency for Palestinian Refugees. UNRWA, established in 1949 by the General Assembly, is the second largest organ with responsibility for assistance to refugees. Its staff of 17,600 makes it larger than any other United Nations body. The bulk of the staff is locally recruited at the field offices in Beirut, Amman, Damascus, the West Bank, and the Gaza Strip and is mainly composed of teachers (approximately 10,000), health workers (approximately 4,000), and individuals engaged in the administration of camps and social services. In fact, to a large extent UNRWA's activities resemble those of a national administration—in this case, one that administers to a people without a territory. The number of refugees registered with UNRWA in mid-1983 was 1,957,061. Medical care is provided at UNRWA's 98 health units throughout the area, with preventive medicine, mother and child care, and health education given particular emphasis. It maintains clinics specializing in chronic and degenerative diseases and 26 dental clinics.

At the beginning of the 1982–83 school year there were 336,207 pupils in UNRWA's 651 elementary and preparatory schools. In addition, vocational and technical training was being provided to 3,948 young people, and 1,310 were receiving teacher training. During the 1982–83 academic year UNRWA awarded 349 scholarships to Palestinian refugees for study at Arab universities.

Relief services concentrate on providing food and other welfare assistance to destitute refugees. This is a new program, replacing the general distribution of basic food rations that was discontinued in 1982. Some 90,000 refugees were benefiting from the new program in mid-1983.

As a result of the events in Lebanon in early June 1982, tens of thousands of Palestinian refugees were left homeless. An emergency operation that brought relief services to some 178,000 Palestinian refugees has since been phased out, a process that began in May 1984 with the suspension of food rations. The reconstruction program, however, as well as other projects to improve the living conditions of the refugees, is continuing.

The budget of UNRWA is approximately $270 million a year. Only $10 million is financed through the U.N. budget; the rest is composed of voluntary contributions.

Kampuchea (Representative of the Secretary-General for the Coordination of Kampuchean Humanitarian Assistance). The activities of the program of humanitarian assistance to the Kampuchean people consist mainly of the distribution of food and the provision of health services, especially to the refugees along the Thai-Kampuchean border. The resources earmarked for this operation amounted to $33 million in 1984–85 and $40 million in 1986–87.

Of the total resources of the U.N. proper, humanitarian activities represent 39.4 percent. These activities are essentially funded through voluntary contributions. The part included in the budget of the U.N. ($38 million) is negligible (see Table I, 1, column 1).[7]

2. The Forum of Discussion and Negotiation and the Services of Public Information ($348 million in 1984–85; $367 million in 1986–87, mainly from budgetary resources. See Table I, 2)

The U.N. is a major forum for discussions and the exchange of views and negotiations among diplomats, representatives of national administrations or institutions, and governmental experts. Its intergovernmental machinery is complicated, having proliferated over the years through the creation of new subsidiary bodies of the main organs mandated by the Charter and of subsidiary bodies of subsidiary bodies. Special international conferences on a number of subjects (population, women, water resources, etc.) are also convened. The U.N. intergovernmental bodies belong to the following groups:

• The General Assembly and its seven main committees, its ad hoc and standing committees (Advisory Committee on Administrative and Budgetary Questions, Committee on Contributions), plus 15 subsidiary bodies, among them the International Law Commission, the Committee on Peaceful Uses of Outer Space, the Committee of 24, the U.N. Council for Namibia, the Conference of Disarmament, and the Law of the Sea Preparatory Committee
• The Security Council and its standing committees
• The Economic and Social Council and its six functional commissions (Statistical Commission, Population, Social Development, Human Rights, Status of Women, Drugs), its six standing committees (Committee on Program and Coordination, Natural Resources, Trans-

national Corporations, Human Settlements, Non-governmental Organizations, Negotiation with International Agencies), a number of standing expert bodies (Crime Prevention, Committee of Development Planning, Tax Treaties, Transport of Dangerous Goods), and its five regional commissions (ECE, ECA, ECLAC, ESCAP, and ECWA)[8]

- The numerous subsidiary organs of the five regional commissions (ECE, for example, has 16 "principal subsidiary bodies" for Coal, Electricity, Gas, Chemical Industry, Timber, Trade, Water Problems, and so forth)

- UNCTAD and its subsidiary bodies; the Trade and Development Board and its six main committees on Commodities, Manufactures, Shipping, Transfer of Technology, Economic Cooperation among Developing Countries, and Invisibles and Financing Related to Trade; and other bodies and working groups on various matters, ad hoc bodies, and preparatory groups, particularly those concerned with 17 individual commodities (cocoa, coffee, cotton, rubber, sugar, tea, etc.)

- The executive boards of programs related to ECOSOC, such as UNHCR, UNICEF, UNDP, WFP, UNEP, UNFPA, UNFDAC, and INCB[9]

To this intergovernmental machinery should be added the interagency machinery, which, under the auspices of the Administrative Committee of Coordination, brings together representatives of the executive heads of the agencies of the U.N. system (CCAQ, CCSQ,[10] the Organizational Committee, and a large number of subsidiary working groups). Finally, the special international conferences already mentioned bring together important technical delegations of member states.

The secretariats of the U.N. and the entities related to the U.N. support the work of this machinery through the preparation of reports, studies, and documents. Their substantive work is described in the other sections of this chapter. Direct support to the functioning of the forum is provided by the Conference Services Department ($266.6 million in 1984–85; $279.1 million in 1986–87), which consists mainly of translation (384 professionals), interpretation (205 professionals), editing (55 professionals), publishing (59 professionals), and library services (65 professionals). The small Office of Secretariat Services for Economic and Social Matters (37 staff, of whom 20 are professionals) deals mainly with the servicing of meetings and the program and calendar planning ($3.6 million in 1984–85; $4.2 million in 1986–87).

Information. The Department of Public Information ($76 million in

1984–85, $82.2 million in 1986–87; a staff of 828, of whom 266 are professionals; 66 Information Centres in various countries) has as its primary objective the promotion of "an informed understanding of the work and purposes of the U.N. among the peoples of the world." It ensures that the press, radio, television, and other news-gathering organizations are supplied with full information about the activities of the U.N. To this end it provides press releases, radio programs, photographic material and leaflets; prepares several publications (among them the *Yearbook* and *Basic Facts*) and periodicals (for example, *Development Forum* and *U.N. Chronicle*); sponsors training programs and editors' roundtables; and ensures coordination of information in the U.N. system. Its work is reviewed by the Committee on Information.

3. Administrative Services ($364 million in 1984–85; $391 million in 1986–87. See Table I, 3)

The administrative activities of the United Nations do not need to be described in detail: They are comparable to those of any corporation or national administration. Such activities are concerned with matters of personnel, finance, and general services at a cost of around $20 million for personnel services; $17.5 million for financial services; $156 million for the office of general services at Headquarters, New York; $53 million for administrative and general services in Geneva and $32.5 million in Vienna; and $74 million for various other expenses. Extra-budgetary resources of $26.2 million represent reimbursements made by other U.N. organizations, the UNJSP Board, and various extra-budgetary programs for the support given to them. The corresponding staff includes 244 (102 professionals) for Financial Services, 200 for Personnel (75 professionals), 812 for General Services (62 professionals, 334 for General Services, 222 for Security Services, 194 for work in various skilled trades), 20 for the Administrative Management Services (11 professionals), 53 for the Audit Office (34 professionals), and 55 for electronic data processing (28 professionals). Among the budget items of General Services are rent and the maintenance of premises ($40 million), communications ($16.4 million), and utilities ($19 million).

The staff in Geneva consists of 515 persons, of whom 58 are professionals, and 480 are general service staff. In Vienna there are 272 staff members, including 12 professionals, 161 general service staff, and 99 who fall into other categories. There are separate administrative services in each Regional Economic Commission. Administrative units in the U.N. have to overcome specific difficulties: a multilingual, multicultural environment; an international staff that includes all nationalities; the management, in cash, of money of all countries; the enormous complexity and variety of functions of the Organization; and worldwide travel and communications.

4. *Economic and Social Programs ($474 million in 1984–85; $517 million in 1986–87. See Table I, 4 column showing budgetary resources)*

The U.N.'s economic and social "programs" correspond to very different types of activities with very different types of objectives. In general, they seek to promote the establishment of common norms or standards, to facilitate the convergence of national policies that will contribute to the definition of common principles, and to assist developing countries in the definition of their development policies. The units in charge of these programs prepare studies, documents, and publications in support of the work of the intergovernmental or expert machinery or to distribute to national services, other users, and sometimes to the public at large. In addition, these units support operational activities (described later in this chapter).

The economic and social programs of the U.N. are distributed among 12 main departments or entities and five Regional Economic Commissions. The 12 units are the Department of International Economic and Social Affairs, Department of Technical Cooperation for Development, UNCTAD, International Trade Center, U.N. Centre for Human Settlements, U.N. Environment Programme, Centre on Transnational Corporations, U.N. Disaster Relief Co-ordinator, the International Drug Abuse Commission, the World Food Council and its secretariat, and, finally UNIDO, now an independent agency. The five Regional Economic Commissions are located in Africa, Europe, Latin America and the Caribbean, Asia and the Pacific, and Western Asia. The list of major economic and social programs is given in Table II (which provides a list of all major programs of the U.N. and the number of programs [central and regional and subprograms]). The number of economic and social programs amounts to 38, and regional programs 65.

The range of United Nations economic and social programs is one of great complexity, and its relationship with the economic and social activities of the other agencies in the United Nations system is not very well defined. The main categories can be differentiated:

Table 2

Breakdown of United Nations "Major programs" into "programs" and "subprograms" Number of Professionals assigned to them (according to Medium-Term Plan 1984–89)

Major programs	Central progs.	Central Subprogs.	Regional progs.	Regional Subprogs.	Total progs.	Total Subprogs.	Number of Professionals			
							Central progs.	Regional progs.	Total	By Subprog.
Political and Security Council affairs	2	8	—	—	2	8	108	—	108	13
Special political affairs	1	3	—	—	1	3	19	—	19	7
International law	5	21	—	—	5	21	60	—	60	2.9
Trusteeship and decolonization	3	9	—	—	3	9	60	—	60	7
* Disaster relief	1	4	—	—	1	4	24	—	24	6
* Human rights	1	4	—	—	1	4	48	—	48	12
* International narcotics control	2	8	—	—	2	8	33	—	33	4
* Refugees	2	10	—	—	2	10	473	—	473	47.3
Public information	1	4	—	—	1	4	227	—	227	56
* Development policies and problems	2	11	5	19	7	30	88	186	274	9.1
* Energy	2	5	5	13	7	18	23	32	55	3
* Environment	1	10	5	8	6	18	48	26	74	4
* Food and Agriculture	1	1	5	12	6	13	16	60	76	6
* Human settlements	1	8	5	17	6	25	90	34	124	5
* Industrial development	3	13	5	12	8	25	328	66	394	15.5
* International trade	9	19	5	21	14	40	156	88	244	6
* Natural resources	2	7	5	12	7	19	11	48	59	3
* Population	2	9	4	14	6	23	55	78	133	6
* Public administration and finance	1	5	2	4	3	9	24	11	35	4
* Science and technology	2	7	5	13	7	20	36	18	54	2.7
* Social development	1	11	4	9	5	20	58	46	104	5
* Statistics	2	8	5	13	7	21	97	60	157	7.5
* Transnational corporations	1	3	—	—	1	3	37	13	50	17
* Transport	2	6	5	26	7	32	22	61	83	2.6
TOTAL	50	194	65	293	115	387	2141	827	2988	7.7
* Economic and Social programs	38	149	65	293	103	342	1667	827	2494	7.3

A. Major programs of *general reflection on economic and social development and of support for negotiations in these areas:*

• the "Global Development Policies and Issues" program of the Department of International Economic and Social Affairs and the Regional Economic Commissions: 7 programs, 30 subprograms, 97 professionals
• the UNCTAD program "Money, Finance and Development": 4 subprograms, 39 professionals
• UNIDO Program No. 2, "Industrial Studies and Research," which also includes a subprogram on "Global and Conceptual Studies and Research": 11 professionals
• the whole of the major program on statistics: 2 programs, 21 subprograms, and 157 professionals. In addition to its value to the international business community, this program may be seen as indispensable support for the exercise of general reflection.

B. *Sectoral programs*
The sectoral programs: (a) are quite unequal in terms of the volume of resources assigned to them; (b) are managed by units of very different size and status—divisions, departments, centers, small units in the Regional Economic Commissions, and nearly independent international organs, such as UNCTAD, UNEP, or UNIDO (now a specialized agency); and (c) deal generally with the problems concerning each sector; only two of them (Drug Abuse and Disaster Relief) are centered around a specific problem. The sectoral programs address the following issues:

• Energy: 7 programs, 18 subprograms, 57 professionals
• Environment: 6 programs, 18 subprograms, 74 professionals
• Food and Agriculture: 6 programs, 13 subprograms, 76 professionals
• Human Settlements: 6 programs, 25 subprograms, 124 professionals
• Natural Resources: 7 programs, 19 subprograms, 59 professionals
• Population: 6 programs, 23 subprograms, 123 professionals
• Public Administration and Finance: 3 programs, 9 subprograms, 35 professionals
• Science and Technology: 7 programs, 20 subprograms, 54 professionals
• Social Development: 5 programs, 20 subprograms, 104 professionals

- Transnational Corporations: 1 program, 3 subprograms, 50 professionals
- Transport: 7 programs, 32 subprograms, 83 professionals
- Marine Affairs (ocean economics and technology): 1 program, 4 subprograms, 11 professionals
- Human Rights: 1 program, 4 subprograms, 48 professionals
- Industrial Development (UNIDO, now a specialized agency, plus Regional Economic Commissions): 394 professionals
- the major program on Drug Abuse: 2 programs, 7 subprograms, 33 professionals
- the major program on Disaster Relief: 1 program, 4 subprograms, 24 professionals
- international trade (UNCTAD plus Regional Economic Commissions): 244 professionals.

The U.N.'s major international trade activities include the program of Money, Finance, and Development already mentioned and eight central programs concerning Commodities (3 subprograms, 43 professionals); Manufactures (2 subprograms, 26 professionals); Economic Cooperation among Developing Countries (4 subprograms, 18 professionals); Trade among Countries Having Different Economic and Social Systems (2 subprograms, 10 professionals); Least Developed, Land-locked and Island Developing Countries (2 subprograms, 15 professionals); Insurance (1 subprogram, 5 professionals); and Trade Promotion and Export Development (ITC) and five regional programs (21 subprograms, 69 professionals).

The language used for describing these activities in the six-year "Medium-Term Plan" (MTP) and the gap that exists between program objectives and day-to-day activities of these units renders the understanding of what the U.N. is doing in these economic and social sectors particularly difficult.

According to a report of the Joint Inspection Unit of September 1982 (U.N. Document JIU Rep. 82/10),

the style used in the various chapters of the plan reveals that the preparation of the MTP has not been taken seriously by many of those requested to engage in it. Many "strategies" consist largely of a statement that "the Secretariat will continue, as required, to study and report on various competent inter-governmental organs. . . ." Vague, routine formulas fill up entire paragraphs. We find "the devising of speical measures will increasingly call for collaboration, not only with Governments of recipient countries, but also with potential donors of voluntary contributions . . ."; "assistance will continue to be provided in identifying priority areas for . . . so as to permit the formulation of appropriate plans and policies": "information will continue to be provided on . . . to help the developing countries to . . . to prepare and distribute publications highlighting the problems, options and strategies . . . etc.": "issue-oriented, in-depth studies at both national and regional levels will be undertaken. . . ." The proportion of descriptions filled in this way with vague formulas would easily, for many programs, stand at 100 per cent, since they often consist of an accumulation of commonplaces about the "internal and external constraints facing developing countries," the "challenge confronting the international community," the United Nations contribution to the international development strategy" or "the vital nature of development of the . . . sector, since growth in other sectors hinges on it." Too many passages in the Medium-Term Plan are thus swamped in a flood of verbalism that this exercise was, in fact, designed to eliminate.

In the following pages, this chapter will try to provide a clearer picture of the content of some of these programs, comparing their ambitious objectives to real outputs and estimating their efficiency. The examples chosen are: first, some sectoral programs that deal with "remote control advice" (Public Administration) or the search for better understanding among member states (Population), the diffusion of norms and intercultural values (Human Rights), or various objectives at the same time (Environment, Drug Abuse); next, programs using a multidisciplinary approach and concerned with general reflection (Global Development Issues and Policy; and Money, Finance and Development); and, finally, the regional programs of the Regional Economic Commissions.

• *Public Administration* ($3.2 million in 1984–85, $3.6 million in 1986–87; staff 38, of whom 21 are professionals; supporting unit, Department of Technical Co-operation for Development. Included in figures related to DTCD in Table I, 4):

According to the Medium-Term Plan, this major program is aimed at improving the public administration and finance capabilities of developing countries. Its objectives are, among others, "to strengthen and enlarge mutual cooperation among developing countries at the subregional, regional, and interregional levels, to develop administrative infrastructure in the various development sectors in developing countries, to develop and improve the managerial and administrative capabilities of developing countries, to enhance the performance of their public managers, etc."

The program is divided into five subprograms concerning the "collection and dissemination of information, management of mutual cooperation among developing countries, management of sector development programs, human resources development for public management, public financial management for development.''

The budget indicates that the program in 1986–87 will have 11 outputs: two reports to the Economic and Social Council on the role of the public sector in promoting economic cooperation among developing countries and on the meeting of experts on public administration; seven publications on the "changes and trends in public administration and financial development," on "problems in joint ventures between public enterprises," on "management information systems for major development programs," on "development administration," and on "management of public current expenditures"; and a newsletter and publication on "training packages for financial management."

An evaluation of this program made in 1978 by the Joint Inspection Unit[11] showed that the publications of this division were, in general, of doubtful value for users in developing countries and that the intended users were, in general, unaware of the existence of these studies.

This type of program is an example of the methodology of the "remote control advice" given by professionals located at Headquarters to national services in developing countries. It would appear that this methodology should be reconsidered.

• *Population* ($4.3 million in 1984–85, $5 million in 1986–87; staff 68, among whom 39 are professionals. Included in figures shown for DIESA in Table I, 4):

The "analysis of world population" implemented by the Population Division of the Department of International Economic and Social Affairs is one of the main programs dealing with population in the U.N. (Other programs dealing with population exist in all Regional Economic Commissions and in the Department of Technical Cooperation for Development [for support of Technical Co-operation Programs]; moreover, one of the main affiliates of the U.N., the United Nations Fund for Population Activities, has a program of $271 million in this field.)

This program deals mainly with research and studies aimed at implementing the recommendations of the World Population Plan of Action and of the World Population Conference held in Mexico in 1984. The studies bear on: improvement of demographic statistics; preparation of world population estimates and projections; preparation of technical handbooks and methodologies that could be useful in demographic evaluation and data analysis; and international migrations, mortality, population policies, the relation between population and development, population plans, etc.

This work is carried out through eight subprograms: World Demographic Analysis, Demographic Projections, Populations Policies, Population and Development, Monitoring Review and Appraisal, Facts Affecting Patterns of Reproduction, Dissemination of Population Information, and Program Support.

The budget of 1986–87 lists approximately 25 outputs, consisting mainly of publications, studies, and reports to the Population Commission (an intergovernmental subsidiary body of ECOSOC with 27 members) and ad hoc information services.

The historical record of this program shows its usefulness as a result of its contribution to the development of population statistics, to an increasing awareness of population issues among governments of all countries, to the definition of population policies in developing countries, and, finally, in cooperation with UNFPA, to the changes in population trends in the Third World. Population policies, which contribute to the lowering of birth rates, have been developed in the last decade in numerous countries in Asia, particularly China and India, and are now being undertaken in Africa and Latin America. The first results are beginning to appear in statistics on birth rates.

• *Environment* (budgetary resources $9.9 million in 1984–85, $11.4 million in 1986–87; extrabudgetary resources, $78.5 million in 1984–85, $84.3 million in 1986–87. See Table I, 4):

This program is managed by a semi-independent unit, the U.N. Environment Programme, created in 1972 as a follow-up to the first U.N. Conference on Human Environment held in Stockholm in June 1972. The objectives of the program are "to monitor significant changes in the environment and to encourage and coordinate sound environmental practices." UNEP, with headquarters in Nairobi, has its own governing council. The program of UNEP involves: global monitoring through various surveillance networks—Global Environment Monitoring System, Computerized Research Services (INFOTERRA), and the International Register of Potentially Toxic Chemicals; a plan of action against desertification; anti-marine pollution programs for the Mediterranean, the Red Sea, the Gulf of Aden, the wider Caribbean, and various other regional seas; and pilot projects in the field of energy, etc.

The main outputs of UNEP are preparation of international conventions, the development of guidelines and principles, the collection of publications and information, the distribution of information, and coordination of action of international agencies. The U.N. has, through this program, contributed to the development of awareness of environmental problems throughout the world.

- *Drug-Abuse Control* ($5.4 million in 1984–85, $5.6 million in 1986–87. See Table I, 4):

Drug-related problems are studied in the U.N. by an intergovernmental body, the Commission on Narcotic Drugs (a subsidiary body of ECOSOC), and by an expert group, the International Narcotics Control Board. The Division of Narcotic Drugs, situated in Vienna, provides substantive support for the commission. A fourth entity, the U.N. Fund for Drug-Abuse Control, established in 1971, assists governments by helping to finance country projects aimed at reducing the illicit supply of and demand for drugs.

Through this relatively complex organization the U.N. carries out its work in the field of drug control, a program that includes: the preparation of conventions (Single Convention on Narcotic Drugs, 1961; Convention on Psychotropic Substances, 1971; Protocol of 1972, amending the Single Convention); surveillance of the implementation of the provisions of the treaties; amendment (on the advice of a WHO expert group) of the scope of the international treaties in order to bring new addiction-producing substances under international control; and an international campaign against traffic in drugs.

It is difficult to measure the effectiveness of these various actions. A general evaluation of the U.N. drug-control system seems necessary.

- *Human Rights* ($11 million in 1984–85, $10.8 million in 1986–87; staff of the Centre For Human Rights 81, among whom 48 are professionals. See Table I, 4):

Among the major achievements of the U.N. are the adoption by the General Assembly on December 10, 1948, of the Universal Declaration on Human Rights, and on December 16, 1966, of the International Covenant on Economic, Social and Cultural Rights and the Covenant on Civil and Political Rights and its Official Protocol.

The program of the Centre for Human Rights is mainly designed to service the work of an important piece of intergovernmental machinery that includes 24 different bodies: the major policy organs (General Assembly, Economic and Social Council, and the Commission on Human Rights) and their subsidiary organs; one expert committee and two working groups for the General Assembly, one working group for the Economic and Social Council, eight working groups for the Commission on Human Rights, the subcommission on Prevention of Discrimination and Protection of Minorities and its six working groups; and the Human Rights Committee and one working group.

The program includes four subprograms: Implementation of International Standards, Instruments and Procedures; Elimination and Prevention of Discrimination and Protection of Minorities and Vulnerable Groups; Advisory Services, Technical Assistance and Publication; Standard Setting, Research and Studies.

The main purposes of the program are to press for implementation of the international instruments and standards for the promotion and protection of human rights, to examine violations of human rights described in complaints received by the Commission on Human Rights and its Subcommission on the Prevention of Discrimination and Protection of Minorities, to disseminate to people throughout the world information on the international instruments and standards on human rights, and to elaborate international human rights standards in areas in which there is a need for better definition (torture, for example, and the rights of migrant workers, children, minorities, and noncitizens).

The main outputs of the Centre for Human Rights consist of documents for the intergovernmental machinery, reports to these bodies, and substantive reports and studies mandated by the policy-making organs. One report of the Joint Inspection Unit described the center's results in the following way:

> Some moral constraints, exclusively relating to civil and political rights, have thus been exerted on various Governments, and these constraints have been developed by the constant pressure of a large number of nongovernmental organizations.
>
> The concrete results have been fairly limited. The situation is, however, distinctly different in relation to each of the two main aspects. With regard to civil and political rights, the principles proclaimed have been given official recognition by virtually all Governments. Systematic violations of these rights have been made more difficult in certain cases. A margin of hypocrisy has, of course, subsisted on the part both of Governments whose regimes were at variance with the recognition of these rights and of countries which apply the principles within their own territory but prefer to close their eyes to what is happening in countries which do not respect them, so as to protect commercial interests or political alliances. With regard to economic and social rights, the recognition in the Declaration or the Covenants of the rights to education, employment, recreation, and social security have not borne any practical fruits. In the absence of a sufficiently strong feeling of solidarity at world level enabling economic and social measures to be taken to secure respect for these

rights, the situation in this regard remains one of hypocrisy and longwind-edness.[12]

The efforts of the U.N. in this field of definition of intracultural values remain, nevertheless, very important.

Programs of Global Development Issues and Policies.
• DIESA's *Global Development Issues and Policy* program ($11.4 million in 1984–85, $12.2 million in 1986–87; staff 109, among whom 64 are professionals. See Table I, 4) is divided into six subprograms: Development Perspectives; Policies for Broad Based Development; Adjustment of Global Patterns of Production and Consumption; Developing Countries: Problems and Prospects; Fiscal and Financial Issues; and, Monitoring and Assessment of Emerging Trends and Problems.
• UNCTAD's *Money, Finance and Development* program ($8.3 million in 1984–85, $8.4 million in 1986–87; staff 80, among whom 43 are professionals. See Table I, 4) has four subprograms: External Financing; Debt Problems of Developing Countries and International Monetary Issues; Interrelationship among Trade, Money and Finance; Contributions to the Implementation of the International Development Strategy; Economic Prospects of Developing Countries; and Statistical and Computer Services.

It is obvious from the titles of these subprograms that the subjects treated by the two programs are essentially the same. Both deal with the preparation and the implementation of the International Development Strategy.[13] Both produce an annual report dealing with the description of the world economic situation of the previous year: *The World Economic Survey* by DIESA, the *Trade and Development Report* by UNCTAD.

Other outputs of programs consist of studies on "changes in the structure of production, employment and trade, and the flow of external resources" (DIESA), contributions to the International Development Strategy (UNCTAD), reports to the Committee on Review and Appraisal of the Implementation of the International Development Strategy (DIESA), reports on immediate measures in favor of developing countries (DIESA), short-term and medium-term economic prospects of developing countries and regions (UNCTAD), etc.

The similarity of the two programs can be explained by the fact that the main task of both programs is the servicing of the two main intergovernmental bodies dealing with the problems: ECOSOC and UNCTAD. The program of DIESA serves ECOSOC and its subsidiary bodies, such as Committee of Development Planning, the Ad Hoc

Expert Group on Tax Matters, as well as the General Assembly and its Committee on Review and Appraisal of the International Development Strategy. The UNCTAD program serves the UNCTAD Conference, the Trade and Development Board, the Committee on Invisibles and Financing related to Trade, and its Committee on International Monetary Issues, etc.

Global reflection on economic and social problems in the U.N. could be the main form that the search for a better consensus among member states might take, if the search were conducted in an interdisciplinary manner and oriented toward the identification of emerging world problems and the study of possible complementarity among national economic policies. Yet this becomes quite difficult when responsibility for that search is split between two different main bodies and given fewer manpower resources than the sectoral programs.

• *Economic and Social Programs of the Regional Economic Commissions* ($174.4 million; staff 2,542, among whom 898 are professionals. (See Table I, 4):

The list of the programs of the five Regional Economic Commissions is approximately the same as the list of central programs, with some exceptions. For example, the Regional Economic Commission for Asia and the Pacific mandates the following programs: Food and Agriculture, Marine Affairs, Development Issues and Policies, Environment, Human Settlements, Energy, Industrial Development, International Trade and Development Finance, Natural Resources, Population, Science and Technology, Statistics, Transport I: Communications, and Transport II: Shipping, Social Development.

The programs of the five commissions are strikingly similar: Their subprograms deal with general problems and issues (special measures in favor of least-developed countries, development planning methods, surveys and information on economic and social development, etc.); and the outputs are technical studies and publications, such as the study of long-term employment in Asia or of the management of tropical forest resources. Each regional economic commission publishes an annual economic and social survey of the region and, generally, a monthly economic bulletin. Support is given to a number of operational projects.

The style of the Economic Commission for Europe is slightly different. A number of subprograms refer to a branch of industrial or production activity: timber, steel, water, coal, electric power, gas, etc.; and the outputs of the numerous groups of experts serviced by the secretariat are common guidelines, harmonization of norms or of national policies, etc.

5. Operational Activities ($706 million in 1984–85, $775 million in 1986–87. See Table I, 4, columns showing extrabudgetary resources)[14]

The operational activities, financed through voluntary contributions, consist mainly of expert services required for technical cooperation "projects." A technical cooperation project involves the identification of a relatively precise and generally modest objective (in the field of training, institution-building, definition of methods or systems, etc.) and the organization of a team of experts and of delivery of some supplies to reach this objective. This fragmentation of technical assistance does not fit easily with the definition of programs or plans in individual countries. There are generally too many small projects, and it is generally agreed that the objectives could often be better defined and thus easier to evaluate and that the experts could be better qualified and better acquainted with the problems of the countries concerned. Moreover, at the U.N. there is no comprehensive document giving a description of the nature, objectives, and types of projects by sector.

As shown in Table I, the total amount of extrabudgetary funds for operational activities in the economic and social fields amounts to $706 million for 1984–85 and $775 million for 1986–87. The regular program of technical assistance also covers operational activities, mainly short-term advisory services. This brings total resources for operational activities to $734 million for 1984–85 and $810 million for 1986–87. The breakdown given in Table I indicates the units managing these projects. Annex 7C of the 1986–87 budget gives the following breakdown by sector:

Sector	1984–85	1986–87
Industrial Development	195.2	202.8
Development Issues and Policy	63.2	70.0
Natural Resources	80.2	90.9
Environment	71.2	76.3
Human Settlements	42.9	42.5
Energy	35.8	47.4
Statistics	32.9	36.1
Population	32.1	33.6

Public Administration and Finance	23.9	25.3
International Trade	17.4	18.2
Transport and Tourism	15.7	13.2
Social Development	9.4	7.5
Food and Agriculture	5.2	4.2
Other (Transnationals, Science and Technology, etc.)	8.9	11.3

This presentation by sector (by addition of central programs and regional programs dealing with the same subject) shows that the bulk of operational activities for the U.N. is in the field of industrial development, Development Issues and Policies, Natural Resources, and Energy and Human Settlements.

The information provided in the program budget on the utilization of these funds is scarce and limited. For the Department of Technical Co-operation for Development, for example, and for the Development Issues and Policies program, the following description is given:

Technical Assistance: At the beginning of the biennium, 140 technical assistance projects in the field of integrated development planning and planning execution will be in existence in 40 countries. Thirty of the projects will be finalized and 40 new projects will be undertaken during the biennium 1986–87.

A more precise description and evaluation of the numerous small projects is obviously necessary.

6. Legal Activities: International Court of Justice, International Law, Trade Law, etc. Office of Legal Affairs ($25 million in 1984–85, $26 million in 1986–87; staff 170, among whom 81 are professionals)

The U.N.'s main legal activities are the juridical settlement of disputes by the International Court of Justice and the progressive development of international law and its codification. Since the inauguration of the International Court of Justice in 1946, states have submitted over 50 cases to it, and 17 advisory opinions have been requested by international organizations. Fifteen of the cases submitted by member states were for various reasons withdrawn or removed from the list; and in 10 other cases the Court found that it lacked jurisdiction to decide upon the merits of the case. In the remaining 25 cases to date, covering a wide range of topics, final judgments have been rendered in all but 4.

These statistics tend to show that, on average, the 15 judges of the Court render one final judgment per biennium, which does not seem to be a very high rate. Cases have involved questions of territorial rights, law of the sea, and treaty interpretation. Several cases have concerned Namibia.

Legal operations are mainly handled by two commissions: the International Law Commission and the U.N. Commission on International Trade Law. A number of conventions have been prepared and adopted by member states—for example, the Vienna Conventions and the Conventions on the Law of Treaties and the Succession of States; and, in the field of trade law, on international sales of goods, international payment, and arbitration in regard to international trade law and seaborne transport. But it seems that the two commissions of lawyers have preferred, on the whole, to codify or at most to itemize rules already recognized rather than to develop the international law. Law of the Sea and Law of Outer Space have been developed through specialized committees and conferences that are classified in the budget under political activities.

Other legal activities are conducted by the Administrative Tribunal. The Office of Legal Affairs provides legal advice to the Secretary-General and servicing and documentation for the various commissions.

7. Political Activities: Peace and Disarmament ($150 million in 1984–85, $152 million in 1986–87). Peacekeeping Operations ($309 million in 1984–85). Secretariat professional staff working for these activities and servicing the political committees 229. See Table I, 6, and legend i.

The political activities of the United Nations are well known and need not be described in detail. They fall into six main categories:

• political interventions of the Security Council through its resolutions and of the Secretary-General through "good offices" or personal action

• negotiations on disarmament that have led to the adoption of a number of treaties and conventions dealing with nuclear weapons-free zones and the prohibition of various types of armaments

• negotiations of a legal and political character on the peaceful uses of outer space and on the Law of the Sea

• gathering and dissemination of information on disarmament, apartheid, decolonization, Namibia, etc.

• management of peacekeeping operations in Cyprus, the Middle East, and between India and Pakistan

• trusteeship and decolonization. Support to decolonization in the 1960s is generally considered as one of the main achievements of the U.N. The problems still on the agenda are primarily those of Namibia and apartheid. As far as trusteeship is concerned, only one territory— the Pacific Islands—is still under this status.

Conclusion

A general review of the use of U.N. resources makes clear the extreme diversity of the Organization's activities. Some of the features of the present situation are:

• the number of semi-independent organs dealing with a great variety of sectors and programs
• the absence of a clear vision of the role of the Organization
• the fact that the greatest part of the U.N.'s resources is allocated to operational and humanitarian activities (on a biennial basis, $5.4 billion of the $6.7 billion resources of the U.N. group)
• the sectorialization of the research work and the lack of attention given to a multidisciplinary approach in the search for consensus.

This situation is a result of an historical accretion in which the following factors seemed to have played an important role:

Initial Constraints. The member states acknowledged, soon after the adoption of the Charter, that it was impossible to implement its disposition in the political field—particularly the military Articles, 42 to 49, of Chapter VII—and that, in order to survive the failure of a political alliance, the U.N. had to look for consensus in other fields. Consequently, development of activities has taken place in fields in which there was already a certain degree of consensus. But the role earlier given to Bretton Woods institutions (and to GATT) in the field of money, finance, trade, and Third World assistance has limited the scope left to the U.N. for developing its own role in these fields.

Development of Activities in Fields in Which Consensus Was Easier to Reach. It has been easiest to achieve a degree of commonality in the field of humanitarian activities, owing to the general support of public opinion, enhanced from time to time by the publicity given by the media to catastrophic situations. The development of a very limited amount of technical assistance has also been a kind of compromise solution to North-South problems, a way of acknowledging their existence without having to reach a consensus on the majority of them.

Distortion Due to the Use of Voluntary Funds. Although the use of voluntary funds has made it possible to overcome obstacles created by a lack of consensus, this type of funding has too often contributed to modifying the order of priorities for bureaucratic, rather than substantive, reasons. Thus, in the U.N. system at large as well as at the U.N. proper, the funds for operational activities are not pledged to programs but to institutions or departments, such as UNDP, UNFPA, and UNICEF, and even to divisions and departments of the U.N., such as Natural Resources and Population. This means that the personal fundraising skills of executive heads, or of departmental division chiefs, sometimes play a more important role in the distribution of funds than do the order of priorities given by member states to such problems or sectors. Of course, the main reason for any rearrangement of priorities lies in the preference of individual member states for certain programs to which they are ready to lend their financial support.

For budgetary funds, the initiatives for the creation of new programs—frequently small programs with limited resources—have often been ideological or have represented compromise solutions to impasses in negotiations.

Absence of Restructuring or Rethinking of the role of the Organization. Despite various efforts in this direction, no real restructuring or rethinking of the role of the Organization has ever been achieved. Even attempts to eliminate obsolete or marginally useful activities or programs have never succeeded.

A reappraisal of the role of the world organization has now become crucial. To understand that role today, it is useful to distinguish between the activities dealing with the search for a better consensus among member states and those involving the conversion of consensus into some substantive action—for example, technical cooperation and humanitarian assistance.

It is possible to place in the first category the forum of discussions and negotiations, political activities, and the research part of the economic and social programs; in the second, humanitarian and operational activities and "remote-control advice" for developing countries, which represents an important part (probably more than half, on average) of the economic and social programs.

A rethinking of the methods for reaching consensus, on the one hand, and a reexamination of the role of multilateral aid, on the other, would appear to be conditions for reaching a better definition of the role of the world organization.

Notes

1. The term "United Nations system" generally has two different meanings: first, to designate all the organizations, including the "financial" organizations represented in the Administrative Committee on Coordination (ACC), which bring together the heads of the agencies under the chairmanship of the Secretary-General of the United Nations; and, second, to designate only the nonfinancial organizations.

In actual fact, the System, in the broad sense, includes three types of global or near-global organizations, with very different functions and types of activities:

A. The organizations with overall competence and some major agencies that, although theoretically in charge of a particular economic or social sector, have in fact a tendency to deal with all aspects of economic and social problems. It is possible to include in this group: (1) the United Nations, which itself constitutes a complex system, including the United Nations Industrial Development Organization (UNIDO, now in the process of being turned into a specialized agency), the United Nations Conference on Trade and Development (UNCTAD), the major operational and humanitarian programs like the United Nations Development Programme (UNDP), the United Nations Children's Fund (UNICEF), the Office of the United Nations High Commissioner for Refugees (UNHCR), the United Nations Relief and Works Agency for Palestinian Refugees (UNRWA), the World Food Programme (WFP), and some 30 juridically independent funds, institutes, centers, or councils; and (2) the United Nations Educational, Scientific and Cultural Organization (UNESCO), the Food and Agriculture Organization of the United Nations (FAO), the International Labour Organisation (ILO), and the World Health Organization(WHO).

B. The "functional" or "technical" organizations, intended essentially to establish rules and ensure cooperation among national services in such fields of common interest as postal services, telecommunications, and transport. In this category are the Universal Postal Union (UPU), the International Telecommunication Union (ITU), the International Maritime Organization (IMO), the World Meteorological Organization (WMO), the World Intellectual Property Organization (WIPO), and the International Atomic Energy Agency (IAEA). With a few exceptions, all countries, including the USSR and the socialist countries, are members of these organizations.

C. The "financial" organizations, also called the Bretton Woods Organizations (the site of the negotiations that led to the establishment of most of them): the International Monetary Fund (IMF), the General Agreement on Tariffs and Trade (GATT), the International Bank for Reconstruction and Development (IBRD), or World Bank, and its affiliates; the International Development Association (IDA) and the International Finance Corporation (IFC). The USSR is not a member. These organizations use a weighted voting system and do not accept the common rules adopted by all the other agencies for staff management and salaries. Their object is essentially to provide a framework for monetary and trade relations and for granting development loans.

Lastly, the International Fund for Agricultural Development (IFAD), established in 1974, with functions comparable to those of the financial organizations.

In this inquiry the term "United Nations system" is used to designate all U.N. bodies other than the International Fund for Agricultural Development (IFAD) and the "financial" institutions.

2. All the figures given in this document are those of the program budgets. For 1984–85 it is possible to find more precise figures in the Program Budget Performance Report: AC/C.5/40/50, Part II of December 9, 1985 and its 36 addenda.

3. The following definitions may assist the reader of this chapter:

Humanitarian activities: help given in emergency situations.

Operational activities: assistance given through expert advice and supply delivery to facilitate the development of a country. Operational activities take place in the countries themselves; they are also called "field activities" as opposed to "headquarters activities."

Technical cooperation: specific programs of operational activities.

Substantive activities: research work, support to negotiations. This work takes place generally at Headquarters (New York, Geneva, Vienna) or at the headquarters of the Regional Economic commission.

Budget activities: activities financed through assessed contributions.

Extrabudgetary activities: activities financed through voluntary contributions.

4. The figures given here for the resources and expenditures of the U.N. affiliates and the specialized agencies are to be found in various documents:

• Report of the Director-General for the Policy Review of Operational Activities for Development (U.N. Document A/41/350, E/1983/108), and its updating by Document E/1986/CRP.1 of July3, 1986.

• Budget Estimate of UNDP for 1986–87 and revised budget estimates for the biennium 1986–87 (U.N. Document DP/1985/57 of May 2, 1985)

• Report of the Administrative Committee of Contributions on the Expenditures of the Organization of the United Nations System Related to Programmes (U.N. Document E/1984/70 of July 6, 1984).

This last document is the only one presenting a complete picture of the expenditures of the entire U.N. system. Unfortunately, it contains some serious mistakes.

5. The U.N. affiliates are independent entities; they have their own resources pledged for each of them by member states and their own budget and executive board (with the exception of UNFPA, which has the same executive board as UNDP). WFP is an affiliate of both the U.N. and FAO; half of the members of its executive board are elected by the Economic and Social

Council, the other half by the executive board of the FAO. The budgets of these entities are submitted for review and recommendation to the Advisory Committee on Administration and Budgetary Questions (ACABQ), which is a subsidiary expert body of the General Assembly, but they are not submitted to a vote by the General Assembly. A report on their activities is distributed to the Economic and Social Council. Other semi-independent entities, like UNEP and UNHCR, have their own executive boards that approve their budgets, but parts of these budgets are funded through assessed contributions in the U.N. budget and this fact gives to the General Assembly an important possible instrument of control.

The activities and semi-independent programs included under the heading of the U.N. proper, combined with those entities included under the heading of U.N. affiliates, are referred to in this chapter and in the chapter on *"The U.N. at 40: The Problems and the Opportunities"* as the "U.N. group."

6. Slightly different percentages would be obtained if the expenditures of WFP were attributed to the "UN group" for only one half, taking into account that WFP is an affiliate of the U.N. and of FAO. On the other hand, the part of UNDP is slightly underestimated by taking into account only the amount of its administrative budget in these calculations. But the order of magnitude is the same, whatever method is used.

7. Voluntary funding provided for Namibia through three trust funds (U.N. fund for Namibia, Trust Fund for the Nationhood Program for Namibia, and Trust Fund for the Institute of Namibia) and for Southern Africa through two trust funds (U.N. Trust Fund for Southern Africa and U.N. Trust Fund for the Education and Training Program for Southern Africa) sometimes appears under the heading of humanitarian activities. The main function of these programs is to provide fellowships, scholarships, workshops, and seminars.

8. ECE: Economic Commission for Europe
ECLAC: Economic Commission for Latin America and the Caribbean
ECA: Economic Commission for Africa
ESCAP: Economic and Social Commission for Asia and the Pacific
ECWA: Economic Commission for Western Asia
9. ECOSOC: Economic and Social Council
UNFDAC: U.N. Fund for Drug Abuse Control
INCB: International Narcotics Control Board
10. CCAQ: Consultative Committee on Administrative Questions
CCSQ: Consultative Committee on Substantive Questions
11. Joint Inspection Unit Report 78/2, U.N. Document GA/A/33/227.
12. Joint Inspection Unit Report 85/9, U.N. Document GA/A/40/988, paragraphs 116–19.

13. The International Development Strategy is a document negotiated and approved by the General Assembly every 10 years. It enumerates the principles to be followed and the objectives to be reached during a "Development Decade." It indicates, in particular, the rates of growth and the level of aid to

be attained during the corresponding period. International Development Strategies have been developed for the first, the second, and the third Development Decades in 1960–69, 1970–79, and 1980–89, respectively.

14. The figures given in Table I for the extrabudgetary activities of the economic and social programs relate mainly to operational activities. However, they comprise some substantive activities (such as those described for the program of Environment) and some overhead cost.

ABOUT UNA-USA

The United Nations Association of the United States of America is a national organization dedicated to strengthening the U.N. system and the U.S. role in that system so that the U.N. will be better prepared to meet the critical challenges ahead. UNA-USA carries out its action agenda through a unique combination of policy analysis, public outreach, and international dialogue. Through the Multilateral Project, the Economic Policy Council, and the Parallel Studies Programs with the Soviet Union, China, and Japan, UNA-USA is producing practical answers to pressing political, economic, peace and security issues.

UNA-USA achieves nationwide public outreach through a unique network of chapters, divisions, and affiliated organizations. The Association provides special information and education services on U.N.-related matters and international affairs for student groups, the media, Congress, and policymaking groups. It also supervises and coordinates the annual observance of U.N. Day in hundreds of communities across the nation under the leadership of a National U.N. Day Chairman appointed by the President of the United States.

The United Nations Association is a private, nonprofit, nonpartisan national organization. It is supported by contributions from foundations, corporations, labor unions, individuals, professional associations and other national organizations, and by income from its publications, conferences, special events, and membership dues.

Elliot L. Richardson
Chairman of the Association

Orville L. Freeman
Chairman of the Board of Governors

Cyrus R. Vance
Chairman of the National Council

Edward C. Luck
President

Staff
U.N. Management and Decision-Making Project

Peter Fromuth
Project Director

Ruth Raymond
Research Associate

Maurice Bertrand
Senior Consultant

Marilyn Messer
Program Administrator

Frederick K. Lister
Consultant

Ema Herman
Secretary